The Vagina:
A Literary and
Cultural History

The Vagina:
A Literary and
Cultural History

Emma L. E. Rees

B L O O M S B U R Y

NEW YORK · LONDON · NEW DELHI · SYDNEY

2013

Bloomsbury Academic

An imprint of Bloomsbury Publishing Plc

1385 Broadway	50 Bedford Square
New York	London
NY 10018	WC1B 3DP
USA	UK

www.bloomsbury.com

First published 2013

© Emma L. E. Rees, 2013

Library of Congress Cataloging-in-Publication Data
Rees, Emma L. E.
The vagina : a literary and cultural history / by Emma L.E. Rees.
pages cm
Includes bibliographical references and index.
ISBN 978-1-62356-871-9 (hardcover : alk. paper) 1. Vagina in literature.
2. Vagina in populare culture. I. Title.
PN56.V26R44 2013
700'.4561–dc23
2012050836

ISBN: HB: 978-1-6235-6871-9
ePDF: 978-1-6235-6789-7
ePub: 978-1-6235-6066-9

Typeset by Newgen Imaging Systems Pvt Ltd, Chennai, India
Printed and bound in the United States of America

For my mother (Lizzie) and for Sue

Contents

Figures

Colour Figures

Acknowledgements

Special thanks go to Ally Jane Grossan at Bloomsbury for her professionalism, good humour and patience. The two readers for Bloomsbury made incredibly generous and enabling comments which generated many interesting thoughts and made this book better than it would have been without their input. I'm also hugely grateful to my own three 'readers', who gave their time to comment on the manuscript: Lucinda Mitchell, Bryony Page and Nick Riddle. Artists and scholars who have given me invaluable help include: Virginia Braun, Keith Briggs, Judy Chicago, Robert Coover, Simon Croft, Tom DeSimone, Matthew Hunt, Mitchell Litchtenstein, Helen Knowles, Julia Kunin, Marcia Pointon, Annie Sprinkle, Jonathan Waller and Naomi Wolf. Those who have helped in other ways are too numerous to mention, but among them are: Jac Armstrong, Jon Cooke, Melissa Fegan, Judy Hayden, Clare Haynes, Barbara Holliday, Greg Hulsman, Ali Hutchinson, Bekky Jennings, Bianca Lisowski, Dawn Llewellyn, Anna Mackenzie, Chris Walsh, Chris Wood, Deborah Wynne and Louisa Yates. I also owe an immense debt of gratitude to all of the staff of the wonderful Gladstone's Library in Hawarden, North Wales. Additionally, I'd like to thank the many students through my years at the University of Chester who have always displayed just the right mixture of curiosity, disbelief and respect whenever I talked to them about this book.

This book is dedicated to two remarkable women: my mother Lizzie Rees and her partner, Sue Foster. Other family members have also shown me love and support when it has been most needed. I'm thinking here of my mother-in-law, Alexis Waitman; my sister-in-law Charlie Weinberg; and my husband's father and stepmother, Tony and Gill Wilson. Finally, two people may have felt that they had no choice but to help with this book, because they were on the 'front line' of the writing process: my patient, loving and supportive husband, Richard E. Wilson, and our beloved daughter and feminist force of the future, Sapphire Rees-Wilson. Thank you.

1

Revealing the Vagina: Introduction

The mother of invention

Serendipity, not necessity, is the mother of invention. How else would a nice girl like me end up writing a book like *this*? In the summer of 1995, while driving through the borderlands of England and Wales in a Volvo so old that it imposed a leisurely pace on us, we saw an unremarkable sign pointing to 'Kilpeck Church'. Turning off the road, we found an extraordinarily quirky Romanesque church in a fairly deserted spot. We parked, and wandered round on foot, our gaze drawn upwards to the ornate, Celtic-style stone carvings which dominated the grey façade. Dolphin-like swirls gave the weathered stone the appearance of effortless motion; a flow, as though waterborne. A line of gargoyles (which, I was later to learn, were actually 'corbels') was wrapped around the little church like a taut line of bizarre stone bunting (see Figure 1.1).

Very few of the 70 or so corbels which have survived the assaults of the weather, the Reformation, and, anecdotally, at least, the parasols of censorious Victorian women, depict recognizably conventional religious images. There are two very equine-looking representations of the Agnus Dei (Lamb of God), and human faces which, at a push, might be Adam and Eve, but most of what we saw that hot summer's day in 1995 mystified us. Here, a weirdly cartoon-ish carved rabbit had, for over 800 years, been squashed next to a stone dog whose droopy ears projected an air of weary resignation; a bird-like monster was captured greedily eating a wide-eyed human being; and a knot of serpents bit

Figure 1.1 *Kilpeck Church showing the Corbel Table.* Photo credit: Jon Cooke

down on their tails, their writhing at a standstill for the eternity the stonemason wanted them to represent. And then we saw *her*: a bald-headed, primitive figure crouched on the corbel table, her blank eyes somehow fixed on her observers, and her hands, inside her knees-akimbo, spreading her proportionately massive labia, exposing her vulva. What was *she* doing on this church? On *any* church? How could an image of such full-on femaleness *possibly* bear a sufficiently hallowed message? Did she justify her place on that sacred building through some sort of code which Hugh of Kilpeck's stonemasons had understood in the twelfth century, but which was lost to us in the twentieth? (Figure 1.2)

We went into the cool, dark church to buy a guidebook, dutifully dropping our coins into the wooden honesty box where they made a hollow clang, briefly hushing the birdsong. Along with the guidebook came a reprint of an extract from a nineteenth-century guide written by G. R. Lewis. Blinking into the sunlight we used Lewis's meticulously illustrated guide to point out to one another the 'meanings' of the different corbels we could see. All was going well until we reached that perplexing female figure. Here, Lewis's meticulousness roundly failed. His illustration of the corbel – number 26, as he called it – clearly showed the same bald-headed figure with the staring eyes. Lewis's

Figure 1.2 *Kilpeck Church Sheela-na-Gig (front view)*. Photo credit: Jon Cooke

figure, though, had its hands pointing *out*wards, to the sides, at complete odds with what we could see. Arms, tailing off into those deceitful little stone hands, seemed somehow to have replaced legs. What were evidently, albeit astonishingly, labia, had been transformed into an unobtrusive, shield-shaped mark. This nineteenth-century antiquarian's illustration might be flawed, we reasoned, but what of his written description? '26 represents a fool', wrote Lewis, 'the cut in his chest, the way to his heart, denotes it is always open and to all

Figure 1.3 *Kilpeck Church Sheela-na-Gig (side view).* Photo credit: Jon Cooke

alike'.[1] 'That's no chest!' we said to one another, and 'that's no cut!' The puzzlement and indignation stuck with me, and a few years later I wrote an essay on G. R. Lewis's encounter with our stony puzzle, more properly called *Sheela-na-Gig* (Figure 1.3). She was, I discovered, a didactic figure found on church façades throughout Europe, silently warning about the dangers of fornication for hundreds of years.[2] What did it *mean*, I wondered then, and still wonder now, for the female genitalia to be so very visible, and yet to be so blatantly and unapologetically eradicated?

The psychologist Virginia Braun has written brilliantly on what it means to research the vagina (I mistyped 'vagibna' there – the demure spellchecker only offered me 'vagabond'), not from a medical, but from a representational perspective, and what it means to bring 'private issues into public discourse'.[3] I understand precisely Braun's point when she writes that, in discussing her research with new acquaintances, 'I admit to making judgements about whether people can "handle" the information. Which leads to lies and omissions. By omissions I refer to my "parent-friendly" account of my research'.[4] In more academic settings, Braun recounts how she would introduce her research in such a way as to invite laughter which, nonetheless, 'reinforces [her . . .]

observation that the vagina is a "troublesome" topic. It remains private in a way that makes its appearance as a topic of social science surprising and illegitimate, at least initially'.[5] Braun's thoughts on what it means – in academic and 'civilian' settings – to want to research and write about the cultural vagina vividly reflect my own experiences in writing this book. I know, for example, that at least one (male) colleague believes my research to be somewhat ridiculous and to fit absolutely with the stereotypical image he has of the 'feminist academic'.[6] Gladstone's Library in North Wales, where I've spent many happy hours writing, has a largely ecclesiastical client-base: at communal meal-times, when asked what I was working on, coyness shamed me into saying something woolly along the lines of 'representations of the female form in literature and art', as though I were some bluestocking researching the ancient Greek sculptures of Praxiteles, rather than a writer concerned with the epistemology of Sarah Lucas's 'Chicken Knickers'. My own mother, always my biggest fan, has a collection of pieces I've written down the years, which she wheels out whenever an unsuspecting guest asks after me, and is perhaps just a little disappointed that I couldn't have found a more 'respectable', or at least easily explicable, topic for this book.

The naming of parts

My earliest encounter with the word that dare not speak its name was when I was very young, at that age when summers seem perpetual and one inhabits one's body with an easy, sensual grace. In my green and white striped dress I must have looked the epitome of a British schoolgirl. The school itself was mainly housed in a large redbrick Victorian house in the suburban English Midlands. Around the house were extensive grounds (which seemed *huge*, to a seven-year old) made up of some wooded areas, some grassy and the slumped mound of a long-disused air-raid shelter. It was one of those prickly and oppressive summer afternoons when the playful yells of schoolchildren scatter the air, together with the far-off whirring of lawnmowers, the hollow 'bokk' of tennis balls and the overhead hum of distant aeroplanes. Hunkering down in the long, brittle grasses, Peggy Lucas and I animatedly exchanged words.

It was one word in particular that we shared that day. But it was in some way *more* than a word, too: it was a jewel, a token of infinite worth, a treasure to be shared and considered and repeatedly turned over in our minds and on our tongues. The word was 'cunt'. An odd little word – harsh-sounding and somehow replete. Consonantal and spat out. We had no idea, Peggy and I, as to what the *thing* might be to which 'cunt' referred, but we knew that the word itself had a magic, and a deliciously taboo aura. It wasn't to be said in front of adults, and friends would have to beg to be allowed into our exclusive semiotic clique. We *owned* that word; it was a code word or cipher. At lunch and in assembly we knew that we knew. In Maths lessons and in English classes we knew that we knew. Changing for PE, and washing brushes in a jam jar in Art, we knew that we knew. We were initiates into a hushed world of words from which adults must be protected, and into which we, in turn, would invite only the most popular girls, those who had, perhaps, another word to trade with us. But no other word could quite reach the potency of 'cunt'. It was a word with the enchanted power of a smooth pebble pressed into the palm of a trader and clasped tight, protectively; a linguistic charm, more powerful even than the Beagle's Captain Robert FitzRoy's buttons, traded for Patagonian children in the late 1820s. And so I learned early on about the currency of language; of its almost talismanic power both in use and in exchange.

For Peggy Lucas and I, then, in the long, dry grass in the heatwave of 1976, 'cunt' was our currency. It was a word whose shared taboo bonded our friendship. The odd part is that, after so many years, I forget who had 'brought' the word to school that day. What I do recall vividly is how it would have felt like betrayal for one or other of us independently to trade our currency with anyone else (in that innocent world of clandestine linguistic commodity exchange I would have been delighted – although somewhat bemused, of course – to have read the *OED*'s description of the 'restricted *currency*' of 'cunt'). This necessity for a restriction, or control, of usage is certainly something grasped by almost any English-speaking person. That the *OED* lists as its first definition of 'cunt': 'the female *external* genital organs' is problematic for those of us who know that the female genitals are made up of numerous components, both internal and external. The alternative word, 'vagina', is clinical-sounding – and actually very anatomically specific, referring as it does to the birth canal. Virginia

Braun and her colleague Sue Wilkinson have explored the differences between academic and lay interpretations of the word: 'the referent of the term "vagina" does not necessarily mirror its anatomical referent. Vagina is frequently used as a shorthand term to encompass women's genitals as a whole, or the more visible vulva.'[7] So – do we need to develop a new language for women's bodies? Or somehow rehabilitate the old one? 'Cunt' is, the *OED* aside, the most *inclusive* term, referring to the vulva, labia, vagina and clitoris. As Germaine Greer somewhat whimsically puts it, should we talk about 'the whole box and dice'; or, as Gloria Steinem writes, about the 'power bundle'; or, for Eve Ensler, 'the package [. . .] the entire deal'?[8] If we don't say 'cunt', then we aren't speaking the truth. In the same TV programme where Greer conjures up that gaming image (one which, somewhat uneasily, reminds me of playing Yahtzee with my grandmother many years ago), the irony is that she doesn't actually *say* 'cunt' very often. When she does, as in reading out lurid verses by the seventeenth-century libertine the Earl of Rochester, she forcefully emphasizes the word's guttural ruggedness. Greer's documentary, broadcast in 2006, was a segment of the popular etymological BBC programme, *Balderdash and Piffle*. Despite the programme showing footage of Greer painting a huge orange-red word 'cunt' onto a whitewashed wall, it's not until more than two minutes in that the word is actually *said* at all – and that's by a man in a vox pop survey. Greer describes how in the 1970s she set about rehabilitating the word, because the word 'vagina', in its omission of 'all the bits that make it fun', felt offensive, not least in its violent sexist etymological roots associating it with a 'sword sheath'. She also suggests that there's something inherent in the *sound* of the word 'cunt' that conveys most forcibly the *power* of women's genitals in a way that 'vagina' simply cannot. 'Cunt', Greer argues, 'demands to be taken seriously'.[9]

However seriously we take a word, however, there are *some* words which are so potent and yet so frangible that they need to be handled reverentially. They are philological nitroglycerine. In this sense, 'cunt' is the older linguistic sibling of the equally hazardous 'nigger'; both words possess the power to shock, and both polarize their advocates and detractors. 'Cunt' is the 'nigger' of the gender wars.[10] It 'has never been innocent', argued the late linguist Ruth Wajnryb, 'at least not for a good number of centuries'.[11] Even Mellors's attempts in *Lady*

Chatterley's Lover to normalize the word are, according to Wajnryb, doomed, because 'taboo words [. . .] are overly invested in connotative or emotional associations rather than descriptive or dictionary meanings'.[12] Is the battle for reclamation already lost, then? Has the connotative freight of social disgust become simply too great for the little word to bear?

Greer argues that in the twentieth century 'cunt' 'became the most offensive insult one man could throw at another'.[13] But Wajnryb also pointed out that 'the more people hear a word, the weaker its taboo, and, therefore, its shock value becomes'.[14] She suggested that cunt is still a relatively *fixed* word – its noun usage is far more widespread than its adjectival usage, for instance (unlike the wonderful versatility of the word 'fuck') – and this both reflects and maintains its taboo status. Reclamation is a way to 'subvert the male-endowed perniciousness of the word'.[15] In this book, I'm not so much holding out hope for a restored *denotative* (i.e. straightforwardly indicative) role for the word that might neutralize its *connotative* (implied) associations, as Greer sought in the 1970s, as exploring how and why it became pejorative (derogatory) in the first place. Is 'cunt' a word that *can* be moved from the dysphemistic (the polar opposite to 'euphemistic') to the purely orthophemistic (plain-spoken) realm of language? Or is this, as linguists Keith Allan and Kate Burridge somewhat dismissively call it, 'a wish that is impossible to grant'?[16] In the same documentary, Greer visited Bart's Sexual Health Centre in London to ask about the psychological impact having 'no acceptable word' for women's sexual organs has on women: the route to the appropriate denotative term is compromised by the social potency of the word itself. In a clinical setting, responses to the socially acceptable, yet anatomically erroneous, 'vagina' are bound to be far more positive than to the problematic 'cunt', yet both denote the same *thing* (one more accurately than the other, in fact). The 'obscenity lies in the actual words themselves – what they *connote* – and not in what they denote', write Allan and Burridge: taboo words can trigger a physical response in us.[17] Greer claims to be pleased that her efforts at reclamation in the 1960s didn't work, because it allowed the word 'cunt' to maintain its clout, becoming 'sacred', a 'torpedo' and 'a word of immense power – to be used sparingly'.

Even when the word itself isn't used, the 'torpedo' effect can still be manifest. In 2004, the British Library commissioned 52 artists and writers to pair up so that each pairing would illustrate one letter of the alphabet for an exhibition. Of the 26 letters, only one – and yes, it is the predictable one – seemed to spark media coverage. Morag Myerscough and Charlotte Rawlins, responsible for illustrating the letter 'C', produced a pink neon sign immortalizing the question (best spoken out loud): 'Has anyone seen Mike Hunt?' The reactions of the press are as interesting as the exhibit itself. Writing in the fairly right-of-centre *Evening Standard*, a London-based daily newspaper, Luke Leitch's piece had the headline 'Workers "C" red over word-play at library'.[18] Leitch began with a short list of the Library's 'treasures', straightaway mentioning the 8,000 schoolchildren – that's 8,000 corruptible minds – who visit each year. Next, Leitch implicitly criticizes the cost of the exhibition (£5,000) before mentioning this 'art' exhibition at the '£511 million library'. Unnamed BL staff, reports Leitch, who were already 'up in arms' because of proposed redundancies, were 'outraged' by the 'adolescent [. . .] ridiculous and offensive' artwork. The BL, according to Leitch, clarified that 'school parties will be kept away from this particular learning experience'. Rawlins herself explained that 'C, after all, is almost unique in having its own word. The C word. The hardest word of them all. In fact, there's only one other letter that has its own word and that's F. . . but no one is that scared of using the F-word these days [. . .] Our aim isn't to shock, it's just to have a bit of fun with our letter and say that we don't think the C-word is such a bad word after all'. By contrast, the left-of-centre national daily newspaper *The Guardian*, rejoiced in precisely the 'adolescent' humour Leitch renounces. 'Library show for word rhyming with hunt', is the headline for Maev Kennedy's piece, which expresses none of Leitch's outrage (the exhibition's extravagant waste of money, and its near-paedophilic threat to the nation's youth).[19] Instead, Kennedy softly mocks the possible responses of the exhibition's visitors: 'If you must laugh, please do it quietly. Should you feel a snort of outrage coming on, please bury it in a handkerchief [. . .] And if Mike Hunt is out there, or anyone who admits to knowing him, he might just like to drop in the British Library, where he may be surprised to find his name up in lights'. Kennedy describes Rawlins as 'unrepentant' – even in this largely positive piece, the idea of *penance* for dabbling with the 'C-word' is conjured up, albeit playfully.

Another 'torpedo' word is, as I have already mentioned, 'nigger'. In his *Nigger: the Strange Career of a Troublesome Word*, Randall Kennedy quotes Justice

Oliver Wendell Holmes: 'a word is not a crystal, transparent and unchanged [but is] the skin of a living thought [that] may vary greatly in color and content according to the circumstances and the time in which it is used'.[20] '*Nigger*', writes Kennedy, 'is fascinating precisely because it has been put to a variety of uses and can radiate a wide array of meanings'.[21] Kennedy's exploration of the power of language as indicator of social class or as 'a tool of demagoguery' has much in common with the debates that circulate around the word 'cunt'; he claims for 'nigger' the status of 'superlative racial epithet – the *most* hurtful, the *most* fearsome, the *most* dangerous'.[22] Such weighty dysphemistic baggage makes any attempt at reclamation exceptionally fraught, and, as Kennedy argues, 'necessarily involves comparing oppressions and prioritizing victim status'.[23]

Can the words 'cunt' and 'nigger', regarded by so many as *so* despicable, ever enter common linguistic currency? Sticks and stones do break bones – of women, of people of colour – but words hurt them, too. If you're being beaten up, does it really make any difference what your attackers are *calling* you? Can some words 'hurt' more than others? I think they can. Precisely because a word *can* 'radiate a wide array of meanings', its specific, situational usage really does matter. Both 'nigger' and 'cunt' are 'rhetorical boomerangs': at some stage thrown out, but returning to the lexicon, having amassed altered meanings along the way.[24] What Kennedy identifies as having happened is that beleaguered minorities have 'thrown the slur right back in their oppressors' faces'.[25] Is it the case that either word *can* connote positivity, depending on setting and speaker? Are some words 'owned' by specific people, but are off limits for others? If the speaker of the word 'nigger' is white, or the speaker of the word 'cunt' identifies as male, do the words automatically assume a new potency and impact? However, if language is an agreed, culturally shared system of communication, it is problematic to place so much emphasis on the specifics of context and speaker: that self-same specificity denies the possibility of universal 'ownership' of language. As Allan and Burridge write, 'offensiveness is never an intrinsic quality of a word, and the choice between alternative expressions will always depend on context'.[26] I'm extremely fond of the word 'fuck' because of its multivalence – it can be a noun, verb or adjective – and most of its meanings have shaken the signifier free from its originary signified.[27]

Similarly, someone might profess to love the word 'nigger'. Kennedy quotes the musician Ice-T on how reclamation of the word was, for him, about reclaiming a history and identity: 'I'm a nigger not a colored man or a black or a Negro or an Afro-American.'[28] How far might we draw a parallel between this 'boomerang' moment and that of the word 'cunt'? On one crucial level, we can't. When Ice-T embraces the word 'nigger', he's adopting an *entire* identity; for a woman similarly to reclaim 'cunt' is to describe only (although 'only' seems inappropriate given its magnitude) her embodied *sexual* identity. While an individual may be a 'nigger', to call a woman a 'cunt' is to take us straight back into the perilous and essentialist inaccuracies of the dysphemistic realm.

The 'indecent' nature of 'cunt' was completely established by the nineteenth century. And, as the cultural historian Lisa Sigel argues, it was then that 'the application of labels such as pornography, obscenity, and indecency hinged upon access. It was presumed that certain people could look at representations with limited emotional, social, and legal consequences while others could not. Objects became indecent through the act of viewing or reading.'[29] So, while *I* may use 'cunt' and am doing so from an informed perspective, *you* may not. The problem is that 'access' to the word cannot be controlled. Is the *word* obscene, then? Or the *thing* itself? Or is it – again – the *context* which is key? What does it mean for a woman not to be able to use the only word that can accurately denote her genitalia? How has that word become 'socially unacceptable'? What does it mean that in many cultures, the most terrible insult is the word for a woman's sexual organs? What makes bad language 'bad' anyway? The plethora of slang terms for female genitals can be seen as an attempt to divert attention away from the reality of women's lived sexual experiences. We don't 'look' at the 'cunt' itself; slang offers a convenient distraction. The 'c-word' is unseen, ob/seen, and, to borrow Freudian terminology, is both totem and taboo (*Sheela*, as I've shown, was in a sacred space, literally elevated). In an important way it's this dilemma that's the focus of this book. If 'she' does have a 'cunt', is she actually entirely at odds with a culture that sees only obscenity in a word, rather than anatomical accuracy? Is it the case that, no matter how much a woman endeavours to reclaim the word, the boomerang comes back too swiftly, so that it knocks her over, shattering her identity? The answer from the writers and filmmakers and artists I consider in *The Vagina* seems to be 'yes'. Each of them tries, in their own way, to make the woman's body whole again: to identify, and to some extent pacify and assimilate, the autonomous cunt. That's a key similarity between the different texts I consider in this book: in each of them, in one way or another, the 'cunt' has become separated from the 'woman'. In some cases, this separation is violently literalized. But we're getting ahead of ourselves.

Numerous alternatives, slang epithets, have been dreamt up for the vagina, not least because of the pervasively pejorative tenor of the word 'cunt'. As Mark Morton puts it, 'calling a woman a *cunt* is far more taboo than talking about her cunt'.[30] But Morton somewhat misses the point here. It is precisely because the term has become an insult that the actual cunt has to be talked *around*: replacement terms, euphemisms ('the product of a human mind confronting the problem of how to talk about something for which there is a dispreferred expression they wish to avoid') or crude slang, conjure up 'cunt', but it is rarely heard about positively.[31] The paradox of the signifier 'cunt' becoming so freighted that it gets in the way of the woman's signified body was noted in the early 1970s by the American artist Carolee Schneemann. In her London letters, mock-outraged pieces ostensibly from '*Cuntalee Snowball, London NW3*', Schneemann writes that: '*Some men are discussing another man who has betrayed them, they detest him and sum up his character as* "An utter cunt." *My questions: is a "cunt" something that makes men angry? Or afraid?* [. . .] *Do English men who say* "You cunt," *caress, stroke, kiss, put their fingers on and in a real cunt?*'[32] A decade later, Kathy Acker expressed a very similar sentiment in *Algeria: A Series of Invocations Because Nothing Else Works*, when she argued that men 'who say they want cunt find real CUNTS frustrating'.[33] More recently, the British artist Cosey Fanni Tutti has said: 'I hate the word "cunt". It has too many negative connotations. I prefer the less prissy and unapologetic term of "Devil's triangle". It suggests power, control and "otherness".'[34]

Does what Kennedy fears might be the internalization of 'white racism' in the appropriation of 'nigger' have a corollary in an internalization of misogyny in the appropriation of 'cunt'?[35] Can self-hatred, a 'tendency towards racial self-abnegation' really be the motivation behind any such potent act of linguistic reclamation?[36] Language thus becomes central to a 'counterstrategy' that seeks to 'seed black cultural expression with gestures that are widely viewed as being off-limit to whites'.[37] Is 'cunt', by this logic, only acceptable when spoken by a woman? In terms of *representation*, how would we reconcile this idea with the idea that the 'author' is 'dead'? Is all artistic output the product of a specific, individuated consciousness? Will 'cunt' *always* be ensnared in a cultural history of nastiness and aggression when uttered by a man, no matter how well-meaning his intentions? I'm thinking here, for example, of Stewart Home's thoroughly unpleasant novel, *Cunt*, which deploys the term in both an anatomical and a colloquial way, and Inga Muscio's magnificent feminist treatise, also called *Cunt*, which uses the word quite differently (see Figure 1.4).[38] Spike Lee's anger at Quentin Tarantino's use of 'nigger' in his films highlights this problem: what if we didn't *know* Lee is black and Tarantino white? Would we watch the films differently? Free of bias or expectation? Would we be better off in a world where the 'eradicationists' had their way?[39] In short, is Muscio's *title* less offensive than Home's, because of what she then goes on to write about *and* because she is a woman?

Crimes and Ms Demeanours

Might 'nigger' always be a more powerful word than 'cunt', since it's 'not merely a symptom of prejudice but a carrier of the disease', a sometimes fatal contaminator?[40] Possibly. But the associations with disease are perhaps even more literalized in the case of 'cunt'. Sigel has argued that '*Cunt* in the eighteenth century had far more bawdy and ribald connotations than it does today' and 'in the context of the late nineteenth century [the word 'cunt' implied] the linguistic pollution of the vaginal area for the sake of men's pleasure. *Cunt* brings that connotation to women's bodies, whereas all other terms seem to conceal it'.[41] Kennedy writes that:

> There is nothing necessarily wrong with a white person saying 'nigger', just as there is nothing necessarily wrong with a black person saying it. What should matter is the context in which the word is spoken – the speaker's aims, effects, alternatives. To condemn whites who use the N-word without regard to context is simply to make a fetish of *nigger*.[42]

And so we're brought back to the errant twins of context and intent. In 1942, the US Supreme Court 'established the fighting-words doctrine' which identified words which 'by their very utterance inflict injury or tend to incite an immediate breach of the peace'.[43] Again Kennedy cites 'ideological baggage' as crucial in understanding the specific resonances of 'nigger'.[44] Does 'cunt' have the same baggage? If a US citizen is denied the right, as happened in 1992, to change his name by deed poll to 'Mister Nigger', would a UK citizen be denied the same right?[45] Might one, should one so choose, legally become 'Ms Cunt'? What if a man wanted to be 'Mr Cunt'? In short, who has a *right* to a *word*?

There's no direct comparison in the law of England and Wales to the fighting-words doctrine, but there are other laws, such as those around breaches of the peace, which can be invoked when certain words are used. However, the rulings relating to such laws are strongly context-dependent. I might attract little attention at a football match were I to call the referee a 'cunt', and I would almost certainly not be arrested. I could argue in court that, in the heat of the match, such emotion-laden words spontaneously overflowed from my mouth. Consider the long-standing debate over fans of North London's Tottenham Hotspur Football Club calling themselves 'Yids', or 'the Yid Army'. Some prominent figures, most notably the British Jewish author and comedian David Baddiel, have been vociferous in their criticism of this particular act of linguistic reappropriation. Others, however, argue that the adoption of the name by supporters (importantly, *not* by rivals) of a club whose roots lie in London's Jewish community is a tribute to a proud history.[46] To return to that fictitious football match: were I to call the referee or one of the players a 'nigger', no matter – and this is crucial – no matter what my *intention*, I would probably be prosecuted under those laws which limit free speech on the grounds of discrimination (i.e. racism, incitement or others). Were I to shout *either* 'cunt' or 'nigger' in a different context, at a primary school, for example, or in a supermarket, the context would be deemed entirely inappropriate and the police would be called. Were I to call someone a 'cunt' or a 'nigger' in my own home, a 'dwelling' as defined by the Public Order Act (1986), Section 8, however, then 'no offence is committed where the words or behaviour are used [. . .] by a person inside a dwelling and the other person is also inside that or another dwelling'.[47] In the United States, federal courts use three 'tests' (based on the gender of both speaker and hearer; on the utterance's sexual content; and on whether the words were specifically directed at an individual) to determine whether or not a speech act should 'amount to actionable conduct'.[48] To return to 'Ms Cunt', it is the case that a name change is not permissible under English law if the name is 'vulgar, offensive or blasphemous'.[49] But what if *I* don't deem the word 'cunt' to be 'vulgar, offensive or blasphemous'? What if I could demonstrate to the Deed Poll Service that the word had a specific denotative meaning? My suspicion – and it's going to take a braver woman than I to test it – is that the definition would not influence the Service's decision, because it's simply too implicated in the messiness of connotative language.

Ultimately, Kennedy argues, in the case of 'nigger' we are 'taming, civilizing and transmuting' the word so that it may be converted 'from a negative into a positive appellation'.[50] If one uses a taboo word, be that 'cunt' or 'nigger', one has to understand that in the moment of utterance or writing, the word leaves us. How it is heard or read by another person is beyond one's control. This is a major drawback in attempting to reclaim the word 'cunt': one woman's linguistic salvage is another woman's 'vulgar, offensive or blasphemous' poison. When we use the word 'cunt', or even when we use its euphemistic 'C-word' synonym, there's no escaping the fact that we are conjuring up not only an anatomical truth but, in fact, centuries of misogyny, hatred and ugliness. The British journalist and author Peter Silverton writes movingly of the impact on him of a powerful scene in the 1997 film *Nil By Mouth*, as a man beats up a woman: 'With each kick, he shouts-spits-screams "cunt!" The rhythm is brutally sickening: cunt-kick, cunt-kick [. . .] This is hatred. For his wife. For her femaleness. For his desire for her femaleness. For his knowledge that he came from such femaleness [. . .] That's cunt for him.'[51] It is a word banished to the linguistic hinterlands, returning only in various covert manifestations, or as a literalizing of its own dubious metaphoric inheritance: as an autonomous, somehow separate entity, occupying a space that both is and is not part of a woman and putting women into an almost impossible position as a result. Such contradictions provide creative possibilities for the writers, performers and artists whose work is the focus of this book.

Mapping 'bad' language

That citadel of language, the *Oxford English Dictionary*, has 'Gropecuntelane' as its first-recorded usage of the word 'cunt', dating from around 1230. Eilert Ekwall's gem of a book, *Street-Names of the City of London*, is the *OED*'s source. Ekwall explains that 'Gropecuntelane is the lost name of a lane in St. Pancras and St. Mary Colechurch.'[52] He also records earlier usage in other British towns and cities, 'sometimes varying with the euphemism Grope Lane': Oxford, Northampton, Peterborough, Stebbing (Essex), Chipping Barnet (North London), Bristol, Worcester and York are listed by Ekwall as having streets with similar names.[53] By St Andrew's Hall and Cinema City in Norwich was once 'Gropecunte Lane'; Oxford's 'Gropecuntelane' – the earliest recorded instance of the thoroughfare's name, dating from c. 1230 – became Magpie Street; and Nelson Street in Bristol started life as the rather less patriotic 'Gropecountlane'.[54] 'The name is an indecent one', declares Ekwall, somewhat prudishly: 'ME *cunte* means "cunnus"'.[55] Presumably once the reader has worked out how 'cunnus' helps to elucidate the surely more suggestive 'cunte', the fact that the street's listed in a section of 'Lanes named from some activity carried on there' should dispel any further doubts.[56] Recent research suggests that Ekwall may have been leaping to the wrong conclusion in his assumption of indecency, however. In an article from 2009, the place–name expert Keith Briggs explored the sources and frequency of occurrences of the 'Gropecuntelane' phenomenon. Briggs persuasively rejects Ekwall's Latin root *cunnus*, considering it an error for *culus*, 'arse'; the Latinate periphrases (words that talk around, rather than about, their object) *uerētrum* and *pudendus*, in their associations with 'awe' and 'shame' respectively, suggest that an 'ambiguity of attitude [around the word "cunt" . . .] has always existed', and the 'existence of numerous by-names recorded in the medieval period would argue against a taboo operating then'.[57] Place names such as Clawecuncte, Clevecunt, Cruskunt, Fillecunt, and Twychecunt existed, as did the name Bele Wydecunte, and my own two personal favourites from Briggs's list: Bluthercuntesaker and Fockynggroue.[58] Rather delightfully, the Dorsetshire town of Sandford Orcas, Briggs claims, probably got its name originally from the Old French *Oriescuilz*, which translates as 'golden ballocks'.[59] This excerpted list alone is compelling evidence to support the idea that what might now be regarded as 'obscene' place names were, in actual fact, relatively common.

Briggs has uncovered some 24 instances of 'Gropecunte Lane' or its variants, not including the many variants of 'Grape Street' which plausibly had the same origins.[60] His contention that the academic and ecclesiastical atmosphere in many of the places where variants of 'Gropcunt lane' have been found suggests a certain playfulness to the point where he posits that 'the name originates as academic slang'.[61] This linguistic mischievousness may also explain how, if we adopt Ekwall's assertion that 'grope' may actually derive from the Old English *grōp*, *grēp* or *grēpe*, meaning 'a ditch', or 'a drain', then streets were called 'Grope' or 'Grape' because of a central sewerage gully, and 'the addition of a middle syllable to give Gropecuntelane was a jocular alteration of this'.[62] The British expert on slang, Jonathon Green, also looks for origins in 'ditch', by going to the Sanskrit *cushi*; and the Greek *kusos* and *kusthos*.[63] Green relates how John Florio's 1598 dictionary cites Boccaccio as a source for *val cava*, defined as a 'woman's private parts, a hollow cavity or valley'.[64] The numerous examples of similarly named streets, however, do lead Briggs to assert, quite cogently, that it is 'much more probable that every Gropelane *is* a "cleaned-up" version of a Gropecuntelane'.[65] Nevertheless, the theory that original 'groped cunt' place–names came from the Old English for 'gully', possibly inviting associations between topographical features and the taboo of the female genitalia, is provocative. There is little evidence to support the claims of many (Ekwall among them) that the names related in some *direct* way to these areas being red-light districts.[66]

Briggs also finds a tenth-century usage (predating the *OED*'s discoveries): members of Hampshire's East Horton Golf Club might well be shocked to discover that in AD 960 King Edgar's Charter records in roughly that location a roadway or path called *cuntan heale* or (*halhe*), or 'cunt hollow' (possibly suggested by the confluence of two streams there).[67] Briggs's essay is irresistible. Who, on looking at a map of related place–names, would *not* want to visit the former locations of 'Cuntewellewang' in Lincolnshire, or to 'Shavecuntewell' in Kent?[68] Indeed, six '-cunte-' names are clustered in Lincolnshire, and these could have Scandinavian origins.[69] Briggs's photographs show vulva-shaped densely wooded gullies or clefts where these place–names were, again suggesting a strong topographical connection.[70] What Briggs's essay proves above all else, however, is that if one starts one's etymological journey with the *OED* alone, a wealth of information will be missed. Briggs has used *The Middle English Dictionary* as a key resource but remarks, tantalizingly, that it's in looking at place–names, in addition to dictionary definitions, that we will find so many provocative, if not yet fully understood, early usages of the word 'cunt' in everyday conversation, where it was, perhaps, playful, maybe even a little saucy, but not taboo.

The *OED* additionally cites one particular proverb from the Middle English (1325) verse manuscript *The Proverbs of Hendynge* (or *Hending*).[71] This is roughly how the proverb goes: '[Give] Þi cunte to cunnig and craue affetir wedding', or 'Give thy cunt with cunning and make your demands after the wedding'. There's a potential pun around the word *craue* here (we can see its etymological affinity with 'crave'), since as well as meaning 'demand' or 'request' it could also hint at the Middle English *crawe*, meaning a throat (a 'craw' is a bird's oesophagus or gullet). In the Northumbrian *Cursor Mundi*, a lengthy Middle English poem written around 25 years before *Hendynge*, women are, perhaps for the first time in English Literature, compared to birds.[72] It was a motif to which both Chaucer and the *Pearl* or *Gawain* poet were to return later in the fourteenth century. The meaning of the pun – if, indeed, there is one – is lost to us, but it might refer to cultural assumptions about women's propensity to speak too much, or might even have sexual connotations of fellatio. A very late fourteenth-century (c. 1400) translation of *Chirurgie*, a text by the Milanese surgeon Lanfranc (d. 1315), is also cited by the *OED*, even though the usage's interiority seems to contradict the very definition ('the female *external* genital organs') it's supposed to illustrate: 'In wymmen Þe necke of Þe bladdre is schort, & is maad fast to the cunte.' Up until the sixteenth century it appears that 'cunt' was being used – in certain contexts, at least – denotatively, without always having an 'obscene' association. In about 1552, the dramatist David Lindsay used the word in his morality play *Ane Satire of the Thrie Estaitis*: a stage direction shows an elderly man and his young wife. '*Heir sall he lok hir cunt*', states the direction, '*and lay the key under his heid; he sall sleip*'.[73] The *OED* lists several other literal usages, before three figurative examples from Rochester, Joyce and D. H. Lawrence.

In terms of etymology, the *OED* suggests the Middle English *cunte,* *count(e)*, related to Old Norse *kunta*; Old Frisian, Middle Low German and Middle Dutch, *kunte*; and possibly, although there's some doubt about this, the Germanic *kunton*. The *OED* also draws a comparison with 'quaint', *queynte* in Middle English, suggesting that it may have been a euphemistic substitution for cunt. The best-known example is probably that found in Chaucer's late-fourteenth-century rambunctious *Miller's Tale*: the scholarly Nicholas attempts to seduce the miller's wife, and 'prively [. . .] caughte hire by the queynte'.[74] Chaucer's use of *queynte* may suggest, in spite of the examples from Lanfranc and Lindsay, above, that *cunt* was indeed unacceptable by the time of *The Canterbury Tales*. However, *queynte* may simply have been his spelling of 'cunt', and intended denotatively. The etymology is certainly contested, then. There's a possibility that *cunt* has Latinate and not Germanic roots at all, and is derived from the Latin for a rabbit hole, *cuniculus*, suggestive of the Latin *cunnus*, 'vulva'. *Cunnus* was American feminist aficionado Barbara Walker's etymological choice, and she also introduced the possibility of the word originating in the 'Yoni of the Uni-verse', Kunda or Cunti, the 'Oriental Great Goddess'.[75] The slang word *cunny*, as a diminutive of 'cunt', is found in 1719, in the first volume of Thomas D'Urfey's *Wit and Mirth: Or Pills to Purge Melancholy*, where the playful associations with *cunicula, cony*, or 'rabbit', are exploited. 'The Charms of *Cunny* by Sea and Land', goes one of D'Urfey's *Songs Compleat, Pleasant and Divertive*, 'Subdues each human Creature;/And will our stubborn Hearts command,/Whilst there is a Man in Nature'.[76] Another possible source for the word is the Latin *cuneus*, meaning 'triangular wedge'; Wajnryb also proposed the Icelandic *kunta*; Eric Partridge plumped for *cu*, 'sacred cow'.[77] According to Green, Partridge was something of a 'cunt' pioneer: he thought it ridiculous for a lexicographer to refuse to have an entry for a word in common usage and included it, albeit with a coy asterisk replacing its second letter, in his 1937 *Dictionary of Slang and Unconventional English*.[78] The *OED*, Green points out, first listed 'cunt' as late as 1972, despite having included 'prick' since the early twentieth century. At the risk of complicating the word's etymology even more, it should be mentioned that Partridge thought 'cunt' derived from *konnos* (trinket, beard or tuft), and was not related to *cunnus* at all.[79]

The antiquarian and amateur lexicographer, Francis Grose, first published his *Classical Dictionary of the Vulgar Tongue* in 1785. It went to many editions both during his life and posthumously, and it is only in the 1788 imprint that he attempts to define the word 'cunt'. 'Attempt' is the right word here, for Grose combined misogyny and what he no doubt felt was humour, along with censoriousness in that volume. 'C**T', runs the entry: 'The Κόννος ["Konnos"] of the Greek, and the *cunnus* of the Latin dictionaries; a nasty name for a nasty thing'.[80] This is a perfect example of the 'pejorization' of the cunt, resulting 'from society's perception of a word's tainted denotatum contaminating the word itself'.[81] Grose also associates the vagina with danger, and in the same volume in which 'C**T' does(n't) make an appearance, we learn that 'a Biter' is 'a wench whose **** is ready to bite her a_se. A lascivious rampant wench', and that 'a Bite' is 'a cheat, also a woman's privities. The cull wapt the mort's bite; the fellow enjoyed the wench heartily'.[82] While the modern *OED* describes 'cunt' as 'Applied to a person, esp. a woman, as a term of vulgar abuse' (the earliest recorded instance of this comes from the Australian writer Frederic Manning's controversial 1929 novel, *The Middle Parts of Fortune*), for Grose, 'Bitch' was 'the most offensive appellation that can be given to an English woman, even more provoking than that of whore'.[83]

The word 'vagina', as I've already mentioned, comes from the Latin for a 'sheath' or 'scabbard' and anatomically has an entirely functional meaning, according to the *OED*, where it is defined as 'the membranous canal leading from the vulva to the uterus in women and female mammals'. The usually prim *OED* does, surprisingly, supply a fairly long list of synonyms for 'vagina', ranging from 'quaint' and 'tail' in the fourteenth century; to 'tuzzy-muzzy' and 'placket hole' in the eighteenth century; and 'jelly roll' in the late nineteenth century. In the twentieth century the phrase *vagina dentata* is first used, deriving from the Latin for 'toothed' and meaning, again according to the *OED*, 'the motif or theme of a vagina equipped with teeth which occurs in myth, folklore, and fantasy, and is said to symbolize fear of castration, the dangers of sexual intercourse, of birth or rebirth'; the *OED* credits anthropologist Robert Lowie with the phrase's first usage, in 1908, in an article on Native American rituals and stories published in the *Journal of American Folklore*. But there will be more of the *dentata* myth in the next section, 'Antecedents'.

In the 1960s, Ashley Montagu, the humanist anthropologist, rather wonderfully described someone uttering an obscenity as being 'like a smuggler cautiously making his way across a forbidden frontier. This is the pathos of profanity'.[84] He also described swearwords as 'astringent' and as having an 'assaultive function'.[85] Montagu attributed the rise in swearwords to an increase in secularization: 'as life becomes more secularized the demythologization of the elements of spiritual power, the pantheon of the gods and their minions, will serve to empty most of the swearer's traditional words of their proscribed potency'.[86] He argued that 'so long as Western societies cling to their chaotically unhealthy attitudes toward sex, the swearer will never want for four-letter words'.[87] He also wrote that '*Fuck* is, indeed, the nonpareil of all the foulest and most inadmissible of all swearwords, four-lettered words or otherwise.'[88] In 1967, for Montagu, then 'fuck' was '*the* four-letter word'.[89] And cultures decide what *the* word should be – it's not fixed. Culture and class are key for Allan and Burridge, too, in their discussion of the MCPC ('Middle-Class Politeness Criterion'), opposed to which is 'coarse' language which is, 'by association, that of the vulgar classes, untrammelled by the middle-class politeness criterion'.[90] Now 'fuck' is far more common, just as 'motherfucker' has shaken itself free of the racial group to whom it's initially attributed by Montagu: 'It may be predicted that this Negro invention will spread quite rapidly to a great part of the English-speaking world.'[91]

Forty years later, Montagu's ironically offensively worded prediction (ironic since 'Negro' is in some ways now more offensive than 'motherfucker') has been borne out, in one study, at least: 'fuck' is now a 'strong' word; the category of 'very strong' is reserved for 'cunt' and 'motherfucker'.[92] However, 'very strong' words were shown, in the same study, to be overused by men more than women, with 'cunt' appearing only 5.51 times per million words spoken by women, but 11.18 times per million words spoken by men.[93] In conducting this research, however, Tony McEnery was acutely aware that his gut instincts and the data he collected were not enough from which to extrapolate. 'I need', he wrote, 'access to something like a Richter scale for BLWs [Bad Language Words]'.[94] One way McEnery found this was to amalgamate pre-existing surveys and data from the BBFC (the British Board of Film Classification). The BBFC supplied a 'scale of offence', from 'very mild' words (*crap, damn, tart*), via 'mild' words (*arse, shit, tits*), to 'moderate' (*gay, nigger, paki, spastic*), strong (*fuck*) and 'very strong' (*cunt, motherfucker*) words.[95] McEnery's findings confirmed that women were less likely than men to use 'strong' or 'very strong' BLWs, and that 'Males direct BLWs at a male target far more often than they do at a female.'[96] In other words, women are less likely than men to use the word *cunt* – *their* word, if you will. Women will seldom use 'their' word as a term of abuse directed at other women. The word is culturally off-limits for women. And yet its origins are exclusively feminine. Most provocative, however, is McEnery's finding that 'the word *cunt* is directed exclusively at males by females. It is a pure intergender BLW for females. This is not true for males, who, while showing a strong preference for directing the word at males, do also direct it at females.'[97]

The word appears 213 times in the British National Corpus (BNC), a collection made in the 1980s and 1990s of around 100 million words from written texts (90%) and informal speech recordings (10%).[98] Each usage is contextualized, and I'd estimate that of the 213, around 175 are dysphemistic. About 13 are denotative, the remaining 25 or so are also denotative *but* are from pornographic contexts. In the dysphemistic group, the word is most often accompanied by 'you' or 'you [*insert adjective of choice*]', or a variant of these. It's used as a name or as an insult, and some of the contexts certainly suggest a degree of, if not affection, then at least non-aggression, in its usage.[99] Its ambiguous connotative/denotative status can also be a source of humour. I'm reminded, here, of an anecdote about the American actor Ethel Merman's (1908–84) very short-lived marriage to Ernest Borgnine (also American, b. 1917). After an audition, Borgnine asked Ethel how it had gone.

> 'Well,' Ethel laughed, 'they were *mad* about my 35-year-old body, my 35-year-old voice, and my 35-year-old face'.
>
> 'Is that so?' said Borgnine. 'And what did they think of your 65-year-old c**t?'
>
> Ethel glared at him. 'You weren't mentioned once.'[100]

For 'cunt' to move to the orthophemistic realm, a seismic linguistic and cultural shift would need to take place. If, as the linguist J. R. Firth astutely put it, 'You shall know a word by the company it keeps', then might positive collocations (words that seem naturally to be bonded together: 'eggs and bacon', '*Cagney and Lacey*', 'beautiful cunt', 'moist . . .', 'tight . . .') overtake dysphemistic ones ('fucking cunt', 'cheating . . .', 'lying . . .')?[101] Or are even restorative collocations too implicated in pornographic associations and connotations ever to regain a widely positive status? British journalist Victoria Coren has argued *against* reclamation, since it would diminish *cunt*'s 'visceral power', and 'to neuter it with daily use, to make it "acceptable to all and sundry"' would be 'an act of terrible vandalism, like demolishing Stonehenge'.[102] Coren's article was prompted by the BBFC's decision to grant director Ken Loach's 2012 film *The Angels' Share* a '15' certificate (thereby cashing in on 15–17 year-old viewers, who would be legally excluded from an '18' movie) *only* if it (in Loach's account, at least) contained no more than seven usages of the word 'cunt', only two of which were allowed to be 'aggressive'. Coren acknowledges that there is 'a feminist argument' to reclaim the word, but concludes that she is 'rather proud that its potency lies in a fear that female sexuality was a dangerous force. It reminds us where we have come from, in at least two ways at once'. While I can see a rationale for Coren's argument, it does miss the point that '*dangerous* forces' (not '*powerful* forces', note) inexorably attract ruthless suppression, and so misogyny finds a rationale.

Down under

If there's this fundamental problem with how to talk about 'it', then there's a real conundrum for companies who want to sell us products to tame, control, and subdue 'it': 'to talk about menstruation in contemporary Western culture is to articulate its secretive, emotionally laden, and shame-filled aspects'.[103] TV ads which show blue liquid being poured from a chemistry-set beaker onto a sanitary pad are commonplace. And, with women in the western world menstruating for the equivalent of six or seven continuous years of their life, there are big bucks to be made.[104] This is not a book about cultural representations of menstruation – Karen Houppert has already done an excellent job with that in *The Curse* – but it *is* about how much, growing up in the 'developed' world, women are exposed to the idea that 'it' is hateful, unruly, unloved, uncharted, unincorporated, even un*named*.[105]

Church and Dwight is an international pharmaceutical company founded in 1846, now employing 3,500 workers, and with net sales of around \$2.6 billion.[106] They're probably best known for their 'Arm and Hammer' products, and market numerous ranges of home and health merchandize, including 'Femfresh' 'personal care' products in the United Kingdom. The Femfresh website shows skinny white women in bright block-colour shift dresses and high heels, throwing back their long hair and laughing the laugh that only the pure joy of having a well-behaved fanny can allow.[107] Some of them even appear to be levitating with the excitement of it all. And if the word 'fanny' grates (probably quite rightly – and puzzlingly, if you're an American reading this), then look at the website. 'Expert care for down there' is the tagline, and then we have: 'Mini, twinkle, hoo haa, fancy, yoni, lady garden [. . .] femfresh is the kindest way to care for your va jay jay, kitty, nooni, la la, froo froo!', and we're told: 'whatever you call it, love it'.[108] But the message is a contradictory one, since were we *actually* to 'love it' then we'd be able to talk about it honestly, and not worry about its potential for betrayal, for leaking, for staining, or for being malodorous in a culture which demonizes menstruation and attempts to fill women with self-hatred. Femfresh's products are 'gynaecologically tested' and 'pH-balanced for specific intimate care', but the words 'vulva', 'clitoris' and 'labia' never appear and even 'vagina' makes a pretty poor show. It's covert visibility in action: *we* (the advertisers) know that *you* (the bleeding ladies) will work out what your intimate *nooni* is, so we don't need to tell you. On one of Femfresh's fact sheets for schoolgirls (if you can instil feelings of shame and inadequacy at a young enough age then you've probably got a consumer for life), a London-based (female) professor of Obstetrics and Gynaecology is quoted, explaining that 'hormonal changes [. . .] alter the pH-balance of our intimate area'.[109] 'Our intimate area'? Is this really the best a gynaecologist can think of?

In five press releases, one fact sheet and ten garish webpages from Femfresh, the words 'vagina', 'vulva', 'clitoris' and 'labia' are conspicuous by their absence. In Femfresh's ten detailed answers to 'FAQs', the word 'vaginal' is – finally (hurrah!) – used, twice, as is the word 'vagina'.[110] By contrast, the word 'intimate' is used more than 20 times in the webpages (not including the press releases and fact sheets). Women have 'intimate skin', 'an intimate environment', engage in 'intimate washes' of their 'intimate areas', need 'intimate care', 'intimate hygiene products' and an 'intimate pH' to fight 'intimate irritants'. If Femfresh's products (and there are many like them on the market, from a range of manufacturers) can 'leave you feeling fresh and confident', then your 'confidence' must, logically – dare I say, *intimately* – be tied not to your intellectual or workplace or family achievements, but to your vaginal 'freshness' attained through using a 'Feminine [. . .] Deodorant' which 'helps limit the development of odour'.[111] Women frequently 'experience menarche as something [. . .] happening *to* them, as something outside of themselves', which they call '"it," giving an illusion of a self that was fragmented'.[112] Such fragmentation is – if you'll forgive the expression – the lifeblood of companies like Femfresh who actively promote it in their literature: 'The pH-balance of the *intimate* skin is different to the pH of *body* skin'.[113] No, Femfresh, my labial skin *is* my 'body skin' because my cunt *is* part of my body. We go everywhere together, my cunt and I. We've known each other for many years and we're very – here's that word again – *intimately* acquainted, thank you. So, 'whatever you call it, love it'. I call 'it' a cunt, or labia, or vulva. I might even acknowledge the clitoris. And I do love 'it', and that's precisely why I don't call 'it' – well – 'it'. But if all women – from the schoolgirls targeted by Femfresh to have a fear of 'odour', to post-menopausal women targeted by Femfresh to dread 'dryness' and 'irritation' – *really* came to love their cunts, then what would happen to that $2.6 billion net sales figure? My mind – for I do have one, Femfresh, even though you want me to call my cunt a 'lady garden' – boggles.

'Lysol' is the brand-name of a disinfectant manufactured by Reckitt Benckiser, a company founded in the 1840s in the United Kingdom, and specializing in cleaning products with operations today in more than 60 countries. Reckitt Benckiser's net revenue for 2011 was £9,485 million (roughly equivalent to $15 billion).[114] Their emphasis is on hygiene: 'RB hygiene brands help promote both personal hygiene for well being and home hygiene to create a safe haven for you and your family'.[115] From the 1920s to the 1950s, however, Lysol's advertising emphasis was less on the safe haven of the home and more on making the vagina a safe haven for men. In a series of extraordinary print advertisements, vaginal douching with Lysol was promoted as a necessity for maintaining a heterosexual relationship. In 1928 'she' could be 'still the girl he married' because, 'during the years following her marriage, she has protected her zest for living, her health and youthfulness, and "stayed young with him"' by using Lysol as a douche; in another ad, from 1934, one 'Dr Helene Stourzh' reassures a woman ignorant of 'the proper method of marriage hygiene' that using Lysol in the 'hidden folds of the feminine membranes' will establish 'a sense of confidence and trust that turns wretched marriages into happy ones'.[116] As late as 1948, 'Married Folks Only' were invited, in a Lysol advertisement, to take a 'Love-quiz'.[117] A picture shows a distraught woman, hands clasped tightly under her chin, turning away from her husband who, coat over arm, is walking out of the door. 'Why does she spend the evenings alone?' asks the ad. Her 'crime' is that she 'neglects that one essential . . . personal feminine hygiene'; here, indeed, is the 'shameful' *pudendum*. In another ad from the same year, Lysol helps a wife to 'hold her lovable charm', and, in the 1950s, 'the other you' (the one who doesn't regularly spray caustic disinfectant into her vagina) 'could wreck your marriage'.[118] Actually, your marriage was far more likely to be 'wrecked' when the potentially harmful effects of Lysol's ingredients were taken into consideration: 'cresol (a distillate of coal and wood), or mercury chloride, either of which, when used in too high a concentration, caused severe inflammation, burning, and even death'.[119] Lysol's efficacy as both marriage-saver and contraceptive was, happily, utterly invalidated in the 1960s, but the *idea* propagated by the manufacturers, that the vagina is somehow not 'good' enough in and of itself, still obtains.

During menstruation, women are encouraged by yet another multinational corporation, Procter and Gamble, to purchase products enhanced with trademarked 'ActiPearls', which make 'period smells [. . .] a thing of the past'.[120] Procter and Gamble, like Reckitt Benckiser, and Church and Dwight, were founded in the early nineteenth century. They now operate in 80 countries worldwide and their 2011 sales figures were a whopping $82.6 billion (around £53 billion).[121] But Procter and Gamble also want women to purchase products when they're *not* menstruating. They want year-round consumers, hence their dogged emphasis on the ever-imminent 'odour' of what Femfresh referred to as the 'froo froo'. Your 'nooni', remember, is a cunning cunt. It will produce odours and generally be an impediment to your health and happiness unless you show it who's boss. Time, then, to 'Feel nothing but beautiful freshness with Always Dailies – every day! They are our thinnest daily pantyliners that keep you and your underwear feeling beautifully fresh.'[122] Further, they're the must-have accessory, a lifestyle choice: 'Like wearing deodorant or lip gloss, using a pantyliner is another nice thing you can do to look after yourself every day.'[123] On a large British supermarket's website in autumn 2012, daily-wear pads like these cost on average 6 pence each. If, out of 365 days a year, a woman menstruates for 84 days and wears pantyliners every day when she's *not* menstruating, that amounts to almost £17 and – more worryingly from an ecological perspective – almost 300 pads per woman per year on landfill sites. And those figures, remember, don't include sanitary towels or tampons. You can't even escape when you're 'Fulfilled and Experienced', post-menopause, since there are problems (which you may not even have known *were* problems) for which you need to buy a solution, because: 'You've been there, done that and got a few grey hairs to prove it [. . .] You're loving life and you're definitely not going to let anything stop you from loving it even more.'[124] For a western woman's entire life, from her first menstrual period to her death, her 'la la' is a moneymaking machine for the big businesses who want to cultivate her 'lady garden'. It's an incommodious house-guest in any woman's body; the independent, unpredictable enemy within. Taking that culturally persistent idea to its logical conclusion is a mesmerizing challenge for the writers, filmmakers and visual artists in whose works the cunt becomes *literally* separated from the woman. The imaginative accounts of that separation form the basis of this book.

What are we to do, then, if we don't have a vocabulary for talking about our own bodies? The lack of a vocabulary deemed 'appropriate' for polite conversation – or even for the doctor's surgery – is distinct. 'Cunt' becomes spectral, haunting our lips as we try to speak of our *lips*. We might talk of our 'pudenda' but the *OED*'s etymology tells us that that means 'that of which one ought to be ashamed'. Is my body shameful? Is my body taboo? Is my body dangerous? Is my body able to maim? Essentialist arguments aside, if I *am* my body, rather than *occupying* my body, the absence of a language silences me. A radical split is forced on me by a culture which dares not speak my name. I *am* my body, but I am also not: 'Our experience of the world is embodied, deeply physical, and sensory, but we also conceive of ourselves and our bodies as separate entities – I and it – that exist in a relationship whereby "I" am the presumed subject and "it" is the presumed object [. . .] We are never entirely its and it is never entirely ours, which makes the body a theater of romantic conflict wherein is staged a sense of impossibility, of "never knowing".'[125] Repeatedly the writers, filmmakers, performers and artists I write about in *The Vagina* confront the 'never knowing' (and sometimes 'never *known*') body. The tension between the polarities of *me* and *my body* grows until body and self are ruptured. The vulva becomes autonomized, 'it' finds a life of its own and its *I* is left flailing in misapprehension and fear. This process of psychical breakdown is one the quirky Slovenian philosopher Slavoj Žižek identifies in his (rather over-enthusiastically detailed) description of heterosexual pornography's 'change of the body into a desubjectivized multitude of partial objects' as 'The woman's body is thus transformed into a multitude of "organs without a body", machines of *jouissance*.'[126] The artist Faith Wilding expresses how, in the 1960s in California, Fresno-based artists were 'doing images of "cunts" – defiantly recuperating a term that traditionally had been used derogatorily and thereby opposing the phallic imagery developed by men [. . .] Making "cunt art" was exciting, subversive, and fun, because cunt signified to us an awakened consciousness about our bodies and our sexual selves.'[127] This is not a new idea. The idea of the cunt – the autonomized cunt in particular – which we'll see in a variety of manifestations in the course of this book, actually forms part of a lengthy literary tradition – the French *fabliau*, or fable – which is as old as *Sheela* herself. In 'Antecedents', I look more closely at this lively literary tradition, tracing the autonomy of anatomy from the *fabliaux* to Denis Diderot, and beyond.

Virgin sticks and cock thieves

To see the contradictory messages circulating around the idea of the cunt, and to understand the contempt in which it's held, one need look no further than that thermometer of the cultural zeitgeist, eBay. A 'worldwide' search on eBay for 'vagina' (press 'Search' even though the search box says 'No suggestions') will produce roughly 2,000 items for sale. In the 'Health and Beauty' category there will be around 200 results on average, including creams, capsules, douches and pessaries which treat the vagina as though it were an object in need of improvement. Most of the items listed here promise to 'tighten' the vagina, or to remove 'odours' from it. The scarily named phallic 'Virgin Stick' is shipped from Malaysia and is sold as a natural herbal product which should be inserted into the vagina for 30 seconds about 15 minutes before intercourse. Even more worrying are the tablets – again from Malaysia – which one should take in order to 'reduce, tighten and further warms [*sic.*] the female intimacy [. . .] Prevent breast and uterine cancer'. Well over 1,000 items are listed in the 'Clothes, Shoes & Accessories' category. Most of these are fairly aggressive T-shirts: 'Your hole is my goal' says one; 'Vagina makes me smile', says another, or 'National Organisation of Pussy Eaters', or 'Vagitarian'. If you prefer, you could have 'Vagina friendly' emblazoned across a 5XL T-shirt, or 'Team Poon'. Also on sale – presumably for those who aren't acquainted with the myth of the *vagina dentata* – are knickers printed with the words 'Cock Thief' or 'Fear My Vagina'. In other categories you can buy silicone, stone or metal sculptures of the labia, some of which are made into jewellery.

For people who don't get out much, there are numerous 'authentic' vaginas; soulless little plastic sex toys which, looking amputated or excised, come packaged in diminutive cardboard product boxes. The 5" 'super sexy realistic pussy' called 'Muffie' is made of 'Love clone material'. On the packaging we read: 'slide it in hard baby! You're in for the time of your life!'. 'In for the time of your life' with no actual woman around, just a pink plastic – sorry: a pink 'Love clone' – handheld object, a house shared with your mother and your unfulfilled dreams for company. From Germany you might choose to import another excised set of genitals, this time on red plastic clockwork feet: you can wind it up and look at it go. Apparently it's a really amusing 'Partygag'. Another German seller will supply you with a vagina moulding kit so that you can fashion a 'Clone-A-Pussy' in the privacy of your own home. Many of the 200 or so 'Books, Comics & Magazines' for sale are copies of Eve Ensler's *Vagina Monologues*, although you can also buy old medical textbooks and some fiction. In the 'Music' section there are CDs from chart-toppers Criminal Vagina ('In Cunt We Trust'), Vagina Dentata Organ and Carnivorous Vagina, or, if you prefer, 'Under the Sign of the Vagina' by Magistral Flatulences. In other categories there are lollipops, specula, anatomical models and bovine semen collection sleeves for sale. It's a pretty unedifying experience, searching these listings: there's a heterosexual bias and women are reduced to vessels, acquiescent pink, excised organs which can be put away when the fun's over (the policies of many of these sellers, mercifully, say that no returns are accepted). Where women are *not* 'reduced' they're defective: too pungent or too 'loose'.

The tangible, commodified, autonomized cunt need not, however, always be a monstrous entity. The self-styled 'Vulvalutionary', Dorrie Lane, made her first vulva puppet in 1993. Her puppets now sell worldwide and are stocked in the United Kingdom by Sh!, the 'Women's Erotic Emporium'. Sh! describes them as: 'beautifully crafted fabric puppets/cushions of the vulva [for . . .] sex education classes, and discussion of women's health and sexuality'.[128] It's certainly refreshing to have a company *calling* a vulva a vulva. It's a politically sound product, too – no Chinese 'Cock Thieves' production lines are in operation here: 'Vulva Puppets are manufactured by hand, by a women's Co-operative in Manchay, Peru, from high quality fabrics'. The choice of locale is significant: Manchay is one of Peru's largest shantytowns, and it's also the setting for Claudia Llosa's award-winning 2009 film *La Teta Asustada* (*The Milk of Sorrow*).[129] Llosa's work portrays the viciousness meted out on numerous indigenous women raped in Peru's civil war in the 1980s and 1990s. There's something profoundly moving about the intensely healing potential for brutalized women, in stitching these puppets, 'made from wine-red velvet and lavender silk, [. . .] as gorgeous to touch as to behold!' Ultimately, this autonomized organ has an altogether different audience: it's a celebratory *objet d'art*, a healing tool, not a masturbatory fantasy. As Sh! proclaims: 'Vulva puppets make lovely presents for daughters, sisters, lovers, mothers and friends. The Vulva Puppet is sufficiently detailed to be used [. . .] educationally and elegant enough to have pride of place in your home – a vulva puppet on your sofa will certainly be a talking point!'[130]

Covert visibility

In 1785, *The Gentleman's Magazine and Historical Chronicle* published an account of an encounter between Samuel Johnson and 'a literary lady [who was] expressing to Dr. J. her approbation of his Dictionary and, in particular, her satisfaction at his not having admitted into it any *improper words*; "No, Madam," replied he, "I hope I have not daubed my fingers. I find, however, that you have been looking for them.""[131] This is a wonderful example of 'covert visibility'; the paradox which structures so many of the texts and images which are the focus of *The Vagina*. In searching for the 'improper words' the 'literary lady' had to have known what those words were. Yet, for the sake of propriety, she had to appear to have been relieved not to have found them, but in so admitting, she exposes herself to Johnson's gentle ridicule. Both Johnson and the woman know what words cannot be mentioned, or printed in his Dictionary, and in discussing their absence from the book are conjuring them up. The words are hidden and yet open: covertly visible.

The idea of the 'covert visibility' of the 'cunt' is an enduring one. So, Johnson and his companion choreographed their conversation around it in the mid-eighteenth century; and it's still in evidence today. *Will & Grace*, a multi-award winning NBC TV show which aired for 8 series from 1998 to 2006, is, of course, worlds away from the literary salons of Johnson's day. Yet the motif endures. In one episode, the perpetually wasted Manhattan socialite Karen (Megan Mullally) gets engaged to wealthy Lyle Finster (John Cleese). Karen's relationship with Finster's adult daughter, Lorraine (Minnie Driver), is strained: 'I've been like a mother to that girl', Karen protests in another episode, 'I've locked her in her room; I've told her she was fat; and once even left her in a store'.[132] As Karen rows with Lorraine, telling her, 'Hit the road, you syphilitic toad!', Finster warns: 'Karen! If there's one thing I will not tolerate, it's rhyming insults.'[133] Undeterred, Lorraine shouts 'Sow!' to which Karen immediately responds 'Cow!'. When Lorraine straightaway retorts with 'Runt!', it is only thanks to Finster's intervention 'Stop it!', while pointing his finger at Karen's open mouth that Karen does not respond.

The extraordinary moment of 'covert visibility' on an extremely successful American TV show known for its gentle sexual innuendo, here dances around the danger-zone of 'cunt'. Covert visibility defines the 'seen unseen' or the 'heard unheard'; in its not-being-said the word 'cunt' looms large above the characters on the screen. As audience members we conjure it up and delight in its imaginary presence while the television programme maintains its wholesome-but-raunchy primetime image and resists scaring the advertisers away. It's a great example of humour as participation – we're not passive receptors of others' linguistic play but we instead delight in our ability to invoke the taboo word. In the next season, for example, Jack (a homosexual man, played by Sean Hayes), is irritated by Grace's (a heterosexual woman, played by Debra Messing) sexual frustration.[134] 'Well, you'd better do it soon', he tells her, 'you know what they say: if you don't use it, it falls off'. To this, Grace replies in a hesitant tone: 'What . . . exactly . . . will fall off?' 'I dunno', replies Jack, 'I dunno what you guys have down there!' Again it is down to Karen to provide the punchline. 'Let me explain', she softly begins, 'Imagine the most beautiful flower you've ever seen, its petals opening as it's gently touched by the sun [. . .] Now imagine a vagina next to that.' Karen's abrupt closing down of the metaphor confounds expectations and makes the unseen momentarily visible. Significantly, it leaves Jack none the wiser. Covert invocation functions as a process similar to that described by Allan and Burridge where 'one characteristic of euphemism is that it involves doublethink: in a given context, something tabooed can be acceptably spoken of using a cross-varietal synonym that avoids dysphemism by employing a euphemism'.[135] The audience are holding in their minds simultaneously two quite contradictory ideas: the taboo of the unspoken word and the possibility of its having been conjured up. It isn't an idea that's confined to 'cunt' of course, but it's in its disingenuousness around women's bodies that it's most damaging. 'Fuck' can also be covertly visible: Peter Silverton recalls a psychology lecturer explaining the role of the hypothalamus in controlling 'the four Fs [. . .] Feeding, flight, fight and . . . sexual behaviour'.[136] It's in that ellipsis, in those three little dots, that the word 'fuck' exists, spectral but nonetheless apparent, and sufficiently potent for French Connection United Kingdom to capitalize on, in its FCUKing advertising campaigns.

In the *Guardian* newspaper in 2005, Mimi Spencer wrote about how difficult it was to explain to her then almost-three-year-old daughter how to talk about her own body. 'Where to start?' asked the bemused mother: 'Like tapenade or mortgage repayment, ["vagina"] sounds strange issuing from the lips of a toddler.'[137] In an anecdotal, somewhat unscientific survey of my own, in April 2012, I asked colleagues, family, friends and social-networking contacts to fill in an anonymous online survey I'd written called 'Cultural Attitudes to Female Genitalia'.[138] I had 54 respondents, including 40 women, 12 men and 2 people who chose not to identify themselves as either male or female – 27 were aged between 21 and 35 years of age; 19 were 36 to 49; and the remaining 8 were 50+. In one question, I asked: 'When you were a child, what words did your primary carer use when talking about genitalia (male and female)?' The answers suggest that the inability Spencer identified in finding an appropriate and accurate name is nothing new. The names ranged from the accurate but restricting ('private parts', 'your bits', 'yourself'); to the anatomically suspect ('front bottom', 'tail [. . .] women had smaller tails than men!', 'down there', 'thingie', 'wee-wee hole'); to the poetically perplexing ('lee lee', 'flower', 'fanny', 'lady garden', 'dupa', 'Ha'penny', 'china', 'Who-ha').[139] Eight respondents did recall their primary carer calling, if not a spade a spade, then at least a cunt a 'vagina'. Dialogue is vital. In their cheery book *Read My Lips*, Debby Herbenick and Vanessa Schick advise their readers to 'Keep talking [. . .] Sometimes even the "not nice" things will get a conversation going. The worst thing we can do to our vulvas is ignore them.'[140]

Later in the same survey, I asked the question: 'How old were you (roughly) when you first heard the word "cunt"?' Approximately the same number of respondents had heard the word before they were 12 (24 people), as had heard it once a teenager (26 people). The remaining four people were 20+ when they heard it for the first time. The youngest recalled contact age was 5; the oldest was 25. The dysphemistic identity of the word was apparent to the respondent who wrote that they heard the word as a term 'of abuse, [aged] about 8; as a descriptive word, about 15'; and to the one who wrote that 'I can't remember! Probably pretty early on in high school, although I'm sure it was a long time before I realized it was a word for vagina and not just a terrible insult. I probably became more aware of it when I read Irvine Welsh's books at about 15/16.' For another respondent, the word's restricted currency emphasizes the 'ownership' aspect of the word: 'I can't remember[;] probably around 10 YRS, heard my older brother say it.' While 61.1 per cent of respondents said they did not use the word 'cunt' regularly, in answering another question, 35.2 per cent of all those who completed the questionnaire said they 'liked' the word, but 29.6 per cent thought it an 'ugly' word. 16.7 per cent reported having no strong feelings one way or another about the word. Covert visibility is arguably at play in the creation of slang terms which must stand in for the female genitalia when 'cunt' can't do. Slang operates in specific communities whose members coin their own linguistic constructs and understandings. Slang both protects the speaker and typically denigrates the spoken *of*. Here's a selection of slang terms, gathered from the somewhat unedifying urbandictionary.com:

pussy, twat, beaver, taco, camel toe, muff, snatch, fuck-hole, oven, penis-glove, cock sock, cock pocket, hoo-hah, slit, trim, quim, pooter, love rug, poontang, poonanie, cooch, tunnel of love, bearded clam, cookie, honey pot, cunny, vag, meat curtains, hatchet wound, putz, fur burger, box, front bottom, gash, kebab, kitty, minge, snapper, catfish, vertical smile, lovebox, love canal, nana, black hole, sperm sucker, cock warmer, whisker biscuit, carpet, deep socket, cum craver, cock squeezer, slice of heaven, flesh cavern, the great divide, cherry, clit slit, fuzz box, fuzzy-wuzzy, glory hole, grumble, man in the boat, mound, peach, the furry cup, wizard's sleeve, cock holster, cockpit, snooch, sniz, grassy knoll, rosebud, curly curtains, furry furnace, velcro love triangle, nether lips, altar of love, Cupid's cupboard, bird's nest, bucket, cock-chafer, fun hatch, pink circle, silk igloo, Republic of Labia, juice box, Golden Palace, Holiest of Holies, yo-yo smuggler, mumbler, crotch waffle, crack, Melvin, beaver teeth, hungry minge, welly top, fortune nookie, conch shell, crack of heaven, jelly roll, lobster pot, bunny tuft, knish, enchilada of love, queef quarters, holy grail, pole hole, Wombsday Book, field of dreams, bean, cooze, old catcher's mitt, devil's hole, Lawrence of a Labia, the promised land, cha-cha, the shrine, bitch ditch, yoni, grandest canyon, happy valley, wand-waxer, Hairy Potter, jaws of life, Pandora's box, Cuntzilla, mystical fold.[141]

The Canadian comedian and musician Jon Lajoie has experimented with the numerous sobriquets for the cunt in his song 'Vaginal Hubris', which is dedicated, delightfully inappropriately, to his fictional sister-in-law.[142] 'She's proud of her pussy, her peach', he raps: 'her bearded clam is well-groomed. / Thinks that she's the real deal, all other pussies are cartoons. / Her vagina is a church and her clit is the steeple; her vulva's one of Barbara Walters's most fascinating people'. The chorus informs us that: 'She's got vaginal hubris, vaginal hubris. / According to her vag all other pussies are useless. / Vaginal hubris, vaginal hubris. / Her pussy confidence is unbreakable like Bruce Willis.' Later, we're told that 'If her pussy made movies, it'd be Stanley Kubrick [. . .] She assumes that her Muffhammed Ali never loses.' Lajoie revels in the linguistic possibilities of the spoken/unspoken cunt – albeit in a naughtily puerile manner. Were 'cunt' less dysphemistic, might the slang substitutions for it be dropped, or rendered unnecessary or would new terms enter the linguistic currency? Nature abhors a vacuum; if we legitimize 'cunt', something else dysphemistic will take its place. That's both the beauty and insufficiency of language. It evolves, becomes freighted with nuance and connotation. *Denotation* is less malleable, but even that is beyond our control to some extent. Above all, it can be said with some certainty that such slang terms render the female body even more divided and ruptured linguistically, metaphorically and psychically.

Armed to the teeth

The fear of the word *cunt* both derives from, and reflects, the fear of the thing, and the two – sign and signified – enter into a dizzying, cyclical relationship one with the other. Freud's legacy is nowhere more in evidence than here: in his revivification of the ancient – and multicultural – myth of the *vagina dentata*, the 'toothed vagina', he endorsed the demonization of the cunt. We do not, of course, need to buy wholesale into Freud's work to find in his terminology a useful way of framing the issues which lie at the heart of the artists' work as discussed in this book. Terms which conjure up the image of the *vagina dentata* are numerous. Epithets include 'snatch', 'dickmuncher', 'snapper', 'grabber', 'penis fly trap', 'black hole', 'grinder', 'vicious circle'.[143] But the taboo around the word 'cunt' is a reasonably recent invention. The fear of the *vagina dentata* may be primeval at its core, but the demonization of the *word* 'cunt' as dysphemistic comes far later – how else might one explain the proliferation of 'cunte' place names? We also need to ask what's at the root of the dysphemism.

Its taboo status certainly has anthropological, psychological origins which are enmeshed with its linguistic sources. Castration anxiety (more properly 'amputation' anxiety) has a large role to play, here. The myth of the *vagina dentata* (and, to a far lesser extent, its punitive mythical corollary, the *penis aculeatus* ('the spiny or prickly penis')), has served universally for millennia to perpetuate a morbid fear of women's genitals. I explore this in more depth in 'Antecedents', next.

The cunt is taboo, and it also has a powerful, almost sacred totemic status. The sensual encounters with Christ's wounds experienced by the eighteenth-century Moravian Protestant Nikolaus von Zinzendorf suggest a powerful eroticization of the holy body assimilated into a visualization of the vagina. As Craig Atwood has drolly noted, 'familiarity with Freud is not required to recognize that the side wound is a vaginal symbol, especially since Zinzendorf himself repeatedly identified it as a womb or birth canal'.[144] Atwood argues that a community (such as Zinzendorf's *Gemeinde*, or congregation) *needs* to create a metaphorical, ritualistic orifice – often with vaginal associations – through which new members may enter. As the anthropologist Mary Douglas writes, 'the human body is always treated as an image of society and [. . .] there can be no natural way of considering the body that does not at the same time involve a social dimension. Interest in its apertures depends on the preoccupation with social exits and entrances, escape routes and invasions'.[145] Religion, as a systematized set of rules, perhaps most powerfully counsels the imposition of this 'unnatural' social dimension on the body; the Virgin Mary can have no vagina, for this would be to pollute her. By contrast, Mary's son, in the Moravian tradition, for example, wears vaginal insignia to signify precisely such a pollution and invasion, but of the *male* body – a body which is ultimately redeemed.[146]

The apparent cultural ubiquity of the cunt, whereby it is pathologized or eroticized, can hide its resistance to these polarities of representation. As in the anecdote from *Will and Grace*, the cunt is less the 'c-word' (that euphemistic abbreviation so many of us encountered as children) than the don't-*see*-word. Its reality is hidden in the overt exposure of pornography and in the controlling discursive practises of medicine. It's even been suggested that canonical medical textbooks, such as Gray's *Anatomy*, do not accurately name or explicate the female genitalia, the clitoris specifically.[147] What the artists whose work is going to be looked at in this book at have in common is a desire to confront the paradoxical hidden-ness of the cunt in modern culture. The cunt is omnipresent, but the same societies which produce and consume pornography in immense quantities are the same ones which mask – or silence – the thing itself. From the sailor-consuming *vagina dentata* flowers in Peter Jackson's lavish 2005 remake of *King Kong* to the chomping Kraken of *Pirates of the Caribbean: Dead Man's Chest* a year later, we are invited to gaze on the primordial cunt, a cunt which is not seen truthfully or in an enabling way for women. This means that many western women are brought up to dislike their own cunts. Inga Muscio summarizes the situation in her characteristically no-nonsense way: 'The fact that women learn to dislike an actual, undeniable, unavoidable region of ourselves results in a crappy Sisyphean situation [. . .] My cunt is *mine*.'[148] Germaine Greer rightly bemoans the fact that 'femininity is still compulsory for women and has become an option for men, while genuine femaleness remains grotesque to the point of obscenity', and remarks, evoking covert visibility's cultural machinations, that 'Advertising of sanitary protection can no more mention blood than advertising of toilet paper can mention shit.'[149]

The scope of *The Vagina*

At the heart of my book, as this Introduction has proposed, are two key tenets. These are the notions of covert visibility, and of the autonomized cunt, and they are manifest in many and varied forms and combinations. What happens to that paradoxical unseen-c-word when it is rendered visible in artistic and imaginative representation? What happens to women when their psychical and physiological identities come apart and the hitherto unspeakable and unseen cunt both speaks and is seen?

There are – of course – many other books about female genitalia. But my approach is different. It moves away from, for example, books by Catherine Blackledge and Jelto Drenth. Blackledge's aim in her *Story of V: Opening Pandora's Box* was to look at 'vaginal variance across species'.[150] Her frame of reference differs from my own as, in fewer than 300 pages, she attempts to explore vaginas cross-culturally, across species, and trans-historically. Her background is in science, and this is very apparent since she looks at representation only in passing, and in relation to a select few texts. She focuses on the sexual organs of fruit flies. Her work here is thorough, but since my own knowledge of them begins and ends with Groucho Marx ('Time flies like an arrow. Fruit flies like a banana'), my focus will not be entomological. My book also differs from Drenth's *Origin of the World: Science and Fiction of the Vagina* where, once more, the emphasis is on anatomy and function rather than on how cultures *represent* that anatomy and function.[151] Drenth's chapter titles indicate this, ranging from 'The Anatomy of the Female Genitals: the Facts', through 'On Reproduction', to 'Idealization and Worship of the Female Genitals'. His title is a nod to Gustave Courbet's famous painting of 1865 – a painting which I also discuss in 'Antecedents'. A year after Drenth, Carol Livoti and Elizabeth Topp published their *Vaginas: An Owner's Manual*.[152] While this is a readable (and, in places, enlightening) book, this mother and daughter writing team again come at the topic with a practical, rather than analytical, goal in mind, and have also been criticized for factual, gynaecological inaccuracies in their writing.

More recently, Naomi Wolf's *Vagina: A New Biography*, a book which met with a storm of controversy on publication, examines the relationship between cognition and sexual response.[153] Wolf synthesizes autobiography, culture and neuroscience in her book, which appeared at an extraordinary time, for 2012 was the year when Michigan State Rep. Lisa Brown was officially admonished for using the word 'vagina' in a debate about abortion; the feminist 'Pussy Riot' activists in Putin's Russia were imprisoned for hooliganism; and Missouri's Todd Akin made remarks about 'legitimate' rape. It seems that never before have women's bodies been so globally debated, and never before has the 'personal' been quite so 'political'. The enduring popularity of Eve Ensler's *Vagina Monologues* continues, of course, to maintain the presence of the cunt in popular culture.[154] In *The Vagina* I ask some challenging questions about Ensler's work in thinking about vaginas and performance art later in this book. One critical text worth mentioning because it examines medical discourses of the vagina while also considering, for example, Annie Sprinkle's work and the films of 'cinematic surgeon' David Cronenberg, is the brilliantly titled *Public Privates: Performing Gynecology From Both Ends of the Speculum* by Terri Kapsalis.[155]

It's also important in this Introduction, in considering what this book is *not* explicitly about, to consider where it might lead, and in *The Vagina's* conclusion I anticipate what interventions theoretical discourses might make in the activist sphere. The issues considered there, then, are obscenity, female genital mutilation (FGM), labiaplasty procedures, menstruation, pornography and, far more optimistically, the transgendered body. I could, of course, devote an entire book to any one of these topics alone, but that has not been my project here. Instead, the theoretical dualism I do establish over the course of the next 300 or so pages – covert visibility and the autonomous organ – is unquestionably enmeshed with activism, since we need to understand *how* women have been denied access, in terms of control or autonomy, to the 'truth' of their own genitals. The global disempowerment of women reflects the fact that physical brutality is both a theoretical discourse and a corporeal reality in the lives of millions.

I wrote that my concluding thoughts on the transgendered body were 'optimistic'. This is because the other directions in which the conclusion points are 'problems': how do we understand the rapidly increasing demand for labiaplasty procedures? What are the effects of pornography on women's lives? How do we stop FGM (and, controversially, *should* we? Who has the right to say that one culture's traditions are 'wrong' and another's are 'right'?)? My conversations with transsexuals during the writing of this book have made it clear to me that the 'problems' they experience are due to fundamental cultural prejudices. In thinking about performance art, I look at the work of transgendered performers to see how they wrest with issues of essentialism and social bias. Who has a 'cunt'? Can gender reassignment surgery gift, or remove, a cunt? I will not view gender and sexuality through the unquestioning prism of what Morgan Holmes terms 'absolute dimorphism'.[156] Nor will I fall into the trap of critiquing one hegemonic binary only to capitulate to another which traps intersexed people in an uncongenial place somewhere between 'normality' and 'monstrosity'.[157] In any discussions such as the ones my book undertakes, it's crucial to read the body as both symbolic and anatomical. It's Holmes who, again, summarizes this idea beautifully, in positioning the body not only as a 'biological *fact* but as a historically contingent and culturally bounded *diagnosis*'.[158]

In *The Vagina*, I trace the origins of the idea of the uncontrollable or self-governing cunt back to the myth of the *vagina dentata* – a story with an astonishing geographic and chronological reach. I explore how bawdy medieval French fables have a potent thematic afterlife in today's novels, plays, films and TV programmes. There's a vast range of literary genres that experiment with notions of covert visibility and the autonomized cunt, and that ask challenging and important questions: What happens when the female body is put on display, and 'cunts' somehow 'speak'? What are we to do if we don't have a name for a woman's genitals? Where are her labia left if her lips are silenced? *How* artists – writers, painters, sculptors, filmmakers and performers – contend with the connected issues of representation, obscenity and authenticity, in representing women's bodies, is central to *The Vagina*. This is, above all, a book about the emancipation of the 'cunt' from passivity and objectification into the far more positive realms of creativity and self-determination.

Notes

1   G. R. Lewis, *Illustrations of Kilpeck Church, Herefordshire: In a Series of Drawings made on the Spot. With an Essay on Ecclesiastical Design, and a Descriptive Interpretation* (London: Pickering, 1842), p. 15.

2   See Emma L. E. Rees, 'Sheela's Voracity and Victorian Veracity', in Liz Herbert McAvoy and Teresa Walters (eds), *Consuming Narratives: Gender and Monstrous Appetite in the Middle Ages and the Renaissance* (Cardiff: University of Wales Press, 2002), pp. 116–27.

3   Virginia Braun, 'Breaking a Taboo? Talking (and Laughing) about the Vagina', *Feminism and Psychology*, 9.3 (1999), pp. 367–72 (p. 367).

4   Braun, 'Breaking a Taboo?', p. 368.

5   Ibid., p. 370.

6   This is the same colleague who, after a scholarly presentation I gave on the ubiquity of the myth of the *vagina dentata*, loudly declared – twice, in case he hadn't been heard by sufficient numbers of people the first time – 'Well! That's it! I'm only going to masturbate from now on!'

7   V. Braun and S. Wilkinson, 'Socio-Cultural Representations of the Vagina', *Journal of Reproductive and Infant Psychology*, 19.1 (2001), pp. 17–32 (p. 28, n. 1).

8   Germaine Greer, *Balderdash and Piffle* (BBC2, first broadcast 30 January 2006); Gloria Steinem, 'Foreword' in Eve Ensler, *The Vagina Monologues* (London: Virago, 2001), pp. ix–xix (p. xix); Ensler, *The Vagina Monologues*, p. 89.

9   All quotations in this paragraph are from Greer, *Balderdash and Piffle*.

10   I'm conscious here of the debt this phrase owes to John Lennon and Yoko Ono's 1972 single 'Woman is the Nigger of the World' (John & Yoko/Plastic Ono Band, *Some Time in New York City*, Apple/EMI, 1972).

11   Ruth Wajnryb, *Language Most Foul: A Good Look at Bad Language* (Sydney: Allen and Unwin, 2005), p. 42. Wajnryb's book was republished in the United States as *Expletive Deleted: A Good Look at Bad Language* (New York, NY: Free Press, 2005), having appeared in the United Kingdom as *C U Next Tuesday. A Good Look at Bad Language* (London: Aurum, 2004).

12   Wajnryb, *Language Most Foul*, p. 44.

13   Greer, *Balderdash*.

14   Wajnryb, *Language Most Foul*, p. 47.

15   Ibid., p. 51.

16   Keith Allan and Kate Burridge, *Forbidden Words: Taboo and the Censoring of Language* (Cambridge: Cambridge University Press, 2006), p. 11.

17   Allan and Burridge, *Forbidden Words*, p. 242, my italics. The idea that 'cunt' is less 'disturbing' in other languages is suggested by the fact that 'although French *con* and Spanish *coño* have the same origin and literal meaning as *cunt*, their extended uses are much less dysphemistic', p. 52. On the distinctions between euphemism ('sweet talking'), dysphemism ('speaking offensively') and orthophemism ('straight talking'), see p. 1.

18   Luke Leitch, 'Workers 'C' Red over Word-Play at Library', *The Evening Standard* (22 October 2004), www.thisislondon.co.uk/news/workers-c-red-over-wordplay-at-library-6943080.html.

19   Maev Kennedy, 'Library Show for Word Rhyming with Hunt', *The Guardian* (23 October 2004), www.guardian.co.uk/uk/2004/oct/23/education.arts?INTCMP=ILCNETTXT3487.

20   Justice Oliver Wendell Holmes, summarizing *Towne v. Eisner* (1918), quoted in Randall Kennedy, *Nigger: The Strange Career of a Troublesome Word* (New York, NY: Random House, 2003), p. 44.

21   Kennedy, *Nigger*, p. 27.

22   Ibid., pp. 9, 23.

23   Ibid., p. 23.

24   Ibid., p. 29.

25   Ibid., p. 38.

26   Allan and Burridge, *Forbidden Words*, p. 104.

27   The relationship between signifier and signified was articulated in the early 1900s by the Swiss linguist Ferdinand de Saussure: 'language is a convention, and the nature of the sign that is agreed upon does not matter'. Ferdinand de Saussure, *Course in General Linguistics*, trans. Wade Baskin; ed. Perry Meisel and Haun Saussy (New York, NY: Columbia University Press, 2011), p. 10.

28 Kennedy, *Nigger*, p. 35.

29 Lisa Z. Sigel, *Governing Pleasures: Pornography and Social Change in England, 1815–1914* (New Brunswick, NJ: Rutgers University Press, 2002), p. 4.

30 Mark Morton, *The Lover's Tongue: A Merry Romp through the Language of Love and Sex* (Ontario: Insomniac Press, 2003), p. 132.

31 Allan and Burridge, *Forbidden Words*, p. 239.

32 Carolee Schneemann, 'Two London Letters', in Carolee Schneemann (ed.), *Imaging Her Erotics: Essays, Interviews, Projects* (Cambridge, MA: The MIT Press, 2002), pp. 95–6 (p. 95).

33 Kathy Acker, *Algeria: A Series of Invocations Because Nothing Else Works* (London: Aloes Books, 1984), p. 5.

34 Cosey Fanni Tutti, personal email correspondence with the author, 31 May 2012.

35 Kennedy, *Nigger*, p. 36.

36 Ibid., p. 37.

37 Ibid., p. 40.

38 Stewart Home, *Cunt* (London: The Do-Not Press, 1999); Inga Muscio, *Cunt: A Declaration of Independence* (New York, NY: Seal Press, 2002).

39 Kennedy uses 'eradicationist' to describe those who 'seek to drive *nigger* out of rap, comedy, and all other categories of entertainment even when (perhaps *especially* when) blacks themselves are the ones using the N-word', *Nigger*, p. 36.

40 Kennedy, *Nigger*, p. 48.

41 Sigel, *Governing Pleasures*, p. 5.

42 Kennedy, *Nigger*, p. 41.

43 Ibid., p. 54; *Chaplinsky v. New Hampshire* (1942), cited in Kennedy, *Nigger*, p. 54. As Allan and Burridge argue, 'Insults are normally *intended* to wound the addressee or bring a third party into disrepute, or both', *Forbidden Words*, p. 79, my italics for emphasis.

44 Kennedy, *Nigger*, p. 56.

45 On Russell Lawrence Lee's unsuccessful attempt in 1992 to change his name legally to 'Mister [actually 'Misteri'] Nigger', see Kennedy, *Nigger*, p. 88.

46 See Murray Wardrop, 'Anti-Semitic Abuse "rife among football fans"', *The Telegraph*, 14 April 2011. Peter Silverton writes compellingly of Tottenham fans' appropriation of the term, and of how fans of other clubs still use it pejoratively: 'their voices and hearts are still filled with hatred. As with nigger, it's the thought that counts, not the word'. Peter Silverton, *Filthy English: The How, Why, When and What of Everyday Swearing* (London: Portobello Books, 2009), p. 248.

47 Le Vine v DPP, Royal Courts of Justice, London, 06 May 2010. Neutral citation number: [2010] EWHC 1128 (Admin). Co/4271/2010. Special thanks are due to Jac Armstrong of the University of Chester for helping me with this aspect of my argument.

48 Christopher M. Fairman, 'Fuck' (March 2006), pp. 1–74 (p. 53). Ohio State Public Law Working Paper No. 59; Center for Interdisciplinary Law and Policy Studies Working Paper Series No. 39. Available at SSRN: http://ssrn.com/abstract=896790

or http://dx.doi.org/10.2139/ssrn.896790. See also cases cited by Fairman where, in 1993 and 1989, US courts found 'bitch', 'slut', 'cunt', 'twat' and 'bitch' to be gender-specific, but 'sick bitch' to be a 'not [*sic.*] gender-related term'. Fairman, p. 54, n. 296.

49 UK Deed Poll Service official website, accessed 27 March 2012: www.ukdps.co.uk/AreThereAnyRestrictionsOnNames.html. The same set of rules mandates against names which are 'impossible to pronounce'. This is extremely subjective: *you* might be able to pronounce a name, but for *me* it's 'impossible'.

50 Kennedy, *Nigger*, p. 139.

51 Silverton, *Filthy English*, p. 69.

52 Eilert Ekwall, *Street-Names of the City of London* (Oxford: Clarendon, 1965), p. 164.

53 Ekwall, *Street-Names*, p. 165.

54 Keith Briggs, 'OE and ME *cunte* in place-names', *Journal of the English Place-Name Society*, 41 (2009), 26–39 (29).

55 Ekwall, *Street-Names*, p. 165.

56 Ibid.

57 Briggs, 'OE and ME', p. 26.

58 For this wonderful list and more see Ibid., p. 27.

59 Ibid. To the best of my knowledge no globally famous footballer has ever lived in Sandford Orcas.

60 Ibid., pp. 28–31.

61 Ibid., p. 29.

62 On the plausibility of *grōp*, *grēp* and *grēpe* meaning 'a ditch, [or] drain', see Ekwall's work on the origins of the name of the Cheshire town of Grappenhall, in Eilert Ekwall, *The Concise Oxford Dictionary of English Place-Names* (Oxford: Clarendon, 1936), p. 193; Briggs, 'OE and ME', p. 31.

63 Jonathon Green, *The Cassell Dictionary of Slang* (London: Cassell, 1998), p. 301.

64 Green, *The Cassell Dictionary of Slang*, p. 301.

65 Briggs, 'OE and ME', p. 31, my italics.

66 In *Balderdash and Piffle*, Greer visits EC1, near St Pancras, which she claims was an infamous haunt for prostitutes, and that *this* was how its name, 'Gropecunte Lane', came into being. If it did, then it was almost certainly because of a waste channel running along it and, through some misogynist metonymy, the prostitutes' bodies and the gully became synonymous. As Briggs writes of the *Gropecuntelane* names, 'hard evidence for or against prostitution has yet to be found'. Keith Briggs, email correspondence with the author, 16 February 2012.

67 Briggs, 'OE and ME', p. 27. Were the golfers ever to find out the origins of their course it might well lead to 'a hole in one' taking on a whole new meaning.

68 For this glorious map of the place-names discussed in his essay, see Briggs, 'OE and ME', p. 32. On a more serious note, however, one must bear in mind Briggs's (frustratingly undeveloped) claim that 'Shavecuntewelle' (or 'Shauecuntewelle') might once have been 'a site of humiliating punishment of women'. See Ibid., p. 33. Briggs writes that 'this case has been known to toponymists for decades and no new

information has turned up'. He bases his theory on the parallels in tone with the punishment of women using stocks or ducking stools, but no hard evidence that an equally debasing activity did go on at 'Shavecuntewelle'. Keith Briggs, personal email correspondence with the author, 16 February 2012.

69   Briggs, 'OE and ME', p. 34.

70   Of course, one must be aware that the aerial views we can obtain of the landscape today were not available to our ancestors, but even from a land-based distance, some copses and clefts may, nonetheless, have looked suggestive.

71   *The Proverbs of Hending* has been dated at the earlier 1260, collected by the compiler of the Harleian manuscript in about 1315. See Thomas Oliphant, *The Old and Middle English* (London: Macmillan, 1878), p. 338. It is dated to around 1300 in Kenneth Jackson's *Studies in Early Celtic Nature Poetry* (Cambridge: Cambridge University Press, 1935), p. 147.

72   I'm indebted to Greg Hulsman of Trinity College, Dublin, for his help with the *Cursor Mundi*.

73   See Gordon Williams, *A Dictionary of Sexual Language and Imagery in Shakespearean and Stuart Literature* (London: The Athlone Press, 1994), p. 724. 'Here shall he lock her cunt', the translation goes, 'and lay the key under his head; he shall sleep'.

74   Geoffrey Chaucer, *The Miller's Tale* in *The Canterbury Tales* in Larry D. Benson et al. (eds), *The Riverside Chaucer* (Oxford: Oxford University Press, 2008), p. 69, l. 3276.

75   Barbara G. Walker, *The Woman's Encyclopedia of Myths and Secrets* (San Francisco, CA: Harper Collins, 1983), p. 197.

76   Thomas D'Urfey, *Wit and Mirth: Or Pills to Purge Melancholy* (London: Pearson, 1719), p. 322.

77   For the *cuneus* link, as for so much else in this section, I am indebted to Matthew Hunt: www.matthewhunt.com.

78   On Partridge's pioneering stance, see Green, *The Cassell Dictionary of Slang*, pp. 300–01; see also Ashley Montagu, *The Anatomy of Swearing* (London: Rapp and Whiting, 1967), where he recounts how, even as late as 1967, Partridge's *Dictionary of Slang and Unconventional English* could not 'be obtained in many libraries, and in some is kept under lock and key and may be looked at only after special application' (p. 306).

79   Green, *The Cassell Dictionary of Slang*, p. 301.

80   Francis Grose, *A Classical Dictionary of the Vulgar Tongue*, 2nd edn (London: S. Hooper, Facing Bloomsbury Square, 1788), n. p.

81   Allan and Burridge, *Forbidden Words*, p. 54; Silverton, however, I think without much foundation, argues that Grose is merely punning here, since 'nasty was also slang for vagina', *Filthy English*, p. 56.

82   Grose, *A Classical Dictionary*, n. p.

83   *OED*; Grose, *Classical Dictionary*, n. p. Quite how Scottish, Welsh or Irish women reacted to the same word in the eighteenth century remains unrecorded. Manning's novel was also published under the somewhat unfortunate title of *Her Privates We*, a quotation from the same exchange in *Hamlet* that inspired the alternative title. Guildenstern replies to Hamlet's statement that he and Rosencrantz 'live about her waist, or in the middle of her favours', with 'Faith, her privates we'. This is developed

by Hamlet, in a moment of characteristic innuendo, into: 'In the secret parts of Fortune? O, most true – she [Fortune] is a strumpet'. See William Shakespeare, *Hamlet*, ed. Ann Thompson and Neil Taylor (London: Arden Shakespeare, Third Series, 2006), 2.2.227–31. Later, Hamlet speaks the now infamous line to Ophelia: 'Do you think I mean country matters?' 3.2.123. In a performance at the Young Vic in London in November 2011, the actor Michael Sheen delivered this line with a full pause after the first syllable of 'country'. The audience's shock was audible. A similarly crude 'cunt' pun appears in the letter Maria has sent to Malvolio, having forged Olivia's handwriting, in *Twelfth Night*. 'By my life', exclaims the duped steward, 'this is my lady's hand. These be her very c's, her u's and her t's, and thus she makes she her great P's'. See William Shakespeare, *Twelfth Night*, ed. Roger Warren and Stanley Wells (Oxford: The Oxford Shakespeare, 2008), 2.5.82–85. The endurance of these mischievous linguistic motifs is exemplified by the endeavours of British retail marketing expert and government adviser, Mary Portas, to revivify the British manufacturing industry by launching her retro-styled, handmade 'Kinky Knickers' in 2012 with 'a hidden message in the gusset encouraging wearers to Love Your Country'. Portas is not known for her timidity: the pun was certainly intentionally there. Source: www.liberty.co.uk/fcp/content/kinky-knickers-mary-portas/content.

84 Montagu, *The Anatomy of Swearing*, p. 2.

85 Ibid., pp. 4, 151.

86 Ibid., p. 300.

87 Ibid., p. 301.

88 Ibid., p. 303.

89 Ibid., p. 305, italics in original.

90 Allan and Burridge, *Forbidden Words*, p. 37.

91 Montagu, *The Anatomy of Swearing*, p. 314.

92 Tony McEnery, 'A Scale of Offence', in *Swearing in English: Bad Language, Purity and Power from 1586 to the Present* (London: Routledge, 2006), p. 36.

93 McEnery, 'Words preferred by males and females in the BNC [British National Corpus] ranked by LL [Log-likelihood] value', in *Swearing in English*, p. 35; Allan and Burridge also demonstrate that 'males swear more often than females', but that in some studies 'the idea that swearing and malediction is largely male behaviour eschewed by girls and women has been shown to be false', *Forbidden Words*, pp. 78, 89.

94 McEnery, *Swearing in English*, p. 35.

95 Allan and Burridge interpret the BBFC's findings differently, arguing that 'more than 50% of respondents rated slurs such as *nigger*, *paki*, *spastic* and *Jew* with *cunt* and *motherfucker* as inappropriate for transmission at any time', *Forbidden Words*, p. 108. I'm not convinced by Silverton's somewhat distasteful assertion that 'pakis are the new cunts', *Filthy English*, p. 239.

96 McEnery, 'Patterns of Male/Female-Directed BLW Use', in *Swearing in English*, p. 38.

97 McEnery, *Swearing in English*, pp. 38, 40; Allan and Burridge argue that 'A speaker is more likely to use "off-colour language" in the company of members of the same gender. Even so, men and women used dirty words differently', *Forbidden Words*, p. 89.

98 See: http://corpus.byu.edu/bnc/.

99   In a town on the Kent coast in the summer of 2011, my husband overheard a conversation between two elderly men at a pub bar. 'Evening, you old cunt!' said one to the other. 'Less of the *old*, if you don't mind', came the swift reply.

100 Nicky Haslam, 'Getting a Kick', review of Geoffrey Mark, *Ethel Merman*, in *The Spectator* (9 February 2008), p. 34.

101 J. R. Firth, 'A Synopsis of Linguistic Theory, 1930–1955', *Studies in Linguistic Analysis* (1957), pp. 1–32 (p. 11).

102 Victoria Coren, 'Keep Our Curses in Rude Health', *The Observer* (27 May 2012).

103 Janet Lee, 'Menarche and the (Hetero)Sexualisation of the Female Body', *Gender and Society* 8.3 (September 1994), pp. 343–62 (p. 344).

104 Sheila Greene, *The Psychological Development of Girls and Women: Rethinking Change in Time* (East Sussex: Routledge, 2003), p. 84. Women in economically secure societies average around 450 menstrual periods during their lifetimes. With increases in life expectancy in the United States, it is now fairly safe to assume that most women living in America 'spend at least one-third of their lives postmenopause'. That leaves plenty of time after menarche and pre-menopause for women to menstruate, and to need to buy products accordingly. See E. W. W. Sonnendecker, 'Menopause', in T. F. Kruger and M. H. Botha (eds), *Clinical Gynaecology* (Cape Town: Juta and Co., 2007), pp. 332–52 (p. 332).

105 Karen Houppert, *The Curse. Confronting the Last Unmentionable Taboo: Menstruation* (London: Profile Books, 2000).

106 Church & Dwight Co., Inc., *2010 Sustainability Report*, www.churchdwight.com/pdf/SustainabilityReports/2010SustainabilityReport.pdf, p. 5.

107 It's worth remembering that in British English 'Fanny' means 'cunt', not, as it does in American English, 'behind'. Hence my puzzled look when a dear American friend once told me that she'd dropped her 'fanny-pack' in central London.

108 Femfresh, 'Whatever You Call It, Love It', www.femfresh.co.uk/love-it.

109 Femfresh, 'Feel Body Confident with Femfresh: Essentials to Get You Through the Term Ahead', www.femfresh.co.uk/pdf/back-to-school.pdf.

110 Femfresh, 'FAQs', www.femfresh.co.uk/expert-care-for-down-there/faqs/3.

111 Femfresh, 'Feminine Freshness Deodorant', www.femfresh.co.uk/femfresh-care-range/feminine-freshness-deodorant.

112 Lee, 'Menarche', p. 349.

113 Femfresh, 'What Causes Irritation to Intimate Skin?', www.femfresh.co.uk/expert-care-for-down-there/faqs/2, my italics for emphasis.

114 RB Press Release, '2011: Full Year Targets Exceeded', 08 February 2012: www.rb.com/2011-Full-Year-Results.

115 See 'Hygiene Is the Foundation of Healthy Living': www.rb.com/Media-investors/Category-performance/Hygiene.

116 These adverts from 1928 and 1934 appeared first in the United States in *McCall's* magazine. Reproductions of the print adverts can be found at the online 'Museum of Menstruation and Women's Health', www.mum.org.

117 Lysol 'Love-Quiz . . . For Married Folks Only', 1948: www.mum.org/Lysol48.htm.

118 For these and other adverts in a similar vein, see: http://vintage-ads.dreamwidth. org/tag/lysol.

119 Andrea Tone, 'Contraceptive Consumers', in Elizabeth Reis (ed.), *American Sexual Histories* (Oxford: Wiley-Blackwell, 2012), pp. 247–69 (p. 252).

120 For more on 'ActiPearl' technology, see the 'Always' site, at: www.always-info.co.uk/ whats-new/always-acti-pearls-pads.aspx.

121 See: 'P&G Corporate Newsroom', http://news.pg.com/about.

122 See: www.always-info.co.uk/product/Liners/product-pantyliners.aspx . To give it its due, the Always publicity does use the words 'vagina', 'vulva' and 'lips'. There are companies which treat menstruation in a healthy, matter-of-fact *and* sustainable way. However, even Mooncup (www.mooncup.co.uk/), a praiseworthy company in so many respects, applies somewhat dubious criteria to its sizing strategy. As one respondent to my 'Cultural Attitudes to Female Genitalia' survey (April 2012) wrote: 'I have yet to contact the manufacturers of Mooncup, who do their product in only two sizes. Apparently when over 30 you need the large size, even if you have not had children. I want to ask them whether every woman's vagina gets wider on their 31st birthday regardless, for instance, of sexual activity'. Anonymous respondent to online 'Cultural Attitudes to Female Genitalia' survey (April 2012); comment posted 2 April 2012, 18:05 hours.

123 See: www.always-info.co.uk/lifestage/every-woman/liner/my-daily-hygiene/ pantyliners-vaginal-discharge.aspx.

124 See: www.always-info.co.uk/lifestage/fulfilled-and-radiant/later-lifestage-symptoms-of-menopause-period.aspx.

125 Jane Blocker, *What the Body Cost: Desire, History, and Performance* (Minneapolis, MN: University of Minnesota Press, 2004), p. 7.

126 Slavoj Žižek, *Organs Without Bodies: On Deleuze and Consequences* (London: Routledge, 2004), pp. 172–3. There's a philosophical genealogy for Žižek's idea, stemming from the 'Bodies Without Organs' of Derrida in the 1960s, via Deleuze, to Žižek's own 'Organs Without Bodies', in 2004.

127 Faith Wilding, 'The Feminist Art Programs', quoted in Laura Meyer, 'From Finish Fetish to Feminism: Judy Chicago's *Dinner Party* in California Art History', in Amelia Jones (ed.), *Sexual Politics: Judy Chicago's 'Dinner Party' in Feminist Art History* (Berkeley, CA: University of California Press, 1996), pp. 48–74 (p. 56).

128 Sh! Women's Erotic Emporium: www.sh-womenstore.com/Sensual+Pleasures/ Touch/Vulva_Puppet.html. Special thanks to Bekky Jennings for bringing this must-have soft furnishing accessory to my attention in May 2012.

129 Claudia Llosa (dir.), *La Teta Asustada* (*The Milk of Sorrow*, 2009). Fausta, the film's protagonist, grows ill, having inserted a potato into her vagina, imagining it to be a form of self-protection against rape.

130 Sh! Women's Erotic Emporium.

131 Anon, 'Dr Johnson at Oxford, and Lichfield', in 'Sylvanus Urban' (ed.), *The Gentleman's Magazine: And Historical Chronicle*, Vol. 55 (London, January 1785), p. 288; the anecdote is also mentioned in Montagu, *The Anatomy of Swearing*, p. 307.

132 *Will and Grace*, Season 6, Episode 16, 'Flip-Flop: Part II' (first aired March 2004).

133   *Will and Grace*, Season 6, Episode 15, 'Flip-Flop: Part I' (first aired February 2004).

134   *Will and Grace*, Season 7, Episode 10, 'Queens for a Day' (first aired November 2004).

135   Allan and Burridge, *Forbidden Words*, p. 53.

136   Silverton, *Filthy English*, p. 6.

137   Mimi Spencer, 'The Vagina Dialogues. It's time to stop hiding behind euphemisms, for our children's sake', *The Guardian*, 18 March 2005.

138   'Cultural Attitudes to Female Genitalia' survey (April 2012): hosted by Survey Monkey.

139   Of all these epithets, it's 'front bottom' that I find most troubling: the 'bottom', as the site of the evacuation of waste from the body, is, in a Kristevan sense, 'abject' (I'll come on to discuss this concept of Julia Kristeva's 'abjection' in relation to Catherine Breillat's film *Anatomy of Hell*). For the child to grow up believing, on some level, that there's a corollary between her 'bottom' and her 'cunt', is to make her 'cunt' subliminally, at least, repulsive to her.

140   Debby Herbenick and Vanessa Schick, *Read My Lips: A Complete Guide to the Vagina and Vulva* (Lanham, MD: Rowman and Littlefield, 2011), p. 254.

141   See: www.urbandictionary.com/define.php?term=vagina&defid=2278413.

142   Jon Lajoie, 'Vaginal Hubris', as performed on Jeff Schaffer (dir.), *The League* (FX, 2009). My thanks to Deborah Wynne of the University of Chester for telling me about Lajoie.

143   See Mark Morton, *The Lover's Tongue: A Merry Romp through the Language of Love and Sex* (Ontario: Insomniac Press, 2003).

144   Craig D. Atwood, 'Deep in the Side of Jesus', in Michelle Gillespie and Robert Beachy (eds), *Pious Pursuits: German Moravians in the Atlantic World* (Oxford: Berghahn Books, 2007), pp. 40–64 (p. 57).

145   Mary Douglas, *Natural Symbols: Explorations in Cosmology* (Harmondsworth: Penguin, 1973), p. 98.

146   This suggestive conjunction of Christ and vaginal symbolism was totally unintentionally realized in the 1990s when a band called Cradle of Filth sold T-shirts which announced in very large letters that 'Jesus is a Cunt'. Had the imagery of Christ's wounds been broached with the band, or had the word 'cunt' been dysphemized, then the shock value of the shirts would have been neutralized.

147   See Helen O'Connell, K. V. Sanjeevan and J. M. Hutson, 'Anatomy of the Clitoris', *Journal of Urology*, 174 (October 2005), pp. 1189–95.

148   Muscio, *Cunt*, p. xxviii.

149   Germaine Greer, *The Whole Woman* (London: Doubleday, 1999), pp. 2, 37.

150   Catherine Blackledge, *The Story of V: Opening Pandora's Box* (London: Weidenfeld & Nicolson, 2003), p. 4.

151   Jelto Drenth, *The Origin of the World: Science and Fiction of the Vagina* (London: Reaktion Books, 2004).

152   Carol Livoti and Elizabeth Topp, *Vaginas: An Owner's Manual* (London: Fusion Press, 2005).

153   Naomi Wolf, *Vagina: A New Biography* (London: Virago, 2012).

154   Eve Ensler, *The Vagina Monologues* (London: Virago, 2001).

155   Terri Kapsalis, *Public Privates: Performing Gynecology from Both Ends of the Speculum* (Durham, NC: Duke University Press, 1997), p. 138.

156   Morgan Holmes, *Intersex: A Perilous Difference* (Cranbury, NJ: Associated University Presses, 2008), p. 13.

157   On the 'Normalcy/Monstrosity' binary, see Holmes, p. 17.

158   Holmes, p. 107; my italics for emphasis.

2

Revealing the Vagina: Antecedents

The supposed oral tendencies of the vagina have featured in diverse cultures for a very long time indeed. Whenever a twentieth- or twenty-first-century writer or artist claims to have invented an innovative, transgressive, wittily postmodern creation by somehow autonomizing female genitals, giving them oral qualities, they are, in fact, simply making the latest contribution to a long-established tradition. I'm going to start exploring the idea of the independent sexual organ by going back to some of its earliest antecedents. The fantasy of the lethal qualities of the vagina has its roots in the primal myth of the *vagina dentata*. The human mouth has many meanings because it can do many things. It was associated with that other powerful bodily orifice, the vagina, long before the term *vagina dentata* entered psychological and anthropological discourses, and an early manifestation of it appears in twelfth-century French *fabliaux*.[1] These popular fables featured courtly, chivalric characters, and the tales' gravity was often undercut by risqué motifs, among them the talking vagina. This motif was still in vogue some 600 years later, when the scholarly, sometimes bawdy, writer, Denis Diderot, revived it in his outlandish novel, *Les Bijoux Indiscrets* (1748). It's the influential mid-nineteenth-century painting *L'Origine du Monde*, by another Frenchman, Gustave Courbet, which provides a visual illustration of the idea of the independent or autonomized cunt (Courbet does not include the woman's head or limbs in his image). And the process of representation continues into rather more modern, ephemeral engagements with the lips/labia homology in music videos.[2] Taken together, then, four antecedents – the myth of the *vagina dentata*, the *fabliaux*, Diderot's novel, and Courbet's painting – create an influential thematic foundation for the works of the writers, directors, artists and performers which form the subject matter of *The Vagina*.

Something to get your teeth into

The threat of castration (more accurately, perhaps, of *amputation*), although a fiction, can be used to justify the maiming of women's bodies, and the primitive legend of the *vagina dentata* – the toothed vagina – still functions to legitimize, or even to promote, misogynist practices such as female genital mutilation.[3] Some years ago I visited what was then an enchantingly ramshackle museum of anthropology in Oxford. Wandering from display case to display case, I was struck by how ancient peoples, geographically separated by tens of thousands of miles, and with no means of traversing those miles, independently came up with similar tools – a simple clock, or sundial; musical or writing instruments; farming implements and weaponry. Just as material objects can have an inter-cultural presence, seemingly without any means of direct communication or transmission, so, too can ideas. Every civilization has, for example, its own creation myth. Most have unique, often apocalyptic, eschatological (end-of-days) visions too. The same stories, created in an attempt to explain inexplicable events, to articulate fears and dreams, or at least to organize them into a linguistic framework, often emerge from cultures which are both chronologically and physically remote from each other. The myth of the *vagina dentata* comes into this category.

The myth is, for example, vividly illustrated in a design on an ornate eleventh-century Pueblo Native American Mimbres myth bowl, which is in many ways a more reliable source than the few Nahuatl (Aztec) texts that survived the vigorous censorship of the Christian Church.[4] The bowl shows a figure with a toothed vagina and rather wide eyes sitting on a male figure whose penis, resembling nothing so much as a hockey stick, penetrates her. One Nahuatl narrative which has survived is the sixteenth-century 'Legend of the Suns', or *Xiuhnel, Mimich and the Star Demon*.[5] Here, the hapless Xiuhnel, out hunting deer with his brother, Mimich, is consumed by the insatiable

'Obsidian Butterfly' goddess, Itzpapalotl, who, in later representations, features as the orally menacing toothed serpent goddess.[6] Mimich escapes to get revenge and, presumably, in order to pass on the story. Vampiric women feature in a twentieth-century Zuni (New Mexican) myth, too, where twin brothers encounter an old, predatory woman whose eight granddaughters they outwit by copulating with false penises made out of wood so that, by morning *'the teeth of these women were all worn out. They were broken in pieces . . . These women never killed men any more'.*[7] In such traditions, castration fantasies are violently enacted and retold.

The Jimson weed, or *Datura meteloides* is in the same family of plants as Belladonna, or Deadly Nightshade, and is used in some Native American Hopi (Arizonan) rituals for its hallucinogenic qualities, which can be fatal.[8] *Tsimona*, a kind of madness or sexual frenzy associated with the seeds of the Jimson weed, becomes personified in a Hopi narrative where the plant's spiny seedcases come to represent the toothed vaginas of the sexually voracious 'Tsimonmamant' women. As in the New Mexican Zuni myths, wooden phalluses are used to knock the teeth out of these monstrous females' vaginas:

> *At first they fucked them with their cottonwood penises. For it was true: the girls' cunts were simply grinding away on their cottonwood stalks. The creatures just couldn't get enough. So the men kept fucking them there. Finally the time came when the teeth of their vaginas were worn down. Now the men used their real penises. Eventually the girls became bored. So the men resorted to their cottonwood stalks once more and fucked them all night long. In this manner they killed all of them. Whenever someone had fucked his girl to death, he stopped. When all of the girls were dead, the men went home. They had really enjoyed themselves.*[9]

In another version, from as recently as the 1970s, a 'Spider Woman' provides a potion which literally petrifies the 'Tsimonmamant'.[10] The Amazonian Yanomami have a myth that the first woman had a toothed vagina; there are Chavín (Andean) illustrations on a similar theme; and Mundurucú (Brazilian) men called the vagina the 'crocodile's mouth'.[11] What's emerging is a cultural ubiquity for the myth.[12] The castration which the *vagina dentata* effects is symbolic then, and, in some versions of the story, is a literal amputation. In the

Madhya Pradesh region of India, a myth of the Baiga people tells of how a woman is unaware that she has three teeth inside her vagina (the fact that her lovers' penises are cut into three pieces doesn't seem to be enough of a clue). A wealthy landlord, determined to conquer the woman, orders four men of other castes to have intercourse with her first: a Brahmin priest, a Gond, a Baiga and an Agaria.[13] The Brahmin loses his penis immediately and the remaining three men hatch a plot. In a violent rape,

> The Gond held the girl down, and the Baiga thrust his flint into her vagina and knocked out one of the teeth. The Agaria inserted his tongs and pulled out the other two. The girl wept with the pain, but she was consoled when the landlord came in and said that he would now marry her immediately.[14]

The idea of the marriage of consolation is almost as shocking as the idea that a woman's sexuality and identity must be somehow forcibly tamed.[15] In another story from Madhya Pradesh, a young man has his penis reinstated by the woman whose vagina amputated it; in return he extracts her 'teeth' with the rather domestic remedy of a length of string (whether or not the other end of the string was tied to a door handle, as in picture postcards, remains unrecorded).[16] In a ground-breaking participant-observer anthropological article of the early 1940s, the missionary-turned-anthropologist Verrier Elwin cited many examples of the retelling of the *vagina dentata* myth arising from his extensive travels in the Indian subcontinent. Most of the tales originate with the Baiga people and, each time, despite a little local colour (a human penis prophylactically sheathed in coarse horse hair; bestiality with a stallion; a booby-trapped vagina which results in a castrated penis being eaten, mistaken for a fish, by a brother-in-law), the vagina is a dark and vicious place.[17] Again in Madhya Pradesh, the wife of an Agaria is attacked by a group of young men; a snake emerges from her mouth and is killed; penises magically regrow when sprinkled with ground-up vaginal tooth powder; and a woman is cooked in a broth, the aroma of which kills the men.[18]

Elwin's accounts also feature phallic objects which are used to neutralize the *vagina dentata.* In a town called Dantinpur (the ominously-named 'Tooth City'), a custom-made iron penis dislodges offending fangs; and an angry tigress-woman is transmuted into a Chamgedri (a being with one orifice for all bodily functions). In Rewa State (bordering Bengal), Elwin learned of an autonomized penis, again mistaken for a fish, which leapt into a woman's mouth, emerged from her vagina, having first killed her, before visiting her mother, whom it killed in the same grisly way. In Chhattisgarh (again in the Madhya Pradesh region of India), a widow is delighted when a cucumber farmer (alarm bells should *surely* have started ringing at that point) sells her an independent penis called Chanduwa; a passing farmer gets an unexpected surprise when he calls to one of his bullocks, also named Chanduwa, and the eager penis turns up instead.[19] Repeatedly, the stories focus on the necessity of subduing women; of violently forcing them into death or marriage, having first – usually – sadistically knocked the teeth out of their vaginas. The lips/labia correspondence pervades these myths: an assertive, articulate woman is an unruly, transgressive, one. The phallic vagina (less a contradiction in terms than we may initially think, tunnels and dark caves being considered) is also a recurrent motif. This is logical enough, considering the number of snakes Elwin and his storytellers would have encountered in the terrain of central and eastern India. In another story from Chhattisgarh, a snake enters a woman via her vagina (her head is in a furnace at the time, so she fails to notice), and bites off the penis of a young man who attempts to rape her. Three of his brothers meet the same fate; it is up to the youngest one to extract the snake with a stick, on condition that it magically reinstate his brothers' penises as the young woman kicks each bereft young man in turn.[20]

Another traditional Native American folktale follows these by now familiar formulae, but the neutralization of female sexuality comes with additional elements of shape-shifting, murder and necrophilia.[21] The Canadian sons of 'Good Weather' were believed to have disarmed an elderly woman's toothed vagina with hammers.[22] Another account has Maori origins: Maui, a traditional Maori folk hero, must penetrate Hine-nui-te-po, the elderly chieftainess, until he is 'on the point of coming out of her mouth', which has teeth 'as sharp and hard as pieces of volcanic glass'.[23] Two of Maui's bird companions, a Tiwakawaka (fantail), and a Tatahore (whitehead) laugh and dance at the sight, waking Hine-nui-te-po, who promptly squeezes Maui to death. In some versions of the story it's Hine-nui-te-po's *pataka* (storehouse) which a man may enter head first. Should he be seen 'standing upright in his canoe', however, he will be 'pressed to death' by Hine-nui-te-po, just as the night 'swallows the evening' and in turn is 'burnt to death by the dawn of the morning'.[24] In numerous such systems of symbology, what are portrayed as negative female sexual character-istics are exaggerated, and male ones are downplayed. Feminine symbols are, as the theologian Jill Raitt writes, 'rendered terrible by the projection onto the feminine of the killing negative masculine, i.e., an invaginated penis aculea-tus [spiny] or tooth or snake'.[25] In following Raitt's logic, we can understand that St George did far more than merely slay a 'dragon' whose fearsome jaws breathed deadly fire (that he used his long lance to subdue his foe and, in so doing, saved the virginal princess-bride, scarcely needs further analysis here).

Even if the vagina is not believed to have teeth, it's still often constructed as a talismanic entity in folklore. In Transylvania, farmers would purify cows' milk by pouring it through a hole in a piece of wood known locally as a 'witch's vagina'. As witches were believed to have tainted the milk in the first place, to pour it *back* into a symbolic body via a 'vagina' was one way of reversing the taint.[26] Skirt-lifting as a way of warding off evil spirits appears as a motif in numerous folktales, too, since even when it is toothless, the vulva is a source of terror. In Germany, everything from ghostly huntsmen to malevolent cats can be warded off by women who, encouraged by their husbands, expose them-selves. The Hugarian anthropologist Géza Róheim, active in the first half of the twentieth century, read tales like this in psychoanalytical terms: 'I, the dreamer, do not suffer from castration anxiety. I get the miller's daughter or the princess' and the anxiety is transferred to the father who appears as, for example, the huntsman.[27] In specific cultures, then, there is a subtle but important differ-ence in how the phenomenon of the *vagina dentata* might best be understood. Another anthropologist, the American Melford Spiro, argued that while psy-chiatrists treat the *vagina dentata* as 'an unconscious, privately constructed fantasy', anthropologists offer an alternative reading, tending to regard it as 'a conscious, publically shared fantasy, that is, as the motif of a wide range of folk tales'.[28] In Burmese culture, for example, Spiro recorded how the vagina was long regarded as a fearful, dangerous entity. He reflected on the inherently paradoxical nature of this fear: the internalization of the 'empirically ground-less' belief that women are dangerous grants them the (albeit folkloric) power to threaten what is constructed as an innate and indisputable male superiority or 'hpoun'.[29] This 'hpoun' is located in the right shoulder, and in some Burmese communities Spiro observed the belief that a woman's genitals should never be placed higher than this point (in other words, a woman should not be standing if a man is seated). Spiro also argued that a focus on the 'degraded, dirty, or repulsive', or 'dangerous or harmful' vagina, transmutes unconscious castration fears into conscious, active beliefs (and specific cultural practices).[30] In other words, one may explicitly articulate a defence against the potency of unconscious fears; the vagina is seen not as a castrat*ed* organ, but as a castrat*ing* one. If the vagina is seen as inherently dangerous (but not castrat*ed* in the Freudian sense of being a 'lack'), then its potency as a symbol of amputation is neutralized, but, as Spiro acknowledges, it is an 'asymmetrical' process, and is 'hardly an effective defense, for it merely replaces one anxiety-arousing fantasy (the fantasy of castration) with another (the fantasy that the vagina is harmful to one's powers)'.[31]

The academic theologian Margaret R. Miles has shown how 'In S. Francesca Romana's lurid fifteenth-century vision, hell was "a lurid and rotting uterus"', and argues how, in 'menstruation, sexual intercourse, and pregnancy, women's bodies lose their individual configuration and boundaries'– the *vagina* is the common denominator in these three 'grotesque' processes, in Miles's formulation, and so becomes both the source and the result of this breakdown of boundaries.[32] For Miles, the 'grotesque' is crucially gendered, and 'massive male sexual organs are figures of pride, self-assertion and aggression; massive female genitals, however, are likely to represent women's dangerous propensities for threatening men's self-control, autonomy, and power'.[33] In works of art where the mouth of hell was depicted looking like a vagina – a theme to which I return later, in discussing the vagina on film and TV – the *oral* lips have a distinct correlation with the vaginal ones: 'open when they should be closed, causing the ruin of all they tempt or slander'.[34] In the West, particularly in the world of film, the *vagina dentata* myth has had numerous incarnations. The Australian academic Barbara Creed provides a persuasive analysis of the lips/lips homology; 'the mother's facial mouth and her genital mouth' both threaten – or promise – to internalize the child.[35] Indeed, the French title of *Jaws* (1975) is *Les Dents de la Mer* (*The Sea's Teeth*). This last word, to my ears at least, is a homophone for *la mère* ('the mother'). *Jaws* signals the ocean as bloody womb/tomb; teeth pull victims to a twentieth-century version of the fleshy female uterine hell envisaged 500 years previously by St Frances of Rome.[36] In psychoanalytical terms, the '(M)other is understood as having the ability to swallow an emergent identity' and so 'the vagina, that which brought life, is looked on as dangerous, murky, and ravenous'.[37] In a similar vein, Ahab's systematic pursuit of Moby Dick has been read as his revenge for his symbolic castration (the loss of his leg).[38] The boy-child's terrified refusal to confront the absence of the mother's penis (for to do so would 'prove' the existence and possibility of amputation and loss), results in the focus instead on a fetish-object, most likely 'the subject *last* glanced upon before seeing the woman's genitals' and so the dominant 'phallic woman' is created, imagined to possess some kind of penis in order to calm the fetishist's fear of what its absence would signify for him.[39]

In the movie *Basic Instinct* (1992), a brief flash of the female protagonist's genitals during a police interview signifies a moment of Medusa-like power and 'virtually turns her inquisitors to stone'.[40] The eponymous creature in *Alien* (1979) has been described as 'a monstrous phallus combined with *vagina dentata*' and, even more powerfully, as a 'bestiary of sexual organs and associations', a combination which (un)naturally 'exceeds the logic of a human (sexual) identity predicated on genital difference'.[41] Creed's work on the symbolism of the *vagina dentata* shows its pervasive presence in horror films, where 'close-up shots of gaping jaws, sharp teeth and bloodied lips play on the spectator's fears of bloody incorporation – occasionally with humour', as, I would argue, Mitchell Lichtenstein achieves in his film *Teeth* (2007) and Neil Gaiman in his novel *American Gods*.[42] In music, the snake is not always a phallic emblem but can be vaginal, too. The rock band Whitesnake may, through their name and iconography, be celebrating phallic domination, but their album artwork tells another story. In 1981, they released the album 'Come An' Get It'. The black cover is dominated by an image of a large, translucent apple; curled up inside this is a snake whose head is thrust towards the viewer, eyes fixed, and mouth wide open. The mouth, despite having two upper fangs, and two lower, is striking; there's no forked tongue here, but instead there's a fleshy, maroon vulva with a dark elongated oval core. The lips/labia homology is explicit. Another album, the fifth from the band Metallica, known as

'The Black Album' (1991), also features a coiled serpent on its cover. The song 'Don't Tread On Me' includes the lyrics: 'Liberty or death, what we so proudly hail/Once you provoke her, rattling of her tail/Never begins it, never, but once engaged.../Never surrenders, showing the fangs of rage/[...] Love it or live it, she with the deadly bite.'[43]

Freud thought that Medusa, with her hair made of coiling serpents, was the epitome of the fetish-object. She was the terrible made visible; her writhing, serpentine hair was the observable manifestation of her hidden genitals. Each phallic snake's mouth is a gaping toothed vagina, and sometimes her mouth is gaping, too, as in Carlos Schwabe's watercolour painting 'Medusa' (1895), where 'With her claws poised, her cat's eyes staring, her mouth wide open, and her snake hair coiling into a bright bouquet of poison-toothed pink labia, this Medusa is a veritable nightmare visualization of woman as predatory sexual being'.[44] The possibility that the hiddenness of the genitals and the privacy of the 'private parts' are at the root of the terror of the *vagina dentata* was explored by Ruth Wajnryb, too. 'After all', she wrote, 'if it were *all* about not being seen, the middle ear is also hidden, but few would cast aspersions in *its* direction [...] the CUNT is the place where deception and betrayal transpire [...] the male ego would feel sufficiently threatened to need to deride and denigrate the female quintessence'.[45] In Freudian psychoanalysis, dreams about the loss of teeth symbolized castration; vaginal intercourse; or an anxiety about the safe post-coital withdrawal of the penis from the woman's body.[46]

Elwin, too, albeit in an article some 70 years old now, identified a ubiquity of the gorgon-like castrating power of the female in the central and eastern Indian communities he observed, where the Poison Maid Vishanghana's beauty was such that simply to gaze on her was to risk death; her serpentine venom is, once more, portrayed as being enormously threatening. In some versions of the stories that surround her, just her sweat can kill a man; in other versions a cut or a bite, especially on the victim's lip, proves lethal. Elwin sees a congruity in the myth of the *vagina dentata* and of Vishanghana. '*Why* is sexual intercourse dangerous?' he asks, 'The first and obvious answer is that hymeneal blood has always been regarded as magically toxic and to be avoided.'[47] It's an idea he dismisses, however, since 'after nearly ten years' experience of these peoples [of

India]' he has 'no hesitation in saying that no girl approaches her husband as a virgin'.[48] Menstrual blood is also dismissed as the origin for the myths, despite the various taboos surrounding it in many cultures; gonorrhoea, too, while possibly producing feelings in the penis like being bitten or scratched during intercourse, is not believed by Elwin to be a convincing explanation for the endurance of the myth. He concluded that it was the primal association of castration with death that motivated the narratives and, while noting their global presence, demonstrated what to modern readers is a remarkable condescension to the Indian communities in which he lived (and into which he married), for they are the 'more-child-like and primitive peoples that have survived into our machine age'.[49] So much of Elwin's fieldwork remains invaluable; happily so many of his cultural prejudices have long since been superseded.

Clitoridectomy and other forms of FGM may have originated in these myths of pacifying the threatening *vagina dentata*.[50] In such practices, the 'teeth' are metaphorically knocked out of the women in a way no less a barbaric than that described in the folklore I've discussed. The *dentata* myth is literalized by the Kenyan Nandi people for whom the clitoris continues to represent a tooth sufficiently that it necessitates excision; similarly, in Mali, the Dogon continue to practise FGM.[51] Some genital rituals are so violent, including the repeated sealing and opening of the vaginal opening, that they are 'indeed a killing and remaking of the woman, depriving her of sexual pleasure and reducing her to a reproductive instrument of her husband's pleasure [. . .] Why is this done? To render the woman harmless to men'.[52] Thus the folkloric tales of *the vagina dentata*, for all mythological and metaphorical narrative qualities, are not remnants of some age so distanced from our own. They are the lived reality of many women's lives today, and, as I discuss in my conclusion to this book, they cannot be dismissed merely as 'safe' fictions recalling long-outdated traditions, because the primitivism is still there:

> Women are then cut and shaped, quite literally, into a 'female character' as defined by men. Whatever seems to be 'male' in them must be cut away. Although in some stories the vagina is thought to be inhabited by a poisonous snake, in all cases the phallic nature of the dangerous part of the female sex organ is stressed. Women are then bound into a female character.[53]

Across cultures and across time, then, the myth of the *vagina dentata* has added weight to cultural practices designed to subdue women and has allowed men to fashion themselves as conquering heroes. The *vagina dentata*, it would seem, exists mainly in the imagination of the – often extremely anxious – beholder. Its influence, however, is still deeply felt today.

The Knight's party trick, or: Labile labialalia[54]

Fables, or *fabliaux*, recounted by itinerant *jongleurs* (poet-minstrels), were immensely popular in Medieval France. Around 160 of these popular *fabliau* texts, some dating from the early twelfth century, are still in existence.[55] While many of these poems engage with bawdy topics, the mid-thirteenth-century *Du Chevalier Qui fit les Cons Parler* ('The Knight Who Made Cunts Talk'), by the enigmatic *jongleur* Guerin (sometimes 'Garin'), goes further, and – as do so many of the manifestations I'll be looking at in this book – has the motif of the *vagina loquens* (the talking vagina) at its core.[56] *Fabliaux* share key structural and thematic motifs with fables, often significantly adapting them, so that the fables' animal characters become human protagonists, and the moral message fables generally have is ousted in favour of cheap laughs.[57] The *Du Chevalier fabliau*, undoubtedly an influence on the writer Denis Diderot, as we'll see, maintains the tradition's playful preoccupation with the human body but pushes it further: the 'magic' in this particular tale is an ability to make women's genitals speak.[58] For if the vagina can be toothed like a mouth, why might it not also speak like a mouth? *Fabliaux* revel in wordplay. Female genitalia might be represented as 'a fountain, a horse named Morel, elsewhere a piglet, a *pertuis* (hole), a doorway, a ring, a valley, a wound, and a little mouse (*sorisete*)'.[59] *Du Chevalier Qui fit les Cons Parler* is a story which does seem to carry a moral, focused on the virtue – for a woman – of silence over speech. In itself, of course, this is a playful irony: Guerin is dependent on an audience's complete attentiveness to the words he speaks; being silenced is of no use to the storyteller.[60]

Within the space of the opening 20 lines of the *fabliau*, the Chevalier's 'rare ability' is explained in a wonderfully matter-of-fact way: 'he could make a cunt converse/by calling on it, and coerce/the asshole in the crease to do/the very same when spoken to'.[61] Guerin reveals that the Chevalier, or Knight, acquired the skill 'the year/that he was dubbed a chevalier', having found himself idle in peacetime.[62] The Knight has pawned his fine clothes and spent 'a quite extended stay' drinking wine.[63] However, he's shaken out of his torpor by news of a major tournament due to take place in Touraine, La Haye and sets about persuading his rather more level-headed squire and confidant, Hugh (very much the Sancho Panza to the Knight's prototypical Don Quixote), to help him get his items out of hock. Setting out for the tournament, Hugh rides on ahead and comes across an idyllic valley, where he sees 'a clear, bright pool revealed./The stream that fed the pool was large,/the undergrowth along its marge/leafed out and green and in its prime'.[64] In this blissful bower, three women of overwhelming beauty (to Hugh, at least) are bathing, unaware of their onlooker who's busy being captivated by their 'bare white flesh, their shapely forms,/their well-proportioned flanks and arms'.[65] Hugh swiftly steals the bathers' clothes and rides rapidly away in search of the Knight, to whom the bathers complain, in tears. Ever pragmatic, Hugh at first refuses to return the clothes, thinking of the money they could raise if sold, but the chivalrous Knight is having none of it: 'I don't desire the sort of pay/which tarnishes my good repute'.[66] Governed by similarly courtly ideals, the by now apparently supernatural bathers insist that the Knight's good turn should not go unrewarded; they call him back and one of the women promises: 'I will give you a very valuable gift, and be certain that it will never fail. You will never go anywhere where everyone will not welcome you, and everyone make joy over you, and give up to you everything which they have'.[67] The second to speak explains *her* gift: 'You'll not encounter, far or near,/a female creature any place/that has two eyes upon her face/whose cunt will not, when spoken to,/be honor bound to answer you'.[68] Seeing that the Knight is both embarrassed and unconvinced, the third bather steps forward and delivers – as it were – the bottom line: 'if the cunt perchance should be/obstructed any way whereby/it cannot make a prompt reply,/the asshole ought to take its place,/no matter whom it may disgrace'.[69]

The Knight rides away from the three women to find Hugh (the strange encounter is an offbeat precursor of the meeting of Macbeth and Macduff with the weird sisters, in Shakespeare's play more than 300 years later), in order to recount his story. The two men meet a 'miserly and tight' priest on horseback who – magically in keeping with the first bather's promise – offers them his hospitality.[70] Hugh and the Knight see the priest's mare as the perfect animal on which to test the other aspects of the women's 'gifts'. 'Sir cunt' begins the Knight, addressing the priest's mare, '"where is your lord going?" [. . .] "Faith, sir knight, he's going to see his girlfriend"'.[71] Fearing the devil's work, the priest flees, dropping his money in his haste. The late expert in medieval French Literature, Brian Levy, identified a latent misogyny (and coined a wonderful word in the process) in this 'first clinical test of this magic vagineloquism', since it is 'duly and successfully carried out on an animal' intimating that 'the noble ladies who subsequently encounter the knight are just as much "mares" as is the priest's steed: woman and animal are equated through their sexual parts'.[72] Jubilant that the 'clinical test' was successful, then, the two companions continue on their journey, next arriving at a castle lived in by a count and countess.

Overcome with the desire to offer such hospitality as the fairy-bathers promised, the castle's inhabitants crowd in on Hugh and the Knight; the count embraces the Knight and kisses his face, and the countess sets up the castle's most well-appointed chamber for him, secretly ordering 'a maid in waiting,/ the worthiest, most captivating' to seduce him.[73] The Knight asks of the damsel: 'Sir Cunt, let's have a prompt reply:/I'd like for you to tell me why/your mistress came here to my side.'[74] The masculine gendering – 'Sir Cunt' – is interesting for a number of reasons. In a sense, it's an oxymoron; but in this case we need to remember that 'cunt' is a masculine noun in French: *le* con. Second, Guerin may be having an additional laugh at the expense of his 'victims': not only does the woman suffer the indignity of having a speaking cunt, but the cunt is *so* alien to her that it's even gendered differently. The maid is thus fragmented in several ways by the bathers' gift. Finally, this usage of 'Sir' could be an hierarchical construct: the woman is a maid-in-waiting not just to the countess, but also to her own autonomous anatomy. She is horrified as her cunt reveals that the countess had ordered her to come to the Knight's bed: as is so familiar in this motif in all its manifestations, from film to painting to modern literature, the cunt's lips are the lips which – unlike a woman's other lips – speak the unexpurgated truth. Although the countess is disbelieving of the maid's report the next morning, she's also intrigued, so asks the Knight to stay at the castle a little longer. Medievalist E. Jane Burns has explored how the 'Old French homophony between *con* (cunt) and *conter* (to tell a tale) reinforces linguistically the bond between the woman's lips and labia when the maiden later explains to her lady how her vaginal lips had been made literally to speak to the knight: "mes cons li conta" ("my cunt spoke to him/my cunt told him a good story")'.[75] One might extend this paronomastic (punning) mischievousness to consider how it's in a castle of a count (*le comte*) and countess (*la comtesse*) that the cunt (*le con*) tells a tale (*un conte*).

At dinner that night, the countess – significantly, given the *fabliau*'s conflation of lips and labia – 'broke in enthusiastically' to the assembled knights' 'rambling conversation' to reveal that her house guest 'possesses the ability/ to make cunts talk and give him answers'.[76] A wager ensues, as the countess 'spoke – she wasn't any/backwoods simpleton or ninny –/ "Sir Knight, whatever may ensue,/I'd like to make a bet with you./I'll wager forty pounds my twat/will never play the fool or sot/and say a single word for you"'.[77] The countess, cunningly, 'took in hand some cotton wool/and with it stuffed her cunt quite full/and plugged it tightly to the crown,/then used her fist to tamp it down'.[78] Guerin proceeds to emphasize the labial homology – the countess's cunt is represented as having a 'gullet', 'choked' with the cotton, its autonomy rendered impotent in its inability to reply to the Knight's repeated questioning of 'Sir Cunt'.[79] It's Squire Hugh who steps in, reminding the frustrated Knight of the gift the third bather gave him. The Knight then demands of the couness's anus why her cunt is being so quiet, and the anus reveals the countess's duplicity: 'Its throat is absolutely full/of cotton, or perhaps of wool,/my lady shoved into her womb/when she went upstairs into her room.'[80] This idea of cunt and anus having autonomy and separate identities inside the countess's body is one which the creators of *South Park* exploit in the episode 'A Million Little Fibers': presumably they thought they were outrageously, innovatively, pushing boundaries of aesthetics and taste. As it transpires, they were continuing a tradition which had been in existence for hundreds of years, as I show in my discussion of Film and TV later.

Guerin's parodic project is designed to ridicule the flimsiness of courtly conventions, shocking refined society into unrefined dirty jokes. The

Knight has won his bet with the countess and Guerin wins, too, as the fabler who exposes the hypocritical hollowness of decorousness.[81] Not only are the countess's organs autonomous, they are also overruled by the count who 'wheeled round to bid/the countess set it free, post haste./She didn't dare refuse, and raced/to give her cunt its freedom'.[82] Using a crochet hook, an appropriately domestic tool, the countess removes the cotton wadding, returns to the court and her cunt speaks, effectively losing her the wager. The countess who thought she could foil the Knight is the loser, because he's silenced her lips.[83] The countess's humiliation is as much in losing the bet as it is in having been forced to allow her cunt to speak. 'The count, who heard the whole affair,/guffawed, as did his company', recounts Guerin, 'then told the countess pointedly/to say no more; she'd lost the bet', and the tale concludes.[84] The countess's cunt has experienced a temporary autonomy in speaking the truth. Ironically, in trying to silence her own body, the countess was actually perpetuating the idea of it as a docile, insentient organ, essentially 'different from the visible, public mouth', since, when stuffed with cotton, it 'bears no necessary connection to the brain. Rather than emitting words or sound, it takes in the penis in a wholly corporeal gesture that could not be more mindless'.[85] The Knight has given it a 'mind', autonomy and identity – against the wishes of the countess.

Mangogul and the ring of confidantes

> We have but one means for fixing transitory but purely conventional things: it is to compare them to constant entities; and here there is no constant base other than the organs that do not change, and which, like musical instruments, will yield *approximately* at all times the same sounds, if we know how to manipulate their tension or length like an artist, and properly direct air into their cavities: the trachea and the mouth form a sort of flute, for which we must constitute the most scrupulous notation.[86]

This is Denis Diderot's entry for 'Encyclopedia' in the massive *Encyclopédie*, the epic project to which he dedicated a quarter of a century of his life. The first volume was published in 1751 when Diderot was 38 years old; three years earlier he had published the rather less influential and far more obscure bawdy fantasy, *Les Bijoux Indiscrets*. Diderot scholars have tended to view *Les Bijoux* as an aberration; a blip in an otherwise philosophically credible writing career, an ironic and psychologically unconvincing 'antinovel', yet a text which, in terms of style and concerns, may be regarded as a blueprint for Diderot's later, more accomplished works.[87] In prison in 1749, Diderot apologized to the authorities – albeit as a stratagem designed to show himself in a favourable, suitably contrite light – for his first three publications: *Pensées Philosophiques*; *Les Bijoux Indiscrets*; and *Lettre sur les Aveugles*, all of which, he said in a letter to Berryer, the Lieutenant General of Police at Vincennes, could be attributed to youthful irresponsibility, being 'intempérances d'esprit qui me sont échapées' ('outbursts which quite escaped me').[88]

Diderot's definition of an encyclopaedia, in its insistence on ideas of orality, has immediate relevance to *Les Bijoux*, a significant literary antecedent for so many of the literary and visual texts which feature in this book. His declaration that sense-perception is the 'constant base' for knowledge is indicative of a stance derived from the writings of the Enlightenment philosopher John Locke. It's interesting that he's citing the *voice* as the most 'constant entity', coming as it does from 'organs that do not change', when the plot of *Les Bijoux* has precisely this transformative quality attributed to the oral. The body is also, in Diderot's definition, an instrument controlled not by God but by the individual who can 'manipulate [. . .] like an artist', playing the vocal chords like 'a sort of flute, for which we must constitute the most scrupulous notation'. This image of the musician controlling his or her instrument is a very persuasive one in terms of identity and selfhood: the body – like an instrument – is subordinate to the will or intention of the individual. What happens, then, when the body is rendered subordinate to the will or intention of an*other* individual? What if the body itself becomes an Other, rebellious and self-destructive? In other words, what happens when an organ becomes autonomized, when, to quote Julia Kristeva, 'Uncanny, foreignness is within us: we are our own foreigners, we are divided?'[89] *The Vagina* is, really, an investigation into how deeply culturally inscribed this 'foreignness' is. The various texts (literary and visual) all have in common the theme of the autonomized organ, the rebellious body, and the mind at war with the body.

At the heart of *Les Bijoux* is a rather indolent Congolese sultan named Mangogul. Lounging in his seraglio in the capital city of Banza with his favourite, Mirzoza, he soon runs out of things to occupy his mind. 'You are bored' says Mirzoza, having exhausted her store of amusing stories and rumours.[90] Mangogul replies:

> We may both imagine, if you will, the adventures of the women of my court, and find them very entertaining. [. . .] But even if they were one hundred times more so, what difference would that make if it is impossible to know them?[91]

This empirical will-to-*know* pervades the rest of the novel. The resourceful Mirzoza recommends that Mangogul ask the genie, Cucufa, by what means such 'adventures' might actually be heard. This focus on the sense of *hearing* is crucial in understanding what Diderot is doing in *Bijoux*. It also prevents the novel from seeming too much of an anomaly in terms of the rest of Diderot's oeuvre, since it was his intensely materialist *Lettre sur les Aveugles* ('Letter on the Blind'), his third publication, about sense-perception and the existence of God, which finally precipitated his arrest in 1749, and *not* his licentious *Bijoux* of the previous year. Cucufa, as all good genies should, comes up with the goods: 'Your wish shall be satisfied':

> 'You see this ring?' he said to the sultan. 'Put it on your finger, my son. Every woman toward whom you turn the stone will recount her intrigues in a loud, clear, and intelligible voice. But do not imagine that they shall speak through their mouths.'
>
> 'From whence,' cried Mangogul, 'shall they then speak?'
>
> 'From the most honest part of them [*la partie la plus franche qui soit en elles*], and the best instructed in the things you desire to know,' said Cucufa. 'From their jewels.'[92]

The literary motif of the sexually charged magic ring was a popular one, not least because of the object's near-vulvar shape. Diderot's contemporary, Marie-Jeanne Riccoboni, reversed the male agency celebrated in *Les Bijoux*, in her novel of 1757, *Les Lettres de Mistriss Fanni Butlerd*. Riccoboni gave her heroine, Fanni, a powerful ring not unlike Mangogul's, which allowed her to enter her beloved's bedroom unseen. Fanni delights in the erotic possibilities the magic ring supplies. Writing at midnight, she reports:

> Vous croyez que je dors peut-être; j'ai bien autre chose à faire vraiment. On ne fut jamais plus éveillée, plus folle, plus . . . je ne sais quoi. Je songe à ce merveilleux anneau dont on a tant parlé ce soir: on me le donne, je l'ai, je le mets à mon doigt, je suis invisible, je pars, j'arrive . . . où? devinez . . . dans votre chambre : j'attends votre retour, j'assiste à votre toilette de nuit, même à votre coucher.

> [Perhaps you reckon I'm asleep; but really I've got something far better to be getting on with. I couldn't be more awake, crazier, more . . . I don't know what! I'm thinking about that magic ring which was spoken about this evening: it was given to me. I've got it, I've put it on my finger, and I'm invisible! I go, I come . . . where? Guess! . . . Into your bedroom! I await your return; I help you wash; I help you get into bed!]⁹³

Michel Foucault wrote that everyone is, on some level, like the voyeuristic Mangogul: 'each one of us has become a sort of attentive and imprudent sultan with respect to his own sex and that of others'.⁹⁴ In Diderot's tale, the ontology of the 'jewels' – their 'nature' – is intriguing in relation to the women unlucky enough to have the stone of Mangogul's magic ring turned on them. In Riccoboni's take, Fanni 'jubilantly uses the ring to turn her gaze onto the body of what turns *her* on'.⁹⁵ Mirzoza, the Sultan's favourite, is not unlike Fanni. She's an assertive and intelligent archetype of the Enlightenment scholar, and serves in the allegory to represent not only Louis XV's mistress, Madame de Pompadour, but also Diderot's own mistress, Madeleine de Puisieux (the wife of one of his colleagues on the *Encyclopédie*).⁹⁶ Significantly, from the start, Mirzoza warns Mangogul about trying the ring on her: 'the favourite paled, trembled, pulled herself together, and beseeched the sultan in the name of Brahma and all the pagods of the Indies and the Congo not to test on her a secret power that showed so little faith in her fidelity'.⁹⁷ In turn, Mangogul swears that he will not use the ring on his beloved.

Mangogul has little difficulty in choosing his first 'victim', a woman called Alcina. She has aroused his suspicions because: 'She was making sport with her husband, which seemed unusual [. . .], for they had been married for more than eight days.'[98] Mangogul turns his ring on Alcina, whose playful conversation with her husband is rudely interrupted by 'a murmuring noise [. . .] from beneath her petticoats: "Well, now I have a title. I am truly glad of it. There is nothing like having a station. Of course, if she had listened to my first advice, she could have found me something better than an emir"'.[99] Alcina, her husband having fled at the jewel's first words, rather pragmatically capitalizes on the situation, winning money in a game she's playing with the other women of the court, who are by now too distracted to be able to concentrate. News of the talking jewels spreads, and Mangogul turns his ring on many more women as the novel proceeds. The members of the Academy of Sciences in Banza debate the phenomenon and, in a chapter advertised in its subtitle as being 'Less Scholarly and Tedious than the Previous One', they challenge the witless anatomist Dr Orcotomus: 'Why has each jewel spoken but once?', concluding that 'there is every reason to believe that it is involuntary and that these parts would have remained mute had it been within the power of their owners to silence them'.[100] The involuntariness of the bewitched organs suggests something powerful about the 'jewels'. They speak with the voice of nature, unrestrained and honest, and the muzzles which the scientific virtuosi design for the court's women prove useless. The fragile façade of the courtly milieu is shown to be at odds with the voices of the women's *mouths*, since, as we saw in the equivalence of 'mare' and 'maid' in the *fabliau*, unrestrained women are coarse and bestial; 'feminine' propriety is only an act.

Physical body and textual body both incorporate contrasting narrative styles. The mouth speaks a quite different narrative to the 'jewel'. The jewels' confessions disrupt the narrative flow itself, since the voice of the controlled, learned author contrasts with the jewels' more chaotic, spontaneous vocalizations, creating '"dialogisme": the confrontation of two narrative styles at once necessary yet mutually exclusive'.[101] The ring has a democratizing power: its lack of respect for social boundaries is curiously positive, since 'jewels' are equal in a way that the courtly women are not. Listening to many women's 'jewels' distracts Mangogul from the only story that really matters to him – that of his beloved Mirzoza's jewel. Until the end of the novel, he remains in thrall to what this silent organ might yet utter.[102] Mirzoza's refusal to have the ring turned on her suggests her superior understanding of its powers (superior to Mangogul's, at least, although this comes as no shock to the reader). The ring is implicated simultaneously in two opposing narratives: one of the will to know; and one of the *angst* of knowledge, of the deep-seated (unconscious) desire *not* to know. This schism mirrors the two opposing stories the women's bodies hold, and the frustrations to which this fact gives rise for Mangogul.[103] As Jacinthe Morel claims, 'la curiosité a installé le doute et l'inquiétude chez Mangogul en meme temps qu'elle lui a offert, par l'intermédiaire de l'anneau, le moyen de dissiper ses soupçons. La curiosité aura pour consequence première de romper l'harmonie du couple' ('curiosity has put Mangogul into a state of doubt and anxiety while simultaneously offering, through the ring, the means of dispelling his suspicions. The chief effect of that curiosity will be to destroy the couple's contentment').[104] Morel argues that Diderot maintains in the reader a level of erotic curiosity to rival Mangogul's, and sees in the structure of the novel a reflection of its themes: 'caractère polymorphe du texte répondant en quelque sorte à la nature multiple et débridée de la curiosité et du désir de savoir' ('the polymorphous nature of the text corresponds in some way to the multiple, unbridled nature of curiosity and of the desire to know').[105] The danger which inheres in this tension between not-knowing and desiring-to-know has been seen by Diderot scholar James Fowler as having an Oedipal basis, centred on Mirzoza: 'the text manifests a fixation on the mother with whom subsequent objects are either identified (Mirzoza) or contrasted (women in general)'.[106] The double-bind of Mangogul's ring, the epistemological anxiety to which it gives rise, is partly what drew Foucault to the novel. In the fourth part of his now-classic *History of Sexuality*, 'The Deployment of Sexuality', he declared that his aim was to 'transcribe into history the fable of *Les Bijoux Indiscrets*. Among its many emblems, our society wears that of the talking sex. The sex which one catches unawares and questions, and which, *restrained and loquacious at the same time*, endlessly replies'.[107]

Diderot's is, on some levels, a relatively benign tale of the phenomenon of the autonomized vagina. Despite its heterosexual male-fantasy setting, the novel is not an entirely misogynist text. While women challenged by the ring speak only of sexual incontinence, thereby recalling centuries of beliefs about the excesses of the female libido, the figure of Mirzoza, rational and calm, functions to represent a more complex figuration of femininity in the text. In the concluding chapter of the novel, Mirzoza, 'to whom lies gave the vapors', passes out during the (presumably falsely hyperbolic) funeral oration for the grand vizier Sulamek.[108] In a panic, Mangogul turns his magic ring on his beloved whose jewel (somewhat melodramatically, considering she's merely fainted) declares eternal constancy to the sultan. Coming round, Mirzoza overhears her jewel and realizes that Mangogul has betrayed his promise that he would never use the ring on her. 'Ah, madame' begins Mangogul:

> do not attribute to shameful curiosity the impatience that only the despair of having lost you suggested to me. I did not test my ring on you; but I thought I might, without breaking my promises, make use of a resource by which to restore you to my vows and assure you of my heart forever.[109]

The novel concludes with Mirzoza accepting Mangogul's explanation, and Cucufa taking his ring back. Mirzoza's involvement with Cucufa's ring presents a more unified female persona than the novel has hitherto offered, since there is no discrepancy between what she professes and the truth. The uncanniness about which Kristeva wrote, in enunciating one's own 'foreignness' to oneself is, in the body of Mirzoza, neutralized and absorbed. She is at home in her own skin. Narrative expectations have also been reversed – Mirzoza's ardent wish not to have the ring turned on her is not, as the reader was led to suspect, because of secret infidelities, but because she is, ultimately, the one testing Mangogul, seeing whether his fidelity to her is as strong as hers to him. Her fidelity, the 'silent speech' of Mirzoza's body 'communicates more efficiently than the speech of the *bijoux libertins*'.[110] She has played – and almost won – a game with the predominantly masculine court.[111] Why only *almost* won? Her hidden spaces have been made as known to Mangogul as those of all of the other Congolese women. Although she maintains bodily integrity and control until the penultimate page of the novel she is, in the end, compromised and revealed. In a sense *what* her 'jewel' speaks is irrelevant; it is the act of being *forced* to speak that counts. Mirzoza has maintained, through the course of Diderot's tale, a solemn wisdom about the deficiencies of language, believing that any 'truth' is both elusive and perilous.

I began this section by suggesting that sense perception was central to Diderot's understanding of the purpose of his crowning achievement, the *Encyclopédie*. He used the language of physiology (the mouth and the trachea, specifically) to illustrate an idea about truth. In his novel, various learned men try and fail to force a classificatory structure, or taxonomy, on the varieties of 'jewels' in Mangogul's realm. Mary Douglas wrote about the kind of relationship between bodily and social control which emerges in the novel. She argues that 'abandonment of bodily control in ritual responds to the requirements of a social experience which is being expressed. Furthermore, there is little prospect of successfully imposing bodily control without the corresponding social forms.'[112] Taxonomies, or attempts to impose order on chaos, are core to the *Encyclopédie*. Indeed, *Les Bijoux* functions on at least one level as an analogy, hinting at the encyclopaedia compiler's desire for *structured* knowledge. Mangogul can, in this way, among others, be read as a manifestation of Diderot himself.[113] In her influential work on film and explicitness, *Hard Core*, Linda Williams argues that the movies are the modern equivalent of Cucufa's ring: they enable viewers 'to satisfy themselves about sex directly, to locate themselves as invisible voyeurs', being 'positioned to *view* the sex "act" itself, rather than only hearing about it'.[114] Like Mangogul, we experience pleasure and, perhaps, a feeling of power, at glimpsing on screen 'the previously hidden, and often sexual, "things" of women'.[115] *How* these 'things' are mediated in a variety of media is the concern of much of *The Vagina*.

L'Origine du Monde

Courbet's oil, *L'Origine du monde*, was owned
by Madame Jacques Lacan and through some tax
shenanigans became the Musée d'Orsay's.
Go see it there. Beneath the pubic bush –
A matted Rorschach blot – beneath blanched thighs
of a fat and bridal docility,
a curved and rosy enclosure says, '*Ici!*'

John Updike, 'Two Cunts in Paris'.[116]

In 1955, the psychoanalyst Jacques Lacan and his wife Sylvia purchased a painting by the nineteenth-century revolutionary French artist Gustave Courbet. Called *L'Origine du Monde*, the painting, which now resides in the Museé d'Orsay in Paris, measures just 55 × 46 cm. Slightly larger than life-sized, it shows a white woman's torso; her head, legs and arms can only be imagined, lying as they do outside the frame, at the centre of which are her genitals (see Figure 2.1).

Here, glistening labia are just visible through that 'matted Rorschach blot', thick, dark pubic hair. It seems that the painting was commissioned in 1865 by the former Ottoman ambassador, art collector, and Parisian *bon viveur*, Khalil Bey. Described by Maxime Du Camp as 'a small picture hidden under a green veil' showing a woman 'moved and convulsed', it had quite a chequered journey through several small galleries and private collections in France, before it reached Lacan's house in Guitrancourt, about 50 km (31 miles) to the north-west of Paris.[117] In 1995, having been feared lost for many years, it was 'found' and passed to the Museé d'Orsay. Lacan organized for his brother-in-law, the surrealist painter André Masson, to create a screen, depicting an abstract reworking of the painting, to cover it. Courbet's 'decapitation' of his muse may be read in radically contradictory ways: whichever way it is interpreted, this woman is separated from her 'I'; her body and mind are not granted reconciliation by the artist and nor are they seen as occupying the same space simultaneously. The subject of the painting – the object of our gaze – may or may not be looking at us, meeting that gaze. The ambiguity of whether or not we too are being watched is potentially disempowering for *us*. It is a characteristically uncanny Lacanian dilemma: does that at which we gaze also gaze at us? Alternatively, the rigidity of the painting's frame may deny the woman it encompasses any agency at all. Her unknown-ness is not enabling, removing as it does her subjectivity and identity from the triumvirate relationship of artist/model/viewer. It's perhaps utterly fitting that a work of art which can give rise to such profound questions around selfhood and the gaze of the other should have been owned by Lacan, since he is today perhaps best known for his engagement with such issues.

Before thinking in more depth about *L'Origine*'s last private owner, I want to consider another of Courbet's paintings. The startling, penetrating gaze of

La Clairvoyante unflinchingly meets ours and the framing of that image invites us to concentrate on her face, since the artist bisects her at the bust line (see Figure 2.2).

She is virtually the other half of *L'Origine*. The observer, Courbet seems to be telling us, if we put these paintings side by side, cannot simultaneously gaze on the cunt *and* be gazed upon by the model. Our eyes move from one to the other and there is a choice to be made. The mysticism of the sexual organs is echoed in the mysticism of the clairvoyant's gaze. Her chin is tilted slightly downwards and her dark eyes fix on us, her mouth set in a stern line. Here is a woman who is not presented solely as a sexual object, but who is mysterious, dangerous and darkly erotic. Courbet's version of disembodied female genitals recurs throughout *The Vagina* in various manifestations, whether it's a novel's protagonist who possesses both the composure of Courbet's *Clairvoyante* but also the fragmented status of his *Origine*; or a piece of performance art that confronts issues of bodily integrity; or a birth image. Many ideas about the cunt, it would seem, return in one way or another to the origin.

Lip reading

What's emerging quite powerfully is the idea that there are 'lips' and '*lips*'; it's a symmetry that has, for centuries, proven alluring to all kinds of artists. There's not only the homology, or likeness, at stake here, of course, as acknowledged in the analysis of the *vagina dentata*, but the associations with cunnilingus should also be considered: the word is made up of *cunnus* (which we met in the introduction), and *lingus*, from the verb *lingere*, 'to lick'. It's entirely possible that the artistic potential for the lips/*lips* playfulness appears in a very early British Latin poem, St Aldhelm's (c. 639–709) *Carmen de Virginitate*, which has the line: 'Mellea tunc roseis haeres*cunt* labra labellis' ('her honeyed lips then clung to his rosy lips').[118] The likeness is replayed widely in popular culture. In 1973, the Rolling Stones released a single called 'Angie', the continental European release for which featured a photograph of a naked woman's breasts and abdomen.[119] In a grotesque move, an enormous yellow-blond wig has been placed around the woman's body to represent hair, and her breasts have been painted to represent eyes, with her nipples as pupils. A pair of large, red cartoon lips, puckered up, with a black hole at their centre, has been painted just above her *mons veneris*. In the image, we both are, and are not, looking at a woman's 'lips'. The Colorado-based electro-pop band duo 3OH!3 enjoyed modest chart success in 2008 with their song 'Don't Trust Me' (the song subsequently (and somewhat depressingly) went platinum in 2009). 'She wants to touch me', the song goes, 'She wants to love me [. . .] She'll never leave me [. . .] Don't trust a ho, never trust a ho [. . .] Shush girl, shut your lips / Do the Helen Keller and talk with your hips'. Despite some radio stations in the United States censoring the Helen Keller references (or maybe because of it) the single has been downloaded over 3 million times since its release. The lyrics are set to a jaunty rhythm and the song has a brightly coloured video reminiscent of songs by other frat-rock bands like Blink-182 or the Bloodhound Gang. The women in the video, of course, all conform to this troublingly misogynist Helen Keller 'ideal' – they gyrate in their underwear in settings including a high-school wrestling match and on the back of a stuffed buffalo in a cartoony stone age, *Apocalyptica*-like setting. It's all good fun – allegedly – but the explicit message that a woman's 'lips' should be closed; that her 'hips' should be open; and that she's a 'ho' (whore), is troubling given the demographic of the band's fan base of, broadly speaking, young men who, as these things go, will grow up to be tomorrow's adult men.

Jamie Foxx is another singer with a 'lips' fixation. In 'Storm (Forecass)', from the album *Unpredictable* (2006), as reviewer Alexis Petridis moistly puts it, Foxx 'deals with a topic hitherto overlooked even in the lubricious lexis of the urban loverman: vaginal mucus'.[120] 'Let me feel the raindrops falling down all over my love', he sings, 'I want it soakin' wet all over the bed; I want the rain to come. / Girl, the weatherman said: / "It's cloudy skies, right there between your thighs."'[121] Live, Foxx serenades his audiences (having moved the women to the front), picking one (oh-so-lucky!) woman and singing 'Let me kiss your lips between your hips' to her.[122] A similar fascination is present in the lyrics to the somewhat whiny-sounding 'Good Girls, Bad Guys' from Falling in Reverse's debut studio album: 'How you look when you are wet / Is something I can't forget / I just wanna kiss your lips / The ones between your hips.'[123] Female pop stars, too, play with this supposed, culturally engrained homology. Lady Gaga's video for her 2011 hit 'Born This Way' is, as are so many of the things in which she's involved, designed to shock and provoke strong reactions. The birth idea of the song's title clearly suggested to the producers of the 7-minute version of the song's video a series of birthing images which are interesting because in them Gaga appears to be giving birth to herself; to be producing a series of versions or reimaginings of her identity (she is, in her desire for gratuitous reinvention, very much this century's Madonna). Graphic and calculatingly shocking though she may set out to be (experimenting in her music videos with images of lesbianism but also of bondage, and violence), everything about her is cynically contrived to garner attention and, consequently, dollars. Cascading pink triangles appear at the beginning and end of her 'Born This Way' music video, not being deployed as queer symbols but as representing her vagina. 'This is the manifesto of mother monster' the voice-over intones, introducing a series of weird alien births which, viewed through a series of symmetrical mirror images, squelch their way towards the viewer. What is being delivered of Lady Gaga is, as the soundtrack drones: 'a race which bears no prejudice, no judgement, but boundless freedom'.[124] As the voice-over gains momentum and the colour palette becomes saturated with blood-red tones, the viewer witnesses 'the birth of evil': a woman perched on HG Wells-inspired spindly, futuristic gynaecological stirrups, pulls dimly lit entities from her own crotch to the swelling sound of a 1950s B-movie orchestra. Three minutes in, the more conventionally choreographed pop-music video starts. 'Don't be a drag, just be a queen' sings Gaga, appearing as an androgynous zombie in tuxedo and bowtie, with skull-face and half her head covered in a long pink wig. It's an almost Platonic version of the creation myth that she presents in the song: two halves – a symmetry – a sense of relentless searching and toil. The symmetrical birthing imagery is then returned to and, as the video draws to a close there's another return, this time to the pink triangle frames of the opening. Gaga's vagina is being presented as parthenogenetic – autonomous – a gateway from which not only good and evil, but also the universe, emerge in a kind of binary fission, from a complex surreal space.

The French *fabliaux* tradition played with the lips/labia homology centuries before these modern representations. That tradition's predication on the basis that a woman's incontinent speech reflected her sexual incontinence is clear, and the female body's supposed labial symmetry collapses distinctions between the 'mouth', on the face and that of the genitals. I've written elsewhere about early modern preoccupations with this 'rhetorical elision of "lips" and "labia"', and have argued that 'the similarities in appearance of Renaissance objects designed to control and contain "unruly" women: chastity belts and so-called "scolds' bridles"' are far from accidental.[125] The potency of a woman's lips – of her 'vulvo-morphic logic' – has been characteristically commented upon by Luce Irigaray in her poetical–theoretical exegesis, *This Sex Which is not One*.[126] 'In what she says, too, at least when she dares, woman is constantly touching herself', writes Irigaray: 'if "she" says something, it is not, it is already no longer, identical with what she means. [. . .] Their desire is often interpreted, and feared, as a sort of insatiable hunger, a voracity that will swallow you whole'.[127] In the next section, I'll be considering the extraordinary ways in which novelists and playwrights have represented the capacity of these lips to swallow, speak and subsume.

Notes

1 On the symbolic significance of 'the moist hole at the center of our faces [. . .] filled to choking with meanings, functions and associations', see Jane Blocker, *What the Body Cost: Desire, History and Performance* (Minneapolis, MN: University of Minnesota Press, 2004), p. 19; on linguistic origins of the phrase *vagina dentata*, see my Introduction, where I briefly discuss anthropologist Robert Lowie's 1908 article about the phenomenon in the *Journal of American Folklore*.

2 According to the *OED*, an 'homology' is an 'homologous quality or condition; sameness of relation; correspondence'. In Biology or Comparative Anatomy it's a 'special homology, the correspondence of a part or organ in one organism with the homologous part in another (e.g. of a horse's 'knee' with the human wrist)'. Further, 'lateral homology' refers to 'the relation of corresponding parts on the two sides of the body' – I'd extend this to include the two 'ends' of the body, hence the lips/labia analogy.

3 On the 'gynocidal masculine' impulse, see Jane Caputi, *The Age of Sex Crime* (Bowling Green, KY: Popular Press, 1987), p. 147.

4 See Pat Carr and Willard Gingerich, 'The Vagina Dentata Motif in Nahuatl and Pueblo Mythic Narratives: a Comparative Study', in Brian Swann (ed.), *Smoothing the Ground: Essays on Native American Oral Literature* (Berkeley, CA: University of California Press, 1983), pp. 187–203 (p. 187).

5   Carr and Gingerich, 'The Vagina Dentata Motif', p. 189. A transcription of the entire story appears on p. 190 of their essay.

6   Ibid., p. 194. On Cihuacoatl showing 'a huge open mouth and teeth, a symbol interpreted as the *vagina dentata*', see, Grisel Gómez-Cano, *The Return to Coatlicue: Goddesses and Warladies in Mexican Folklore* (Bloomington, IN: Xlibris, 2010), p. 182.

7   Ruth Benedict, *Zuni Mythology* (New York, NY: Columbia University Press, 1935), quoted in Carr and Gingerich, 'The Vagina Dentata Motif', p. 196.

8   See Ekkehart Malotki, 'The Story of the "Tsimonmamant" or Jimson Weed Girls: A Hopi Narrative Featuring the Motif of the Vagina Dentata', in Swann (ed.), *Smoothing the Ground*, pp. 204–20.

9   Translation by Malotki, from a narrative told by Herschel Talashoma, 'The Story of the "Tsimonmamant"', p. 213.

10   Ibid., p. 208.

11   See Mark Miller Graham, 'Creation Imagery in the Goldwork of Costa Rica, Panama and Colombia', in Jeffrey Quilter and John W. Hoopes (eds), *Gold and Power in Ancient Costa Rica, Panama and Colombia* (Washington, DC: Dumbarton Oaks Research Library and Collection, 2003), pp. 279–300 (p. 290).

12   On this ubiquity see also Barbara Creed, 'Medusa's Head: The Vagina Dentata and Freudian Theory' in her *Monstrous Feminine: Film, Feminism, Psychoanalysis* (London: Routledge, 1993), Chapter 8, pp. 105–21.

13   For a partial transcription of the Baiga story see Jill Raitt, 'The *Vagina Dentata* and the *Immaculatus Uterus Divini Fontis*', *Journal of the American Academy of Religion* 48.3 (September 1980), pp. 415–31 (p. 416).

14   As transcribed in Raitt, 'The *Vagina Dentata*', p. 416.

15   On how sexuality can figure as 'metonymy for full personhood', see Alexandra Juhasz, 'It's about Autonomy, Stupid: Sexuality in Feminist Video', *Sexualities* 2.3 (1999), pp. 333–41 (p. 334).

16   Verrier Elwin, 'The Vagina Dentata Legend', *The British Journal of Medical Psychology*, 19.3–4 (June 1943), 439–53 (p. 439).

17   For fuller transcriptions of these Baiga stories, see Elwin, 'The Vagina Dentata Legend', pp. 439–40.

18   Ibid., p. 441.

19   Ibid., p. 445.

20   Ibid., p. 443.

21   See Raitt, 'The *Vagina Dentata*', p. 417.

22   Géza Róheim, *Fire in the Dragon and Other Psychoanalytic Essays on Folklore*, ed. Alan Dundes (Princeton, NJ: Princeton University Press, 1992), p. 119.

23   Raitt, 'The *Vagina Dentata*', p. 417.

24   Wilhelm Dittmer, *Te Tohunga: The Ancient Legends and Traditions of the Maoris* (London: G. Routledge, 1907), p. 34.

25   Raitt, 'The *Vagina Dentata*', p. 419.

26   Róheim, *Fire in the Dragon*, p. 20.

27 Ibid., p. 110.

28 Melford E. Spiro, 'The Internalisation of Burmese Gender Identity', in L. Bryce Boyer and Simon A. Grolnick (eds), *The Psychoanalytic Study of Society*, Vol. 15, *Essays in Honour of Melford E. Spiro* (London: Routledge, 1990), pp. 45–68 (p. 58).

29 Spiro, 'The Internalisation', p. 45.

30 Ibid., p. 57. In his analysis of taboo practices, Spiro argues that the avoidance of the vagina can lead Burmese men 'either [to] abjure sex altogether, or else [. . .] turn to males – persons without a vagina – for sexual gratification' (p. 57).

31 Spiro, 'The Internalisation', pp. 59, 60.

32 Margaret Miles, 'Carnal Abominations: The Female Body as Grotesque', in James Luther Adams and Wilson Yates (eds), *The Grotesque in Art and Literature: Theological Reflections* (Grand Rapids, MI: Eerdmans, 1997), pp. 83–112 (pp. 86, 93).

33 Miles, 'Carnal Abominations', p. 97.

34 Ibid., p. 99.

35 Creed, *Monstrous Feminine*, p. 113.

36 Caputi discusses *Jaws* in *The Age of Sex Crime*, p. 147.

37 J. C. Smith and Carla J. Ferstman, *The Castration of Oedipus: Feminism, Psychoanalysis, and the Will to Power* (New York, NY: New York University, 1996), p. 234.

38 See Jane Caputi, *Goddesses and Monsters; Women, Myth, Power, and Popular Culture* (Bowling Green, KY: Popular Press, 2004), p. 29.

39 Creed, 'Medusa's Head', p. 116.

40 Caputi, *Goddesses and Monsters*, p. 329.

41 See Robin Wood, quoted by Kelly Hurley in 'Reading Like an Alien: Posthuman Identity in Ridley Scott's *Alien* and David Cronenberg's *Rabid*', in Judith Halberstam and Ira Livingston (eds), *Posthuman Bodies* (Bloomington, IN: Indiana University Press, 1996), pp. 203–24 (p. 210); Caputi, *Goddesses and Monsters*, p. 70; Hurley, 'Reading Like an Alien', p. 210.

42 Creed, 'Medusa's Head', p. 107. A similar horror/humour effect is achieved in an episode in Neil Gaiman's novel *American Gods*. Bilquis, posing as a prostitute, demands of a male client that he worship her as a goddess when they fuck. 'I worship your breasts and your eyes and your cunt. I worship your thighs and your eyes and your cherry-red lips . . .' says the unsuspecting punter. As he climaxes, 'He thinks, grasping for thought and reason again, of birth [. . .] This is what he sees: He is inside her to the chest [. . .] He slipslides further inside her [. . .] He feels the lips of her vulva tight around his upper chest and back, constricting and enveloping him [. . .] she pushes him inside her. Her labia pull slickly across his face, and his eyes slip into darkness [. . .] Her belly is flat, her labia small and closed'. Neil Gaiman, *American Gods (Author's Preferred Text)* (London: Headline, 2005), pp. 31–3.

43 Metallica, 'Don't Tread On Me', from 'The Black Album' (Elektra, 1991). 'Bite', in Francis Grose's *Dictionary*, as I mentioned in my Introduction, meant 'a woman's privities'. Grose, *A Classical Dictionary*, n. p.

44 Bram Dijkstra, *Idols of Perversity: Fantasies of Feminine Evil in Fin-de-Siècle Culture* (Oxford: Oxford University Press, 1986), p. 310. There's a wonderfully surreal take

on the Medusa myth in the second episode of the animation series *Drawn Together*. Clara, a Disney-like princess character, reveals that, instead of a vagina, she has a large green, talking octopus (which she calls an 'Octopussoir'), with teeth at the end of each of its tentacles. She finds true love when a bachelor kisses one of the tentacles; he promptly grows a large octopus – this time a grey one – in lieu of *his* genitals. However, the romance is short-lived, as Prince Charming blows off his head with a shotgun. The episode ends with a chorus of the 'Labia' song (since the only sensible thing to do in such a predicament is to sing): 'La la la la labia: baby you got something for me (in your wizard's sleeve) [. . .] Hoochie coochie gitchy gitchy yeah yeah yeah / Gotta snatcha gonna catcha yatcha yeah yeah yeah / Binja minja bearded clam / Furry burger smiley sam [. . .] Fluffy muffy stuffy in the yeah yeah yeah / I gotta fever for the beaver weaver yeah yeah yeah / Honey pot peachie pie / Take it to the Y-clef / Bushy bushy fishy squishy yeah yeah yeah / Smelly jelly underbelly yeah yeah yeah / [. . .] Cookie nookie slitty kitty yeah yeah yeah / I diggy giggy murky wiggy yeah yeah yeah / La la la la labia baby you got something for me'. Octopussoir himself (he has a male voice) joins in with the singalong. Dave Jeser and Matt Silverstein, 'Clara's Dirty Little Secret', *Drawn Together* (Season 1, episode 2, 2004).

45   Ruth Wajnryb, *Expletive Deleted: A Good Look at Bad Language* (New York, NY: Free Press, 2005), p. 80. In a *Daily Beast* archived *Newsweek* article by Kathleen Deveny called 'Why the C Word is Losing its Bite: Rethinking the Most Taboo Term in English', Wajnryb's quotation has, in a delicious irony, been expurgated: 'the c---', readers learn, is, indeed, 'the place where deception transpires'. See Kathleen Deveny, 'Why the C Word is Losing its Bite: Rethinking the Most Taboo Term in English', *Daily Beast* (as an archived *Newsweek* article) first printed on 29 August 2009 and available at www.thedailybeast.com/newsweek/2009/08/28/why-the-c-word-is-losing-its-bite.html (accessed 16 February 2012). Clearly the cunt's 'bite' is still too painful for some editors.

46   See Creed, 'Medusa's Head', p. 119.

47   Elwin, 'The Vagina Dentata Legend', p. 448, my italics.

48   Ibid., p. 449.

49   Ibid., p. 453.

50   At the time that Elwin was writing, in the 1940s, clitoridectomies were no less common than 'the cutting off of the nose as a penalty for adultery [which was . . .] common all over India', and the 'Gond and Baiga punish a riggish ['promiscuous', *OED*] woman by putting chili [*sic*.] and salt into her vagina. Stories in which a crab catches and sometimes excises a woman's clitoris are very popular'. See Elwin, 'The Vagina Dentata Legend', p. 447.

51   See Raitt, 'The *Vagina Dentata*', p. 420.

52   Ibid.

53   Ibid., p. 421.

54   I've constructed the word *labialalia* from *labia* (genital lips) and *lalia* (speech or chatter). *Labile* means 'changeable', with an associated meaning of lapsing into sin. The phrase as a whole captures the core motifs of the *fabliaux*, and of modern representations, too.

55 See Charles Muscatine, 'The Fabliaux, Courtly Culture, and the (Re)Invention of Vulgarity', in Jan M. Ziolkowski (ed.), *Obscenity: Social Control and Artistic Creation in the European Middle Ages* (Leiden: Koninklijke Brill, 1998), pp. 281–92 (p. 290). R. Howard Bloch contends that there are around 170 extant *fabliaux*. See R. Howard Bloch, 'Modest Maidens and Modified Nouns: Obscenity in the Fabliaux', also in Ziolkowski (ed.), *Obscenity*, pp. 293–307 (p. 295).

56 Roy J. Pearcy, *Logic and Humour in the Fabliaux: An Essay in Applied Narratology* (Cambridge: D. S. Brewer, 2007), p. 11.

57 Pearcy, *Logic and Humour*, pp. 12, 151, n. 4. Pearcy regards *Du Chevalier Qui fit les Cons Parler* as a parody of the more conventional – and less licentious – courtly *lai* verse form. On some commentators' attempts to bowdlerize, 'sometimes ludicrously so', the titles of *fabliaux* so that, for example, *Le Chevalier Qui Fist Parler les Cons* became *Du Chevalier Qui Fist Parler les Dames*, see Brian J. Levy, *The Comic Text: Patterns and Images on the Old French Fabliaux* (Amsterdam: Rodopi, 2000), p. 20, n. 58.

58 George Ellis, 'Preface' to M. Pierre Jean Baptiste Le Grand d'Aussy, *Fabliaux or Tales, Abridged from French Manuscripts of the XIIth and XIIIth Centuries* (London: Bulmer and Co., 1796), pp. i–xxxvi (ii). Ellis's choice of the word 'quaint' to describe Diderot's novel is intriguing, given its etymological associations with the word 'cunt'.

59 R. Howard Bloch, 'Modest Maidens and Modified Nouns: Obscenity in the Fabliaux', in Jan M. Ziolkowski (ed.), *Obscenity: Social Control and Artistic Creation in the European Middle Ages* (Leiden: Koninklijke Brill, 1998), pp. 293–307 (p. 301).

60 That some of the language and images of the *fabliaux* had accrued obscene associations by the eighteenth century may be gathered from the prefatory remarks to an early, bowdlerized anthology. 'In perusing the original fabliaux', writes George Ellis at the end of the eighteenth century, 'it is impossible to repress our astonishment at the indelicate and gross language to which our ancestors of both sexes appear to have listened without the least scruple or emotion', and 'it is not the language only, but the whole tendency of many of the fabliaux, which is highly reprehensible'. Further, 'From the account that has been given of the fabliaux, it is evident that they were perfectly unfit to be presented in their original state to modern readers. Some indeed were so faulty, that M. Le Grand was constrained to suppress them as quite incorrigible'. See Ellis, 'Preface', pp. xxxii, xxxiii–iv, xxxv–vi.

61 Guerin, *Du Chevalier Qui fit les Cons Parler*, in Robert Harrison (trans.), *Gallic Salt: Glimpses of the Hilarious Bawdy World of Old French Fabliaux* (Berkeley, CA: University of California Press, 1974), pp. 218–55 (p. 219).

62 Ibid., p. 221.

63 Ibid.

64 Ibid., p. 225.

65 Ibid., p. 227.

66 Ibid., p. 229.

67 This prose translation was done in 1999 by the scholar and Knights Templar expert, Helen Nicholson: http://homepage.ntlworld.com/nigel.nicholson/hn/indexKnight.html.

68 Guerin, *Du Chevalier*, p. 231.

69 Ibid., p. 233.

70 Ibid.

71 Helen Nicholson's translation.

72 Levy, *The Comic Text*, p. 56.

73 Guerin, *Du Chevalier*, p. 241.

74 Ibid., p. 243.

75 E. Jane Burns, *Bodytalk: When Women Speak in Old French Literature* (Philadelphia, PA: University of Pennsylvania Press, 1993), p. 55.

76 Guerin, *Du Chevalier*, p. 247.

77 Ibid., p. 249.

78 Ibid., p. 251.

79 Ibid., pp. 251, 255.

80 Ibid, p. 253.

81 For a fascinating insight into the heterogeneous identity of the original readership of the *fabliaux*, and into how 'obscenity' is a culturally contingent concept, to the point where it might be argued that 'fabliaux are the only substantial body of evidence that gives us reliable insight into contemporaneous everyday speech', see Muscatine, 'The Fabliaux', p. 286.

82 Guerin, *Du Chevalier*, pp. 253–55.

83 See E. Jane Burns, 'This Prick Which is Not One: How Women Talk Back in Old French Fabliaux', in Linda Lomperis and Sarah Stanbury (eds), *Feminist Approaches to the Body in Medieval Literature* (Philadelphia, PA: University of Pennsylvania Press, 1993), pp. 188–212.

84 Guerin, *Du Chevalier*, p. 255. Other iterations of the tale, along with Diderot's more famous *Les Bijoux Indiscrets*, include the thirteenth-century German *Der Rosendorn* (sometimes called *Der weisse Rosendorn*) in which, again, it's a male character who is responsible for reuniting a woman with her wayward, talking vagina; see Sebastian Coxon, *Laughter and Narrative in the Later Middle Ages: German Comic Tales 1350–1525* (London: MHRA Legenda, 2008), especially p. 46.

85 Burns, *Bodytalk*, pp. 54–5.

86 Denis Diderot, 'Encyclopédie', in *Encyclopédie ou Dictionnaire raisonné des sciences, des arts et des métiers*, Vol. 5 (Paris, 1755), pp. 635–48A, as translated by Philip Stewart in *The Encyclopedia of Diderot & d'Alembert: Collaborative Translation Project* (Ann Arbor, MI: Scholarly Publishing Office of the University of Michigan Library, 2002). http://hdl.handle.net/2027/spo.did2222.0000.004.

87 Stephen Werner, *The Comic Diderot: A Reading of the Fictions* (Birmingham, AL: Summa, 2000), p. 25. Werner argues that the 'central and most prominent features' of later works 'first saw the light of day' in *Les Bijoux Indiscrets*, p. 29.

88 Jonathan I. Israel, *Enlightenment Contested: Philosophy, Modernity, and the Emancipation of Man 1670–1752* (Oxford: Oxford University Press, 2006), p. 841.

89 Julia Kristeva, *Strangers to Ourselves*, trans. Leon S. Roudiez (New York, NY: Columbia University Press, 1991), p. 181.

90 Denis Diderot, *The Indiscreet Jewels*, trans. Sophie Hawkes (New York, NY: Marsilio, 1993), p. 11.

91 Diderot, *Indiscreet*, p. 11.

92 Ibid., p. 13. Almost as an afterthought ('I forgot to mention', says the narrator), the reader learns that the ring also grants invisibility to its wearer. See Diderot, *Indiscreet*, p. 14. For more on eighteenth-century *bijoux* as symbolic of the female genitals, see Marcia Pointon, *Brilliant Effects: A Cultural History of Gem Stones and Jewellery* (New Haven, CT: Yale University Press, 2009).

93 Marie-Jeanne Riccoboni, *Les Lettres de Mistriss Fanni Butlerd*, 'XXVe Lettre', *Oeuvres Complètes de Mme Riccoboni*, Vol. 4 (Paris: Foucault, Libraire, Rue des Noyers, 1818), p. 27. For more on Fanni's 'magically assisted voyeurism', see Elizabeth Cook, *Epistolary Bodies: Gender and Genre in the Eighteenth-Century Republic of Letters* (Stanford, CA: Stanford University Press, 1996), p. 132; my English translation.

94 Michel Foucault, *The History of Sexuality*, Vol. 1 (Harmondsworth: Penguin, 1990), p. 79.

95 Miller, p. 13, my italics for emphasis.

96 On Puisieux as Mirzoza see P. N. Furbank, *Diderot: A Critical Biography* (London: Secker & Warburg, 1992), p. 43. Furbank relates how Diderot wrote the book in a fortnight in an attempt to prove to Puisieux how easy he found such genre fiction as *le roman galant*. See Furbank, p. 43.

97 Diderot, *Indiscreet*, p. 15.

98 Ibid., p. 17.

99 Ibid., p. 18.

100 Ibid., p. 32.

101 Werner, *The Comic Diderot*, p. 17.

102 For more on the novel's 'untold story', see Thomas M. Kavanagh, 'Language as Deception: Diderot's *Les Bijoux Indiscrets*', *Diderot Studies XXIII*, ed. Otis Fellow and Diana Guiragossian Carr (Geneva: Librairie Droz, 1988), pp. 101–14 (p. 109).

103 On how Mangogul is 'obliged to content himself with partial truths tied to each individual and discrete object of inquiry', see Suzanne Rodin Pucci, 'The Discrete Charms of the Exotic: Fictions of the Harem in Eighteenth-Century France', in G. S. Rousseau and Roy Porter (eds), *Exoticism in the Enlightenment* (Manchester: Manchester University Press, 1990), pp. 145–75 (p. 157).

104 Jacinthe Morel, 'De la Curiosité dans *Les Bijoux Indiscrets*: Propositions de lecture', *Diderot Studies XXV*, eds Fellow and Guiragossian Carr, pp. 75–88 (p. 78); my translation into English.

105 Morel, 'De la Curiosité', p. 88; my translation into English.

106 James Fowler, *Voicing Desire: Family and Sexuality in Diderot's Narrative* (Oxford: Voltaire Foundation, 2000), p. 20.

107 Foucault, *The History of Sexuality*, p. 77; my emphasis.

108 Diderot, *Indiscreet*, p. 266.

109 Ibid., p. 367.

110   Jennifer Vanderheyden, *The Function of the Dream and the Body in Diderot's Works* (*The Age of Revolution and Romanticism: Interdisciplinary Studies*) (New York, NY: Peter Lang, 2004), p. 108.

111   Linda Williams, *Hard Core: Power, Pleasure and the 'Frenzy of the Visible'* (Berkeley, CA: University of California Press, 1999), p. 4.

112   Mary Douglas, *Natural Symbols: Explorations in Cosmology* (Harmondsworth: Penguin, 1973), p. 99.

113   Additionally, Mangogul's predilection for hearing the sound of his own voice may be read as being about the author, for Diderot was 'an exceptional conversationalist. When launched, he seems to have talked inexhaustibly, moving unpredictably from one subject to another'. Peter France, *Rhetoric and Truth in France: Descartes to Diderot* (Oxford: Clarendon Press, 1972), p. 203.

114   Williams, *Hard Core*, p. 2; my emphasis.

115   Ibid., p. 4.

116   John Updike, 'Two Cunts in Paris', in *Americana: And Other Poems* (New York, NY: Knopf, 2001), p. 56.

117   Maxime Du Camp, *Les Convulsions de Paris* (1889), quoted by Susan Kandel in 'Beneath the Green Veil: The Body in/of New Feminist Art', in Amelia Jones (ed.), *Sexual Politics: Judy Chicago's 'Dinner Party' in Feminist Art History* (Berkeley, CA: University of California Press, 1996), pp. 186–200 (194); see also p. 199, n. 21. For more on the painting's 'chequered journey' to Guitrancourt, see Linda Nochlin, 'Courbet's "L'origine du monde": The Origin without an Original', *October*, Vol. 37 (Summer 1986), pp. 76–86.

118   Michael Lapidge, *Anglo-Latin Literature, 600–899* (London: Hambledon, 1996), p. 247. Keith Briggs imagines that, despite his outward shows of piety, Aldhelm may have constructed his verse in such a way that 'haere*scunt*' naughtily suggested 'her is cunt'. See Keith Briggs, 'OE and ME *cunte* in Place-Names', *Journal of the English Place-Name Society*, 41 (2009), pp. 26–39 (p. 37).

119   The Rolling Stones, 'Angie', *Goats Head Soup* (Rolling Stones, 1973). In the United States and the United Kingdom, the single was issued in a standard Rolling Stones label sleeve. The *Goats Head Soup* album cover shows Mick Jagger's veiled face apparently situated in the 'V' of a woman's crotch; his famously thickly lipped mouth is not accidentally situated.

120   Alexis Petridis, Review of Jamie Foxx, *Unpredictable*, in *The Guardian*, 21 April 2006.

121   Jamie Foxx, 'Storm (Forecass)', *Unpredictable*, 2006.

122   Caroline Sullivan, Review of Jamie Foxx, live at the Café de Paris, London, in *The Guardian*, 25 April 2006.

123   Falling in Reverse, 'Good Girls, Bad Guys', *The Drug in Me Is You*, 2011.

124   Lady Gaga, 'Born This Way', from the eponymous album, 2011.

125   See Emma L. E. Rees, 'Cordelia's Can't: Rhetorics of Reticence and (Dis)ease in *King Lear*', in Jennifer C. Vaught (ed.), *Rhetorics of Bodily Disease and Health in Medieval and Early Modern England* (Surrey: Ashgate, 2010), pp. 105–16 (p. 106).

126 On Irigaray's 'Vulvomorphic Logic', see Jane Gallop, *Thinking Through The Body* (New York, NY: Columbia University Press, 1988), p. 95. Gallop also writes insightfully on Diderot's novel, pp. 71–9.

127 Luce Irigaray, *This Sex Which is Not One*, trans. Catherine Porter (New York, NY: Cornell University Press, 1985), p. 29.

3

Revealing the Vagina in Literature

In camera

The twentieth-century Spanish filmmaker Luis Buñuel delighted in making the unseen seen. Ideas of metamorphosis and illogicality pervade his works, as do bodily organs behaving in surreal ways, religious irreverence and composure in the face of the grotesque. These themes fascinate and influence the work of writers, too. In the American–Greek Eurydice Kamvyselli's novel *f/32* (1993), for example, a wounding takes place which is as shocking and corporeal as that performed in Buñuel's 1929 short film *Un Chien Andalou*, in which a razor slices into an eyeball in close-up. The juxtaposition of the vagina and the blasphemous is emphasized in Robert Coover's play, *A Theological Position*; and Susanna Kaysen's deployment of the idea of a 'camera' owes a debt, like Kamvyselli's, to Buñuel. The surrealism of novels by Maureen Freely and Nicholson Baker arguably influenced what has come to be known as the 'Bizarro' genre – another focus of this chapter – and can also be better understood in the light of Buñuel's artistic experimentation. In considering the literary vagina, we'll also meet the playwright Jane Arden, the polemicist Periel Aschenbrand, the novelist William S. Burroughs and the fiercely avant-garde writer Kathy Acker.

The prestigious Palme d'Or at the 1961 Cannes Film Festival was awarded to Luis Buñuel for his exuberantly irreverent *Viridiana*.[1] The film's cynical examination of what happens when charitable acts go badly wrong, is surely a swipe at the Spanish dictator General Franco's own gesture in inviting Buñuel to return from Mexico to make any film he liked. *Viridiana*, described by Víctor Fuentes as 'the greatest and most divine erotic orgy on film', was the result, and, despite Franco's initial magnanimity, it was swiftly banned in Spain and condemned by the Vatican.[2] *Viridiana*'s disturbing images of sexual assault and assorted other grotesque moments culminate in a graphic parody of Leonardo Da Vinci's 'La Última Cena'. This 'Last Supper' is played out in an ornate dining room in a temporarily deserted country house. Viridiana is a novice nun, and niece of Don Jaime, the debauched mansion owner. After Don Jaime's suicide, the charitable Viridiana invites a group of beggars into the house, where they run amok. Order and civility disappear, and what should be a refined meal has become instead a beggars' banquet. One particularly eccentric beggar addresses another, called Enedina: 'Senorina? [. . .] Take a portrait as a memento'. 'With what camera?' asks another beggar, to which Enedina replies: 'Con una máquina que me regalaron mis papás' ('With a camera my parents gave me!'). As the men laugh, Enedina undertakes the role of director: 'If you don't quieten down, no portrait! When I'm close, no-one is allowed to move! Come on! [. . .] We must see your face! [. . .] Come on, let's be still!' A cock crows, and the beggars freeze in specific poses, on one side of the table in a tableau – in a theological position, one might say – imitative of Da Vinci's 'Last Supper'. Satisfied that her subjects are correctly assembled, Enedina lifts her skirts with a flourish, and 'takes the picture'.

The riotously blasphemous imagery is self-evident, but there is more going on in this scene than that. Enedina uses the colloquial 'una máquina' for 'camera', but, in Spanish 'la cámara' can mean both 'camera' and a little chamber, or orifice. By directing and then filming the beggars, Enedina has assumed Buñuel's role, but instead of the phallic gaze of the *auteur*, she has a *vaginal* gaze all her own.[3] Buñuel expert Juliàn Gutiérrez-Albilla has written that 'Enedina's literal "cut" (namely her vagina) executes the "click" of the shutter. Hence, the irruption of the female genitals perversely challenges the notion of sacredness conventionally attributed to the celebrated scene.'[4] Everyone laughs once the 'picture' is taken, and a leper starts playing the 'Hallelujah Chorus' on an old gramophone player before disappearing to change into Don Jaime's dead wife's wedding dress. A blind beggar called Don Amalio took the role of Christ at the centre of Enedina's 'photograph', and explodes into a jealous rage when he's told that another beggar is sexually assaulting Enedina behind a sofa on which one of her daughters sleeps. In a literal blind fury he smashes the glasses and crockery on the dining table, destroying whatever shreds of decorum might have remained. The cock crow which had been audible when Enedina took her picture symbolizes the beggars' outrageous betrayal of the pious Viridiana's well-intentioned opening of the doors of her dead uncle's mansion to people who 'embody most of the seven deadly sins. If pride is absent, it is simply because they have none'.[5] The director and his characters are alike both in their iconoclasm and in their explicit rejection of the thin veneer of social propriety.

Buñuel's fascination with the scopophilic (the desire to *look*) was established in his first film, *Un Chien Andalou* (1929). In the 16-minute film, Buñuel plays with a series of Freudian dreams and nightmares. Any logic of time, place or theme is dispensed with, and the film's refusal to succumb to the restraints of anything closely resembling a linear narrative is strategic in terms of its purpose and themes. Looking at an object cannot, in and of itself, secure understanding of, and meaning for, it; similarly, the film becomes the object of *our* consideration as the characters within it observe one another in a variety of bizarre vignettes. Just as Enedina's 'camera' confounded viewers' expectations of what a woman can perform, so Buñuel's camera refutes our interpretive attempts. At least three of the central images of *Un Chien* seem to me to be so deliberately invoked in the writing of authors who use the vagina as a central motif, that they're worth establishing here.

The first image is that of the eye, and its ramifications for the 'I'. The short, silent film opens with Buñuel himself sharpening a cutthroat razor while watching a small cloud bisect a full moon. This movement is replicated as he holds open the left eye of the 'Young Girl', here played by the French actor Simone Mareuil, and apparently draws the blade across it, cutting it in two. It's a shocking image to watch, since it fills the entire frame and is disturbingly convincing (in fact, the eye of a dead animal was used, no doubt much to Mareuil's relief). Later, Mareuil stares – again Buñuel plays with the urgency of the ocular impulse – at a death's-head moth, motionlcss on a wall. We, too, watch, and decipher, as if we were Mareuil's collaborators. In another scene, we watch a crowd which has gathered to watch a woman calmly and methodically poking at a severed hand. A police officer intervenes, disperses the crowd, calmly picks up the hand and puts it into a striped box which he hands back to the young woman. This striped box – the oddly incongruous container for the amputated organ – is the second image from Buñuel's film which, it seems to me, reappears in various forms in writing about the vagina. The third fundamental image is, unsurprisingly, perhaps, Buñuel's fascination with the bodily orifice. We have already seen how Enedina's 'camera' performs a gaze which controls and redefines a group of rowdy beggars, to the point where she threatens to usurp the *auteur's* own role. In *Un Chien Andalou*, a swarm of ants emerges from a stigmata-like wound in the right palm of a character's hand. This hole fades into an image of an armpit which, in turn, becomes a prickly sea urchin. A man's lips also disappear, apparently wiped from his face and then reappear as a phenomenally pubic-looking armpit in the middle of his face. Mareuil retreats, sticking out her tongue as she goes to a beach (distance, like time, is as meaningless and fluid in the surreal world of this film as it is in the world of dreams). And this is in a film where the audience has previously witnessed a cyclist dragging across the room towards Mareuil two grand pianos, two stone tablets bearing the Ten Commandments, two dead donkeys, and two Catholic priests (one played by Buñuel's collaborator on the film, Salvador Dali).

Without this context, the title of Susanna Kaysen's 2001 novella *The Camera My Mother Gave Me* is inexplicably odd.[6] In a sense, it's a poetic way of describing mother–daughter heredity. That Kamvyselli, as we shall see, also chose a photographic reference for the title of *f/32* maybe points to something more. An introspection, perhaps? Turning the lens inwards? Specularity? Kaysen is probably best known for her autobiographical account of her mental illness, *Girl, Interrupted*.[7] However, in her 2001 novella *The Camera My Mother Gave Me*, she is focused on the interconnections between physiological and psychological disease. The book documents, over a fairly ambiguous time period, the experiences of a narrator who is trying to heal her vulvodynia (vulvar pain). The medical profession – just about every branch of it, from traditional medicine to a fair share of quackery – is at a loss and can't cure it. The narrator's friends seem to believe it's the narrator's relationship with an abusive male partner which is causing the pain. In other words, the negative psychological impact of that relationship is evident in physiological symptoms.

Recalling Enedina's flamboyant 'photographic' gesture as it does, Kaysen's odd title is immediately aligned with Buñuel's particular mode of portraying disconnectedness and illogicality. Kaysen's narrator learns that she needs to regard her cunt as, somehow, less autonomized or separate, and as more integral to her*self*. She objectifies it at the same time as seeing it as – understandably – central to her erotic activity and sense of herself as a sexual being: 'I've become a vagina! I said. I can't stand it. There's got to be more to me than that.'[8] Her doctor agrees that she shouldn't take 'antiviral stuff' if she doesn't want to, but she remains conflicted: 'Is it okay? I asked. Is it okay that I want to stop trying to fix it?'[9] When she recounts the visit to the doctor in a prickly argument with her boyfriend, she images that 'During this conversation, my vagina was carrying on an internal monologue that went, Zing, sting, yow.'[10]

As the story progresses, the narrator begins to heed her friends, wondering whether her boyfriend's treatment of her isn't in fact rape. Her intellectualism and, crucially, her separation of her mind and her body, is getting in the way of her seeing the relationship for what it really is. 'Did he manhandle you?' a friend asks.[11] '*Manhandle*, I said, that's an interesting word. Forget about that stuff, she said sharply.'[12] The friend's 'sharpness' stems from her frustration that the narrator has become so separated from her embodied sense of self that she can view it objectively, rather than *feeling* it, too. The narrator gradually comes to believe that she has lost all vaginal sexual sensation. In a chapter called 'The Dead Vagina' she describes how her 'vagina had curled up into itself like a hedgehog, cool, dry, and unresponsive', and describes herself as having exiled, starved and ultimately killed it:

> I wanted my vagina back [. . .] I wanted unpredictability, upset, waywardness. I wanted the world to regain the other dimension that only the vagina can perceive. Because the vagina is the organ that looks to the future. The vagina is potential. It's not emptiness, it's possibility, and possibility was exactly what was missing from my life.[13]

Once she finds a new lover, the narrator fantasizes about a sexual encounter in which 'I am floating or pivoting around my vagina, which has become the fulcrum of my existence', but having misread the signs with this potential lover, she declares to her close friend Paula, 'I think my vagina's lost its mind.'[14]

The end of the novella is very open-ended and unsatisfactory because of its narrative ambiguities. There's no sense or suggestion of an accurate diagnosis of the narrator's condition, nor of a cure for it. Instead, there is a loosely metaphysical-sounding ending to the book which makes it sound as though the narrator does not have the closure or the sense of wholeness she's been seeking and which she here appears to advocate:

> Our unit of existence is a body . . . Disease is one of our languages . . . My vagina keeps trying to get my attention . . . I'm still listening.[15]

This is a tale of the non-assimilated experience of female sexuality, of the brokenness of the female psyche. As the narrator suggests, 'I pulled away inside myself, so that the events on the bed were far from where "I" was, and the pain was far away also. That worked, but I didn't like doing it.'[16] The narrator is not a unified (w)hole at the novel's conclusion; her cunt is demanding, insistent, even – one might say – autonomized.

The political vagina

At the cutting edge of British theatre in the late 1960s was Jane Arden, an actor and playwright whose *Vagina Rex and the Gas Oven* was first performed at Jim Haynes's Art Laboratory on Drury Lane in London in February 1969. Arden's concerns were with what she saw as the connections between women's mental health and their social status. In her introduction to the 1971 published play script, she stated her hope that the 'political and personal are beginning to cleave unto one another and yesterday's "deranged" females are emerging as today's radical leaders'.[17] The play's experimental use of projections, voiceovers, lighting and nudity gave it a distinctive, sinister mood which the director, Jack Bond, exploited in making the nameless Man (first played by Victor Spinetti) behave pitilessly towards the nameless Woman (Sheila Allen), at one point jerking her body around as if it were a ventriloquist's dummy. This idea of the fragmented female was established at the play's start, as a disembodied woman's voice is heard saying 'We have no language. The words of women have yet to be written. Woman's use of speech amounts to an assenting silence or an unheard shriek.'[18] The Man, ably aided by a group of 'Furies', continues to torment the Woman, who strips and 'falls to her knees'.[19] The now-naked Furies move her 'into the birth position' and two of them pull a white plastic sheet from between her legs and hold it up so as to form a screen between the audience and her prone body.[20] Onto this screen is projected a close-up of a woman's genitals; onto the main wall is a 'large projection of the rest of the naked woman in labour'.[21] The Furies, one by one, tear their way through the smaller screen and are 'birthed' onto the stage. A robot arrives (it's OK – it's 1969), and tells the distraught Woman that 'Schizophrenics are the result of basic alienation with the mother', which prompts her to run to the back wall where the projection has now changed into 'an enormous gas oven with an open door. Screams of babies are heard'.[22]

It's all very 1960s and avant-garde: the main socio-cultural themes of the day are there, right down to the evocation of space exploration and sci-fi. The vagina is a surrogate projection into the space where the woman's legs are splayed on the stage; it is uncontrollable biology. Its visual comparison with a gas oven emphasizes its role as portal into life, which ultimately is a passage to death; this was emphasized by British psychedelic artist Alan Aldridge's original poster for the play. Aldridge's drawing shows a naked woman with a mask-like face, baby under each arm and mirror in hand, reflecting a skull back at her, with an oven door swinging out of her gravid belly, showing oven shelves inside and a bun in the oven. Thus metaphor is literalized again, and the female genitals bear the brunt of the play's misogyny as enacted by the Man who, stabbing an imaginary woman onstage, 'bends over this invented female body and begins to hack – as though he is dismembering it [. . .] "My *mother* – her breasts – and her cunt"'.[23] The spotlight is then directed onto the Woman who, the stage directions tell us, in language portentous enough to fluster even the most resourceful stage-manager, 'metamorphoses into the omnipotent mother-goddess'.[24] In the world of this play, a woman is trapped in the interstices of biological destiny and mental ill health. As Arden wrote, 'one of the outcomes of the production' was a piece in the *Observer*, which asked '"Are Women Oppressed?"' as though there was still some doubt about the matter.'[25]

In 2005 the American activist Periel Aschenbrand published *The Only Bush I Trust is my Own*, as a summary of her political engagement with the US Presidential elections of the year before. The book is a collection of anecdotal meanderings from a sometimes very humorous (mainly in her vivid evocations of her phone conversations with her mother), but often objectionably self-obsessed, New York writer. The playfulness of the book's title and cover sets the tone for what is to follow – the author on the cover meets the reader's gaze full on; Eve-like, the apple held provocatively in her right hand is unbitten and a leaf hides her own 'bush'. The book's title is printed across the picture, hiding her breasts. This is political pussy at its most challenging and at its most paradoxical – in effect a Pussy Riot in waiting. Aschenbrand does identify the inconsistencies in her political activism herself, most robustly in her vignette on her beloved Prada handbag at LaGuardia airport: 'I paid more for this bag', the writer argues with airport security, 'than what Haitians make in a year, and I need it lest I forget that I live in a social trance and am a complete fashion victim'.[26]

Aschenbrand encourages her female students to 'put our tits to better use' so as to 'make people think about things no one else is making them think about'.[27] 'If Michael Moore made being politically active hip', she continues, 'I wanted to make it sexy'.[28] After experimenting with commercially unsuccessful slogans ('Foucault is sexy' was never going to be a best-seller), she hit upon the witty 'the only Bush I trust is my own', a slogan that at once conjured up female sexuality and the Republican George Bush (no mean feat).[29] This idea developed into Aschenbrand's 'body as billboard [. . .] anti-clothing line' and the 'Bush' T-shirt was worn by 100 women for an anti-Bush poster for the presidential campaign. Susan Sarandon is on the poster, as is Eve Ensler ('arguably the most famous bush in the United States').[30] 'I am', writes Aschenbrand, 'on a mission to change things – one pair of tits at a time'.[31]

Aschenbrand's brand of sexual politics is composed of contradictory and deliberately provocative statements which actually do not amount to much. In the choice of the book's title she makes the 'bush' centre-stage but is arguably more obsessed by 'tits' and 'the anus [. . .] the last taboo of the body'.[32] She never problematizes the way she *uses* the female body to make a political statement, nor of her deployment of playfully controversial language. Hers is less a political manifesto than a half-hearted, solipsistic attempt to provoke people into buying her book.

The Second Coming

William S. Burroughs spent several years in the 1950s voluntarily holed up in a stifling Moroccan hotel room, unapologetically indulging his sexual and narcotic fantasies while writing his infamous *Naked Lunch*. This kaleido-scopically druggy novel ventures into the outlandish and taboo hinterlands of human experience as the characters Dr 'Fingers' Schafer and the sadistic Dr Benway debate how, in the interests of increased efficiency, the human body might somehow be streamlined. 'Instead of a mouth and an anus to get out of order', Schafer proposes impulsively, 'why not have one all-purpose hole?'[33] Burroughs's 'Talking Asshole' vignette, in which Benway recounts what's effec-tively a *fabliau*, is the result. The story centres on a man 'who taught his ass-hole to talk' at first 'like a novelty ventriloquist act' until 'the ass started talking on its own', developing 'sort of teeth-like little raspy incurving hooks' which 'would eat its way through his pants and start talking on the street, shouting out it wanted equal rights'.[34] This autonomized asshole can't be silenced, not even in a *fabliau*-style attempt to stifle it with candles. Instead, maliciously and grotesquely, the asshole slowly kills off its host, leaving his eyes until last, because 'one thing the asshole *couldn't* do was see'.[35] The story, less manuscript, perhaps, than '*anuscript*', can be read as a parable for Burroughs's own anxie-ties over what he thought of as the fractured identity of the professional writer (his unease was, no doubt, exacerbated by industrial quantities of Tangier's finest drugs).[36] In Benway's lurid fable the '*anus dentatus*' ultimately destroyed its host. By contrast, when it's female genitals which writers imagine seek-ing autonomy, the protagonist can sometimes be – ironically – strengthened or even unified, as is the case in Eurydice Kamvyselli's 1993 novel, *f/32: The Second Coming*.[37]

    As we saw in 'Antecedents', at around the same time that Burroughs was wrestling with the narrative complexities of *Naked Lunch*, the French psycho-analyst Jacques Lacan was buying Gustave Courbet's painting *L'Origine du*

Monde. There's a tempting thread of influence waiting to be picked up here: Lacan's work can help to make sense of some of the intricacies of Kamvyselli's radically postmodern novel which depicts a woman torn between possessing analytical power like Courbet's *Clairvoyante* and sexual potency like his *Origine*.[38] Lacan observed the fascination of very young children when they see their own reflection in a mirror and argued that, in crucial mirror *moments* (Lacan resisted the idea of these being *stages*), the individual is aware of himself- or herself-as-image. Of course, human contact and language later come to define the individual, but at this 'primordial' stage, the infant is struggling to develop a sense of 'I' in relation to the reflected self or *imago*.[39] The *imago*-as-version-of-self is the individual's sense of self *before* language or socialization, but it is a fiction or a distortion because it's a reflection or *re*presentation of reality. The *imago* thus presents a distorted, unattainable (because idealized) version of reality. Ela, the adult protagonist of *f/32*, utterly loses any clearly defined status for her 'I' after suffering a brutal sexual assault, and her subsequent quest to repair and unite her body and her psyche is the fundamental focus of Kamvyselli's narrative. For Lacan, the 'subject' (a more fitting word, perhaps, than the unified idea of an 'individual') must end up with the 'assumption of the armour of an alienating identity', in an attempt to hold together an otherwise fragmented or distorted self which is based on that initial mirror identification.[40]

The 'Ideal-I' in the mirror, in its apparent and attractive completeness and strength, is quite at odds with the actual physical helplessness of a human child and remains an 'other', sought after by the individual throughout their entire life. The egos of Lacan's and, by extension, Kamvyselli's, subjects are fractured (quite different to René 'cogito ergo sum' Descartes's seventeenth-century notion of a unified 'I'), and persist in a state of tense agitation, with mirror 'moments' being repeatedly, compulsively revisited in one way or another. Such moments, as conceived of by Lacan, and as fictionalized by Kamvyselli, are crucial in human development, then. But they are also deeply troubling because the infant, as he or she gets older, realizes just how unattainable the perfection and wholeness of the *imago* is, and so experiences dissatisfaction with being but a pale version of the self which cannot live up to the reflected ideal. This profound disappointment is a psychical experience to which the individual is condemned repeatedly to return. The subject's self-image is fissured, and the psychic split or *manque-à-être* (literally, 'lack of being') is often manifest in the guise of mental illness.[41] The mirror is, to use Lacan's terminology, a 'stadium' ('*stade*') in which the subject forever seeks, and is forever obsessed by, her own image. Lacan went so far as to suggest that because *everyone* falls short of the Ideal-I, then everyone is, in some respect, paranoid, trying to make sense of their place in the world and chasing fleeting *substitutes* for the Ideal-I. Kamvyselli evokes this *manque-à-être* through the painful and convoluted relationship Ela has with her temporarily autonomized and voracious 'V': her brutally removed genitals. She imagines a world where the libido is unrestrained and where *Verneinung*, the *denial* or repression of sexual drives and mortality, is a condition of human existence. *Verneinung* allows human impulses a fleeting opportunity for expression, as repressed drives erupt into consciousness in, for example, dreams or hallucinations.[42] In *f/32*, such ruptures persist until they become the totality of the fabric of Ela's universe.

The 'it' of the novel's subsections is ambiguous. We have: '*Why* she lost it', '*How* she lost it', and 'How she *found* it', and there's also a two-page epilogue called '*Why* she found it'.[43] Of course 'it' could refer to Ela's genitals which are 'lost', but with Lacan as our template, 'it' resonates with the building blocks of identity and selfhood. As Ela moves *away* from her initial condition of bodily unity and psychic detachment, she ironically moves *nearer* to a unified identity, quite at odds with the unfortunate, digested host of Benway's tale: 'Who is in control?' Ela asks, 'This cunt or I? Is "it" I?'[44] By the old Frick Museum in New York City, a crowd assembles as a blind man attacks Ela, sawing at her genitals until they are entirely detached from her. Kamvyselli's tone is troubling here. What is being described is the most visceral and bloody of acts; what is conveyed through the magic realist language is otherworldliness, almost objectivity. The language creates a bridge for the reader from what is nearly unimaginable or unrepresentable, to the safer retreat of simile: 'Now blood spurts from Ela's cunt like a scarlet bird, flying across to the blind man's eye.'[45] As language creates a distance for the reader, so Ela experiences for the first time life *beyond* language: 'she no longer has to live in metaphor: this man's knife makes a difference. It makes her aware of herself'.[46] Bizarrely, this act of extreme violence is equated in Ela's mind with an act of love and a spiritual coming into being. In the Lacanian sense it is a moment of epiphany by which the mutilated self spectacularly confronts the *manque-à-être* to the point where Ela actually nears orgasm during the public excision. The novel explores how Ela accommodates this trauma, a process which is hampered in no small part by her genitals' autonomous quasi-celebrity escapades.

Kamvyselli's narrative form is fractured: its choppy paragraphing is the material manifestation of Ela's discontinuous sense of self, and the novel's different points of view reflect its Lacanian fixation on looking, mirrors and lenses. At the narrative's start, Ela is frustrated because she can't *see* her genitals but would like 'to have a good look'.[47] The attempts in the novel's opening pages to find an appropriate vocabulary for describing Ela's body indicate how (sexual) identity precedes language – her body resists the putative stability of linguistic definition. What is taken from her in the attack is the body part that cannot speak its name in a culture (as we saw in this book's introduction) that does not dare to speak its name. For the female protagonist, it is at once her*self* and is unknown to herself. The same men with whom Ela has sexual intercourse, the reader is told, cannot interact with her face – her Gorgon-like, castrating *Clairvoyante* – in the way in which they interact with her *Origine*. Lips, eyes and genitals are pulled into the vibrant account with, at one point, Ela blindfolding herself so that the ideal-I/Eye of her body predominates: 'So Ela ties her panties over her mocking eyes and exposes instead the pure eye of her cunt, which loosens men up'.[48] In this first section of the novel, then, Ela arguably portrays herself as either *Clairvoyante* or *Origine*; she cannot be both simultaneously until the act of extreme violence which wrenches the metaphor of bodily detachment or dissociation and renders it in literal, spatial terms. Paradoxically, this violent separation allows Ela a refreshed subjectivity, empowering her in ways which differ quite radically from the equivocal power she previously had while having sex with men, when 'being owned and being fucked are opposites. Possession is erotic only for that second when I hold a man tightly in me; the annihilation of the self is not itself erotic. An orgasm [. . .] is a crime against the mind'.[49]

Ela's male lovers are her mirrors, and in their reification of Ela-as-*imago*, Ela-as-authentic-identity is lost:

> No one knows who Ela is. So everyone wants her. 'This is the real thing,' men think, and want to rise up to her standards. She embodies everyone's ideals and pretences, for she is arbitrary, like a dream-condensation; that is her freedom [. . .] People exist as fiction for Ela. The world is a second language for her. She contemplates: People can't see that I am normal. No one presumes that I am a subject. I need a sign on me.[50]

Visual or linguistic signification can eradicate, rather than explain, individuals (especially in pornographic or clinical discourses). Ela's anxiety here is not only about the fictionality and futile aspirational gestures of other people, but is also a commentary on the fictionality of the self, a self which has had presented to it an ideal Lacanian *imago* so many times that the 'I' repeatedly experiences insufficiency and alienation. In an important sense it's a manoeuvre that replicates heterosexual pornographic discourses in which the (usually) male gaze is controlling, and the female body is reduced to silenced object, reified and revered while simultaneously being regarded as desirable, threatening and repulsive. Ela's maturation is mapped through the self-reifying act of reflection: 'Her mirror showed her that she was a surprised abyss', with 'abyss' connoting sinister suggestions of emptiness and interiority.[51] However, this traumatized self is also a creative being who deals with the world by escaping into a Rabelaisian *Verneinung* of hallucination and fantasy, seeing 'a rowdy brothel in place of a Byzantine church, an immense phallus held by screeching griffins on the Liberty statue, a family of fat hermaphrodites involved in a complex orgy during maths class'.[52]

During the blind man's attack, Ela laughs 'at the defeat of logic . . . the ridicule of reality'; she even continues with the excision herself once he has stopped.[53] The violent act is very public, and in a vivid metaphor for voyeurism, the hitherto unseen has been rendered visible; the word is made flesh: 'As Ela's cunt drops off, falling with a tiny "slomp" on the ground, the diverse faces crowding around her are possessed by a unified expression of pity and fear. They all sense that they see something which was never meant to be seen. *Presto.*'[54] In a riposte to misogynist clichés, the metaphorical has been bloodily realized: 'The next time any men (including cops) say: "Give me your cunt, baby," I can now reply: "Voilà" and hand it over to them [. . .] Life is interesting only when metaphors become literal.'[55] 'Ela suddenly recognizes it through her tears', writes Kamvyselli: 'it is a wide-angle 35mm camera lens! She takes her 2 & ¼ medium-format Hasselblad from her purse. Her ex-cunt fits perfectly on to it'.[56] Drily, Ela observes that what she's experiencing may be 'normal in decuntations' and her cunt/camera allows her to renegotiate her relationship with the world, not through language but in the visual realm, as she ventures onto the streets to take photographs.[57]

The language Kamvyselli uses in describing Ela's excised organ is quite startling. She uses techniques of defamiliarization to emphasize the schism between self and other. Following the attack, Ela puts her cunt in an empty peanut butter jar. It is a 'hacked plant', 'a bright pretty foetus', and wears 'a roguish smile that reminds Ela of Iago'; it could be carried 'like a shield [. . .] a crown [. . .] the Gorgon's head, an Oscar'.[58] Without her cunt, Ela must renegotiate her sense of self: 'What gender is she now? Does she still have an identity, is she a "she"?', and she begins to 'find' herself in her apartment where there are 'thousands of tiny mirrors that reflect the most interesting surreal fragments of herself'.[59] The roles of Ela, 'I', and the author are deliberately blurred – there is an italicized commentary from an 'I' who may or may not be Kamvyselli, and who watches Ela while experiencing its own crisis, '*wondering: Is my identity at stake?*'[60] These vertiginous crises of identification are further complicated as the Narrator watches Ela who is looking at photographs of the Narrator who experiences horror at the fact that she does not have genitalia in the photographs. This moment compromises the Narrator's previously self-assured voice and all identities are laid open: '*The cunt, not I, is the gap at the centre of this world.*'[61]

After searching for the absconder-vagina in the underworld of New York porn, the Narrator has a sighting of it in a porn cinema, where it is busy mirroring the on-screen actions with a lone penis. Her attempt to abduct both parties fails and she returns to her hotel room to discover just the penis wrapped up in her coat. The Narrator fleetingly considers asking Ela to attach the penis to herself, in order to '*get men's point of view, what they see inside a vagina, why they go mad, all those mysteries*'.[62] Momentarily, then, the instability of identity suggests possibility rather than terror in this increasingly dystopian world. The catalogue of bizarre encounters between the Narrator and the fugitive genitals continues: one moment she is the Statue of Liberty's genitalia, being photographed by delighted tourists; the next, she is masquerading as a topping in Ray's World Famous Pizza (this surely gives 'Hand Tossed' a whole new meaning, in British English, at least). Ela's simultaneous quest, however, which intertwines with that of the italicized Narrator, is grotesquely portrayed as she is mutilated, her tongue cut out by a female child rapist who uses the same knife used in the initial excision or 'decuntation'. Ela identifies this violation as an 'oral castration': this conflation of lips and labia serves to emphasize the precarious vulnerability and fluidity of her sense of self.

Kamvyselli's mischievous play with Lacanian discourses of psychoanalysis is present in the surreal conversation Ela has with a jailer who, following a news report that the cunt is in a shoebox, opens the box to find '*a big hole [. . .]* "*It" is nothing! A signifying absence!*'[63] The cunt, meanwhile, appears on the Letterman Show – and then *on* Letterman (this showbiz career recalls one we'll see later, in Tom DeSimone's film *Chatterbox*). Kitty Kelley, the infamously salacious celebrity biographer, is set to write the cunt's biography, and Johnny Carson names her 'V'. In a solipsistic, mimetic move, Ela decides to write her own book too, called *f/32*, and is given dubious looks at the library as she begins to 'research the history of other cases of violently emancipated cunts'.[64] The use of the idea of emancipation is interesting here: the Narrator is pressing us again to see the liberatory potential of the 'decuntation' rather than to focus on the grim nature of its violence. At the same time that it ('she'?) is being sought, V is free and has freed Ela from the constraints of the patriarchal gaze. The novel has incarnated/incuntated metaphor.

f/32 is situated firmly in the tradition of Diderot, the chevaliers and the motif of the *vagina loquens*. Five years before Eve Ensler published *The Vagina Monologues*, Kamvyselli imagined an autonomous cunt with a celebrity all its own. Like Ensler's V-days, V becomes '*the message of the day. V is the media queen. V is the other half of TV [. . .] V is the new reincarnation of the American identity*'.[65] As the frustrated Narrator declares, '*Read my lips: No more cunt!*', the narrative further folds in on itself as Ela declares her intention to write *f/32* 'with both her mind and her cunt'.[66] The narrative breakdown is soon after echoed by another collapse of identity as the Narrator expresses her frustration at the extreme nature of V's commercialism and fame ('*V is the biggest trend ever [. . .] Even Pynchon's book, V, although unrelated, tops the bestseller lists*').[67] The further the elusive V moves away from Ela, the closer both Ela and the Narrator become in terms of self-knowledge. V is continually being debated, defined and puzzled over by the public – like female sexuality she cannot just 'be' but must instead be re-presented and repackaged through language and popular culture. V is Lacan's unattainable Ideal-I. As the novel draws to a close, '*The old illusion of "I" has died and rotten away and no one new is replacing it [. . .] my reflection has become stronger than me and I have become an image in the mirror.*'[68] Looking in the mirror it is not clear who Ela sees but 'She resembles her cunt. A thought blazes through her mind: Am I my cunt? Am I my own lost cunt?'[69]

Ultimately, after a prolonged pursuit, the novel delivers a joyous reunion: lips meet lips as Ela kisses her cunt; for the narrator this appears to be a moment of reconsolidation too, as she incorporates her cunt and Ela, her alter ego. Story and character; throat and cunt; lips and labia turn in on each other as the moment of reunion or consummation is marked by Ela placing V in her mouth. At that moment, mirrors and glass shatter and the Narrator is left out, blinding herself like Oedipus now that Ela and V are one: '*I possess no [. . .] self to be remembered.*'[70] Ela is consumed by a significantly private, independent sexual climax as the Narrator relinquishes her power. '*Once upon a time the mirror looked in the mirror and desired a fusion*', writes Kamvyselli, '*But, gazing into itself, it saw a blank gap. So then it gazed into the Other, and it shattered. The world has lacked a firm support and a deep root ever since.*'[71] The final section of the book is presented in a pseudo-documentary style, as Ela's autobiographical notes for her version of *f/32*. It's a concluding tone of celebration and unity where the mirror is broken, and the female protagonist can experience an authentic identity: '*My reflection looked at me, not at herself*, and '*The mirror, like a camera, froze my eyes [. . .] Today, I broke the mirror. I didn't know I could.*'[72] Adults must exist in a Lacanian nightmare of a compulsive search for the intangible ideal-I; the *imago* which fascinated us as we stared at ourselves reflected by the mirror or in our mother's eyes. Like naughty children, we are forever kept away from a permanently *authentic* self by the distortions and controls of language and society. What Kamvyselli powerfully imagines in *f/32* is a universe at once utopian and dystopian where the '*real*' is tantalizingly *possible*, but which remains as fleeting and inaccessible as a flash of light refracted by a shard of broken, mirrored glass.

Vagina qui verba facit: The flesh made word

A Theological Position was the American writer Robert Coover's fourth publication, his first successful foray into drama after two novels (*The Origin of the Brunists* (1966), and *The Universal Baseball Association* (1968)) and a collection of short stories, *Pricksongs and Descants* (1969). He recalls the attraction of turning to drama after prose as 'exhilarating' and 'much more fun [than] sitting alone in a gloomy room for hours on end, batting at a keyboard. Writers assume they can do everything, and when the opportunity arose to propose some plays, I couldn't resist, wrote a flurry of them, of which only four ever got finished enough to be produced'.[73] Those four are collected together in his *Theological Position*, first published in 1970.[74] All four plays are weird in theme and action. The first, *The Kid* is a Wild West fantasy, *High Noon*-style pastiche featuring more than 200 'cowpokes' and numerous saloon 'belles' in a peculiar parody of the Resurrection: 'The West will EVER be a place a [*sic.*] grace and glory, / Since the day that they strung up the Kid!'[75] While some of the speech patterns in *The Kid* are naturalistic, in *Love Scene*, the second play in the collection, they are not. In this avant-garde rendering of the Fall, a man and woman are on stage but they say nothing. The only speech is that of the disembodied, rather fractious 'Voice', a peevish stage-manager, omniscient *auteur*-God. Like Blanche Dubois (in *A Streetcar Named Desire*) in reverse, Voice cries out that '*I want REALISM, goddamn it!*' and grows increasingly frustrated, blasphemous and sexually crude as the couple circle and kiss one another, culminating in an offstage linguistic and, one imagines, sexual, ejaculation:

VOICE: No! Can't wait! Tear it off! Faster! I'M TELLING YOU – *TEAR IT OFF!*

The man glances up at the voice, pauses momentarily, then proceeds to tear the woman's blouse.

VOICE: (*continuing*) Go! Rip! Kill! Oh! Come! Faster! Shit! Sorry! Ah!
Please – *Aaahhhh . . . .*

Prolonged silence.[76]

At the play's close, a third actor appears. He mimics shooting the man and woman with the pistol he's holding and '*The actors [. . .] move quietly offstage*', exercising free-will in a deterministic, yet godless universe.[77]

The volume's third play is *Rip Awake*, a lengthy monologue delivered, as its name suggests, by Rip Van Winkle. Its theological position is lampooned in a tedious and, one imagines, unperformable peroration on heaven and hell, with the by-now expected irreligious moments; we learn that his wife's 'last words were: Rip, in the name of Jesus H. Christ, button up your fly!'[78] What it has in common with the other plays in the volume, however, is that even alone (or is it, perhaps, *especially* alone?), human beings need to create narratives of myth, to create icons, to identify a godhead, however inappropriate that figure might be (the feeble Sheriff, the sexually frustrated Voice, the reincarnated Rip, who, without a creator, doubts his identity: 'Maybe *I'm* Peter Vanderdonk, maybe I've been living with my stories so long I've got senile and started believing them').[79] This idea of theological positions as 'stories' which are at once the untenable and yet necessary features of the human intellect is returned to in the volume's concluding play, *A Theological Position*. While the other plays dealt with the godhead, the Resurrection, Eden, identity and iconography, it's the Virgin Birth which is the focus of this one.

Three characters are onstage at the play's start: a Priest ('Our position is fixed'), a Man and an 'obviously pregnant' Woman.[80] From the outset, the Church's intransigence on matters of doctrine is the object of Coover's attack. Because, as the Priest says, 'Our position is theologically indisputable', he demands that the Man penetrate the already-six-months-pregnant Woman so as to prove the impossibility or, rather, to secure the avoidance, of a second virgin birth.[81] Like the other plays in the volume this is, of course, not naturalistic. The Woman is a silent, non-malevolent presence on the stage, an observer, as the two male characters thrash out their religious differences. In the play's strange universe, the men decide that the Priest should penetrate the Woman, who remains utterly silent and compliant as she's positioned on the kitchen table in preparation for his advances. He plays with the Woman's naked breasts and peers up her skirts. As he penetrates her, he chatters nervously and the Man encourages him. The Priest's language grows increasingly esoteric:

> *The* PRIEST's *excitement augments. The* MAN *watches closely the scene of the proximate encounter.*
>
> She. Yes, it might be. She. It is always 'she'. It has always been 'she'. The impossible illimitable unapproachable 'she'. But to dream, to make of that 'she' a 'her', you see, to become at once substantive and verb, and so not only transform 'she' to a knowable 'her' but at the same time transubstantiate the self, yes! Substantive and verb! Matter and spirit! Oh my God, I've got the sweet taste of trinities in my mouth![82]

Like Diderot's sultan, the Priest is positing the female body as the source of truth; the cunt as a gateway to knowledge. The Priest's cuntly encounter is what is really showing the way, the truth and the light: in a perversion of John 14:6, the Priest can come to the father, to the truth, not through Jesus, but through the woman's body.[83] As the Woman tightens her muscles around the Priest's penis he exclaims how mouth-like her vagina is and orality and language become central. Words 'spill' from the Priest: 'Resilient! Elastic! Velutinous! [. . .] Tractable! Sericeous! Edematous! Oooo! [. . .] Buttery! Lubricious! Oleaginous!'[84] Unable to climax, he accuses the Woman of witchcraft and continues to hump away on top of her inanimate body, his excitement growing as he talks about the Church's punishment of witches. As he collapses and, with the Man's help, pulls away, he cries out 'I think she's biting me' and remembers 'a terrible cave I was in as a boy [. . .] They said there was a bear'.[85] Finally, '*A rich husky cascade of laughter issues forth from beneath the* WOMAN's *skirts. Her* CUNT *speaks*.'[86]

It's worth pausing momentarily here in order to consider the staging difficulties of this play. It was first performed in Los Angeles in 1975, and again, by the Odyssey Theatre Ensemble in 1977, starring Linda Toliver and Gary Guidinger. The director Ron Sossi also staged it in New York in July 1979. This performance was on the bill, as the Odyssey's had been, with British dramatist Peter Barnes's theological satire about St Eusebius, *Noonday Demons*. Both plays were presented by Sossi as 'An Evening of Dirty Religious Plays' at the off-Broadway Performing Garage Theatre. The *New York Magazine*'s listing suggests that the run was not a long one, with only a dozen performances taking place: 'This double bill includes *Noonday Demons*, by Peter Barnes and *A Theological Position*, by Robert Coover. Thurs thru Sun at 8, thru 7/15. *Red Riding Shawl*, by John Emigh. Fri, Sat & Sun at 8, thru 6/24.'[87] Despite what I would imagine to be the considerable difficulties in staging such an abstract play, it was revived briefly, in the early 1990s, at the Staatstheater in Kassel, Germany. It does strike me as far more of a radio- than a stage-play, partly on account of its brutality but also because of the autonomized cunt. Like a French *fabliau* made flesh, this is a difficult and at once humorous and profound play. 'Like a child who pats a pile of wet sand into turrets and crenelated ramparts', wrote one critic, 'Robert Coover prods at our most banal distractions and vulgar obsessions, nudging them into surreal and alarming focus.'[88] Coover himself never saw a live production of the play but, in what he recalls as 'that brief engagement with the theater', did see several productions of *The Kid* and *Love Scene* and has, on occasion, performed *Rip Awake* as a reading.[89] He also recalls seeing a filmed production of *A Theological Position* which, appropriately enough, given the play's concerns with the word made flesh, or, here, the flesh becoming the word, made metaphor literal: 'a hand puppet of a talking beaver was used with a projected voice. Amusing, though I don't remember being convinced by the performance itself'.[90] Coover unequivocally believes that the Cunt should have a female voice; the abstraction of not knowing quite *how* that voice is being produced would be lost by the use of the glove puppet, but would certainly take the play into more comedic and therefore, perhaps, more comfortable, territory.

The Cunt's first words literalize another metaphor or, rather, idiom. The Priest wants 'to get to the bottom of this!', and the Cunt responds: 'The bottom of it indeed! Going to kiss the Devil's unguentiferous oleaginous ass, are you, father?'[91] 'I use your language', the Cunt declares, 'having failed with my own'.[92] As if to consolidate the point, the priest exclaims 'My word!' to which the rapid reply comes: 'No, mine! And the word is flux, the bloody simpliciter flux!'[93] This play on the idea of the 'dicto simpliciter', the sweeping generalizations and unquestioning tenets that are the cornerstones of the priest's faith, leads to the

Priest's exclamation: 'Yes: *vagina qui verba facit* [. . .] *Loquax. Vagina lo-.*'[94] As with the other examples of the *vagina loquens* I'm considering in this book, the message of a woman's voice demanding to be heard in the most extraordinary way is somewhat subordinated – not surprisingly, perhaps – to the novelty value of the spectacle. 'Cunt' reveals that the man wanted to put her in a circus while she, on the other hand, wanted to tell her story, 'a history of cunts', to redefine language, since 'only man could hang himself with glossaries, blow his brains out with metaphors!'[95] She (the Cunt) argues that her autonomized speech is the only way in which she (and Coover's inference is very clearly that this is about *all* women) can be listened to and taken seriously, especially in a culture like the priest's where the epitome of good womanhood is the immaculate Virgin. 'We have to stir the senses', she says, 'grab you where it hurts! Any penetration, however slight, is a bloody business!'[96] The allusion here to the *vagina dentata* is striking in its graphic insistence on *penetration*, not just of the intellect or understanding, but of the body, too. The war of words is metaphorically bloody. As we'll see, the film *Teeth* imagines, the *vagina dentata* literally producing blood in its castratory emancipation. The Priest's insidious teachings penetrate women's lives; the Cunt's speech penetrates the Priest's understanding. Shortly, her teeth penetrate his flesh: 'This is the wild bear speaking to you from the terrible cave!' she yells, conjuring up the Priest's childhood fears, and biting him as he attempts to stifle her.[97]

The Priest is so rigidly habituated to his own doctrinal training that he believes demonic possession can be the only plausible explanation for the sudden appearance of an autonomous Cunt. As he talks about the punishment of witchcraft by burning, the Cunt exclaims: 'That's right, anything you don't understand, kill it, that's your road to salvation, your covenant with holy inertia! Kill and codify!'[98] She makes it explicit that it's autonomous female sexuality that the priest and, by extension, the Church – indeed, *all* religious orthodoxies – fear: 'how you shy from something so simple as communication with your own gametes! Hey, I'm calling to your balls, boys!'[99] The Cunt calls it as she sees it: the points she makes about the established church, while being blasphemous and confrontational in the extreme, highlight the Church's hypocrisy and inherent contradictions. The sassy, no-holds-barred talking cunt is another return to the *fabliaux*, and it also resonates with one of the films considered later in this book: Tom DeSimone's soft-core *Chatterbox* (1977).[100] Coover knew the French *fabliaux*, having taught them 'in a class for writers on ancient fictions (an exploration of alternative narrative strategies)'.[101] However, he claims inspiration from what he characterizes as the 'welcome rise in the late 1960s of a more militant feminism, together with the aggressive taboo-breaking of vanguard theater at that time'.[102] This sentiment anticipates the representation of Gloria Steinem in *Chatterbox*: American feminism in the late 1960s was finding its voice, and the *fabliaux* provided the perfect ironic way to express that shock of hearing the hitherto unheard and unheeded. But the object of Coover's attack is clear: 'the hateful Virgin Mary image as perpetrated and perpetuated by dogmatic males'.[103]

The Priest's own dogmatism takes the form of a striking brutality; we see him threaten the heavily pregnant Woman with a bread knife in a crude preamble to an exorcism: 'Think of her as a host! It'll be easier that way! She must be liberated from this demon!'[104] The 'demon' is female autonomy, both sexual (as evinced by the clearly visible pregnancy bump), and intellectual (as insisted on by the articulate Cunt). However, just as the foetus both is and is not a part of the woman herself, so, too, is the Cunt. Both Cunt and foetus have autonomy; both express the Woman without the Woman actually expressing herself: she remains silent throughout. The Cunt continues to threaten the Church by describing things as they really are and highlighting the contradictions that inhere in the idea of the godhead. 'Ah, the unending hope for the diabolical!' says the Cunt, 'I tell you, you show me a *deus et diabolus*, and I'll show you a dirty old man trying to bugger his own brown pink marble fair full snowy rosy red ass!'[105] It's a strikingly graphic image of self-referentiality, of inflexible (despite the image's intimation of physical contortion) boundaries and of unbending narrow-mindedness.

The Cunt demands: 'Do you think you can stay the moving spirit in an alphabet?', as the Priest stabs the Woman in the abdomen.[106] It's a moment of resituating the *Logos* ('Word'), reminiscent of Luce Irigaray's declaration that 'if we speak to each other as men have been doing [. . .] we'll miss each other', and 'Words will pass through our bodies, above our heads. They'll vanish, and we'll be lost'.[107] In this flash of graphic violence, the Woman speaks for the one and only time herself: 'You . . . you have hurt me . . . !'[108] Like Ela in *f/32* it takes an act of such violently misogynist horror for her own voice to be heard, and the Woman collapses. As we'll see in DeSimone's *Chatterbox*, there's a final moment of transference. The penises of the two men begin to speak, the Woman and the Cunt having been silenced. The Priest's Prick speaks to the Man's Prick as the play concludes:

> Man's Prick: Why is it we always become the thing we struggle against?
> Priest's Prick: Because of love . . .
>
>   *Pause.*
>
>   After all, there's something to be said for talking cunts . . .
> Man's Prick: Yes, there's something to be said . . .
>   FADE.

So, what is that cryptic 'something to be said'? Why must the saying of it return at the play's end, to the phallogocentrism, crudely literalized by the talking pricks? Peter Prescott's assessment of *A Theological Position* is somewhat dismissive as he argues that 'it should have been funnier than it is, or more profound, or something' and then, resorting to an almost theological language of his own, suggests that 'Coover takes extraordinary risks and deserves forgiveness for his failures.'[109] Brian Evenson is more attuned to what I think Coover was trying to do. 'The vagina must be shut up', he writes, 'so as to keep the system unchallenged – according to the system, cunts (both literally and as a slang term for women) should not be allowed to have their say; they should sit back and enjoy what they get.'[110] Coover sees the moment of 'something to be said' as indicating, 'idiomatically [. . .] a form of reluctant acceptance.'[111] He continues, still in revealingly religious language: 'The martyred cunt has aroused the pricks, not to sympathy, but to a kind of nascent understanding. Almost literally: Women speaking up boldly is a good thing.'[112] Yet it's not a Woman speaking up boldly; it's a fractured Woman, an autonomized Cunt. And so Coover's play leaves us in something of a conundrum: is martyrdom really a viable mode of seeking sexual equality and authentic selfhood? The martyred body is the dead body. It can pave the way but its *own* agency is as abruptly ended as the Woman's was. What kind of liberation is this?

Simmering chickenshacks and pussyfloss: Imagining *Loveland*

For the traveller who fears they've seen it all, there's a sex theme park called Loveland on South Korea's Jeju Island. I suppose it's more a sculpture park than a theme park, really: over 100 disembodied and sometimes grotesquely distorted sculptures, mostly copulating heterosexual couples, occupy the site. One particularly striking sculpture shows a woman kneeling at the end of a short wooden pier, dangling what looks like a red chilli into the red, fleshy, vulvar core of a giant oyster-shell floating on the lake's surface. There is – mercifully, maybe – at Loveland little of the immersive, hands- (and other organs-) on experiences imagined by the two writers I'm going to focus on now. Nicholson Baker's none-too-subtly titled *House of Holes* is a lurid, episodic novel which is strikingly reminiscent and, in places, almost derivative, of Maureen Freely's much earlier *Under the Vulcania*.[113] However, while Freely uses the motif of a theme-park modelled on sexual fantasies to explore the humanity of Fiona, the central protagonist, in Baker's hands the result is altogether less humane, and certainly less subtle. His concern is with a crude surrealized mechanism of disembodied organs; in Freely's fictional world such disembodiedness is firmly rooted in Fiona's reality.

Under the Vulcania (its title is a nod to Malcolm Lowry's 1947 novel, *Under the Volcano*) is a novella which follows the visits of several women, including Fiona, to the 'Vulcania', a health-spa with a difference. Here, women can act out every conceivable (if that's not too infelicitous a word in this context) sexual fantasy. Fiona, we learn, has been an architect, and the Vulcania itself is a feat of architectural creativity, being a complex with multiple rooms and areas where different sensations can be experienced and desires realized. The 'Specularium', for example, 'called to mind a planetarium, except that the image beamed on the ceiling was the interior of a vagina'.[114] One suspects that Freely is interested in the psychological dynamics of relationships between men and women as much as she is in sexual ones. Fiona is a credible, flawed character. Grazing her leg in the Gardens of Babylon 'had propelled her into racking sobs. She had felt as if she were mourning a death – but whose?'[115] Freely inverts norms of sexual harassment, for example, as female clients roughly fondle the bodies of male prostitutes: 'It was one of those scenarios that made you very, very glad you were not born a man.'[116] In such moments of inversion, the novel functions as a powerful satire of sexual politics – Baker's narrative, too, has such grotesque, Swiftian moments of shock.

The delights on offer in the Vulcania include 'the Appearance and Reality Centre'; 'the Chastity Beltway'; 'the Virtual Reality Challenge' ('basically, there are two black boxes. One offers sex with a real man, and the other offers sex by simulation [. . .] just like the Pepsi Challenge'); 'the Ice-Cream Parlour' ('which catered to women who liked vanilla sex'); 'the Rough Trader Saloon'; 'the Halfway House'; 'the Unofficial Insemination Centre'; and the rather more prosaic 'TV Room'.[117] Some of the Vulcania's 'beaux' (they are mostly students working there in order to pay off their debts) listen to confessions as the female clientele uninhibitedly share their fantasies which are mostly focused on castration 'by truncheon, by scissors, by teeth, by hanging, and through the agency of a baby giraffe'.[118] Such graphic moments complicate Freely's agenda. Vulcania is a place for the expression of women's untrammelled identities, but in moments such as this, the novel functions less as a riposte to misogyny, than as a mere recycling of its own tired ideas that women's 'true' sexual desires are dangerous at worst, and suspect at best. While Raul oversees the day-to-day running of the Vulcania, it's a lawyer called Miranda Simpson who represents the conglomerate which owns the enterprise. Raul 'found her above ground in the – the name still made him wince – the Institute for Continuing Research on Our Bodies, Our Genitals'.[119] She arrives at the Vulcania to rule on a paternity suit and Raul senses her unease at the business's activities: 'if Miranda thought all women were good and nice, how was she going to explain why some women only seemed to feel good and nice when they were treating themselves or someone else as objects? He could sense her disapproval as they made their way down this corridor of perversities'.[120]

Fiona is one such client of the Vulcania who experiences the disjunction Raul senses between female sexual desire and autonomy. It transpires that Fiona and Raul have a history. He had, many years previously, denounced and rejected her for harbouring sexual fantasies – quasi-rape fantasies – which now, ironically, she is paying him to organize. Raul 'had called her a professional victim

[. . .] he hoped it actually happened to her one day, so that she found out what it meant to be degraded, so that she found out what an unreconstructed imagination could do to its deserving owner.'[121] Her recollection of Raul's cruelty taints her *choice* of sexual experience in the Vulcania – sex with eight young men, and her pleas for them to stop are interpreted as part of the experience: 'With the fourth she gave up struggling [. . .] She was here, stuck in a fantasy come true. What was happening was sordid, was giving pleasure to everyone in the hall but herself.'[122] In this moment of the ultimate 'be careful what you wish for', sex is a paradoxically unifying experience for Fiona. She 'tried to devise some escape for her mind. But for once, she couldn't', and she becomes painfully aware of her body as her self (it's significant that Freely hints in the early parts of *Vulcania* at Fiona having recently recovered from some chronic, but never quite defined, illness).[123] Through heterosexual vaginal penetration Fiona feels whole: 'When he entered her, she felt complete again. When she felt his penis pumping inside her, she felt once again alive.'[124] This idea of duality has been established by Freely early in the novel in a passage where Fiona, in a Cartesian ('cogito, ergo sum') moment, recalls 'the best game of all [. . .] to elaborate on the idea that she was the only living person on earth and that all other humans were apparitions placed there to amuse her and keep her from feeling lonely'.[125] On arrival at the Vulcania 'she just wanted to BE here, and not think about it' but she ends up accidentally, as one does, saying to the barman instead: 'I want to suck your cock.'[126] The forthrightness of Fiona's language here might be read in two radically different ways. Is it an empowerment, an opportunity to dispense with 'feminine' niceties and get right, as it were, to the root of the matter? Or does this language signal the degradation of another human body, a desire to fragment *him*, to reduce *him* to his genitals alone? Away from the frenzied debauchery of much of the Vulcania, there is a space reserved solely for women:

> The Chastity Beltway was a flight of stairs away from the Roman Baths. It consisted of twelve suites, arranged in a semicircle, around a marble pool. This pool area was the only part of the Vulcanian labyrinth where women were not allowed to entertain beaux; it was therefore the place where clients who were still breastfeeding received visits from their babies. As Fiona

walked in, two of these mothers were entering the pool for a dip with their six month olds.[127]

In this description, Freely plays with taboo notions of femininity and sexuality. The architecturally classical backdrop powerfully recalls the myth of the Minotaur: here, it's Ariadne who has the agency at the heart of the maze, not a Theseus figure. Further, the labyrinth is not a place of entrapment but of liberation: of life, not death. What's more, these women effortlessly combine sexual activity and maternity, resisting being forced into one role or the other – in the apparently utopian space of the Vulcania, women really can 'have it all'.

In *Vulcania*, the 'soccer mom' clientele arrive in a variety of banal vehicles which, in most instances, they have just used for the school run. In Baker's *House of Holes*, by contrast, the varied clientele travel through circular objects (a finger and thumb touching tips; the seventh hole on a golf course; a drinking straw; the spindle shaft of a peppermill) in order to arrive at the eponymous theme park, presided over by the Director, Lila ('large and pretty in bifocals'), where they can uninhibitedly embark on whatever pornographic encounters they desire.[128] From the outset of *House of Holes*, when, as the chapter title helpfully recounts, 'Shandee finds Dave's Arm', and Dave's Arm has a life of its own, it's clear that this is a magical-realist universe of outlandish and autonomized organs, most of them, of course, sexual. Luna, a volunteer in a soup kitchen, has her feet masturbated over by Alexander Borodin and Nikolai Rimsky-Korsakov as she sits in a 'pussy cradle'. In this episode, relatively early on in the novel, Baker's absurd neologisms are apparent. Luna, we're told, 'ground her pussytwat against the crotchy holder' and 'Chuck's thundertube of dickmeat [. . .] pushed her frilly doilies of labial flesh aside' (Baker's 'quaint' imagery is jarringly inappropriate in its domestic sentimentality, and I couldn't help – most unfortunately – but be reminded of Judy Chicago's Emily Dickinson plate at *The Dinner Party*, which we'll see soon).[129] Baker revels in putting the jism into 'neologism'.

The House is a wonderful mixture of the everyday and the extreme. As readers, we, too, get pulled into the core of its narrative, rapidly accepting the weirdness of its scenarios. The chapter 'Shandee Wears the Sponge Gloves', for example, begins with the sentence 'Shandee left Dave's arm to sleep late in the hotel room'.[130] By this point in the novel there is not much to surprise us about this sentence. We know that we're in a world where a man, desperate for a larger penis, will, voluntarily and temporarily (for this is a high-tech, scientifically futuristic universe of porn) literalize a metaphor and give his right arm for an enlargement procedure.[131] Further, Shandee 'met Zilka for melon and a croissant at the terrace restaurant overlooking the Garden of the Wholesome Delightful Fuckers', reminiscent of *Vulcania*'s own 'Gardens of Babylon'.[132] So disorientating is the novel as a (w)hole that I found myself wondering whether 'melon and a croissant' was an odd or unreal, or even sexually suggestive, combination, while scarcely giving pause to the Boschian 'Garden of Earthly Delights' landscape spread before the two breakfasting women. Similarly, Baker's meticulous attention to minor details has a strange, disconcerting quality which is often strikingly beautiful. Rhumpa looks into a partially dismantled pepper grinder and 'thought, The peppercorns are waiting to be ground up. They're still round, like little dry planets, but not for long'.[133] This unmitigated focus on the everyday produces an almost meditative state which facilitates Rhumpa's journey, like that of a pornographic Alice in Wonderland, to the House of Holes: 'the pepper grinder got bigger and she jumped down into it and fell through tumbling peppercorns, and she smelled a hundred dinner parties of the past'.[134] A similar moment of transcendence is later reached by a male character, Dave, who 'had a big plaid blanket in his canvas bag and a thermos of barley soup, and he unfurled the blanket over some matted grass and lay down and looked up at the clouds till he found one with soft breasts and a leg held alluringly half open'.[135] At one point a character enters the House via his own penis: 'Wade stared at his cockhole and zoomed down into it. It was kind of an odd, juicy, self-referential experience.'[136]

Sometimes it is the vulva itself which is the portal, and the women of the House have a greater connectedness to the way of the (sexual) world than the male visitors. "I'm a portal, silly," said Loxie [. . .] "I'll show you my pussy. That's the hole you're looking for".[137] That said, the House is patrolled by the 'sick bitch', the 'Pearloiner' (a cleverer and more amusing neologism than any of the others in the book) whose habit it is to steal clitorises: 'Zilka got her clit stolen clean away'.[138] Zilka's description of her encounter with the Pearloiner is powerfully reminiscent of Ela's attack in Kamvyselli's *f/32*. At Terminal O at St Louis airport, Zilka is 'fwooshed into a different mind zone' at security where she encounters the Pearloiner:

> She was about forty-five, superpatriotic, big hair, big high heels, big patriotic tits, fake. And she goes, 'I'm sorry, but we've determined that your clitoris is not a carry-on item.' She's like, 'It's swollen and oversized, and it's over the weight limit, and it's a security threat, and I'm going to have to remove it now.' Then she clapped her hand to my crotch, and I felt this sharp painful tugging, and I saw my clit go into a tiny clear baggie, with a numbered label on it, and then a gloved man took the top off a large jar.[139]

The elements are strikingly familiar – the matter-of-fact excision, the jar – but whereas Kamvyselli had a wider agenda in *f/32*, examining the fractured psyche of a woman, quite what is Baker's aim is less clear. If it's a satire on the 'enemy within' mentality of increased airport security post-9/11 then it needed to be sustained to have impact. As it is, the episode is reduced to just one among many in the novel. Whereas both Ela and her vagina were, however bizarre it may seem, plausible 'characters', here the reader has little sympathy for Zilka, a cartoon character in a novel populated by caricatures. The narrator's assumptions about women's sexuality are at times also cartoonish at best, and problematic at worst: 'what woman can avoid feeling a thrill as she unbuttons her shirt in front of an attentive stranger?'[140]

The pleasure dome in Freely's *Vulcania* does have utopian echoes of a Xanadu, but it also houses failures and disappointments, tainting the possibility of uninhibited sexual activity. 'After lunch', Freely writes, 'Jacqui managed to talk Fiona into going along with her to the Palace of Foreplay. It had looked appealing in the brochure, but the reality was smaller in scale [. . .] The Hall of Mirrors was another misnomer'.[141] Jacqui 'could, if she really stretched her imagination to its outer limits, just see that it might be exciting'.[142] This invocation of the imagination – of cerebral processes being so difficult in order to experience bodily pleasure – is a subtlety Baker never manages to achieve. His is a world of puerile punning, lacking in a wider message. In the House of Holes, then, ugly and bizarre neologisms negate the possibility of a psychologically intact or credible woman emerging. Instead, Baker's women are broken down into constituent parts. They have neologistic 'slippy sloppy fuckfountains', a 'simmering chickenshack', 'pussyfloss', a 'famished slutslot', a 'cuntgash' or a 'succulent stovetop'.[143] Women can ride 'the Pussyboard', on which they glide 'along a cable, in a spread-pussy harness', and 'land in a lake of white rejuvenating oil. [They . . .] ski along gently on [their . . .] pussylips over the lake'.[144] When the character Henriette rides the Pussyboard, she experiences sexual intercourse in the heteronormative, retro-pornographic, tired way that is Baker's metier: 'She knelt, breathing in the rich air, feeling better than she had in months, listening to the rustle of stroking men around her. "Come all over me, guys," she said. One man jizzed on her cheek, another on her shirt, two on her lips, one on her nose, one on her shoulder, and another – a cute guy with blond spiky hair – came politely into her cupped hand'.[145] Where other writers (Freely, Kamvyselli, even Diderot, perhaps) use the magical realist settings of their work to *reimagine* possibilities for women's sexual identities, Baker invariably closes down such liberating opportunities in his prose. Henriette's experience is not about understanding herself better, but is to become 'a jizm-covered princess' as though 'jizm' is all women need to enjoy sexual fulfilment.[146]

Baker is as imaginative when it comes to inventing words for male genitals as he is for women's – one character, Dave, for example, has a 'Malcolm Gladwell', presumably in tribute to its orgasmic 'tipping point'; and Nedbody (headless Ned) has a 'pistil head of his manjig'.[147] Friggley the pornmonster inhabits a subterranean lake in the House which is full of all of the bad porn that has been sucked up and disgorged after successful 'pornsucker missions'.[148] The monster is 'a personification of poymorphousness unlike anything the world of human suck-fuckery has ever known', and reaches a hand out of the lake: 'Five penises hung dangling off the forearm – it looked like a bizarre bagpipe. The hand was made up of half a dozen clustered vaginas'.[149] The monster emerges fully at Rhumpa's urging:

> Almost before she'd finished there was a sudden volcanic swirling of the waters. An amalgamation of body parts heaved itself up on the widest part of the ledge and stood dripping. There must have been a hundred penises – some pale pink, some coffee colored – along with breasts and eyes and clits and an enormous mouth at the center. It stood on a mass of arms and legs.[150]

In chapters with names like 'The Story of Prince Bohuslav's Beard' and 'Wade Presses the Sex Now Button and Koizumi Visits', Baker is implicitly acknowledging his novel's debt to earlier literary traditions. Like Diderot's Congolese Sultan, for example, Bohuslav is a powerful ruler who grows tired with courtly life in peacetime, and frustrated with his wife, whose 'perfect beauty and [. . .] perfect goodness made him restless', and who bites Bohuslav's beard at the point of orgasm.[151] Bohuslav supplements his sexual activity by weekly rendezvous with 'Uniques', imperfect, 'ordinary' women, each of whom bites his beard. This quickly enters folklore: 'It was said by some in the court that if you held your ear to his beard, you could hear the pleasure cries of a thousand women.'[152] One night, a Unique snips off Bohuslav's beard, runs away with it and distils it to create a powerful aphrodisiac called 'Gouttelettes de Bonheur, or Droplets of Happiness'; Bohuslav thereafter maintains a monogamous relationship with his wife and 'Seventeen of his penis satchels are on view in the museum of the House of Holes'.[153] In another chapter, we meet Koizumi, a Canadian–Japanese sculptor whose narrative account is reminiscent of Native-American folktales. As a young girl, Koizumi and a friend ate pinecone seeds and expelled 'boy-cones' into the creek, which grew into sleeping, fairytale boys who slowly grew, 'gathered strength, and [. . .] had the most beautiful penises and thatch patches'; subsequently Koizumi produces 'dark polished wood' sculptures of women, one of which she presents to Wade.[154] Elsewhere, in the chapter 'Dennis Explores Mindy's Purse', there is a special chewing gum which, when chewed, gives 'a woman in Estonia [. . .] a singing orgasm'.[155]

In the vertiginous world of the sexual possibilities that the House provides there are often instances of a separation of organ and body. In the 'Hall of the Penises', Polly draws back a green curtain to reveal 'many little toadlike things hanging out from holes in the wall about crotch height'.[156] It transpires that these are male genitalia poking through 'gloryholes' for women. Polly and her two female companions begin to sing and dance and 'soon they began to notice some changes in some of the wall toads. There was a new alertness about their attitude, no question about it. Several of them had started to do a little elongational leaning-forward sort of movement'.[157] Revealingly, the reduction of individuals to their genitalia, is 'kind of interesting and exciting, but also a little sad, because those penises had no clue what Polly, Donna, and Saucie were all about as women – what they believed in, what their plans were'.[158] Elsewhere a female character fellating a headless man called Ned, 'concentrated on his true self, which was his dick'.[159] Like the autonomized cunts which are at the heart of this book, so Baker here reduces the Self to Organ. The reductionism reconfigures Ned's Self, a pattern which will recur (has, indeed, already been in evidence) as *The Vagina* continues. In another episode, Dune and Marcie swap genitals, and Mindy (even the characters' names are like those in tacky porn narratives), documentary film-maker and Ani DiFranco fan, interviews Dune's new genitals: 'Dune pulled his pudendum open. "Mindy, let me ask you: Do you want to interview this pussy?"'[160] The organ is not, however, autonomized, but the scenario is merely an opportunity for Baker to describe yet another penetrative sex scene – 'Mindy eased the condom-covered microphone into Dune's pussyhole'.[161]

House of Holes concludes with an incongruously tender reimagining of the creation myth. The last chapter, 'The Silver Egg Hatches' tells the fictional story of two medieval- or Greek-sounding characters, Gallanos and Mellinnas, Lilliputians in the Swiftian House of Holes, who hatched together from a silver egg laid earlier in the novel by a woman called Jackie. 'Loud sounds blossomed from enormous fleshy flushed faces' of the spectators who watch the little silver people copulate and fall asleep on a 'folded washcloth'.[162] Sexual knowledge precedes language – as Gallanos and Mellinnas instinctively copulate, they push 'against the muteness of their throats until finally a series of small cries came out, strange uncertain sounds that increased in volume and pace until, as they reached the final throes of their lovemaking, they became groans of joy'.[163] Like the Bizarro fiction which I'll shortly discuss in more depth, Baker's writing suggests a multitude of possibilities for identity and sexual experience but it ultimately peddles a depressingly familiar phallocentric, heterosexist narrative in the guise of doing something visionary and innovative.

Acker's *Algeria*

The writer Kathy Acker, like the pirate she dreamed in her fiction of becoming, was a looter.[164] She pillaged and mined language for its most resplendent gems with which she adorned her writing as though it were her own body. 'Acker was never a woman writer', claims novelist Jeanette Winterson, 'but she was a writer who was a woman. Her vulnerability as a woman in a man's world set her to use her body as a text [. . .] She would not deny her own body'.[165] Acker's avant-garde fiction is radically postmodern and knowingly metafictional. Her narratives are exquisite palimpsests that deliberately disrupt conventional narrative structures, techniques and expectations.[166] She sometimes wrote pornographic stories and novels, and frequently mixed up the horror and humour of what it means to be human. Her language at times flowed in a dream-like, surreal stream of ungrammatical, oddly spaced sentences and images, as in 1972's *The Burning Bombing of America*: 'the poor live outside the law. our cunts are silver daggers   we shall live in a new world'.[167] Sometimes the poetic, lyrical qualities of her writing were foremost: 'And then   the city arises   rises from your cunt   golden star'.[168] In their postmodernity, Acker's images were sometimes, ironically, reminiscent of early modern courtly love poetry: 'I place diamonds in the hair of your cunt   you who I can desire'.[169]

Acker's ability to capture a sense of place impressionistically is brilliantly conveyed in, for example, the 1978 novel *Kathy Goes to Haiti*. Here, streets are 'congested', with 'rotting pastel-colored wood walls piled on top of each other, legless and armless beggars on wheels, male and female one-basket merchants, rows of food and leather and plastic shoes and notebooks and hair curlers, one or two scared white tourists, starved children looking for the rich white tourists, non-existent sidewalks and cars, lots and lots of cars'.[170] In Acker's writing, boundaries – between realism and surrealism, between the sensual and the intellectual, between self and other, and even between self and self – melt away and essential truths are transitorily glimpsed in the interstices.[171] In one of Acker's last works, 1996's *Pussy, King of the Pirates*, Pussy feels that her identity is fragmented as she waits for an abortion: 'she was simultaneously and continuously hungry and nauseous, because she wanted the child to remain alive'.[172] Pussy is caught in the fissure between female sexual desire and cultural propriety: 'She didn't know whether or not to tell the stranger that she and he could now have a baby; she decided not to bother him, because by not disturbing him she was being polite'.[173] Later, trying on clothes in an antiques shop, Pussy stares at her reflection in an old mirror, 'a mirror that was also outside' and 'realized [she . . .] was beautiful'.[174] The clinic believes that the abortion might not have been successfully carried out: 'Pussy asked when they might know positively what she was. She, or her body, was confused'.[175] The pivotal 'or' in this sentence is key to understanding Acker's ideas about embodiment. The female body is one which can do autonomous, surprising things – get pregnant, miscarry, fail to abort a foetus – and Pussy has to relinquish control in the face of the inescapable corporeality of this fact. But it is not only her own body which is holding her hostage: 'Pussy' becomes 'the female', the objectified focus of medical scrutiny, as various healthcare professionals debate whether she is, indeed, pregnant or not. Fury at that kind of systematic objectification pervades Acker's work. In her earlier *Don Quixote* (1986), abortion – the elimi- nation of the piece of self-that-is-not-self – is a similarly prominent theme. It is the castratory figure of Medusa who screams: '"What the hell do you know!" [. . .] Her snakes writhe around nails varnished by the Blood of Jesus Christ. "I'm your desire's object, dog, because I can't be the subject. Because I can't be a sub- ject: What you name 'love', I name 'nothingness'. I won't not be: I'll perceive and I'll speak"'.[176] Acker's 'I', like Kamvyselli's, is engaged in an incessant struggle to disrupt the idea that literature (or even *thought*) originates in an uncomplicat- edly unified consciousness. Eventually, Pussy is given a second abortion. 'The doctor who did the suction', Acker writes, 'replied that this time something had come out, but he didn't know what it was'.[177] The narration switches to the first person, from whom potentially contaminative blood pours: 'I couldn't change my pad', says the narrator, 'because there were men everywhere. But if I didn't throw away the old blood, something dreadful, like rot or disease, was going to touch my body [. . .] I no longer cared whether they saw me. And changed the pad in the hallway. Childhood was officially over'.[178] Later, the narrator wryly muses that 'I didn't know how to be a woman. I couldn't make a curtain. A curtain or shroud for the body of my mother'.[179]

In Acker's *Blood and Guts in High School*, one of the protagonist Janey's primitive drawings is labelled 'My cunt red urgh', and she calls herself, during her sexual relationship with her own father, 'tough, rotted, putrid beef'.[180] The female body is a site of corruption, fragmentation and alienation in Acker's works, and for her first-person narrators the process of maturation is a proc- ess of sexual development and awareness in which that body and its urgent, embodied desires can seem unfamiliar, autonomous, even *dis*embodied. In her 1973 novella, *The Childlike Life of the Black Tarantula* Acker's narrator describes how 'I see his eyes fall down on me his finger point the muscles below and beneath my belly begin to quiver I watch myself falling into my cunt,' and, later: 'I see my cunt ahead of me the pear lips pulsing and the thin inner folds. But I can never be certain.'[181] This disorientating lack of certainty pervades Acker's work and has at its core the 'cunt' which is at once familiar and unknown. 'I have no identity', says the narrator of *The Childlike Life*, 'I can feel the hand softly running up down my leg inside the leg against the sand softly spreading my legs,' and, later: 'My body doesn't exist [. . .] I'm not sure if I think of myself as a person.'[182]

Acker's attempts to demystify female desire aren't always celebratory, however. The narrator of the short story 'New York City in 1979', describes the body of an 'old actress', and it's a description which (notwithstanding Roland Barthes's 'death of the author'), had it been written by a male author, could certainly be read as misogynist. 'Her legs are grotesque: FLABBY', declares the narrator, 'Above, hidden within the folds of skin, there's an ugly cunt. Two long flaps of white thin speckled [*sic.*] by black hairs like a pig's cock flesh hang down to the knees. There's no feeling in them. Between these two flaps of skin the meat is red folds and drips a white slime that poisons whatever it touches. Just one drop burns a hole into anything. An odour of garbage infested by maggots floats out of this cunt. One wants to vomit.'[183] It's a striking description which appears to refute Jeanette Winterson's assertion that 'there is no disgust in [. . . Acker's] work.'[184] But who is the 'one' who 'wants to vomit'? The 'one' is not only the observer, but also the inhabitant, of the abject body, here figured as the *old* female body; the body for which culture no longer has need, nor desire; the persistently diseased, hopelessly corporeal body which Acker, in the last stages of the breast cancer which killed her at the age of 50, would come all too vividly to understand. The dominant emotion in the description, then, is not 'disgust' at, but *fear* of, the inexorable deterioration of the ageing body.

In 1984, Acker published the 29-page pamphlet *Algeria: A Series of Invocations Because Nothing Else Works*.[185] The first page is black and, prominently positioned in its centre is the single word in white: 'CUNT'. 'The land in Algeria', it's stated in smaller writing, 'is pink/Life in this/America stinks [. . .] In 1979, right before the Algerian revolution begins, the city is cold and dark . . .'.[186] Divided into seven sections, *Algeria* dips into different genres. It's first-person narrative; it's semi-autobiographical (as, arguably, is much of Acker's work); it's dramatic in places (reminiscent of Coover's early, short plays).[187] Part 1 is called 'The Stud Enemy' and it opens with a first-person account of heterosexual intercourse. The narrator has left a male lover called Kader in Toronto and has gone to New York; the separation is scarring: 'In New York I feel I'm jagged part skin walking down the street. I feel part of my being no longer is. That is disgusting. That is an outrage'.[188] The discourse shifts from the personal to the political; the story of the narrator and Kader is overtaken by an account of the outbreak of the ill-fated Algerian 'revolution' of 1945. Acker's dissolution of the boundary between the personal and the political was perhaps most clearly articulated in her 'A Few Notes' (1989), where she wrote that 'Any appearance of the individual heart is a political occurrence'.[189] Even this historical account in *Algeria* is eroticized, in customary Acker sadomaso-chistic style, as a male French police officer first lusts after, and then shoots, a young, male Algerian protestor. The narrator's yearning to have Kader visit her is interwoven with the historical narrative, and is also aggressively sexual and effects an extreme disaggregation of self and body, as she writes: 'My body desperately wants a cock inside *her*.'[190]

Personal alienation, the message seems to be in this initial section of *Algeria*, is the cost of political oppression. 'The degree of alienation of the people who gave me this world seems frightening to me', writes Acker, 'Alien to aliena-tionation [*sic*.], we now have to live depersonalized or . . .'.[191] Part 2 of *Algeria* is called simply 'Cunt' and provocatively declares that Muslim veiling 'makes the woman anonymous. There is no such thing as a woman. Henceforth a woman is A CUNT'.[192] This is depersonalization at its most raw, and it's a situation which, in Acker's world, is created by the cultural practice of veiling. Acker's substitu-tion of the words 'THE CUNT' for any reference to specific women ('This is the way THE CUNT my mother committed suicide') is shocking, but of course that's Acker's point: in a simple linguistic manoeuvre she's reduced women to an essentialist facelessness.[193] Paradoxically, the problematic and potent cultural foundations of that anonymity are given character precisely *because* of Acker's candid reduction of 'woman' to 'CUNT'. Another peculiar effect of this technique of substitution is that THE CUNT necessarily takes on an autonomous life. Thus 'THE CUNT ate at the most expensive restaurants in New York [. . .] The closer THE CUNT came to no money, the more frenzily [*sic*.] it spent [. . .] THE CUNT was left with no money and no source of money. Its apartment in which it had lived for thirty years was about to be taken away from it because it hadn't paid rent in three months.'[194] This pronoun – 'it' – renders the idea of a straightforward linguistic substitution more problematical than it at first appeared. That THE CUNT is an 'it' and not a 'she' grants it even more autonomy. The potentially painful account of the narrator's (and, possibly, Acker's) mother's suicide is thus delivered in a surreal, almost absurdist, way. Dressed in a blue suit, THE CUNT checks itself into the New York Hilton and overdoses on Librium. Thus the narrator distances the event from herself/itself (this division is further emphasized by the reference in this section of *Algeria* to the narrator's adoption papers). Suicide is presented as the ultimate expression of rebellion, autonomy and protest: 'Suicide and self-destruction is the first way the shitted-on start showing anger against the shitters.'[195]

'The Next Crazy CUNT' is the title of the third section of the pamphlet. Here, 'THE CUNT' is the narrator's wealthy grandmother for whom the narrator maintains a pretence of being married: 'Since it knows Ali and I are married, I have to keep pretending I'm married to Ali.'[196] The dizzying switching between locales and perspectives continues into part 4: 'Omar Meets a Rebel' which takes the reader to 'the Battle of Algiers' in the Arab quarter. It's a filmic piece where the narrator, Omar (here, in typical Acker anarchic fashion, sometimes a woman's name, sometimes a man's), offers a running commentary based mainly in a café, interspersed with violent, incongruent images of THE CUNT exhuming its mother in order to rip the gold jewellery and fillings from her corpse. The café owner, Medjebri, is a police informant and Omar and THE CUNT threaten to shoot a police officer who has just drunk tea there. The hold-up goes wrong, however, as the gun isn't loaded, and Omar and THE CUNT flee. 'If we don't get out of here now', says THE CUNT, 'they'll catch us.'[197] This dialogic style is present in the fifth section of the pamphlet, too: 'Madness Begins'. The scene shifts rapidly from Omar's apartment to a restaurant in Manhattan where, in typically fantastic fashion, Mick Jagger signs

THE CUNT's breast. Acker transforms all of the women around Jagger into 'CUNTs' and then we're back in Algeria where women are also 'CUNTs'. In this scene the fragmentation is played out vividly as police officers detonate a bomb, and viscera and limbs are pulled from the resultant rubble. The atmosphere of the text is febrile: scenes from the European quarter, the residential area where the French police officers live, are juxtaposed with descriptions of Omar watching a performance called 'Black Orpheus'. Omar has become Orpheus, the mythical Greek hero, seeking advice from a shaman in a Native American headdress as to where he might find Eurydice (his wife) who turns out to be a *'short fat CUNT'* who tries, but fails, to follow Omar out of the auditorium.[198] The disorienting effects of the narrative are expounded by the bizarre entry into the text – for one line only – of anthropologist Claude Lévi-Strauss: 'Meaning depends on rules', he says, gnomically, 'Is rules. That's the nature of language'.[199] But life doesn't follow 'rules'; Acker's overwhelmingly postmodernist text doesn't follow 'rules'; fiction can traverse geographical and political boundaries and so language breaks the rules, too. Even to try to speak of the cunt is to distort reality.[200]

The untitled 6th section is set in a porn cinema on 42nd Street. Omar is described as *'a young boy-CUNT'* in the opening stage directions but almost immediately wiggles *'her hips slightly'* while saying: 'I'll be who I am. I AM Omar'.[201] The entire section is given over to a script for a live sex show in which a man called Hacene plays a psychiatrist encouraging Omar (who is playing the role of a Miss Fendermast) to undress. CUNT is briefly a third character, excitedly encouraging Omar's stage ambitions. Hacene blurs the characters of Omar and CUNT as he says: 'Miss Fendermast, it's a common CUNT delusion that men are obsessed with CUNTS. It stems from the CUNT's knowledge that it is genitally inferior'.[202] As the scene draws to a close, Omar has turned into a dog because, in this opulent imaginative realm, such metamorphoses are possible. In the final, short section of *Algeria*, the first-person narrative is returned to. '"I" move so fast, I can no longer feel. Is feeling therefore just self-reflection?' muses the narrator before the story finally switches to third-person narration. CUNT plants a bomb in a bar. 'We are forced together even though we hate each other', *Algeria* concludes, 'because we are so lonely frightened unsure defensive because we have to survive'.[203] In the end, rendered passive and abject in the face not only of the fear and isolation of the human condition, but also of an apparently indefatigable patriarchy, the Cunt tries to escape the insufficiencies of *language* by reducing certainty to rubble through an *act* of terrorism. A recognizably individuated character such as Omar or Hacene could not have carried out this action in Acker's narrative with the same, universal effect which renounces the specificities of time, gender, nationality and identity. The autonomized cunt, unsure even of its status as an 'I', uses a bomb to tear a hole in the fabric of this unreliable universe which is uniquely Acker's in its strangeness, anxiety and, paradoxically, emancipatory potential.

Bizarro jaunts

The arrestingly titled novellas *Razor Wire Pubic Hair* and *The Haunted Vagina* by Carlton Mellick III, are published by Rose O'Keefe's Eraserhead Press. This small independent imprint, along with Raw Dog Screaming Press, Afterbirth Books and Swallowdown Press, is part of a collective known as Bizarro books. But Bizarro fiction is more than a publishing concern; it's a genre with its own anarchic rules (if that's not an oxymoron) and shared and very distinctive thematic and stylistic characteristics. It appears that Bizarro's primary function is to give expression to the more obscure, tasteless, fantasies of the male psyche (most of its authors are men).[204] A glance at the titles of Mellick's publications gives a clear indication of the sort of writing one might expect to find in *The Haunted Vagina*. If his *Razor Wire Pubic Hair* (2003) does not appeal, then why not try *The Baby Jesus Butt Plug* (2004) or *The Menstruating Mall* (2005)? The titles alone suggest something about the writer's puerile desire to shock for shock's sake. The fact that these books claim to be pushing literary boundaries and find in the image of the vagina the ideal object or image through which to express transgression, is revealing in itself. Mellick attempts to overthrow every convention in his writing. A multi-organed character in *Razor Wire Pubic Hair*, for example, 'stops us in the middle of the road to put tiny versions of Jesus Christ inside of her cunts [. . .] stuffing them head first down the cunts, and she keeps grabbing until every vagina has one under its lips'.[205] This deliberate attempt to shock falls flat. Mellick does not have the artistic vision to sustain it, or to make it credible or even disturbing. In short, Mellick is no Acker. *Razor Wire Pubic Hair* is a book which advertises itself on its cover as 'an anti-novel of the future'.[206] What it is, in fact, is a crudely visceral exploration of female sexuality or, more accurately, of what one man imagines that sexuality to be. As with Mellick's *Haunted Vagina*, *Razor Wire* features images of explicit sexual activities, a surreal and nightmarish landscape and a pervasive sense of menace. This threat comes in *Razor Wire* from a group called 'the rapists' (their *modus operandi* is clumsily suggested by their name) and from the skeletal 'Zephrans' in *The Haunted Vagina*. What both books also have in common, however, is a feeling of maternal instinct perverted, and a strong sense of an Oedipal return to the womb. This return is explicitly played out by Mellick whose narrators journey through what's relentlessly portrayed as the terrifying space of the vagina.

Razor Wire doesn't have page numbers but is divided into three 'Acts', each of which features several 'scenes'. Additionally, strange and disturbing black and white drawings of women punctuate the text. In his 'Author's Note', Mellick describes 'the violent-cunt world of Razor Wire Pubic Hair' and delights in a puerile, self-consciously transgressive and self-congratulatory spiel. Act One is called 'My Life as Multi-Sexed Fuck Merchandise'. The set-up is *Matrix*-like but without the carefully thought-through philosophical conundrums of that film. Mellick's narrator lives in a womb – much as he ends up in in the equally dystopian *Haunted Vagina* – and is polysexual, with multiple sexual organs. This vision is of a matriarchal future where the patriarchy has rendered itself extinct because it 'lived [. . .] for sex. Slave to cunts [. . .] Only women and flesh-creations such as yourself can live in today's society'.[207] Procreative sex in this new world order takes the form of the female penetrating the (mostly-) male with 'Tube tendons like snakes of meat' until the male partner is consumed: 'Tubes emerging from her stomach absorb the nutrients from my body, sucking them into her, to feed her egg.' This succubus is smitten with the narrator and decides to keep him for future procreation. Mellick's style is less a flowing, coherent narrative than a series of awkwardly juxtaposed tableaux. The images of consumption and orality (the *vagina dentata*) occur frequently and fuel the narrator's desires as he fantasizes about his female partner's 'mouth cavern':

> My penis becomes a rising tower, poking into the splintery wood of the table, at the thought of becoming food for the women, to be chewed, soaked in their saliva, rolled between cheek and tongue, lips hugging me, sucked on for flavour, imagining the slide down a female throat to become a bulge in their pale-fleshed bellies.[208]

The woman then feeds the narrator from her vagina which is crammed with food, in a perversion of a baby bird being fed by its mother. In this universe of conflation, blurring and boundary-shifting, mouths and vaginas function almost as one. To penetrate one is not just homologous to penetrating the other but is to penetrate what can actually end up *being* the other. Mellick's attempts to be poetic sometimes result in arbitrary sequences of words, as he writes about how 'a want of pin-emotions cricks into my neck, my vagina curling indoors, digits graze threatened, covering shaded cheek skins'.[209]

Deep.

The eponymous character of *Razor Wire Pubic Hair* is the sister of Celsia, the narrator's keeper. The sister has a body covered in what at first appear to be tattoos of vaginas but which turn out to be actual vaginas. The fantasy is not only for a woman to be a sexually aggressive partner but also, it would seem, for her insatiability to lead her to *become* her own sexuality. The sister's body is covered, the narrator tells us, in vaginas 'not just in her crotch [. . .] some on her shoulders, her neck, a small one behind an ear, and one on her forehead so that she can get her brains fucked out'.[210] The sustained metaphor of the transposed vagina, which is not where it 'ought' to be, pervades the novella. Even an act as apparently straightforward as moving along a corridor becomes imbued with vaginal meanings which, in this vertiginous world of surreality and homology, are themselves transformed into an oral image: 'we begin to slide, force-slipping through the greasy passage like food swallowed down a long throat'.[211] Indeed, the dominant image in Mellick's writing is that of the oral mixed in with the genital. At a gathering of the women in *Razor Wire Pubic Hair*, the narrator comes face-to-face with the monstrous Hoota beast, 'a giant vagina with legs, spiky hair on its top and around the sides' which swallows him 'like a mouth with extra thick saliva'.[212]

Act Two of *Razor Wire* is called 'Something Living Inside of Cunts' and again features the idea of a return to the womb. Celsia pulls the narrator (who is apparently unscathed following his close encounter with the Hoota beast in Act One) into a tree trunk where there are 'warm meat and fluids, heating me like a womb'.[213] Indeed, the willing infantilism of the narrator is made clear by his description of himself childishly sitting down 'in some sticky fluids, draw[ing] a picture on the ground. Waiting for someone to take care of me'.[214] The metamorphosis of objects into vaginas occurs again later in the novella when 'a giant cunt' appears in a wall and draws the narrator into 'its plastic-flesh mouth', eventually getting 'irritated' and spitting him out again.[215] In terms of transmogrification and the process of making literal the mouth/vulva analogue, this episode is significant because the 'giant vagina' begins to speak, having first curled 'its lips into the shape of a mouth'.[216] The conversation touches briefly on the nature of the soul which the talking vagina deems 'not all too significant a feature to possess'.[217] '*What is a significant feature?*' asks the narrator. '"A cunt," replies the giant cunt'.[218] By this point in the story, several eyeballs have rolled into the speaking vagina so that it can see itself while it's speaking (the reader's eyeballs also roll frequently while reading Mellick's work).

The third (and, mercifully, final) act of the novella is called 'Quality Time with Rapists and Zombies'. Like the vaginas, the 'Rapists' in Mellick's work are castrators but they meet their match in Celsia's sister whose 'cunt [was] now a frog mouth' consuming them. The will-to-know is vividly played out as the narrator gazes on the sister: 'I see into the cunt on her forehead, see into her mind'. She 'licks her facial lips with a black snake tongue, licking her vaginal lips with a razor wire tongue [. . .] hunting for someone else to feed her cunt'. The lips/lips conflation is finalized in this encounter. That 'someone else' turns out to be the narrator himself, as he brutally disarms the monstrous sister's weapons at her behest. He describes his desire to 'rip through her razor wire pubic hair like weeds, rip them out of their roots [. . .] my cock hammer-ramming through her with sharp teeth [. . .] my cunt sealed up sewn lips shut'. This passage is significant because of its eradication of any androgyny surrounding the narrator up to this point. Here he is all 'man', vengeful and powerful in a fantasy of brutal domination. To all intents and purposes he *is* one of the attacking hordes of 'Rapists'. The brutality of this image is nothing new, of course, and is startlingly like the Native American stories of the Jimson Girls and the Hopi wooden dildo narratives I discussed in 'Antecedents'. For all his protestations about originality and boundary-pushing, Mellick is actually writing in a long-established tradition – and not half so well as other contributors to it. This moment of phallic supremacy is followed by the narrator's trip to the attic of the house where a giant penis totem is surrounded by pictures of naked men covering the walls. These 'frozen images of masculinity' threaten the narrator who decides to climb into the incubator in the kitchen, 'the hairy cunt machine [. . .] curl up into a ball and go to sleep, back to the womb now dead and old and rotten'. The novella's concluding image is of the narrator's own vagina having reopened and talked to him before he is consumed by a serpent which, in a Biblical moment of atonement, turns him into sperm awaiting rebirth and a reunion with Celsia. It is an image of anticipation of a reunion which is replayed in the later book, *The Haunted Vagina*.

The arresting opening sentence of *The Haunted Vagina* launches the reader straight into the action, and introduces the story's pervasive misogyny: 'I've been scared to have sex with Stacy ever since I discovered her vagina was haunted.'[219] Stacy's vagina's initial manifestations are auditory and although she has no control over the sounds that emanate from it, she is familiar with – even proud of – the phenomenon: '"I'm haunted," she said, touching her vagina and smiling'.[220] In the weird universe of Bizarro fiction the extraordinary is quickly assimilated into the realm of the everyday. For all the puerile haphazardness of his work, Mellick is not a writer entirely without talent – when he chooses, for example, to lampoon cultural pretension in *The Haunted Vagina* he is witty and original. Steve (the narrator) and Stacy discuss music: 'we talked about how she planned to give a theremin rendition of Death and the Maiden, and how she wanted to incorporate it into bondage performance'.[221] Significantly, the lovers also share a peculiar orality, a 'quirky way of eating', preparation, perhaps, for the overt *vagina dentata* motif which dominates Mellick's tale.[222] Further, the first malignant, visual manifestation occurs during an oral sex session between the lovers. A skeleton climbs slowly out of Stacy's vagina and

Stacy and the narrator are – as one would be – horrified. The idea of separation is vividly played out:

> Stacy just watches her body in amazement as the hand clutches onto her leg and pulls. Another hand emerges and grabs her other thigh, trying to pull itself out of there.
>
> Then it dawns on her. Yes, Stacy, this is actually happening to you. She looks at me with wide dilated pupils, frightened of her own vagina.[223]

The vagina is being figured in multiple ways here, in this scene where Stacy effectively gives birth to death. The vagina is a terrifying place for the narrator who attempts to rationalize his fear by displacing it onto Stacy, 'frightened of her own vagina'. As with the narrator in *f/32*, Stacy's vagina has a history of having been worshipped, and she, by extension is granted a divine status. The vagina is autonomous and beyond understanding. It moves in mysterious ways, even entertaining other college students: 'She brought magic into their worlds.'[224] The vagina is word made flesh, 'proof that [the students' . . .] drunken philosophical discussions of rebellion against reality were somewhat correct'.[225] Again, as in both *f/32* and, as we'll see, in the film *Chatterbox*, the talking vagina makes money by entertaining incredulous spectators.

The perverse birth figured in the novella's opening chapters is revisited later in a caricature of domestic *mores*, in the form of Stacy's doll houses. In gazing on these, she returns to a time of innocence, much as the narrator does. It's a version of what the narrator does when he sets out on his impossible voyage into Stacy's body, and it recalls not only the schlocky sci-fi movie *Fantastic Voyage* (1966), but also the grotesquely sexualized language of Jonathan Swift's *Gulliver's Travels* (1726). There are shifting and surreal descriptions of a school which has been turned into a pub – again, a motif of innocence and childhood has been appropriated by something very adult – and it's in this setting that Stacy announces, in a coldly matter-of-fact way to the narrator, Steve, 'I want you to go in there [. . .] I think my vagina is a gateway to another dimension.'[226] Steve's promise – 'I'll give it a try' – is indicative of an overwhelmingly Oedipal desire to unearth the mystery of maternal origins. The vagina, the 'abysmal cavity', as Steve calls it, is sexual *and* maternal, nurturing *and* consuming:

> I can feel her holding me inside of her belly as a way to comfort me one last time before my voyage.
>
> I push off with my feet. It seems looser the farther in I get. After a few inches, I feel Stacy's hands grab my ass and shove me from behind. I straighten out as my buttocks go through, now lying inside of her. She grabs my legs and jostles them in. I squirm forward.
>
> The next thing I know, her lips close up around my wriggling toes.[227]

Once inside Stacy's body, Steve imagines himself to be 'like a human penis' in a terrifying world – the vagina's potentiality for procreation means that infinite regress is possible – one vagina might encompass others.[228] Steve is 'born' into the fantasy world to which Stacy's vulva was the portal, tumbling down a cliff, bloodied and disorientated. This is a nightmarish, intimidating landscape full of menace in its dark forests and threatening cliffs. The exact topography of this place inside Stacy's body is never made entirely clear by Mellick, but the presence of 'old dolls. A dozen of them, hiding behind cobwebs', recalling Stacy's doll houses, suggests that this might be Stacy's unconscious.[229] Steve is really getting to *know* her – as Mangogul got to know and, by extension, to possess, the sexuality of the women in his court, in Diderot's tale. Steve's emergence back into reality after his first excursion to what he terms 'womb world' is also figured as a birth: Stacy has a 'humongous pregnant belly' and he is the foetus for whom 'it's tough moving through the fleshy tunnel [. . .] towards Stacy's vagina'.[230] Steve tells Stacy about his adventures in her womb, and then bursts her bubble of pride at housing a whole world inside her, but she resists his scepticism:

> 'The whole world must be some kind of tumor the size of a pea', she says, 'hiding somewhere in my womb'.
>
> 'So I was really just inside of you this whole time?'
>
> 'Uh-huh' she says, smiling.[231]

Like some kind of postmodern, surreal Queen Elizabeth I, Stacy tasks Steve to be her explorer, that is, to boldly go (forgive the split infinitive) back into her vagina after some careful preparation, and to see what he can find there so that she can write a book about it. As was the case on the first trip, the land inside Stacy is a nightmarish one inhabited by reminders of her past. 'There are shelves here filled with dolls' which are 'black and warped' and 'In the next room, there are melty black statues of people. A mother holding a child, the baby dripping through her arms like wet dough.'[232] Indeed, the entire landscape and the narrator's mode of moving through it is like a computer game, a point made explicitly in Steve's encounter with Stacy's imaginary friend, her avatar in womb world who is 'exactly like a CGI character.'[233] This creature, Fig, quickly makes friends with Steve. She lives in a doll house where she takes him to introduce him to other people. There's also a run-in with the evil Zephrans, the skeletal figures who first made an appearance at the beginning of the book by crawling out of Stacy's vagina. As time passes, Steve notices that his body is changing to become more like Fig's CGI-style body. He also notes that Stacy's body is nourishing him as though he were a baby in her womb and this image of in utero self-sufficiency is echoed pages later in a startling image of male parthenogenesis as he effectively 'gives birth' to his own skeleton which, in a startlingly incongruous simile, 'claws at [his . . .] wormy toes like a kitten'.[234] His metamorphosis is complete and he has become, in this Oedipal return, childlike, without body hair and, like Fig, without nipples. Mellick graphically describes the effects of Stacy having sex which results in the narrator being trapped inside her foetus: 'We're no longer inside of Stacy's body, we're inside of her baby's.'[235] The narrator's misogynist rage and sense of being trapped by the all-consuming, unfaithful cunt, erupts as he starts to choke Fig. This is soon neutralized by consensual sex 'like snail sex. Or jellyfish sex. Or Japanese anime sex.'[236]

The concluding four chapters of the novella are a rushed affair. Female sexuality maintains its unknowability. No amount of penetration, fantasy or hypothesizing can ever truly reveal to the male narrator what it *means* to have a vagina and a womb. Mellick's 'irreal' (a word coined by Bizarro writers to sit on the intersection of the real, surreal and unreal) contribution to the theme of the autonomized vagina is an interesting but ultimately reactionary (because it's misogynist) one. His imagination is vivid but is too coloured by the world of graphic novels (of which the Bizarro genre might be said to be a near-relative), and computer games, to enjoy a real originality or freshness. The result is a disappointingly misogynist will-to-know which lacks the finesse or invention of, for example, its eighteenth-century progenitor, *Les Bijoux*. Confronted with the terrifying reality of twenty-first-century life, and yearning rather for irreality, Mellick returns to the womb in an act of doleful Oedipal nostalgia.

Coda

The idea of, to return to Ela's word, 'decuntation', with which many of the writers in this section have experimented, is a profoundly disturbing one because of its brutality and ugliness. It is not, unhappily, *only* the stuff of fiction. In 1845, a Dr Samuel McMinn was called to the Alabama countryside 15 miles away from his practice in Tuscaloosa. There he discovered 'Mrs B', a woman of around 48 years of age, 'floating in blood'.[237] Mrs B had used a razor to cut around her genitals, 'terminating the process by amputating or exsecting [*sic.*] the whole of the external organ'.[238] She had, in effect, performed FGM on herself, and McMinn reports assuming she would die. He found out from her friends that Mrs B's husband had left her on account of a perimenopausal mental breakdown she'd experienced in her early forties; up until the excision, they said, 'she had been crazy for several years'.[239] After this initial visit, McMinn maintained contact and three weeks from his first visit her mood had lifted and 'in about four months the wound completely cicatrized [scarred over]'.[240] Mrs B's husband moved back in with her and they continued to 'live together in peace and good order'.[241] McMinn concludes his report (for the *Western Lancet* originally) by recording visits to three patients exhibiting similar behaviour to that of the original Mrs B. He doesn't draw many conclusions as to whether or not a degenerative disease (perhaps syphilis or gonorrhoea, presumably) had precipitated the psychosis each woman reported. In his medical report, McMinn conflates mid-nineteenth-century ideas about a woman's mental health, physical health and gynaecological aetiology. The woman's sexual organs and insanity are literally – *hysterically* – allied.[242] His presence in the recovery of these women is only ever presented – in his own account – as being incidental – it seems that the administration of cod liver oil, the replacement of soiled dressings with clean ones and the return of a formerly errant husband can 'cure' a woman of her fissured sexual identity. Sometimes fact can be – almost – stranger than fiction.

Notes

1 Luis Buñuel (dir.), *Viridiana*, 1961.

2 Victor Fuentes, *Buñuel: cine y literatura*, p. 139, as translated and quoted in Tatjana Pavlović, Inmaculada Alvarez, Rosana Blanco-Cano, Anitra Grisales, Alejandra Osorio and Alejandra Sánchez, *100 Years of Spanish Cinema* (Oxford: Wiley-Blackwell, 2009), p. 97.

3 On Enedina becoming 'Buñel's own ego', see Julián Daniel Gutiérrez-Albilla, *Queering Buñuel: Sexual Dissidence and Psychoanalysis in his Mexican and Spanish Cinema* (London: I.B. Tauris, 2008), p. 78. A similarly surreal moment in which a camera is intimately associated with the body and the family occurs in Kathy Acker's writing. In her 1976 work *Florida*, one of Acker's characters shares 'irrelevant details' with another. 'When I was two years old', says one character to the other, 'I refused to drink milk. My parents, they were still alive then, were scared I was going to die. My father started to take a camera apart. Only when he started to break the camera, would I drink the milk'. See Kathy Acker, *Florida*, as excerpted in Amy Scholder and Dennis Cooper (eds), *Essential Acker: The Writings of Kathy Acker* (New York, NY: Grove Press, 2002), p. 80.

4 Gutiérrez-Albilla, *Queering Buñuel*, p. 75.

5 Gwynne Edwards, *A Companion to Luis Buñuel* (Woodbridge: Tamesis, 2005), p. 134.

6 Susanna Kaysen, *The Camera My Mother Gave Me* (New York, NY: Vintage, 2001).

7 See Susanna Kaysen, *Girl, Interrupted* (New York, NY: Random House, 1993), and James Mangold (dir.), *Girl, Interrupted* (2000).

8 Kaysen, *The Camera*, p. 105.

9 Ibid.

10 Ibid., p. 108. On how vulvodynia meant for one woman that 'my vulva [. . .] burned unexpectedly and inconveniently. It burned at school. It burned at the grocery store. It burned at the bar. It burned when I ate ice cream. It burned when I drove my car. It burned when I had sex – and that part really sucked', see Katinka Hooijer, 'Vulvodynia: On the Medicinal Purposes of Porn', in Merri Lisa Johnson (ed.), *Jane Sexes It Up: True Confessions of Feminist Desire* (New York, NY: Four Walls Eight Windows, 2002), pp. 259–80 (p. 260).

11 Ibid., p. 115.

12 Ibid.

13 Ibid., pp. 123, 127.

14 Ibid., p. 135.

15 Ibid., p. 149.

16 Ibid., p. 58.

17 Jane Arden, 'Introduction', in *Vagina Rex and the Gas Oven*, Playscript 58 (London: Calder and Boyars, 1971), n.p. (p. 5).

18 Arden, *Vagina Rex*, p. 10.

19 Ibid., p. 53.

20 Ibid., p. 54.

21 Ibid.

22 Ibid., p. 55.

23 Ibid., p. 49.

24 Ibid.

25 Arden, 'Introduction', in *Vagina Rex*, n.p. (p. 5).

26 Periel Aschenbrand, *The Only Bush I Trust is my Own* (London: Corgi, 2006), p. 181.

27 Aschenbrand, *The Only Bush*, pp. 66.

28 Ibid., p. 67; Michael Moore (b. 1954) is an activist filmmaker, and persistent irritant to the Right in the United States.

29 Ibid., pp. 67, 69.

30 Ibid., pp. 72, 104.

31 Ibid., p. 109.

32 Ibid., p. 137.

33 William Burroughs, *The Naked Lunch: The Restored Text* (London: Harper Perennial, 2005), p. 110.

34 Burroughs, *The Naked Lunch*, pp. 110–11.

35 Ibid., p. 112.

36 On the '*anuscript*', see Gaétan Brulotte, cited in Oliver Harris, *William Burroughs and the Secret of Fascination* (Carbondale, IL: Southern Illinois University Press, 2003), p. 230. On how the autonomous bodily organ is not subject to 'an exploitable oral-genital organization', but, rather, suggests 'other forms of social organization implied by different subject-structures', see Timothy S. Murphy, *Wising up the Marks: the Amodern William Burroughs* (Berkeley, CA: University of California Press, 1997), p. 98.

37 Eurydice Kamvyselli, *f/32: The Second Coming* (London: Virago, 1993). The book itself gives little clue to the author's identity, being attributed only to 'Eurudice'.

38 Kamvyselli herself has said: 'I was conscious of Lacan's mirror stage etc. and worked it in the whole structure of the book & more consciously the last short chapter [. . .] My work always is about philosophy & ideas rather than characters or stories in the conventional sense'. Eurydice Kamvyselli, personal correspondence with the author, 27 April 2009. On Kamvyselli as a literary 'thug', see Raymond Federman, *Critifiction: Postmodern Essays* (Albany, NY: SUNY Press, 1993), p. 131.

39   On this process as primordial, see Jacques Lacan, 'The mirror stage as formative of the function of the I as revealed in psychoanalytic experience', delivered at the sixteenth International Congress of Psychoanalysis, Zürich, 17 July 1949, from Jacques Lacan, *Écrits: A Selection*, trans. Alan Sheridan (New York, NY: W. W. Norton, 1977), p. 2.

40   Lacan, 'The mirror stage', p. 4. Lacan refers to these inner and outer worlds by the German terms '*innenwelt*' and '*umwelt*'.

41   Stamelman usefully defines *manque-à-être* as 'the lack and primal loss of oneness with another in which language, desire, and subjectivity have their origins'. Richard Howard Stamelman, *Lost Beyond Telling: Representations of Death and Absence in Modern French Poetry* (Ithaca, NY: Cornell University Press, 1990), p. 79.

42   On the phenomenon of *Verneinung* (negation) as a paradoxical 'avowal of the signifier itself that it annuls', see Jacques Lacan, *Écrits: A Selection*, trans. Alan Sheridan (London: Routledge, 2001), p. 153. It is 'the negation whereby repression is simultaneously maintained and denied' according to Sheldon Pollock in his 'Cosmopolitan and Vernacular in History', in Carol A. Breckenridge, Sheldon Pollock, Homi K. Bhabha and Dipesh Chakrabarty (eds), *Cosmopolitanism* (Durham, NC: Duke University Press, 2002), pp. 15–53 (p. 50, n. 22).

43   My emphases.

44   Eurudice (Kamvyselli), *f/32*, p. 36.

45   Ibid., p. 48.

46   Ibid., pp. 42–3.

47   Ibid., p. 6.

48   Ibid., p. 19.

49   Ibid., p. 23.

50   Ibid., p. 27.

51   Ibid., p. 31.

52   Ibid., p. 33.

53   Ibid., pp. 48–9.

54   Ibid., p. 51.

55   Ibid., p. 56.

56   Ibid., p. 66.

57   Ibid., p. 67.

58   Ibid., pp. 54, 59, 60.

59   Ibid., pp. 58, 63.

60   Ibid., p. 79.

61   Ibid., pp. 86, 107.

62   Ibid., p. 116.

63   Ibid., pp. 128–9.

64   Ibid., p. 133.

65 Ibid., p. 136.

66 Ibid., pp. 139, 141.

67 Ibid., p. 142.

68 Ibid., pp. 150, 151.

69 Ibid., p. 164.

70 Ibid., p. 181.

71 Ibid., p. 184.

72 Ibid., p. 186.

73 Robert Coover, personal email correspondence with the author, October 2011.

74 Robert Coover, *A Theological Position: Plays* (New York, NY: EP Dutton & Co. Inc., 1972).

75 Coover, *A Theological Position*, p. 75.

76 Ibid., pp. 89, 95.

77 Ibid., p. 98.

78 Ibid., p. 111.

79 Ibid., p. 114.

80 Ibid., pp. 126, 125.

81 Ibid., p. 127.

82 Ibid., p. 145.

83 In John 14:6, Jesus says: 'I am the way, the truth, and the life. No one comes to the Father except through me'. King James Version.

84 Coover, *A Theological Position*, p. 150.

85 Ibid., pp. 155, 157.

86 Ibid., p. 161.

87 *New York* Magazine, 25 June 1979, p. 23. Ironically, the magazine's cover had in bold font: 'The meaning of gay [. . .] The church condemns it as a mortal sin'. In the same week that Sossi's double bill opened, LA band the Knack released 'My Sharona' and, in the United Kingdom, Johnny Rotten and Joan Collins both appeared on *Juke Box Jury*.

88 Peter S. Prescott, *Encounters with American Culture, Volume 2 (1973–1985)* (New Brunswick, NJ: Transaction Publishers, 2006), p. 45.

89 Coover, personal email correspondence with the author, October 2011.

90 Ibid.

91 Coover, *A Theological Position*, pp. 160, 161.

92 Ibid., p. 161.

93 Ibid., p. 162.

94 Ibid.

95 Ibid., p. 164.

96 Ibid., p. 166.

97 Ibid., p. 167.

98   Ibid., p. 168.

99   Ibid., p. 169.

100   DeSimone's film was a far less explicit version of Claude Mulot's earlier *Le Sexe qui Parle* ('Pussy Talk', 1975).

101   Coover, personal email correspondence with the author, October 2011.

102   Ibid.

103   Ibid.

104   Coover, *A Theological Position*, p. 170.

105   Ibid.

106   Ibid., p. 171.

107   Luce Irigaray, 'When Our Lips Speak Together', reprinted in Janet Price and Margrit Shildrick (eds), *Feminist Theory and the Body: A Reader* (New York, NY: Routledge, 1999), pp. 82–90 (p. 82).

108   Coover, *A Theological Position*, p. 171.

109   Prescott, *Encounters with American Culture*, p. 46.

110   Brian Evenson, *Understanding Robert Coover* (Columbia, SC: University of South Carolina Press, 2003), p. 102. Evenson's assessment of the play has a political edge to it, which is, presumably, what Coover had hoped for. 'Coover suggests', writes Evenson, 'that more attention should be paid to "the soft letter of the soft law" [. . .] in lieu of choosing an ascetic and restricted "position"', p. 102.

111   Coover, personal email correspondence with the author, October 2011.

112   Ibid.

113   Nicholson Baker, *House of Holes* (London: Simon and Schuster, 2011); Maureen Freely, *Under the Vulcania* (London: Bloomsbury, 1994).

114   Freely, *Under the Vulcania*, p. 63.

115   Ibid., p. 57.

116   Ibid., p. 92.

117   Ibid., pp. 51, 67.

118   Ibid., p. 75.

119   Ibid., p. 62.

120   Ibid., p. 68.

121   Ibid., p. 102.

122   Ibid., p. 104.

123   Ibid.

124   Ibid., p. 59.

125   Ibid., p. 39.

126   Ibid., p. 43.

127   Ibid., p. 85.

128   Baker, *House of Holes*, p. 22.

129 Ibid., p. 20.

130 Ibid., p. 62.

131 And what a depressing, sordid future it is that Nicholson imagines, where the pursuit of science is all for the pursuit of orgasm. In his earlier novel, *The Fermata*, Nicholson imagined a universe which could be momentarily paused by a man called Arno Strine, who uses this extraordinary gift not for altruistic ends, but to undress and sexually exploit women unawares. Nicholson Baker, *The Fermata* (London: Vintage, 1994).

132 Baker, *House of Holes*, pp. 62, 53.

133 Ibid., p. 71.

134 Ibid.

135 Ibid., p. 169.

136 Ibid., p. 95.

137 Ibid., p. 27.

138 Ibid., p. 33.

139 Ibid., pp. 63, 65.

140 Ibid., p. 76.

141 Freely, *Under the Vulcania*, p. 91.

142 Ibid.

143 Baker, *House of Holes*, pp. 23, 91, 92, 93, 185.

144 Ibid., p. 130.

145 Ibid., pp. 136–7.

146 Ibid., p. 137.

147 Ibid., pp. 184, 196.

148 Ibid., p. 238.

149 Ibid., p. 239.

150 Ibid., p. 241.

151 Ibid., p. 83.

152 Ibid., pp. 83, 84.

153 Ibid., p. 85.

154 Ibid., pp. 120, 123.

155 Ibid., p. 139.

156 Ibid., p. 150.

157 Ibid., p. 151.

158 Ibid.

159 Ibid., p. 196.

160 Ani DiFranco (b. 1970), is an acclaimed US feminist singer–songwriter; Baker, *House of Holes*, p. 233.

161 Baker, *House of Holes*, p. 233.

162 Ibid., pp. 261, 262.

163 Ibid., p. 262.

164 For more on Acker's figure of the pirate as 'the revolutionary subject of an entirely economic social world, with the free market imagined as the open sea, the horizon of the possible', see Michael Clune, 'Blood Money: Sovereignty and Exchange in Kathy Acker', *Contemporary Literature* XLV, 3 (2004), pp. 486–515 (p. 487). On Acker's 'textual piracy' as 'feminist guerrilla warfare', see Susan E. Hawkins, 'All in the Family: Kathy Acker's *Blood and Guts in High School*', *Contemporary Literature* XLV, 4 (2004), pp. 637–58 (p. 638).

165 Jeanette Winterson, 'Introduction' to Amy Scholder and Dennis Cooper (eds), *Essential Acker: The Writings of Kathy Acker* (New York, NY: Grove Press, 2002), p. ix.

166 As Joe Moran has written, 'No one could accuse Acker's work of being easy to assimilate: she rejects almost all the conventional means by which readers can orient themselves through a text.' Joe Moran, *Star Authors: Literary Celebrity in America* (London: Pluto Press, 2000), p. 141.

167 Kathy Acker, from *The Burning Bombing of America: The Destruction of the U.S.*, as reprinted in Scholder and Cooper (eds), *Essential Acker*, p. 7. The spaces between words are enlarged here, and in other quotations from Acker, as in the original.

168 Acker, *The Burning Bombing of America*, in Scholder and Cooper (eds), *Essential Acker*, p. 6.

169 Ibid.

170 Acker, *Kathy Goes to Haiti*, in Scholder and Cooper (eds), *Essential Acker*, p. 83.

171 As Martina Sciolino expresses it: 'Acker's writing is [. . .] inserted between [. . .] latent and manifest postmodernisms, challenging their separation in a constructed dream-work of her own'. See Martina Sciolino, 'Kathy Acker and the Postmodern Subject of Feminism', *College English*, 52.4 (April 1990), pp. 437–45 (p. 438).

172 Acker, from *Pussy, King of the Pirates*, in Scholder and Cooper (eds), *Essential Acker*, p. 318.

173 Acker, *Pussy, King of the Pirates*, p. 318.

174 Ibid., p. 320.

175 Ibid., p. 323.

176 Acker, from *Don Quixote*, as reprinted in Scholder and Cooper (eds), *Essential Acker*, p. 220. See 'Antecedents' for more on the enduring potency of the Medusa myth.

177 Acker, *Pussy, King of the Pirates*, p. 324.

178 Ibid., p. 329.

179 Ibid., p. 331.

180 Acker, from *Blood and Guts in High School*, as reprinted in Scholder and Cooper (eds), *Essential Acker*, pp. 116, 114.

181 Acker, from *The Childlike Life of the Black Tarantula*, as reprinted in Scholder and Cooper (eds), *Essential Acker*, pp. 27, 29.

182 Ibid., pp. 29, 37. The same narrator later declares: 'my cunt is my center my cunt is my center my cunt is my center' (p. 32).

183 Acker, 'New York City in 1979', in Scholder and Cooper (eds), *Essential Acker*, p. 143.

184 Winterson, 'Introduction', in Scholder and Cooper (eds), *Essential Acker*, p. ix.

185 Kathy Acker, *Algeria: A Series of Invocations Because Nothing Else Works* (London: Aloes Books, 1984).

186 Acker, *Algeria*, n.p.

187 On Acker's work as less 'autobiographical' than 'autoplagiarist', where the 'autoplagiarist takes the phrase "life story" literally – as a literary term', see Sciolino, 'Kathy Acker', p. 440.

188 Acker, *Algeria*, p. 1.

189 Kathy Acker, 'A Few Notes on Two of my Books', in Ellen G. Friedman and Miriam Fuchs (eds), *The Review of Contemporary Fiction: Kathy Acker, Christine Brooke-Rose and Marguerite Young*, 9.3 (1989), pp. 31–6 (p. 31). Kathryn Hume makes the point that although she is political, Acker is not calling her readers to action. Rather, 'We must make up our own minds on what we want to do'. See Kathryn Hume, 'Voice in Kathy Acker's Fiction', *Contemporary Literature*, 42.3 (Autumn, 2001), pp. 485–513 (p. 499).

190 Acker, *Algeria*, p. 2; my italics for emphasis.

191 Ibid., p. 4.

192 Ibid., p. 5.

193 Ibid.

194 Ibid., pp. 5, 6.

195 Ibid., p. 7.

196 Ibid.

197 Ibid., p. 11.

198 Ibid., p. 18; Acker wrote a sentence of praise for the back cover of Kamvyselli's *f/32* – clearly, the name 'Eurydice' has a special resonance. In myth, Orpheus had to lead Eurydice out of the underworld.

199 Ibid., p. 19.

200 As Clune argues, 'The project of dismantling the self is expressed in language that floats free of sovereign subjects, circulates between individuals, and is available to everybody because it is not identified with anybody – and it is, additionally, not identified with any body either'. See Clune, 'Blood Money', p. 504.

201 Acker, *Algeria*, p. 19.

202 Ibid., p. 22.

203 Ibid., p. 29. Acker was to return to the themes of Algeria and terrorism four years after the publication of *Algeria*, in her novel *Empire of the Senseless*.

204 Will Self's 1993 *Cock and Bull* certainly had some 'Bizarro' elements to it. A male rugby player called John Bull unexpectedly develops an anatomically perfect cunt – behind his knee: 'Bull's vagina really *was* cute. A dear little box. Its lips were just so, flanged just so. The pearly pink of the vagina's internal skin faded into the white,

freckled skin of Bull's leg, just so. And the lips weren't too crinkled, the clitoris wasn't too long'. Will Self, *Cock and Bull* (London: Bloomsbury, 2006), p. 162.

205   Carlton Mellick III, *Razor Wire Pubic Hair* (Fountain Hills, AZ: Eraserhead Press, 2003), n.p.

206   Mellick, *Razor Wire*.

207   Ibid., n.p.

208   Ibid.

209   Ibid.

210   Ibid.

211   Ibid.

212   Ibid.

213   Ibid.

214   Ibid.

215   Ibid.

216   Ibid.

217   Ibid.

218   Ibid.

219   Carlton Mellick III *The Haunted Vagina* (Portland, OR: Eraserhead Press, 2006), p. 7.

220   Mellick, *Haunted*, p. 8.

221   Ibid., p. 14.

222   Ibid., p. 17.

223   Ibid., p. 22.

224   Ibid., p. 26.

225   Ibid.

226   Ibid., p. 31.

227   Ibid., p. 36.

228   Ibid., p. 37.

229   Ibid., pp. 43–4.

230   Ibid., pp. 47, 49, 54.

231   Ibid., pp. 51–2.

232   Ibid., p. 68.

233   Ibid., p. 72.

234   Ibid., p. 88.

235   Ibid., p. 94.

236   Ibid., p. 99.

237   Samuel N. McMinn, M. D., 'Insanity Cured by the Excision of the External Organs of Generation', *The Boston Medical and Surgical Journal*, Vol. xxxii, No. 7 (Wednesday 19 March 1845), pp. 131–2 (p. 132).

238   McMinn, 'Insanity Cured', p. 132.

239 Ibid.

240 Ibid.

241 Ibid.

242 The idea of *hysteria*, the etymology of which lies in *uterus*, is explored by Elaine Showalter in her *Female Malady: Women, Madness and English Culture, 1830–1980* (London: Virago, 1987).

4

Revealing the Vagina in Visual Art (1): Judy Chicago

Eating out

The conservative Catholic writer Alice Thomas Ellis once wrote of 'the old dinner-party conversational rule', which means: 'no mention of sex, religion, politics or money. Just praise the flower arrangement and don't blow your nose on the napkin'.[1] The idea of a 'dinner party' has, to my mind, a tantalizing aura of the 1970s about it, of creamy-pink prawn cocktail, frozen Black Forest gateau and Blue Nun wine. It's a suburban drinks party, after all, which sets the scene for the paralysing comedy of social manners that's so astutely captured by Mike Leigh in his stage play, *Abigail's Party* (1977).[2] In the 1980s, during rapid economic growth, and equally rapid social deprivation, it was aspiration, the Thatcherite '*loadsa money*' mind-set, and mobile phones the size (and value) of a gold bar, which were the trappings of an often spiritually redundant – but financially replete – lifestyle. The playwright Caryl Churchill tapped into this façade of 'wealth' in a devastatingly cynical and provocative way in her 1982 play, *Top Girls*.[3] Marlene, the very model of a 1980s Maggie, is, in Act 1, hosting a party in a restaurant to celebrate her promotion. The main guests, however, are five historical figures, each of whom has her own story to tell, from the vain, courtly Nijo (Lady Nijo, b.1528, a Japanese Emperor's courtesan; later a Buddhist nun); the ninth-century Pope Joan; to the peasant,

Dull Gret (based on the subject of *Dulle Griet*, a grotesque sixteenth-century painting by Pieter Brueghel the Elder). They are joined by Isabella Bird, a nineteenth-century Scottish traveller, and Patient Griselda (the virtuous wife in Chaucer's Clerk's tale).

The play takes its title from a recruitment agency owned by Marlene, and the 'top girls' in the play's capitalist structuring are those who possess an almost Darwinian single-mindedness. Joyce, Marlene's sister, sees the world through altogether more socialist eyes, regarding class as a dominant factor in the oppression of Thatcher's populace – men *and* women. As the play unfolds, the audience learns that the cost of Marlene's 'success' involved handing over her daughter to be raised by Joyce. Churchill's deployment in this opening act of a dinner setting facilitates not only the intermingling of characters from diverse backgrounds, but significantly works to suggest a powerful continuity of the preoccupations which women have shared – but have largely had silenced – through the centuries. The presence of the five historical characters is a visual reminder that *his*tory, so often written by the (male) victors, can offer a new way of understanding, if women's roles within it are aired and understood. All 16 of the characters we see on stage during the play are women, and the impact on their lives of precisely those dinner party taboos (sex, religion, politics and money), cannot go unnoticed by the audience. As one critic observed, 'these women from the past make up a carefully selected group whose dramatic function is to represent different aspects of the female psyche or contrasting female views'.[4] What Churchill ultimately achieved was to reframe the struggle of women in the 1980s to 'have it all' (career, family, financial security), *seeing* women's efforts by viewing history through a feminocentric (women-focused) lens.

You are cordially invited to consider how 'cunt art', with its origins in 1960s West Coast America, resonates today. This food for thought will be served at an iconic dinner party where vital issues will be contested: legacies, identities, histories, births and bodies. Every taboo conversation topic proscribed by 'polite' society will be fair game. The role of the woman artist is under investigation: does the epic exhibit *The Dinner Party* (large tables set with plates which abstractly depict famous women's labia and vulvas) offer the viewer an unfashionably biographical view on how its creator, the artist Judy Chicago, interprets her *own* struggles as a woman artist? If much figurative art produced before *The Dinner Party* suggestively signalled an insistent need for open and honest representations of the female body, then one might argue that *The Dinner Party* offers up a vision of the return of the repressed. But the dual concepts of continuity and heredity complicate that return: what this particular exhibit does is painfully to underscore how there *has* always been a continuum of women's achievements, but that it has been repeatedly stifled by a patriarchy for which the return is too terrifying a thought. 'For every image that we read as *woman*, at least two bodies co-exist in fantasy', writes art historian Griselda Pollock, 'in an uneven continuum the representation of the female body can move between a pleasurable memory of [. . .] the maternal body to the punished and degraded [. . .] fetishism of the female body as the sign of castration and the castrated or castrating other'.[5] Glimpses of a cultural continuum – of tantalizing moments of interconnectedness – will be brought back to light in this section of *The Vagina*, which considers 'cunt art' from its early incarnations. Chicago's *r*epresentations of specific 'guests' at her *Dinner Party* – the heroic Biblical Judith, the Renaissance artist Artemisia Gentileschi, the writer and philosopher Mary Wollstonecraft – function as a way in to considering how women have seemingly always been brutalized and subjugated. They will be the bridge between the first and second of these visual art sections. However, those same women are being relocated in a *tradition* of intellectual strength. The second 'art' section of *The Vagina* starts with the origin of the world: birth. It asks how the *parturient* (in labour) body is represented in art today. How do artists make seen the formerly ob/seen moment of birth?

'There's lots of vagina in our work'[6]

A visitor in the early 1990s to the German town of Kassel (about 200 miles south-west of Berlin, and once home to the Brothers Grimm) might well have headed to the Neue Galerie. This building, although having been nearly destroyed by the Allied bombers, had protected many of its most important artworks by packing them off to Vienna for the duration of the Second World War. It reopened its doors in 1976, and in 1992, the American artist

Zoe Leonard (b. 1961) chose its 'sober, airless' venue for her exhibition.[7] From the walls of the Galerie's seven rooms Leonard removed all paintings which did not feature women prominently (and also, for some reason, left a still life of a fish on display). On the wall-space she had freed up, Leonard hung 19 of her own works: 10" × 8" black and white photographs, each one showing a close-up of a different female friend's genitals. The visual juxtaposition of these explicit photos with the museum's paintings powerfully challenged preconceptions about the historical representation of women's bodies. In a different setting, the photos would not have had the same kind of impact: context was all-important.[8] The art which made the pubic public felt, to the artist, both 'aggressive and irreverent' and 'bolder and more caustic' than work she'd done before.[9] Leonard also recalls that 'Once the genitalia went up, the whole gallery seemed to shift. Relationships between the photos and the [remaining] paintings were amazing to set up. The facial expressions on the people in the paintings all seemed to respond to the photographs. Some were humorous, some poignant, some sensuous.'[10]

What will become apparent in this section of *The Vagina* is that the ground-breaking work of artists like Judy Chicago facilitated interventions, of which Leonard's is a particularly powerful example, into the established art scene. Both artists are preoccupied with making women *seen*, literally and metaphorically, and not *obscene*. Leonard's powerful juxtaposition of, and intertextual play with, 'live' nude photographs and the Galerie's staid male-authored paintings worked, as Chicago's *Dinner Party* had done before it, to humanize, even autonomize, women: 'two hundred years ago', mused Leonard, 'these women [in the paintings] had sex, they had desire, they jerked off, some were lesbians. Some were probably miserable and repressed, but also some may have found great joy and power in their sexuality.'[11] Susan Kandel has called Leonard's intervention 'a gesture both cunning and blatant [. . .] If every art object is a beaver shot in disguise – something to gape at, to possess, something in and through which a sense of the self is derived – then Leonard is merely stating the obvious.'[12] Kandel's argument adopts the language of the postmodernist maven Jean-François Lyotard to express how post-1980s vulvar artists play with the 'unpresentable', 'that which is visible on two registers at once. This simultaneity is its unpleasantness; it is its danger.'[13] In an important sense, in imagining these backstories for the original occupants of the Neue Galerie's walls, Leonard is anticipating a shift from covert to *overt* visibility in her pictures. Because each photograph showed only the genitals, it could be imagined that each somehow 'belonged' to the women whose faces are seen in the paintings that still hang on the walls, but whose sexuality had to remain – until Leonard revealed its *possibility* – covert.

Judy Chicago's earlier works also confront or challenge the viewer, so it's of little surprise that *The Dinner Party* was later received in that way. But we're getting ahead of ourselves. It wasn't until the Fullerton exhibition in 1970 – the same event at which Judy Gerowitz (née Cohen) officially became Judy *Chicago* – that Chicago explicitly identified herself as a 'feminist' artist and her work began to demonstrate a preoccupation with female sexuality. This led to her founding the Fresno State College Feminist Art Program – the first of its kind in the United States.[14] Her 1971 *Red Flag* confronted ideas about representing the vagina (the work's title transmits a plethora of heated associations, from danger, to rebellion, to provocation, to annulling or stopping something). For here is a close-up photograph of a woman pulling a tampon from her vagina. It's a provocative image not only because of the faintly phallic nature of the tampon, but also because it reminds the viewer of the *reality* of many women's embodied experiences. The removal is decidedly non-erotic, for isn't the vagina something *into* which, in traditional representation, objects are customarily placed (speculum, penis, voice), and not a place from which objects are removed? The image challenges assumptions that the vagina should be represented as exclusively 'erotic' in the first place. *Red Flag* captures a private moment – the functional, not the pornographic or pathologized cunt – and makes it *seen*. It's not like a birthing image because it is self-contained: no medical professionals interfere, since the moment is serenely autonomous. No one else is needed. This is a powerful vulva; the tampon's emerging from an equally potent vagina. *She* is in control; it's as though Courbet's *L'Origine* has been secularly transubstantiated, made flesh and allowed to have depth as well as surface. *Red Flag* vividly violates all sorts of taboos, not only the seen/unseen dichotomy of the female body, but also the religious codes of, for example, the Jewish *mikvah*, the immersion pool believed to reinstate both a woman's 'purity' after menstruation, and *taharat hamishpachah*, that of the family home, too.[15] Judith's own *mikvah*, as we shall see in my work on the Biblical story of Judith and Holofernes in the next section, is hinted at in her protracted ritualistic preparations for the trip to the tent of the Assyrian General. The motif of the female 'containment' of menstruation was revisited in Chicago's *Menstruation Bathroom* installation (1972), and had already been explored by Faith Wilding in her complex tableau *Sacrifice* (1971), at the centre of which lay a life-sized model of an eviscerated woman on a table, daubed in cow guts and blood and surrounded by candles and sanitary pads.[16]

In terms of art since the 1960s, Judy Chicago was central to the Californian feminist movement which, as art historian Laura Meyer has claimed, 'sought to establish and theorize a "female sensibility" in art, making use of female body imagery and reclaiming traditionally "feminine" domestic crafts and materials to explore aspects of female identity, an idea that was opposed by many New York Feminists'.[17] Meyer convincingly explores how the revolutionary 'Womanhouse' project in LA (1972; an actual house rebuilt by women artists who then furnished each room in unexpectedly transgressive, feminist ways) was in so many ways a precursor for the thematic and, in some instances, aesthetic concerns of *The Dinner Party*.[18] The artist Faith Wilding also recalls those early days of the 'cunt art' movement: 'Although we did not fully theorize our attraction to cunt imagery at the time, we knew it was a catalyst for thinking about our bodies and about female representation [. . .] *Cunt Art*, made for the female gaze, aimed to reverse the negative connotations of a dirty word with a defiant challenge to traditional depictions of submissive female sexuality.'[19]

'There's lots of vagina in our work, but it is not about vaginas', wrote Wilding in 1980, 'Rather we are inventing a new form [of] language radiating a female power which cannot be conveyed in any other way at this time.'[20] The political tenor of Wilding's artistic statement was unequivocal: 'As women artists we are presenting an image of woman's body and spirit as that which cannot and must not be colonized either sexually, economically, or politically.'[21] Wilding is still fascinated by vulvar images, and says: 'I am amused when I read my passionate arguments for a vaginal imagery, partly because nowadays I prefer to refer to the vulva because it is the non-reproductive, visible, and most pleasurable part of the female sexual anatomy.'[22] Wilding is a founder member of the subRosa feminist collective which unites art and activism, and practises 'a situational embodied feminist politics nourished by conviviality, self-determination, and the desire for affirmative alliances and coalitions'.[23] Wilding has made a short video on labiaplasty called 'Vulva de/reconstructa' and has contributed an essay, 'Vulvas with a Difference' to the subRosa anthology, *Domain Errors*.[24] Here, Wilding critiques the new commodification of the female body which biotechnological 'advances' have facilitated, as they 'make clear that what is lacking or inadequate is the woman's body and the structure of her sexual organs – not medical knowledge and sexual practices'.[25] Another subRosa project is 'Constructa/vulva', an 'interactive sculptural performance' staged at the Regina Gouger Miller Gallery at the Carnegie Mellon in Pittsburgh in September 2000 at the exhibition 'Fusion: Artists in a Research Setting'.[26] The 'Constructa/vulva' was a 6' × 5' soft vulva sculpture accompanied by various pertinent anatomical parts in different shapes and sizes – labia, a cervix, a clitoris. 'Performers costumed as speculums assisted and encouraged audience members to create their ideal vulva' by affixing the different anatomical parts to the main sculpture with Velcro.[27] A portrait of each audience member in, by, or on their ideal constructed vulva was given away (a little like the Log Flume ride at Britain's largest theme park, Alton Towers, but presumably with the subject wearing a less horrified expression). Here, women's genitals have become the stuff of educational, anatomical pantomime, a three-dimensional, participatory homage to the self-investigatory work of Tee Corinne (of *Cunt Coloring Book* fame) et al. in the 1960s and 1970s.[28] Disney does gynaecology – you don't meet Mickey but you can have your picture taken by a woman dressed as a speculum while you stand next to the 6'-high cunt sculpture you helped to make. Despite the bizarre imaginings of the creators of *South Park*, which we'll see in the Film and TV section of this book, they haven't come up with that one. Yet.

Cunt art and butterflies

Second-wave feminism's emphasis on the female artist's agency, on her role as painter, not merely as paint*ed*, focused on 'central core' imagery. Representations by Chicago and other Fresno artists often had at their centre a space which was to be construed not as a void or lack, but as an emblem of the potency of the 'invisible' vagina. In 1973, Miriam Schapiro and Judy Chicago asked: 'What does it feel like to be a woman? To be formed around a central core and have a secret place which can be entered and which is also a passageway from which life emerges?'[29] However, the imagery is complex, as American art historian Amelia Jones has argued, since much 'central core' art actually focuses not on the vagina, but on labial or vulvar images.[30] That's not to suggest that Chicago and other artists don't emphasize the powerful musculature of the vaginal canal: in some of the plates that are part of *The Dinner Party*, that's very much the case. But the idea of '*cunt* art' seems to me (and to artists such as Faith Wilding, it would seem) to be a far more appropriate name in its anatomically inclusive spirit. Wilding declared that 'the notion "cunt is beautiful", like the civil rights mantra "black is beautiful", was about "claiming what has been most derogated as your strength"'.[31] Central core images do not, despite some critics' claims, somehow 'reduce' women to vaginas, holes: they can, rather, make both the literal (the vagina) and the metaphorical (achievements) *seen*, giving women depths, complexities and identities.[32] Looking at the central core concept like this gives us an approach to the art which is neither reductionist nor essentialist, but which in fact advances an opening out or an exploration. The idea that Judy Chicago's *Dinner Party* (at which we'll look closely in a moment), is somehow essentialist – *reducing* women's identities – is wrong.[33] Indeed, the art historian Griselda Pollock is vituperative about projects like *The Dinner Party*, which seek to reposition women in dominant historical discourses, arguing that 'to claim creativity for women is to do more than find a few female names', as if this is all that Chicago achieved.[34] California-based academic Anette Kubitza also claims that since 'male meanings are encoded into representations of women, these representations cannot simply be co-opted by feminist artists without being laid open to misunderstanding'.[35] In the poststructuralist twenty-first century we must be careful not entirely to dismiss as essentialist (and, therefore, somehow naïve or worthless) the attempts at 'female' representation – and reclamation – of the 1970s. In any case, do today's young women know any more than their second-wave 'sisters' of the 1970s? Santoro's 1974 *Towards New Expression*, published by the activist feminist organization Rivolta Feminile, juxtaposed photographs of flowers, shells, vulvas and nude statuary as a way of putting back into art the 'real' meaning of women's sexuality. Such a move has not, however, always been seen as liberating, but could be seen as perpetuating 'the exclusively sexual identity of women, not only as body but explicitly as cunt'.[36]

Central-core exhibitions did shatter taboos and brought female sexuality to the fore.[37] Amelia Jones has argued that possible responses to Judy Chicago's central-core work include the 'far more ambiguous and sexually multiplicitous anatomical "destiny" for women (as well as men)' in other early cunt images by Hannah Wilke, Faith Wilding or Karen LeCocq (whose tactile *Feather Cunt* (1971) cushion both celebrates and rejects domestic kitsch in its playful use of traditionally 'feminine' colours, materials and textures and, presumably, crafts, but which challenges such 'niceties' in its clearly vulvar imagery).[38] The American artist Marlene McCarty's (b. 1957) single, confrontational large printed word, 'CUNT' (1990), is, suggests Jones, an 'alternative to central-core imagery'.[39] McCarty's unequivocal artwork also recalls Chicago's 'Cunt Cheerleaders', Fresno Program students who wore 'letter sweaters spelling "C-U-N-T" and performed cheers in public [which] exemplify the empowering aspect of "cunt" for these women as well as the humor that accompanied its recuperation (a humor that is largely ignored by theorists who dismiss "cunt imagery" as essentialist).'[40] The academic Michèle Barrett has also suggested that the vulvar focus, or 'vaginal iconology', eradicated socio-economic differences between women; differences which became more widely debated and acknowledged in feminist theory in the 1980s.[41] If we argue that 'Woman – capital W – is a fiction and a myth', and refuse 'anatomy as a basis for the determining fictions of sexual identity' then we can ascertain where a certain antagonism to Chicago's approach might come from.[42] However, taking Jones's thoughts on board, too, we might be more receptive to the possibility that paradoxical interpretations can actually co-exist, if not peaceably, then at least uneasily. What's important is that the debates are had, that theories are formulated and that women's bodies are understood in both visual and linguistic terms: the unseen c-word needs to be *seen* in affirmative, healthy ways.

Artist Hannah Wilke, who in 1975 sculpted disembodied vulvas out of chewing-gum and attached them to herself and to members of her audience, thought that Chicago's piece was 'denigrating to women' by reducing them to genital representations.[43] I don't agree: we're back to the *seen/unseen* idea again.

While we won't find out 'which' *The Dinner Party* is – feminist icon or essential-ist exemplar – we can certainly look thoughtfully at its context; at similar work by other artists; and at other *readings*. Jones's take is particularly insightful here. 'There are certainly strong arguments to be made in favour of rethinking certain prescriptive and historically myopic aspects of the theories [. . .] in the 1980s', she writes, but 'at the same time, attempting to recuperate 1970s femi-nist art by simply dismissing poststructuralist or postmodern feminism [. . .] is as limited as the justly criticized tendency among many poststructuralist femi-nists to dismiss body-oriented feminist work from the 1970s as unequivocally and naïvely essentialist'.[44] Jones certainly sees herself as anomalous, being both a poststructuralist *and* a supporter of Chicago's work (and of other 1970s femi-nist artists), since 'the most effective feminist art [. . .] is radical because it is emphatically both erotic *and* theoretical at the same time'.[45] The importance is not in setting out to discover some sort of 'truth' in Chicago's representations, but instead to allow a space for the simultaneity of, at times, contradictory nar-ratives. *The Dinner Party* is, after all, caught between poles, being seen 'as adu-lated icon of feminist utopianism or despised exemplar of essentialism'.[46] Is a woman more than her – albeit tangential, abstracted, symbolic – vagina?[47] Yes, of course, and in looking at *The Dinner Party* we're looking on what should not and *can't* be seen – the cunt and, crucially, at women's achievements since pre-history. Chicago's plates threaten western cultures where porn is widespread and more easily accessible than ever before, but which fear 'honest' representa-tions of women's bodies.[48] The achievement-focus-aspect of *The Dinner Party* when taken as a whole and not just, in a reductionist sense, as a *hole* (i.e. a series of vulvas illustrated on the plates), is a facet of the work which artist Maureen Mullarkey wilfully overlooked, displaying instead an astonishing arrogance and condescension in her criticism. 'The women who file worship-fully past this cunnilingus-as-communion table', wrote Mullarkey, 'see nothing askew in Chicago's decision to represent the stature and variety of women's accomplishments by genitals only'.[49]

The activist-artist Harmony Hammond's (b. 1944) take on central-core imagery in the early 1970s was largely abstracted, and displayed experimen-tation with forms and textures, as in her 'Floor Pieces' (1973), which were labyrinthine paintings on fabric which had been made into circular rugs.

Hammond's vulvar 'Empress' (1979) was a ring doughnut-shaped sculpture, coloured in lustrous pinky-golds, topped with two small black protuberances which look like After Eight mint wrappers concertinaed into tiny wings. The central shape looks as though it's wound in bandages – suggestive, perhaps, of the idea of excision – and the sense of the fabric quality of the piece is strong. It's a larger-than-life piece, too, standing 23.5" tall, and 19"across. There's something at once familiar and repellent about its decontextualized, sinewy presence. Hammond has written about another artist, Julia Kunin, some of whose work, like Chicago's *Dinner Party*, is on display at the Elizabeth Sackler Center for Feminist Art in Brooklyn. Kunin's sculpture 'Crimson Blossom' (1999) from one perspective has the same labial/butterfly qualities as Chicago's *Dinner Party* plates. The floral name of the piece adds to its ambiguities and it's also reminiscent of Robert Mapplethorpe's erotic floral close-ups. Similarly, Kunin's 'Red Suede Saddles' (1993) appear petal-like and *touching*, in an Irigaraian sense (see Figure 4.1).

'Woman "touches herself" all the time', writes Luce Irigaray, 'and moreover no one can forbid her to do so, for her genitals are formed of two lips in continuous contact. Thus, within herself, she is already two – but not divisible into one(s) – that caress each other.'[50] Kunin's petal-saddles exceed interpretive confines. They promise mobility, pivoting on their wires; they are in the process of definition, never resting, interpretively, for the viewer. Kunin sees the piece as 'an expression of visual pleasure', and as a sign of 'bodacious, bawdy lesbian visibility, infused with humor and sensuality. It urges women to ride, and to take the reins'.[51] Her three 'Keyhole Instruments' (1993) also seem erotic and somehow bodily but, like the saddles, they are inanimate objects in an endless state of becoming. This idea of redefinition through context is key to Kunin's aesthetic. In her 'Egg Board' of 1990, she plays with the idea of mundane domesticity transfigured through female sexuality: a wooden chopping board has a circular cut-out middle through which seven breast-like objects protrude. The piece certainly owes a visual debt to some of Chicago's egg/breast motifs from *The Dinner Party*. British artist Sarah Lucas's (b. 1962) photographic self-portrait 'Chicken Knickers' (1997) also plays with ideas of food and female sexuality.[52] An uncooked chicken, pinned to the large white knickers worn by the artist, has shaken itself free of its ontological character and has, through context, become a surreal commentary on women, sexuality and food. It's a powerfully connotative visual image; the positioning of the chicken renders it not a denotative 'chicken', but connotes a suggestively intimate and (for the viewer) unsettling image of nakedness, vulnerability, almost pornography. But it's covert visibility at work again; not linguistically, but visually. We conjure up a full frontal without being shown *anything* of a woman's genitals. It's a brilliant, droll piece of art. The shocking incongruity of images also features in the work of the Austrian artist Elke Krystufek, whose paintings 'Vaginanose (Max Raphael revisited)' and 'Size does not matter, age does matter' (both 2006) place a vulva where facial features should be: a mouth, forehead or nose are all transfigured in Krystufek's work, becoming vulvas, spread open by two or three fingers, 'as an invitation or an indecent gesture'.[53]

Chicago herself describes how, in the early 1970s, she was drawn to the butterfly form because of its image of liberation (and, presumably, vulnerability and beauty) and how this became merged 'with a vulval or vaginal form [. . .] I wanted to universalize from this form, transforming the physically defining characteristic of women into an aesthetic and metaphysical exploration of what it has meant to be a woman'.[54] Before *The Dinner Party*, Chicago had experimented with the radiating butterfly/labial form in other works such as her 'Great Ladies' series (1972–73) and her 30 Porcelain Miniatures of 1974 where 'the Butterfly Vagina [. . .] gets to be an active vaginal form'.[55] For me this is the pivotal moment in Chicago's rationale for her project: the idea that sexual/physiological uniqueness becomes aestheticized and *meta*physical. It's about making the c-word *seen*; it's an insistent, maybe even confrontational, quality which came to characterize her work. In her 1975 *Compressed Women Who Yearned to be Butterflies*, Chicago herself enters the frame for a photograph, standing against her painting, arms and legs stretched out like Vitruvian (wo)man. The 1973 series by Chicago, *Transformation Painting – Great Ladies Transforming Themselves into Butterflies* has a similar motif, as each square is transformed into a circle which, in turn becomes (or, as the title suggests, is subjectively and deliberately *created as*) a butterfly/vulvar shape. It's a challenge to the dominant phallocentric aesthetic of western culture, and Chicago writes that: 'one reason why I used a vaginal or vulval form in *The Dinner Party* was to counter the prevalence of images embodying phallic power'.[56] A journal entry from the 8th March 1971 shows Chicago's pioneering spirit, which, as we shall see, she also identifies in the women represented at *The Dinner Party* – they're not just *other* women, they're each Judy Chicago, too: 'I want to [document] the growth of the first Feminist art ever attempted.'[57] Such comments, while perhaps justifiable, go some way to explaining why the ambitious *Dinner Party* installation remains so contentious. 'As I have often quipped', Chicago writes, and it's this kind of quip that for decades was to land her in trouble with the conservative, Christian 'art establishment' – and, less predictably, perhaps, with many feminists, too – 'my intention was to do a reinterpretation of the Last Supper from the point of view' of its cooks.[58]

The Dinner Party

Amelia Jones's 1996 Hammer/UCLA exhibition catalogue not only collects together essays about Chicago, but it also situates *The Dinner Party* in a feminist art *tradition*. Jones is not afraid of hyperbolizing the installation, claiming that 'the issues it raises are central to an understanding of the politics of modernist, postmodernist, and feminist art theory and art history.'[59] That's an awful lot of -isms. There are many reasons why it's a dinner party setting, as I've already suggested, witticisms about the Last Supper aside, and Chicago herself has said that she used plates to 'convey the fact that the women I planned to represent had been swallowed up' by history.[60] There's also something misleadingly 'safe' about the idea of a dinner party: it's domestic, feminized, even slightly dated. Chicago subverts such 'safety'. The work is peppered with revelatory moments which draw the viewer up short, forcing him or her to confront their preconceptions about women through history. For example, we 'meet' Alpis de Cudot, the astronomer who, some three centuries *before* Copernicus, posited a heliocentric universe. Such achievements are only seen or spoken of because of the challenging, extraordinary nature of the vast installation as a whole.

A large triangle (itself a traditionally feminine form, recently adopted in Eve Ensler's 'V-days') is formed by three 48' long tables. At each of the three points of the triangle is an altar cloth. The installation is a mixed-media work in which crafts traditionally associated with women (textiles, ceramics) have been used, revived from (in some cases) obscurity and re-presented as fine art. The open-centred table is covered in pristine white fabric and on each of the 3 sides there are 13 place settings each comprising a runner, plate, simple cutlery, napkin and goblet. Altogether, 1,038 women are represented in one form or another; 39 of them each have a place setting, from each of which stream women's names, fired into 2,304 handmade porcelain tiles on the 'Heritage Floor'. Each tile has been fired three times to give it a lustre (the entire work is to be seen under controlled lighting and is arrived at via a corridor of tapestry entry banners). Each of those 39 plates is 14" in diameter and although many of the designs are flat, three-dimensionality and a deliberate resistance to geometric conformity start to creep in as the chronological arrangement progresses from the first plate to the last. This gradual evolution of the forms into three-dimensionality expresses 'women's intensifying struggle for equality': each plate, a vulvar motif at its centre, represents a woman's yearning for autonomy and recognition away from patriarchy's eradications and constraints.[61] Every plate sits on its own unique runner which drapes 13" over the front and 13" over the back of the table. This use of 13 recalls the number of attendees at the Last Supper, and is also associated with the 'number of participants at a witch's [*sic.*] coven'.[62] Because of the 'open' design of the entire set-up, from almost any angle one can see an entire 'wing' (one of the sides of the triangle), and the runner backs of at least one of the other two wings. On the runner fronts is embroidered each woman's name in gold; the first letter is heavily and idiosyncratically ornamented, reminiscent of illuminated manuscripts. *The Dinner Party* is a quite remarkable feat of research, collaboration and patience in what – we must remember – was the pre-Google era. From a collection of around 3,000 biographies of women from prehistory to the late twentieth century, Chicago selected the 999 whose names feature on the Heritage Floor.

This monumental exhibit was first shown in the spring of 1979 at the San Francisco Museum of Modern Art. On the exhibition's opening night, 5,000 people turned up. Thereafter, people were prepared to queue for sometimes 5 hours even after the exhibit had been open for some months. Over the next 17 years it was viewed by over a million visitors around the world. In her list of acknowledgements in her book *The Dinner Party: from Creation to Preservation*, Chicago describes the work's journey to its permanent home as a 'long adventure'.[63] And what an adventure it has been. The exhibit was anticipated, as I've already said, in Chicago's works dating from the late 1960s and early 1970s (the *Great Ladies* series and *Female Rejection Drawing* in the *Rejection Quintet* (1974); and *Pasadena Lifesavers* (1969–70)). These works, with their central-core imagery, peeling away petal-like layers, and, some-times, handwritten commentaries, are the ancestors of the *Dinner Party*. Such precursors do not *objectify* the female forms depicted, but vividly offer them as *subjects*. Chicago still tries to understand why – out of a career which spans almost 50 years, and major exhibitions worldwide – it is this one work, this heavily symbolic representation of women's history, which has come to define her so overwhelmingly. Chicago writes about the tremendous sense of isola-tion she felt trying to make it as a female 'Artist' in the United States in the 1960s, becoming a kind of unofficial archivist of women's historical achieve-ments. Finding no readily available, *visible* history for women, Chicago went about creating/reviving/archiving one and her excitement at being at the heart of such an enterprise is almost evangelical; she repeatedly depicts herself as a feminist prophet. *The Dinner Party* makes the viewer consider that which is traditionally hidden from view; not only the vagina, but also an entire canon of women's achievements and their domestic 'crafts' (china painting, for example), unlike men's 'arts'.[64] To borrow a slightly irritating phrase from twenty-first-century corporate-speak, Chicago brings women's bodies, his-tories and, as a result, *identities*, to the table. What becomes confrontational about *The Dinner Party* is not only the repeatedly unexpected vaginal, labial and vulvar imagery, but also what it facilitates, which is a rehabilitative history of women's achievements since prehistory.

Each of the women featured in *The Dinner Party* – many of whom had been 'lost' in history – is presented, not least because of the Heritage Floor, as part of a continuum or network that reaches through time and across dis-ciplines. Similarly, the work itself has recently been situated in the broader context of feminist art history by, for example, Amelia Jones. But what I'm try-ing to do is to move away from the sense that the installation's highly contro-versial arrival on the art scene has hindered it being properly or productively talked about. Looking at some of the plates – making the unseen-seen – might be challenging, but that's the point. These are not the compliant, objectified, inanimate, characterless vaginas that acquiesce to the pornographer's gaze. The scrutiny which Chicago invites us to undertake is markedly different: passivity, objectification and subjugation are forcefully rejected so that women's achievements can be prioritized and celebrated.

Critical responses and the unseen scene

The Dinner Party, because of its open, unapologetic aesthetic and abstracted portrayal of the cunt, attracted venomous vilification (as, of course, had so many of the tables' historical 'guests' in their lifetimes). The late art critic Hilton Kramer's view was that *The Dinner Party* displayed 'an insistence and vulgarity more appropriate [. . .] to an advertising campaign than to a work of art'.[65] Kramer was from that modernist school of thought whose authority was threatened by the work of women artists such as Chicago in the 1960s and 1970s who, the modernists argued, elevated 'kitsch' to the status of 'art'.[66] Indeed, Kramer really went to town on Chicago's piece. In the *New York Times* he described *The Dinner Party* as 'crass and solemn and singleminded', asking who 'would dare to vulgarize and exploit the imagery of female sexuality on this scale and with such abysmal taste?'[67] Kramer claimed that: 'Nothing more obvious or accessible or didactic has been seen in an exhibition of contemporary art in a very long time', since '[t]aste is not Judy Chicago's forte'.[68] He then displays more of his conservatism by having recourse to an enduring question, and despairing at the shock of the new which marks, in Kramer's mind at least, the decline of civilization as we know it. 'Is "The Dinner Party" art?' he asks, continuing: 'Well, I suppose so. After all, what isn't nowadays? But it is very bad art, it is failed art, it is art so mired in the pieties of a political cause that it quite fails to acquire any independent artistic life of its own. To this male observer, it looks like an outrageous libel on the female imagination.'[69] Kay Larson, writing in *Village Voice*, described the exhibition's visitors as participating in 'a ritual of oral consumption, a communion of the spirit in the flesh, a cultural cannibalism in which we're invited to eat from the labia of mythical women and ingest their power'.[70] Such criticisms strongly evoke Eucharistic imagery, a tendency which Amelia Jones cleverly deconstructs, arguing that, in 'dismissing [*The Dinner Party*'s] appeal by linking it to the blind devotion inspired by religious zealots, [. . . critics] downplay questions of their own elitism' – and, perhaps, of their own creative jealousy and artistic frustration.[71]

Negative reviews – based not only on the installation's 'explicitness' but also on its popularity and perceived 'kitsch' (and, therefore, antimodernist) qualities – led to museums cancelling the exhibit despite its evident popularity, forcing it to go into storage. 'What was I to make' queried Chicago, 'of the stark contrast between the outpouring of gratitude and appreciation from so many viewers and the near-total rejection by the art establishment?'[72] She writes that years later she 'would joke that *The Dinner Party* became the piece that everyone wanted to see but no museum wanted to show', and that she didn't 'know of too many artists whose audience insists that seeing their work changed their lives'.[73] This is the empowered, pulsating, producing cunt; like the parturient body, it's one which can terrify people. It 'shouldn't' be seen. Chicago invites us to look, and in that act of looking, of seeing the *see*-word, we also view an entire history which is *kept* unseen because of the perceived shame of the unseen body. If we reveal one (the cunt) to plain sight, then we reveal the other (women's power), too. As Parker and Pollock express it, '[i]n European art the signal omission from the depiction of the female nude is exactly the sign of her femaleness, her difference. Female genitals are almost never exposed'.[74] Kubitza, however, is sceptical that Chicago is a visionary artist: 'the success of Chicago's vulvar imagery with a large female audience seems due in part to the fact that it *can* be faced; Chicago's vulvas are abstract and, perhaps most importantly, they are "clean"'.[75] Kubitza's on to something, of course: *The Dinner Party*'s vulvar plates *are* 'clean' and beautiful in their abstraction. But when we think about the exhibit as the heir of, for example, *Red Flag*, we are forced to reconsider 'cleanliness' as used by Kubitza. I do take issue with Susan Kandel's claim that it's 'the pornographic regime' which is 'sited in the fold between the visible and the invisible'.[76] That's *not* the 'pornographic' regime, for that regime is ubiquitous and obvious; that (internet/online) regime is *very much* seen these days. It's Chicago's vulvar plates that occupy precisely the liminal *seen/not-seen* place because of their abstract qualities. They do not represent the eroticized body, but nor are they pathologized; they are an attempt at finding something *between* extremes.[77] They are lips which, through their multi-layered, pains-taking context, imagery and purposes, speak. They are more than museum pieces: they are feminist apparitions, each one insistently articulating women's experiences.[78]

In important ways, *The Dinner Party* was – and continues to be – strongly emblematic of Chicago's own issues with success, identification and accept-ance – as a 'Female Artist'. I'd say Chicago sees herself most powerfully in the place-setting of the medieval proto-feminist Christine de Pisan. Chicago's work is a modern take on de Pisan's famous *Book of the City of Ladies* (1405), in which historical women find solidarity. Chicago might just as well be talk-ing about herself in writing of de Pisan that she: 'maintained that writing that degraded women exerted an evil influence on people's minds, and offered her own books, which chronicle the contributions of hundreds of women, both as an alternative and as a tribute to the women of her times'.[79]

The Dinner Party: A wing and a prayer (to the goddess)

The first of the installation's three 'wings' marks the achievements of women from prehistory to Rome; the first seven plates evoke the goddess figure and her centrality in gynocentric (women-centred) prehistoric cultures, to suggest to viewers the possibility of a return to such social structures. Significantly, in terms of women's power, it was also a world in which humanity did not under-stand the scientific mechanics of procreation, to the point where women were believed to have powers of parthenogenesis (a process defined by the *OED* as 'Reproduction from a gamete without fertilization', and one which I've already suggested Lady Gaga imitates). Pre-linguistically, the Primordial Goddess was represented by holes or spirals carved into rocks, connoting the vulva (the front runner of her place-setting in Chicago's work has a spiral around the letter 'P'). Her plate symbolizes a powerful, feminized creation myth and what *The Dinner Party* is doing here is what it continues to do as the viewer walks around it: revivify a sense of *connectedness* to shadowy antecedents, suggesting sweeping, invisible, yet binding, connective threads. The Primordial Goddess's plate's inchoate butterfly form has a dark centre, signifying, in Chicago's own words, the 'primal vagina and the sacred vessel'.[80] Kubitza argues compellingly for the work's subversive qualities: 'these women are offered as role models precisely because they had transcended a traditional female role; their potential had not been exhausted in fulfilling reproductive functions'.[81] The Goddess's runner has a dead animal's pelt on it (suggesting how very fine the line is between life and death), and cowry shells are stitched onto it, their angry little spiny teeth conjuring up stories of the *vagina dentata*. As the very first plate in the sequence of 39, it's flat – resting, calm, not needing to resist or rise up. The illusion of a tremendous depth is created at its centre, drawing the viewer in to a dark, maroon pool, inviting a return to the primitive or, indeed, primordial, realm. The amniotic 'pool' at the plate's centre and the animal skin on which it sits, are brought together to suggest a uniquely female perspective on the paradox of life-giving and life-taking. The plate is – obviously – inanimate, but it does represent fecundity and the *possibility* of movement; the animal skin, by contrast, was once part of an animate creature, and is now rendered inanimate. In challenging these boundaries of stasis and action – even of Eros and Thanatos – Chicago is suggesting something really potent about women's bodies and, from some angles, even gives the impression that we're looking *into* the wounded body of the dead animal whose skin we see, dissected. On the Heritage Floor, names written in gold of other goddesses involved in specific cultural creation myths stream from the Primordial Goddess's place setting.

Lustre and tonal qualities make Chicago's plates look three-dimensional and active: they're not passive objects solely for our contemplation, but seem to have an energy and motion. This shift from passivity to subjectivity had been in evidence, as I've already argued, ever since Chicago's 1974 *Female Rejection Drawing*, in which there was 'imagery that visualized the "orgiastic throbbing [and . . .] highly focused feeling of clitoral sensation" that signalled women as desiring subjects rather than mere objects of desire'.[82] Fecundity is emphasized by the egg-like shapes in the design of the Fertile Goddess's plate. Whether they're babies' crowning heads, or breasts or eggs, they're incontrovertibly feminized, and organic in their form. One moment they look as though they're formed from human tissue, and the next, they appear plant-like. Folds of flesh are persuasively suggested through shading on the plate. This organicism and sense of evolution has a momentum from the Fertile Goddess's setting to the next, that of the Mesopotamian fertility goddess Ishtar. There's a similar core motif on this plate, for example, of 'eggs' (or are they breasts?) bursting out again but this time in browns and golds, and the central ovoid (or is it vulvar?) section appears to be containing them. The illuminated capital 'I' of the Ishtar runner front looks toothed, evoking once more the apparently inescapable and culturally and diachronically ubiquitous, image of the *vagina dentata*, an image also evoked by the shell-like central section of the Hindu goddess Kali's plate, as Chicago moves even more decisively into the homological lips/labia territory. Kali herself is 'harmful [. . .] guarding the doorway to death [. . .] a so-called *devouring* female energy'.[83] The artist argues that she took the deci-sion to represent a non-western woman in this study of women in western civilization because the demonization of Kali shows how a powerful female figure can be turned into a figure to be feared. Actually, some of Chicago's imagery on the place-settings does derive from non-western traditions, but most of it is western – even Eurocentric – in form. 'Gradually' writes Chicago, 'and particularly in India, the "death" aspect of the Mother Goddess ceased to be part of a unified and venerated concept, and became instead a separate and terrifying entity. It is this change that the Kali place setting symbolizes'.[84]

It would be an injustice to Chicago to suggest that any one place setting resembled any other, such is the level of meticulous detail in each. The similari-ties that there *are*, though, suggest a natural progression from one to the next, both echoing and producing the matrilineal continuity for which Chicago yearns. Similarly, the Heritage Floor names that *reach* or stream out from each place-setting suggest something potent about the interconnectedness of past, present and future. The plate on the place-setting of the *hetaera* ('courtesan') philosopher Aspasia has a foliate design, but is, according to Chicago, a 'ruffled butterfly' in muted earth colours.[85] This idea of muteness is quite deliberate: Aspasia was put on trial by the Athenian courts for her intrepid eloquence. In depicting *muted* tones, Chicago is expressing something compelling about how, in confronting one set of lips in the plate's labial design, other lips – at last – have a chance to 'speak' to us. *The Dinner Party*'s narrative is about move-ment: it's a static spectacle telling a narrative of 'progress' of a glacial pace. The work's development from one plate to the next emblematizes female resistance, visually rendered in increasingly anxious ways as the viewer moves around the table. The resistance is articulated triply: in the individual narrative of each place-setting; in the Heritage Floor tributaries which emanate from it; and in how one setting relates to the next. The movement propels us towards an autonomized ideal; an empowerment of women, and as such it's not a smooth arc of progression, but a painful labour of coming into being.

The Dinner Party: The second course

The second of the three tables which constitute the triangular structure of *The Dinner Party* runs chronologically up to the Reformation. Chicago argues that here 'the images [become] more active and three-dimensional, visually symbolizing women's struggle to transcend the confines of their historical circumstances'.[86] The German tenth-century poet and playwright Hrosvitha (often known as Hrotsvit) seems to have the image on her plate of the maternal vulva with hands clasped as though to support a belly, but equally in a prayer pose, or possibly in a posture of humility. The runner of Trotula is the most ornate the viewer has encountered so far, if they are walking chronologically around the tables: she's a figure whose precise origins remain obscure, but she was probably an eleventh-century Italian gynaecologist, obstetrician and author of *De Passionibus Mulierum* ('On the suffering of women'). On her runner is a tree of life *trapunto* (padded quilting) design that again evokes a gynaecological theme, or emphasizes how *The Dinner Party* functions as a genealogical matrix onto which women's lives might be mapped.[87] Trotula's plate has something of the spirit of Kilpeck's aesthetic and cultural eclecticism to it: its images are neither exclusively southern Italian nor Byzantine, but mix elements such as a serpent, with Pre-Columbian motifs. This geographical and historical mélange of images suggests something powerful about the cultural ubiquity of female sexual imagery, be that empowering or designed to intimidate. And so we're back in the world of Kilpeck's *Sheela*, and in the tradition of the *vagina dentata* myth. Hildegarde of Bingen, the mystic, was, according to Chicago, 'one of the first people to describe female orgasm accurately', and on the back of her runner is a meticulously embroidered version of her vision of the universe

which is oddly reminiscent of a horizontal rendering of the traditionally vertical Our Lady of Guadalupe.[88] This 'universe' is unmistakably vulvar in shape.
The Dinner Party is not only a *record* of these women, then: it is a *perpetuation*
of a feminocentric tradition which is robustly and defiantly overt in the plates'
vulvar designs.

The Dinner Party: Last to be seated

The third and final wing of *The Dinner Party* documents women's successes
from the American Revolution to the Women's Revolution, an explicit nod to
the idea of the 'battles' inherent in the reclamation of women's history. That's
a history which, as Chicago has made clear since the powerful Goddess plates
of the installation's First Wing, has not been one of smooth socio-economic
progress. An unblinking eye is at the centre of astronomer Caroline Herschel's
plate, where a ceramic butterfly/labial 'wing' seems to be lifting itself upwards,
as if promising to peel away to reveal a mystery imprinted on the white plate
glimpsed beneath.[89] The irregular plate edges (it is not a perfect circle) also
'suggest the lessening of the limits against women in science'.[90] This takes the
narrative in a different direction – as the 'wing' depicted on the plate – just one,
note, not all of the depicted four – pulls away from its surface. The emphasis is
on how the labial-butterfly figure is not yet ready to fly. Progress, a movement
to equality, is a possibility, but it is a slow and painful process, as gradual as
pupal development. The message is clear: women are destined to reinvent the
artistic/intellectual wheel if they don't know what – or who – has come before.
To paraphrase George Santayana, those women who do not know of their past
are doomed to repeat it.

In 1920, the Nineteenth Amendment in the United States gave women
the vote, and was posthumously named after Susan B. Anthony. The plate of
the nineteenth-century American feminist activist has all four 'wings' curling upwards, radiating from a deep, vulvar, burgundy and highly-glazed centre that looks like pooled blood (see Figure 4.2). 'The jarring red coloration
[is] intended to express the anger and determination' of the work Anthony
(1820–1906) did with Elizabeth Cady Stanton (1815–1902).[91] It's the most

dynamic plate so far: fleshly, conch-like flaps lift, and curl up, acanthus-like. It's an immensely tactile plate, with its undulations of smooth, deep ridges. More names on the Heritage Floor emanate from Anthony's place-setting than from others because it is 'meant to remind viewers (particularly young women) of the enormous effort required to achieve the reforms that present generations of women take for granted'.[92] One suspects, not for the first time, that Chicago is projecting her *own* ideas/aspirations here through these historical paradigms, enacting something important, perhaps autobiographical, about heredity, influence, role models and continuity. The Anthony runner is unusual, too, in that it has a large red triangle, emanating from which is a series of names of other women's rights champions. It is as though Anthony, whose runner is emblazoned with the words 'INDEPENDENCE IS ACHIEVED BY UNITY', has a Heritage Floor stream of names not only in fact, but also on her runner. Anthony's place-setting is in marked contrast to that of Emily Dickinson whose setting's colours are pale and dainty with petite, floral stitching and ribbon work. The pale pink-coloured plate has a vulvar core where soft pink folds gently expand outwards and become lacy ruffles (they conjure up tennis-players' knickers from the 1970s or, worse, split-crotch panties. Or perhaps underwear worn at the Moulin Rouge – these are all fairly inappropriate associations to make with Dickinson). The four wings look like two, with a vertical split (the horizontal one is there, too, but is less pronounced), which reinforces the underwear idea. It's hard to read this as an enabling image. If we are gazing on an unseen-seen cunt, it's one which is not so much liberated as clichéd; a frou–frou of frilly lace. This 'lace' is, of course, 'immobile' and 'pale yet strong', presumably more because of its texture than its visual appearance.[93] Chicago sees the lace as a prison for Dickinson, 'a witty and ironic way to present this brave poet', but the irony cannot entirely rescue the plate from its clichéd, eroticized set-up.[94]

Like Anthony's plate, that of Margaret Sanger (1879–1966) seems violently three-dimensional: the design, looking insect- or lobster-like, spills over the plate's limits. It looks like congealed blood, in a deep red shade of glaze. The bloody associations come from Sanger's name ('le sang' is French for 'blood') and the bloody insect/crustacean is a continuation of Chicago's butterfly theme: 'the sangaris', she explains, is 'a blood-red butterfly, which seemed a perfect metaphor for Sanger's work'.[95] The runner, too, has a distinctly vaginal theme, with its red scalloped edges. It's 'an embroidered rendition of a medical drawing of the female reproductive system, transformed into a celebration of the miracle of the female body'.[96] However, the 'miracle' is mitigated by the chain linking mother and child stitched into the 'M' on the runner (see Figure 4.3). The runner back depicts fallopian tubes and uterus and its red tucks and folds and layers make it a part of the plate and vice versa: when we peer into its centre we are looking at the 'truth' of female reproduction. (This peering was anticipated by Chicago in her 1973 *Through the Flower* painting where our gaze is directed through orangey petals into a luminescent green centre, the experience of which one commentator has described as offering 'a vision from *within* the vagina onto a celestial field of light'.[97]) This harmony of plate and runner evokes Sanger's own claim that 'without the right to control their own bodies, all other rights are meaningless'.[98] Sanger's mother had been pregnant 18 times with 11 live births. This, coupled with Sanger's work as a nurse, convinced her that birth *control* was a major first step to liberation and equality for women. This idea of 'control' is powerful: while Chicago controls the images she displays in the installation, she cannot control her viewers' reactions to, or interpretations of, them, as is clear in the accounts I've given of her detractors.

More remarkable women lead off from Sanger's setting on the Heritage Floor – Golda Meir and Eleanor Roosevelt among them, and the other gynaecological trailblazer (and also, unhappily, advocate of eugenics), Marie Stopes, who met with Sanger in July 1915.[99] In Sanger's Fabian Hall speech in London on 5th July 1915, after which she met Stopes for the first time, Sanger spoke of how – and the language evokes Godwin's words on the dead Wollstonecraft (as we shall shortly see) – 'every where [*sic.*] women have shown tendencies to overthrow some of the old regulations of society & [*sic.*] throw off some of the [*fetters*] [*sic.*] which have held them down so long'.[100] One of the last plates of the entire sequence, that of Virginia Woolf, is three-dimensional, with a curling up – Sanger's 'throwing off' – of the design. Deep troughs and ridges cut across the plate's plane both horizontally and vertically; the vaginal centre is filled with what looks like the breast imagery of the First Wing, or like fruits waiting to burst out in ripeness. Interestingly Chicago's original study for the plate makes these curvilinear shapes look far more like leaves of a book, which in turn makes the central objects the stones that weighed down Woolf's coat pockets as she walked out into the River Ouse in Sussex, on the 28th March 1941, aged 59.[101] The 'bursting center' of the plate is a 'symbol of this writer's fecund genius and a reference back to the power embodied in the early goddess plates' of the installation's first wing.[102] This penultimate place-setting completes the striking continuity of Chicago's project, which challenges the proscriptive motions of linear phallic 'progress'. 'History as Judy Chicago writes it', argued Nancy Ring, 'is a jagged-edge circle where past and future meld into the present, disparate parts are unified, and a scattered, divided humanity is made whole'.[103] The triangular structure of the entire installation, rather than, like Donne's compasses, 'mak[ing] me end where I begun [*sic.*]', allows her to illustrate the three eras she's delineating in each of the three wings and to show how women's 'progress' still bears continuities with those first primordial images.[104]

Journey's end?

In her search for a permanent home for *The Dinner Party*, Chicago thought a suitable location had been found at the Carnegie Library (part of the University of the District of Columbia). However, as the late Henry Hopkins (director of the Armand Hammer Museum of Art and Cultural Centre at UCLA when it staged an exhibition centred on and precipitated by Congress's ludicrous, philistinic response to *The Dinner Party* in 1996), wrote, 'all hell broke loose'.[105] Chicago expressed her horror at the idea that 'the then-developing feminist theory was postulating that *The Dinner Party* degraded women by reducing them to "vaginas on plates"', and was infuriated by the issues raised by Congress when she attempted to donate the work to the University of the District of Columbia.[106] Writing in *The Los Angeles Times* in 1990, Richard Mahler reported that the Republican congressman Robert K. Dornan said that *The Dinner Party* 'is not art, it's pornography'; that Rep. Dana Rohrabacher 'denounced the piece as "weird sexual art"'; and that Rep. Stan Parris 'sponsored a measure that sought to *punish* the university by withholding $1.6 million from an appropriations bill'.[107] The House of Representatives – many of whose members involved in the debate had not actually seen the exhibition first hand – intervened, and congressmen labelled the work as pornographic and took to 'excoriating the imagery on the plates'.[108] I'm minded to agree with Laura Meyer's wry aside that 'it was *The Dinner Party*'s moralism, not its immorality, that so threatened the congressmen who declared it obscene [. . .] It has a didactic, preachy quality that can seem quite overbearing'.[109] It was a piece of artwork, then, which involved the US Congress, no less, before ending up in Brooklyn. While the search for a permanent exhibition space was underway, Chicago's next work, the 1993 *Holocaust Project*, was 'pilloried' and suffered 'public ridicule'.[110] The achievements of the women artists, philosophers, doctors, writers, teachers, musicians and activists which Chicago portrayed in *The Dinner Party* as misunderstood, repressed, ridiculed, even punishable, was not for the artist (nor for any of us, perhaps) a purely historical phenomenon. It was, and is, a living, breathing and dangerously powerful misogyny. Chicago's work *matters*. It provides a roadmap and a genealogy for women artists and social pioneers, taking women's experiences and validating them in unprecedented ways. Birth is one such 'experience', and it is to this that the next section of *The Vagina* turns.

Notes

1   Alice Thomas Ellis, *God has Not Changed* (London: Burns and Oates, Continuum, 2004), p. 52.

2   The stage play was adapted in 1977 for BBC TV and featured remarkable performances by Alison Steadman and Tim Stern. Abigail herself is the sulky teenage daughter of one of the guests, and she never actually appears on stage.

3   Caryl Churchill, *Top Girls* (London: Methuen Drama, 2005).

4   Chantal Cornut-Gentille D'Arcy, '"The Personal is Political" in Caryl Churchill's *Top Girls*: A Parable for the Feminist Movement in Thatcher's Britain', in Susanna Onega (ed.), *Telling Histories: Narrativizing History, Historicizing Literature*, Costerus New Series 96 (Amsterdam: Rodopi, 1995), pp. 103–15 (p. 106).

5   Griselda Pollock, *Differencing the Canon: Feminist Desire and the Writing of Art's Histories* (London: Routledge, 1999), p. 148.

6   Faith Wilding, 'How the West was Won: Feminist Art in California', *Women Artists [sic.] News*, 6.2&3 (Summer 1980), pp. 15–16 (p. 15).

7   Zoe Leonard, quoted in Laura Cottingham, 'Interview with Zoe Leonard', *Journal of Contemporary Art*, 6.1 (Summer 1993), pp. 64–77 (p. 73). Also: www.jca-online.com/leonard.html.

8　On how Leonard also 'made interventions in the common practices of museology', see Hilary Robinson, *Reading Art, Reading Irigaray: The Politics of Art by Women* (London: I.B. Tauris, 2006), p. 24. On the importance of context in Leonard's work, see Kerstin May, *Art and Obscenity* (London: I.B. Tauris, 2007), p. 123.

9　Leonard, quoted in Cottingham, 'Interview'.

10　Ibid.

11　Ibid.

12　Susan Kandel, 'Beneath the Green Veil: The Body in/of New Feminist Art', in Amelia Jones (ed.), *Sexual Politics: Judy Chicago's 'Dinner Party' in Feminist Art History* (Berkeley, CA: University of California Press, 1996), pp. 186–200 (p. 191). Kandel also acknowledges Leonard's obvious visual debt to Courbet and discusses the significance of the veil behind which Khalil Bey, the original owner of Courbet's painting, displayed it.

13　Kandel, 'Beneath the Green Veil', p. 198.

14　See Laura Meyer, 'From Finish Fetish to Feminism: Judy Chicago's *Dinner Party* in California Art History', in Jones (ed.), *Sexual Politics*, pp. 48–74 (p. 52). Meyer calls the *Acrylic Shapes* (1967) 'soft' and 'anthropomorphic', suggesting that they 'evoke the vulnerability of human flesh' (p. 53), quite contrary, of course, to the technologically hard-surfaced minimalism of Chicago's 'finish fetish' contemporaries' work.

15　See Barbara Binder Kadden and Bruce Kadden, *Teaching Mitzvot: Concepts, Values, and Activities* (Denver, CO: A.R.E. Publishing, 2003), p. 89. Chicago herself is, according to the back cover of her *Holocaust Project: From Darkness Into Light*, descended from 23 generations of rabbis. See Judy Chicago, with photography by Donald Woodman, *Holocaust Project: From Darkness Into Light* (New York, NY: Penguin, 1993). Jane Ussher has argued that Chicago's photograph subverts 'the function of art as containment of "woman" and her seeping boundaries'. See Jane M. Ussher, *Managing the Monstrous Feminine: Regulating the Reproductive Body* (London: Routledge, 2006), p. 165.

16　Chicago's *Acrylic Shapes*, part of the assertively masculinist 'finish fetish' school of LA (a model which was totally opposed to the collaborative, or more properly, 'cooperative', construction of *The Dinner Party*), now look to me like a collection of gynaecological specula. It's funny how an a posteriori reading can do that. On *The Dinner Party*'s paradoxical engagement with, and distance from, the concept of 'finish fetish', see Meyer, 'From Finish Fetish to Feminism', p. 66. On the key difference Chicago herself has identified between modes of *collaboration* and *cooperation* in the production of *The Dinner Party*, see Amelia Jones, 'The "Sexual Politics" of *The Dinner Party*: A Critical Context', in Jones (ed.), *Sexual Politics*, p. 106. As Jones argues, 'Feminists are clearly held to higher standards here [in terms of the cooperation/collaboration debate], the expectation being that they will achieve some kind of democratization of the creative process'. Jones, 'The "Sexual Politics" of *The Dinner Party*', p. 116, n. 103.

17　Meyer, 'From Finish Fetish to Feminism', p. 55.

18　See Meyer, 'From Finish Fetish to Feminism', on, for example, Womanhouse's *Dining Room*; on Frazier, Hodgetts and Weltsh's *Nurturant Kitchen*; on LeCocq and Youdelman's *Leah's Room*; and on Chicago's own *Cock and Cunt Play* (performed by Faith Wilding and Janice Lester), in Jones (ed.), *Sexual Politics*, pp. 58–60. Meyer does make the point that '*The Dinner Party* was not a collaboration in the same sense that Womanhouse was', p. 69.

19   Faith Wilding, in Laura Meyer with Faith Wilding, 'Collaboration and Conflict in the Fresno Feminist Art Program: An Experiment in Feminist Pedagogy', *n.paradoxa: International Feminist Art Journal*, 26 (July 2010), pp. 40–51 (p. 46).

20   Wilding, 'How the West was Won', p. 15.

21   Ibid.

22   Faith Wilding, private email correspondence with the author, 22 July 2011.

23   See www.cyberfeminism.net/.

24   See Ibid. This includes a DVD of *Vulva De/Re Constructa* and the 'Big Vulva' performances. I discuss the short film on labiaplasty (*Vulva De/Re Constructa*) in my conclusion to *The Vagina*.

25   Faith Wilding, 'Vulvas with a Difference', in Maria Fernandez, Faith Wilding and Michelle M. Wright, *Domain Errors! Cyberfeminist Practices* (New York, NY: Autonomedia, 2002. A subRosa project), pp. 149–60 (p. 151).

26   See www.cyberfeminism.net/projects.html.

27   See Ibid.

28   Tee Corinne, *Cunt Coloring Book* (San Francisco, CA: Last Gasp, 2005 [1988]).

29   Miriam Schapiro and Judy Chicago, 'Female Imagery', p. 11, as quoted in, and commented on by, Amelia Jones, 'The "Sexual Politics" of *The Dinner Party*', in Jones (ed.), *Sexual Politics*, pp. 96, p. 113, n. 55.

30   See Jones, 'The "Sexual Politics" of *The Dinner Party*', p. 112, n. 42.

31   Wilding, quoted in Jones, 'The "Sexual Politics" of *The Dinner Party*', p. 97.

32   Jones, for example, talks about Chicago's 'unified format', but this is to ignore the minutiae of differences between the place settings of *The Dinner Party*, a work which celebrates diversity as much as uniformity. See Jones, 'The "Sexual Politics" of *The Dinner Party*', p. 26. Lisa Tickner has, according to Meyer, seen in *The Dinner Party* a 'fixing' of the idea of 'femininity'. See Meyer, 'From Finish Fetish to Feminism', p. 72, n. 2.

33   On how 'feminist critical practice must resist [. . .] specularity', see Griselda Pollock, 'Screening the Seventies: Sexuality and Representation in Feminist Practice – A Brechtian Perspective', in *Vision and Difference: Femininity, Feminism and the Histories of Art* (New York, NY: Routledge, 1988), p. 181, as cited in Jones, 'The "Sexual Politics" of *The Dinner Party*', p. 90; p. 111, n. 32. As Pollock came to express it some years later, 'I must wonder about what I am looking for and what I see in or read into the work of artists who are "women" when the feminist project is caught in the paradox of deconstructing the category "women" in the name of "women" as feminism's object'. Pollock, *Differencing*, p. 103.

34   Pollock, *Differencing*, p. 102.

35   Anette Kubitza, 'Rereading the readings of *The Dinner Party* in Europe', in Jones (ed.), *Sexual Politics*, p. 158.

36   See Rozsika Parker and Griselda Pollock, *Old Mistresses: Women, Art and Ideology* (London: Routledge, 1981), p. 127.

37   On how these exhibitions effected 'a necessary demystification of female sexuality', see Kubitza, 'Rereading the readings', p. 160.

38 Jones, 'Introduction', in Jones (ed.), *Sexual Politics*, p. 25; Karen LeCocq, *Feather Cunt* (1971, remade 1996), mixed media. Original dimensions 12"w × 10"h × 12"d.

39 Jones, 'Introduction', p. 26.

40 Jones, 'The "Sexual Politics" of *The Dinner Party*', p. 114, n. 62. Jones points out that a humorous verse was printed under the *Everywoman* 2 (7 May 1971) 'centrefold' of this group.

41 On Barrett's stance, see Kubitza, 'Rereading the readings', p. 160. On Barbara Rose's 1974 coining of the term 'vaginal iconology' see Kubitza, 'Rereading the readings', p. 160. See also Barbara Rose, 'Vaginal Iconology', *New York Magazine*, 11 February 1974, p. 59.

42 Pollock, *Differencing*, p. 99.

43 Quoted in Jones, 'Introduction', p. 38, n. 9; Hannah Wilke, *S.O.S. Starification Object Series*, 1974–82; 10 b & w silver gelatin prints and 15 chewing-gum sculptures mounted on board (Collection of the Museum of Modern Art, New York). On how Wilke used 'tiny labia, made from lips' in her art, see Jane Blocker, *What the Body Cost: Desire, History, and Performance* (Minneapolis, MN: University of Minnesota Press, 2004), p. 40.

44 Amelia Jones, 'Power and Feminist (Art) History' (Review Article), *Art History* 18.3 (September 1995): 435–43 (p. 437). The book she's reviewing is: Norma Broude and Mary D. Garrard (eds), *The Power of Feminist Art: Emergence, Impact and Triumph of the American Feminist Art Movement* (London: Thames and Hudson, 1994).

45 Jones, 'Power and Feminist (Art) History', p. 438.

46 Jones, 'Introduction', p. 24.

47 Karen Finley and Bruce Pollack's *Cocktail Party* was an early and crude attempt to critique the 'essentialism' of Chicago's work. As Jones writes, 'a group of invited participants carrying "prick plates" (one plate, e.g., featured a creative rendering of Abraham Lincoln's penis) [. . .] offered a humorous if also acerbic comment on the latter work's historical and symbolic pretensions'. See Jones, 'The "Sexual Politics" of *The Dinner Party*', pp. 86–7. Another satirical take was Maria Manhattan's (Maria Scatuccio) *Box Lunch*. See Kubitza, 'Rereading the readings', p. 154. On Manhattan see Steven Hagar, 'The Box Lunch' in *Horizon* 24 (March 1981) and Judith L. Dunham, '"Dinner Party" Aftertaste' in *Artweek* 10 (25 August 1979), both cited in Kubitza, 'Rereading the readings', p. 174, n. 19. Kubitza offers insight into how European artists responded to Chicago's work in their own.

48 As Jones argues, the female body as 'obscene' challenges 'high art's' status. For Amelia Jones's essay on the 'obscene' female body, 'Interpreting Feminist Bodies: the Unframeability of Desire', see Paul Duro (ed.), *The Rhetoric of the Frame* (Cambridge: Cambridge University Press, 1997), pp. 223–41.

49 Maureen Mullarkey, 'Dishing It Out', p. 211, as cited in Amelia Jones, 'The "Sexual Politics" of *The Dinner Party*', p. 90; p. 111, n. 30.

50 Luce Irigaray, *This Sex Which is Not One*, trans. Catherine Porter (New York, NY: Cornell University Press, 1985), p. 24.

51 Julia Kunin, private email correspondence with the author, 30 October 2012.

52 Sarah Lucas, 'Chicken Knickers', 1997. Photograph on paper, 426 mm × 426 mm, Tate Britain.

53　On Krystufek's work see, for example, Sally O'Reilly, *The Body in Contemporary Art* (London: Thames and Hudson, 2009), p. 84.

54　Judy Chicago, *The Dinner Party: From Creation to Preservation* (London: Merrell, 2007), p. 12.

55　Jones, 'The "Sexual Politics" of *The Dinner Party*', p. 104. Chicago, quoted in Meyer, 'From Finish Fetish to Feminism', pp. 63, 66.

56　Chicago, *Creation to Preservation*, p. 274. The butterfly/labial visual similarity was controversially exploited by the British painter Chris Ofili whose massive *Holy Virgin Mary* canvas was called 'sick' by then-Mayor Rudolph Giuliani, when it was exhibited in New York in 1999. The image shows a black Madonna, and elephant dung was incorporated into the painting's texture. But it was the small 'butterflies' flitting around the Immaculate Virgin that really upset visitors to the Brooklyn Museum: on closer inspection these 'butterflies' were actually collage images of buttocks and vulvas taken from pornographic magazines. For a brief account of the controversy, see Gareth Harris, 'Chris Ofili's The Holy Virgin Mary returns to London', *The Telegraph* (28 January 2010). www.telegraph.co.uk/culture/art/art-news/7093216/Chris-Ofilis-The-Holy-Virgin-Mary-returns-to-London.html.

57　Ibid., p. 10.

58　Ibid., pp. 11–12. In 2001, Rosalind Miles's book *Women's History of the World* was reprinted with the title *Who Cooked the Last Supper?* See Rosalind Miles, *Who Cooked the Last Supper?* (New York, NY: Three Rivers Press, 2001).

59　Jones, 'The "Sexual Politics" of *The Dinner Party*', p. 85.

60　Chicago, quoted in Jones, 'The "Sexual Politics" of *The Dinner Party*', p. 113, n. 53; my emphasis.

61　Chicago, *Creation to Preservation*, p. 15. Three of the plates do not have explicitly vulvar imagery. The Sojourner Truth plate features three faces, the right-hand one of which shows the bared teeth of rage and, which might, at a push, be a representation of the *vagina dentata*. Ethel Smyth's 'piano' plate and Natalie Barney's 'starfish' plate are also exceptions to the dominant vulvar theme of the installation. The original study for Barney's plate shows a deep fissure or slit running across the centre of the image on the plate which is not as visible in the finished item. I take issue with Amelia Jones's statement that 'Those of us who have benefited from being white – like Chicago, like myself – don't tend to see race as an aspect of our femininity'(Jones, 'The "Sexual Politics" of *The Dinner Party*', p. 101). Far from being irrelevant, race, rather, reinforces the hegemonic codes which make covert visibility a reality in women's lives; it is not the truth that Truth's plate somehow denies black women's sexuality; instead it problematizes and redefines all women's identities. Yes, the Truth plate feels incongruous in terms of its placement between two far more graphically vulvar settings (Mary Wollstonecraft's and Susan B. Anthony's), but incongruity can often jar us into asking more questions and into making new connections, and into seeing the covert within the overt.

62　Jones, 'The "Sexual Politics" of *The Dinner Party*', p. 117, n. 124.

63　Chicago, *Creation to Preservation*, Acknowledgements. This book is, fundamentally, a more detailed account of the information the 'Heritage Panels' (also, incidentally, reproduced in the book) provide as part of the installation: they offer a contextual, biographical, historical guide to the 999 women whose names are glazed into the tiles of the Heritage Floor.

64 On the gendered nature of the art/craft binary see Meyer, 'From Finish Fetish to Feminism', p. 61. In her contribution to the same book, Kubitza makes the somewhat disappointingly patronizing observation (with little quantitative or qualitative substantiation) that when *The Dinner Party* was displayed in 'Britain, as in the United States and Canada, the visitors to the show were mostly women interested in the needlework and china-painting techniques or in the piece's feminist message; they were not, by and large, familiar with art world politics and art historical issues'. See Kubitza, 'Rereading the readings', p. 155.

65 Hilton Kramer, 'Judy Chicago's "Dinner Party" Comes to Brooklyn Museum', *The New York Times*, 17 October 1980, as cited in Jones, 'The "Sexual Politics" of *The Dinner Party*', pp. 84–118 (p. 84 and p. 110, n. 3).

66 For more on how 'kitsch' threatened Kramer's modernist – and phallic – tendencies see Jones, 'The "Sexual Politics" of *The Dinner Party*', pp. 88, 92.

67 Hilton Kramer, 'Judy Chicago's "Dinner Party" comes to Brooklyn Museum', *New York Times*, 17 October 1980, Late City Final Edition. Available at: http://grammarpolice. net.archives/001194.php.

68 Kramer, 'Judy Chicago's "Dinner Party"'.

69 Ibid.

70 Kay Larson's 1979 *Village Voice* review, quoted by Jones in 'The "Sexual Politics" of *The Dinner Party*', p. 102.

71 Jones, 'The "Sexual Politics" of *The Dinner Party*', p. 111, n. 20.

72 Chicago, *Creation to Preservation*, p. 27.

73 Ibid., pp. 270, 280.

74 Rozsika Parker and Griselda Pollock, *Old Mistresses: Women, Art and Ideology* (New York, NY: Pantheon, 1981), p. 126.

75 Kubitza, 'Rereading the Readings', p. 175, n. 52, my italics for emphasis.

76 Kandel, 'Beneath the Green Veil', p. 186.

77 Terri Kapsalis has written really insightfully about the binaries which, 'in representation and practice' structure the vagina and vulva, which 'are continually being negotiated, oscillating between the poles [. . .] of sacred-profane, classical-grotesque, pure-dangerous'. See Terri Kapsalis, *Public Privates: Performing Gynecology from both ends of the Speculum* (Durham, NC: Duke University Press, 1997), p. 20.

78 In my use of the word 'apparitions', here, I must acknowledge my debt to Terry Castle who seeks out the 'apparitional lesbian' in texts which might otherwise deny her existence; it is, to my mind, another manifestation of the covert visibility with which I am concerned. See Terry Castle, *The Apparitional Lesbian: Female Homosexuality and Modern Culture* (New York, NY: Columbia University Press, 1995). As Castle puts it: 'Why is it so difficult to see the lesbian – even when she is there, quite plainly, in front of us? In part because she has been "ghosted" – or made to seem invisible – by culture itself'. Castle, *Apparitional*, p. 4.

79 Chicago, *Creation to Preservation*, p. 136.

80 Ibid., p. 34.

81   Kubitza, 'Rereading the Readings', p. 169; I'm not entirely at ease with Kubitza's claim, however, that 'a more pointed criticism of Chicago's approach might be that she does not question the traditional male ideal of public success but, rather, attempts to legitimate women within this ideal' (Kubitza, 'Rereading the Readings', p. 169). 'Success' is, of course, measured in numerous ways. When its antithesis is oppression, silencing and eradication, however, it suddenly becomes the *only* desirable state of being, no matter how 'traditional', 'male' or 'public' that might be.

82   Schapiro and Chicago, 'Female Imagery', p. 11, in Jones, 'The "Sexual Politics" of *The Dinner Party*', pp. 96, p. 113, n. 54.

83   Chicago, *Creation to Preservation*, p. 48, my italics for emphasis.

84   Ibid., p. 47.

85   Ibid., p. 76.

86   Ibid., p. 91.

87   Women gynaecologists continue to be celebrated throughout the work. On the Third Wing, Elizabeth Blackwell's name becomes a visual pun as, on her plate, rainbow coloured wings swirl from (or into?) a black well in the plate's centre. It's not really a vulvar image despite Blackwell's occupation – and that of her contemporary, Elizabeth Garrett Anderson – as a gynaecologist and is, in some senses, probably because of its bright colours, more optimistic in appearance than the settings which precede it (the colours are also rainbow-like, perhaps to signal LGBT (Lesbian, Gay, Bisexual and Transgender) sympathies). Somehow the plate just does not seem as 'angry' as Susan B. Anthony's, for example. Garrett Anderson's runner has a scalloped edge – in itself a mark of shifting away from rigidity and conformity. Oddly, Chicago writes that a grey chiffon overlay is in place on the runner to indicate the 'dreariness of Blackwell's long struggle', but I don't see this at all – the runner colours are slightly muted but the vibrancy of those same colours on the plate undermines this idea of 'dreariness'; Chicago, *Creation to Preservation*, p. 114.

88   Chicago, *Creation to Preservation*, p. 125.

89   The eye/'I' image and its vaginal associations may be traced back at least as far as Georges Bataille's 1928 *Story of the Eye*.

90   Chicago, *Creation to Preservation*, p. 181.

91   Ibid., p. 201.

92   Ibid., p. 203.

93   Ibid., p. 221.

94   Ibid.

95   Ibid., p. 233.

96   Ibid.

97   Meyer, 'From Finish Fetish to Feminism', p. 63.

98   Chicago, *Creation to Preservation*, p. 233.

99   On Margaret Sanger's speech on how 'Feminism should mean [that . . .] women should first free themselves from biological slavery, which could best be accomplished through birth control. This was, generally speaking, the introduction of the term into England', see Margaret Sanger, *The Autobiography of Margaret Sanger* (New York, NY: W. W. Norton (1938), 2004), p. 171.

100 Margaret Sanger, *The Selected Papers of Margaret Sanger: Volume 1: The Woman Rebel, 1900–1928*, ed. Esther Katz (Champaign, IL: University of Illinois Press, 2003), p. 143.

101 Chicago, *Creation to Preservation*, p. 255.

102 Ibid., p. 250.

103 Nancy Ring, 'Identifying with Judy Chicago', in Jones (ed.), *Sexual Politics*, pp. 126–40 (129).

104 For the line that includes 'makes me end where I begun' see John Donne, 'A Valediction Forbidding Mourning', in Theodore Redpath (ed.), *The Songs and Sonnets of John Donne* (London: Methuen, 1983), p. 261. The equilateral triangle has other associations, too. It's a Christian symbol of the trinity, and geometrically suggests autonomy since it's a very stable, self-contained figure. It also figures as an abstraction of the topography of the female reproductive anatomy. My particular thanks go to Clare Haynes for her invaluable input here (and elsewhere).

105 Henry T. Hopkins, 'Foreword' in Amelia Jones (ed.), *Sexual Politics: Judy Chicago's 'Dinner Party' in Feminist Art History* (Berkeley, CA: University of California Press, 1996), p. 10.

106 Chicago, *Creation to Preservation*, p. 279.

107 Richard Mahler, 'The Battle of Chicago: [. . .] Feminist Artist Judy Chicago fires back at critics who call her *Dinner Party* obscene and withdraws her gift of it to a university', *The Los Angeles Times*, 12 October 1990: http://articles.latimes.com/1990–10–12/entertainment/ca-2100_1_dinner-party; my italics for emphasis.

108 Chicago, *Creation to Preservation*, p. 282.

109 Meyer, 'From Finish Fetish to Feminism', p. 74, n. 64.

110 Chicago, *Creation to Preservation*, p. 282.

5

Revealing the Vagina in Visual Art (2): Birth's Wide Berth

Endings and origins

The lives of four very different women powerfully, if surprisingly, intersect in this section of *The Vagina*. Here, I consider the Biblical Judith of Bethulia; the Baroque painter Artemisia Gentileschi (1593–c.1652); the writer and philosopher Mary Wollstonecraft (1759–97); and the painter Frida Kahlo (1907–54). These four women are connected by Chicago's *Dinner Party*, not least in the image of the parturitive (birthing) vagina as powerful, self-determining entity. How are *The Vagina*'s twin themes of covert visibility and the autonomous organ figured in representations of this parturitive motif? And how do visual artists today approach the representational taboo of the moment of crowning (when the baby's head emerges from the vaginal canal)? The birthing image, somewhat cheerlessly described by Julia Kristeva as 'a violent expulsion through which the nascent body tears itself away from the matter of maternal insides', presents us with all kinds of questions about appropriateness, voyeurism, autonomy, agency, point of view and the vagina 'in action', as it were (but in a more naturalistic way than the autonomized vaginas we've already encountered).[1] Does the supine woman, her baby crowning, have as much agency as some of the other images under consideration in *The Vagina*? Vaginal birth is a supreme instance of covert visibility; it's seen *and* unseen.

Everyone knows about it; few people talk about it. We're back at that night-marish middle-class dinner party: like money, sex, politics and religion, vagi-nal birth is not normally construed as being a topic for 'polite' conversation.

The artist Georgia O'Keeffe's (1887–1986) place-setting at Chicago's *Dinner Party* is in some ways the final destination of the installation. And it's certainly one of the most visceral-looking plates: it feels almost voyeur-istic peering into the deep well of the central core (which is emphasized by a deep maroon colour, evoking blood), and at the curling, leaf-like labia (or are they labia-like leaves?) which emit from it (see Figure 5.1). The plate is 'a sculptural translation of one of [. . . O'Keeffe's] paintings, *Black Iris* (1926)' and it has the most relief and height of all of *The Dinner Party* plates.[2] Frida Kahlo's name is one of those emanating from O'Keeffe's place-setting, along the Heritage Floor. Griselda Pollock best articulates the dilemma around how autobiographically inflected Kahlo's art is. Are we 'Seeing the artist or reading the picture?'[3] I must accept that *my* interpretation is a projection of my own *desire* to 'read' images and texts in a certain feminist way; the texts provide the space for me to do this, but that does not mean that they also, somehow, pro-vide the 'truth'.[4] Kahlo's paintings are, for me, about Kahlo. I struggle to read Sylvia Plath's poetry without having my interpretation coloured by the grim corporeal fact of her suicide, and the shadow it casts *back* over her poems. Likewise, Kahlo's physical frailty, caused by a horrifying bus accident which left her permanently disabled, seems to me central to – *inseparable* from – her art, especially in her compulsive revisiting of her own image in numerous self-portraits which appear at once accurate and abstracted. One of these pic-tures is crucial to this discussion: Kahlo's 'My Birth' of 1932, currently owned by Madonna. On a pristine white bed in a sparsely furnished room lies a fig-ure whose top half is shrouded by a sheet. From the hips down, however, she is naked, lying with her feet towards the viewer. Her legs are bent at the knees and are wide open: from between them emerges a grotesquely large, lolling head (its eyebrows, significantly, are exact copies of those Kahlo portrayed in most of her self-portraits), the prone woman's vulva loose around this mon-strous baby's neck. Blood stains the sheets and, on the wall over the bedhead, overseeing the scene, is an image of *Mater Dolorosa* (Our Lady of Sorrows). The miscarried child both is, and is not, Kahlo; likewise the shrouded mother.

It is a grim tableau, at the very centre of which is the distended vulva, threshold, here, to both life and death.

Viewing 'My Birth' is not merely an act of physical positioning, but it's also one of *interpretative* perspective.[5] The physical perspective is especially striking when one moves from Kahlo's portrayal of death in childbirth to another, this time the one stitched into the back of the runner of Mary Wollstonecraft's place-setting at Chicago's *Dinner Party*. For here the image is extraordinarily similar, despite Chicago not knowing 'My Birth' at the time of *The Dinner Party*'s composition.[6] The eighteenth-century gentility (restrictive and fussy, although beautiful) of the stumpwork (raised embroidery) on Wollstonecraft's runner contrasts powerfully with the image on its back (see Figure 5.2).[7] Here, the juxtaposition of life and death is starkly presented. It's a tripartite scene, echoing, perhaps, the formation of a religious triptych, suggesting a representation which is to be read not literally but symbolically. To the left, a young girl (presumably Fanny Imlay, Wollstonecraft's then three-year-old daughter from her affair with the American Gilbert Imlay) is grieving, both hands up to her face. A discarded top hat (her father's?) lies by her feet, indicative of the idea that this is a house of domestic upset. To the right, a man, presumably William Godwin, is dressed in a formal grey suit and holds a baby, Mary (later Mary Shelley), in his arms. He is the only one of those represented in the tableau whose eyes might be meeting ours. On his face, painstakingly stitched wrinkles look more like tears as he cradles his newborn securely, but he looks at us, not at her. The central section of the triptych is dominated by a large bed over which is sprawled a woman's – Mary Wollstonecraft's – body. She died at the age of 38 just 10 days after Mary was born in 1797. This reinforces the notion that the triptych forms not a literal moment but a narrative symbolizing a protracted period of suffering. The bed itself is draped in gold-striped blue curtains and the woman's eyes are closed, her lips nearly black, her hair spread out over the pillows. Across her abdomen lies a carelessly arranged green coverlet from which her spread legs point towards the viewer, her right foot flopping over the end of the bed, almost in the viewer's own space. Red blood runs from between her legs in an image totally opposed to the wealthy social propriety suggested by the other details such as the expensive rug. The perspective is uncannily like Kahlo's.

As Chicago reflected during the construction of *The Birth Project* (begun in 1980), the Wollstonecraft image made her uncomfortable. She recalls that she 'decided to soften the powerful and unfamiliar subject matter of birth by designing everything in such a way as to be translated into and embellished by needlework'.[8] She adds that 'My black-and-white design for the image was exceedingly raw and graphic but, when it was translated into stumpwork, pet-it-point, needlepoint, and embroidery, it was entirely transformed. It seemed to me then that the softening effects of the needle and textile arts might prove beneficial to the topic of childbirth.'[9] But the Wollstonecraft runner back *is* 'raw and graphic'; the traditional needlework techniques, because of their embodiment of what womanhood 'should' be, contrast with the spilling out of the central figure's womb: what women 'shouldn't' be. The *seen* technique points to the silent poignancy of women's *unseen* lived experiences. Here, as in Kahlo's tableau, the vagina is both giver and destroyer of life. It cannot be contained, tucked away, hidden; it bleeds out graphically, uncontrollably, into scenes of domestic propriety. I don't agree with Amelia Jones's idea that Chicago presents 'birth as a heroic yet confining event defining womanhood'.[10] It's not heroism that I see: it's tearing, division, and a bringing forth, the price of which is often (literally for Wollstonecraft, and at least metaphorically for Kahlo) death.

The idea of perspective as *point of view* is central here. Are art's 'known narratives' necessarily phallocentric, to the point where, as feminist viewers, we're left not knowing what we 'should' know or what we 'should' be looking at when we gaze on Kahlo's tableau, or Chicago's tables?[11] Is the phallocentrism of pornography our only lens when we gaze on the displayed vagina? This is where biography is crucial – Kahlo and Chicago (and Artemisia Gentileschi, of whom more shortly) are women artists with agency. They are not mute, and, by extension, their works are not mute either, but engage the viewer in a matrix of ideas, exchanges, conversations and interpretations. When we come to think about the crowning pictures in works by modern visual artists we'll see a new kind of vaginal autonomy that brings with it a shift away from the biographical: the vagina, not the artist, has agency. The artist's role is most often as recorder of events. It's a question of finding an accommodating space in dominant artistic (or literary, performance or filmic) discourses within which the woman artist operates.[12] That 'space' is emblematic (explicitly so, in the case of Chicago) *of* the vagina, or is emblematized *by* it. Is the autonomized cunt the key to understanding this process of the renegotiation of phallocentric artistic and expressive discourses?

Artemisia Gentileschi

The third of these four women who represent the perilous autonomy of the parturitive body is Artemisia Gentileschi. She was born in Rome at the very end of the sixteenth century, and travelled extensively in Italy and beyond, working hard at perfecting the artistic techniques that made her a celebrated artist of the Caravaggist School. She entered into the aesthetic and narrative discourses of painting of the era, reworking those topics (often Biblical in theme) which were preoccupying her male counterparts, including her father, Orazio. Gentileschi's rejection by art academies led to her father enrolling the help of an artist friend, Agostino Tassi, to teach her perspective. Legal records of the period show that in 1612 Orazio accused Tassi of having raped Artemisia the previous year. The protracted and well-documented series of legal interrogations and disputes saw claim and counterclaim, and the torture – both actual (the thumbscrews) and psychological – of Artemisia herself, before Tassi was briefly exiled from Rome. It's a story which, unsurprisingly enough, perhaps, has attracted to it several artists, including Chicago, who seats Gentileschi at *The Dinner Party*. Gentileschi's velvet runner there is distinctive, with what Laura Meyer terms 'vulvar drapery folds', which threaten 'to overwhelm the plate'.[13] It also has a black fabric 'hole' at its core, on which the plate, with its red, orange, rust and green 'undulating forms', sits (see Figure 5.3).[14] When we lift Gentileschi's plate from her place-setting, we see that black gap, the aporia, the absence, which, without the vulvar plate, is a powerful rendition of the complexities of situating women in historical contexts whose parameters have already been so strongly circumscribed by phallocentric logic and discourse. The hole signalled by the black fabric is replete with symbolism. The hole is whole.

What if having biographical knowledge about an artist isn't a reduction, but an *enlargement*, offering us a way in to reading not just an individual artist's life, but also in to understanding something fundamentally important about the socio-political gendered power matrix she inhabited? Thus, as Nanette Salomon suggests, '"Artemisia" is an historically elusive construct' as is Artemisia's subject, Judith (of whom more shortly).[15] Pollock warns against adopting a post hoc, ergo propter hoc ('after this, therefore because of this') biographical interpretation of Gentileschi's life: reading her paintings *only* through the 'sensationalism' of the rape would make them all about 'sexual violence and violation', reducing their impact as contributions to the Baroque debate of the early seventeenth century and 'offering no problems for interpretation'.[16] Instead of this unproblematic biographically inflected reading we should instead seek to destabilize meaning and resist fixity. We thus, according to Pollock, may come to see a 're-vision [. . .] based on stories of the body, the woman's body, the body of the painter, the painted body, the viewing body and the dead body'.[17] In terms of perspective, what Gentileschi's paintings of Judith and Holofernes present to us is similar to the Kahlo and Wollstonecraft images already discussed. Where those representations were of the presence of death in birth, however, Gentileschi's work positions the possibility of a birth image in the midst of a murder. All of these representations – by Kahlo, of Wollstonecraft, and by Gentileschi –share elements both of composition and of content.

I want to think about three of Gentileschi's paintings: her c. 1612–13 *Judith Slaying Holofernes*; the 1620 version of the same painting; and the c. 1625 *Judith with the Head of Holofernes*. In this last, the c. 1625 composition, Judith raises her left hand in an almost balletic way (but open-palmed as though indicating 'stop'), to shade her eyes from the brightly burning candle set to the left of the frame. Her right hand, holding Holofernes's sword, clutches tightly, knuckles pronounced, and hovers over her lap. As Mary Garrard had previously noted, and as Mieke Bal also argues, Judith's pose here might be read as 'a symbolic reference to the [classically ubiquitous modesty of the] Venus Pudica pose, the sword replacing Venus' hand that covers her genitals'.[18] This playful intertexuality is highly suggestive: covert visibility resides in the space between this painting and the two earlier versions of *Judith Slaying Holofernes*, in terms of Judith's positioning and in viewers' responses. 'Seeing, in a glance', Bal continues, writing of the two *Slaying* compositions, 'thighs in Holofernes' arms, imposes a choice of two fictions: either the head is a head, but of a baby, or the head is a penis, and being cut off. These arms/thighs [. . . are] invisible *yet highly visible*.'[19] Gentileschi's representation of the assassination, particularly the 1620 version, is far more bloodthirsty than those of her contemporaries such as Sirani or even Caravaggio: 'she wished to evoke the spectator's fear of the homicidal woman'.[20] *Why*, in 1620, did Gentileschi reproduce almost exactly the same picture as her 1612–13 *Judith Slaying Holofernes*? To use filmic terminology, the 1620 version is less of a close-up, and the gore is more apparent as jugular blood spurts from Holofernes. The sword is longer in the 1620 picture, and Judith is wearing a gold bracelet on her left arm. Each painting displays the intense triangular arrangement of the three faces, and the women's eyes evade the viewer, looking down in absolute 'business-like' concentration.[21] The only possibility of eye-contact is with Holofernes, and his is the only face that registers a sense of panic.

For me, the earlier, 1612–13 painting is the more powerful of the two because of its intensely personal, claustrophobic space (see Figure 5.4). We don't *need* the blood spurts or the longer sword of the later version to understand the horror of the scene. Most importantly, however, in the 1620 version we can see Holofernes's legs to the left of the frame, which immediately eradicates the ambiguity I'd argue for in the 1612–13 version where his arms look like legs, 'split into a 'V' [. . .] characteristic of the 'V' formed by the open thighs of a woman at the point of giving birth'.[22] Gentileschi has positioned the two women in such a way as to suggest a 'shocking conjunction of birth and death', arguably reasserting a narrative of *feminine* supremacy.[23] The introduction of the possibility of a vagina (and there are, importantly, specific details which Gentileschi brings to the painting: in the biblical telling the maid is not there and Holofernes does not wake, far less struggle), and the no-nonsense capability of the women in a birthing scene, serve to give the familiar theme a new angle – quite literally – in Gentileschi's rendering of it. Her retellings of the original story from the *Apocrypha* tell us much about

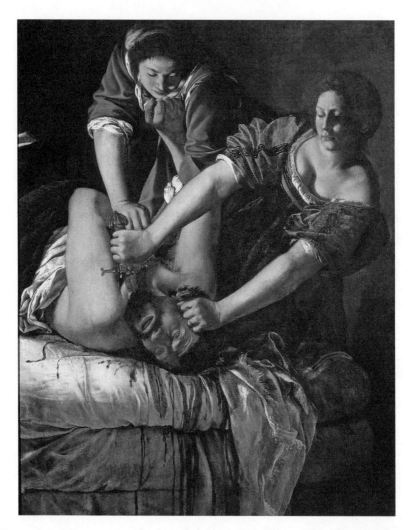

Figure 5.4 *Artemisia Gentileschi,* Judith Slaying Holofernes *(c. 1612–13), oil on canvas, H. 158.8 cm × W. 125.5 cm.* By kind permission of the Ministero per I Beni e le Attività Culturali, Naples (Museo Nazionale di Capodimonte)

'the ambivalence of the bond, at once erotic and funereal, which unites Judith and Holofernes'.[24] The vulva functions as the locus for the 'erotic and funereal' energies in the sexualized retelling of Judith's story – especially if we reframe Gentileschi's suggestively parturient revisioning in the light of Pointon's essay, such that it becomes a 'render[ing of] the murder of Holofernes through the imagery of childbirth. We are not talking here of the Biblical nativity [. . .] but of its counter-type, the raw and physical brutality of parturition'.[25] Moreover, Gentileschi's 'Confusion' of arms and thighs is 'a serious and passionate commitment to confusion, to a complexity over clarity, to mobility over fixity, to collusion over collision, to intersubjectivity over objectivity'.[26] It is a grotesque image, this idea of a man appearing to be 'delivered', but instead being murdered. Judith 'delivers' Holofernes in Gentileschi's 1612–13 painting, but, as on Wollstonecraft's back runner, and in Kahlo's 'My Birth', it's a delivery of death, despite being a rebirth for Judith and for the Jewish people. Further, if we take the biographical approach, we can argue that the painting was a cathartic, retributive act for the raped Gentileschi. Read in this way Gentileschi offers a riposte to traditions of representation (think here of Courbet's *L'Origine* and *La Clairvoyante*, as introduced in 'Antecedents') 'that would "cut off *her* head", silence her difference as a woman and let "woman" function only as a "headless body" – the nude perhaps'.[27] Is it possible that this is to do with one set of lips being silenced, and the other lips, silently, 'speaking'? Pollock says that 'a woman's voice is made': do Chicago's *Dinner Party* labia break the other lips' silence?[28] Are *they* the lips that have a voice and can 'speak', by reclaiming Judith and Gentileschi and Kahlo and all of those other women from matrices of masculinized, phallocentric art history?

The Dinner Party as a whole is a work of perpetual suspended animation – it's a table set for guests who can never arrive, who can never be presented as guests, but who must instead be semiotically *re*presented and whose being resides in their absence from their own party. Instead, Chicago's piece receives viewers or spectators whose specular acts and interpretations work to fill the 'emptied space' not only of the unattended, waiting *Dinner Party* but of each place setting; of each name on the Heritage Floor; and, ultimately of each vulvar/butterfly plate, too. If the piece is read as *not*-masculine rather than as a positive, 'feminine', then the seen/unseen dichotomy comes into play again, because Chicago's work may never be truly 'known' (and nor may Gentileschi's). 'Woman' can never be 'known' in a culture (our own, and that of early modern Italy) where knowledge is phallocentrically organized. Reading *Judith Slaying Holofernes* as a representation of birth (itself, in a sense, an act of the powerful cunt) is, therefore, an interpretive act which may – or more likely may *not* – be informed by biographical information. Many credible critics have, to some extent, isolated Gentileschi's handling of the Judith and Holofernes story from its popularity with so many of her contemporaries (her father, Orzio Gentileschi, painted a version of it in around 1610–12; Caravaggio himself portrayed the theme in 1599), but hers is the only one that can actually make one gasp at its birthing possibilities. Agnès Merlet's biopic *Artemisia* (1998) has – quite rightly – attracted criticism for reconfiguring the Artemisia/Tassi relationship as consensual when historically it is documented as being one of rape and subjugation. Merlet's opening voiceover specifically confuses arms and legs – a confusion which I think Gentileschi *wanted* to convey in her Judith: 'A pointed finger . . . Draped material . . . A raised hand . . . A leg which isn't a leg but an arm . . . A confused ballet of gigantic bodies . . . The sweeping movement of limbs.'[29] This leg/arm confusion is, as we've seen, *key* to my reading of Gentileschi's paintings of Judith and Holofernes. As we watch Merlet's Gentileschi at work on the 1620 'blood spray' version, the voiceover intentionally eroticizes and makes ambiguous the *kind* of bodily contact we're witnessing: 'Legs spread, muscles taut. Faces twisted, upside down. An arm stretches out. A fist is raised. A round breast escapes from its corset. A sword strikes, cutting all along its edge. An eye stares. And the colour red erupts onto the canvas.' In looking at an *essentially* female experience (birth) through the lens of murder, images are distorted; roles are reversed; and literal 'speculation' is redeployed. Indeed, we'll see next how Gentileschi's alter ego and artistic subject, Judith, also pragmatically redrew the boundaries of gendered roles.

Judith and Holofernes

And so, in looking at the last of these four women whose lives or works accentuated the vagina's potential for signalling both life *and* death, we return to the First Wing of Chicago's *Dinner Party*. Judith's plate has a wing- or leaf-like appearance, again vulvar, the female reproductive idea enduring into the fertility images that appear on the runner in the form of pomegranate-decorated coins (see Figure 5.5). Judith's story is consistent with narratives of women not only as victims but as fierce avengers too, especially in the Old Testament and the *Apocrypha*. Judith's status as a widow represents 'a nation lacking the necessary

Figure 1.4 *Cover of Inga Muscio's book* Cunt. By kind permission of Inga Muscio

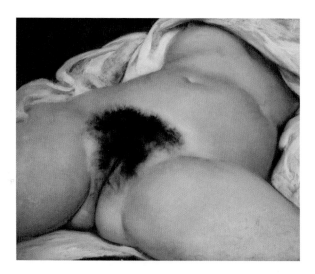

Figure 2.1 *Gustave Courbet*, L'Origine Du Monde *(1866), oil on canvas,* H. 46 cm × W. 55 cm. Photo credit: Gianni Dagli Orti, the Art Archive at Art Resource, NY

Figure 2.2 *Gustave Courbet*, La Clairvoyante *(c. 1865), oil on canvas,* H. 47 cm × W. 39 cm. Photo credit: Erich Lessing, Art Resource, NY

Figure 4.1 *Julia Kunin*, Red Suede Saddles *(1993)*. By kind permission of the artist and of Martin Margulies of the Margulies Collection, Miami, Florida

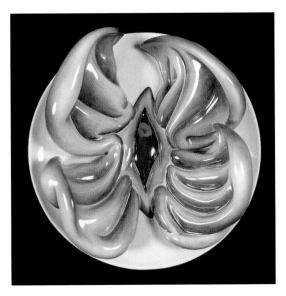

Figure 4.2 The Dinner Party – *Detail*. Susan B. Anthony Plate © Judy Chicago 1979; Collection of the Brooklyn Museum of Art. Photo © Donald Woodman

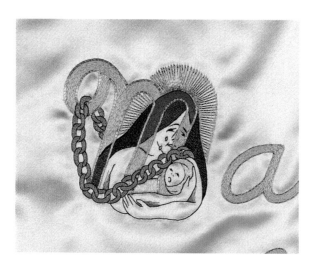

Figure 4.3 The Dinner Party – *Detail.* Margaret Sanger Capital Letter
© Judy Chicago 1979; Collection of the Brooklyn Museum of Art Photo
© Donald Woodman

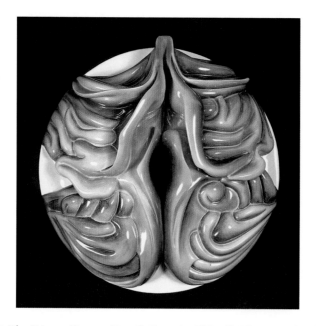

Figure 5.1 The Dinner Party – *Detail.* Georgia O'Keeffe Plate © Judy Chicago
1979; Collection of the Brooklyn Museum of Art. Photo © Donald Woodman

Figure 5.2 The Dinner Party – *Detail.* Mary Wollstonecraft Runner Back © Judy Chicago 1979; Collection of the Brooklyn Museum of Art Photo © Donald Woodman

Figure 5.3 The Dinner Party – *Detail.* Artemisia Gentileschi Runner © Judy Chicago 1979; Collection of the Brooklyn Museum of Art Photo © Donald Woodman

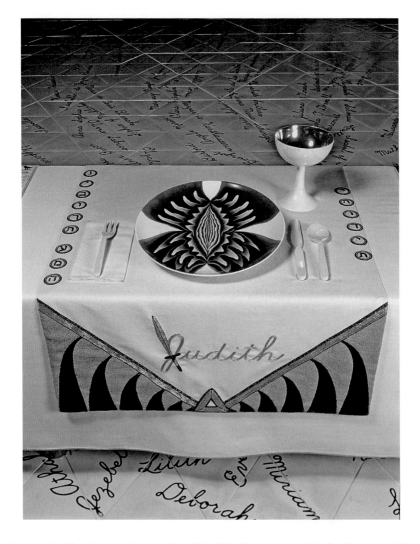

Figure 5.5 The Dinner Party – *Detail.* Judith Placesetting © Judy Chicago 1979; Collection of the Brooklyn Museum of Art Photo © Donald Woodman

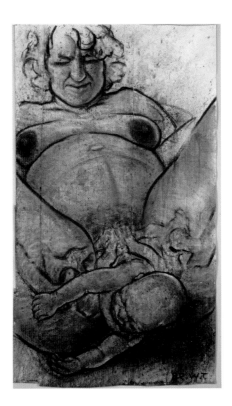

Figure 5.6 *Jonathan Waller,* Mother No. 58, *charcoal, soft pastels, gouache, watercolour, acrylic, shellac and car spray paint on watercolour paper, H. 144 cm × W. 84 cm.* By kind permission of the artist

Figure 6.1 *Pieter Brueghel the Elder,* Dulle Griet *(c. 1562), central detail.*
Photo credit: Gianni Dagli Orti, the Art Archive at Art Resource, NY

Figure 6.2 *'Lips' promo material for* Chatterbox *(1977).* By kind permission of Tom DeSimone

Figure 7.2 *Simon Croft,* There is no Name for it *(2009), A6 size postcard image (148 × 105 mm).* By kind permission of Simon Croft

male warrior-redeemer'.[30] It's worth considering Judith's story in some detail, here, since her ingenious, heroic actions revolve around her understanding of the imagined powers and dangers of female sexuality. *The Book of Judith* is one of the ancient *Apocrypha*, a series of books written after the Old Testament and before the New, between the third century BCE and the first century AD. They are included in both Septuagint (Greek) and Vulgate versions of the Old Testament but not in the canonical Hebrew Bible, despite appearing to have influenced the writers of the New Testament.[31] Protestant Reformers decried the *Apocrypha*, and designated them as being non-scriptural, or even heretical. The etymology of the term *Apocrypha* – from the Greek for *hidden* (hence of *uncertain* authorship) – has, in its suggestion of secrecy, concealment, even shame, much to do with the seen/unseen motif of this book. The Apocryphal *Book of Judith* itself plays with images of concealment and subterfuge; in it we may read a corollary to representations of the vagina which is also concealed, tucked away and distrusted. Some theologians argue that the *Apocrypha* are essential to a full understanding of 'the Jewish environment of early Christian thought, community life, and ethics'; others even contend that 'there is a reasonable likelihood that the author of (an earlier) stage of the book of Judith was a woman'.[32] The Book is predominantly didactic and allegorical, rather than an historically accurate account of a series of events, and Judith's very name, coming from the Hebrew 'Yehudit', meaning 'Judean woman, Jewess', reinforces her status as archetype, emblematic of Israel in her 'name, widowhood, chastity, beauty and righteousness'.[33] What does that archetype convey, then? De Silva sees *The Book of Judith* as telling 'the story of a contest between the dominant Gentiles, with their claims about the gods, and the God of Israel'.[34] By Chapter 8, Judith becomes a startlingly psychologically credible character. This chapter establishes her as a wealthy, beautiful widow whose piety is so pronounced that she has been mourning and systematically fasting in a rooftop tent (probably a semi-permanent *sukkâ*) for more than three years, thereby being distanced from her people.[35]

The fictional city of Bethulia, probably not far from Jerusalem, was under siege by the Assyrians (strictly speaking they were probably actually the Babylonians) who had taken 'into their hands the fountain of water, which issueth forth of the foot of the mountain [. . . and since] all the inhabitants

[. . .] have their water thence; so shall thirst kill them and they shall give up their city'.[36] The gradual starvation of the Bethulians under the command of Nebuchadnezzar's general, Holofernes, is a deliberate strategic decision designed to frighten the city's Elders into capitulating to the besiegers' demands. The rhetoric is intentionally emotive, as the Bethulian men 'and their wives and their children shall be consumed with famine, and before the sword come against them, they shall be overthrown'.[37] It's also symbolic: images of interiority and encircling which are first encountered here have resonances later in the story of Judith where tents, canopies and bags enclose and conceal. If Bethulia is symbolic (and the Hebrew word conjured up by it, *bĕtûlâ*, means 'virgin') then the Assyrians' decision not to penetrate its walls with their phallic swords is significant, too, as is the emphasis on the weak and the vulnerable – those wives and children – who will be the first to die through starvation.[38] It's the male citizens who appeal to Ozias (Uzziah in some versions) to capitulate: 'it is better for us to be made a spoil unto them, than to die for thirst: for we will be his servants, that our souls may live, and not see the death of our infants before our eyes, nor our wives nor our children to die'.[39] Ozias sends the men away, asking them to allow God five more days to intercede on the Bethulians' behalf, after which time they will surrender.

Not all of Ozias's audience were men, however, and at the start of Chapter 8 we finally meet Judith, who has overheard Ozias's decree. In this story of narrative echoes and circles it is significant that Judith has been made a widow because her husband, Manasses, had died more than three years prior to the siege 'in the barley harvest [. . . as] the heat came upon his head, and he fell on his bed, and died'.[40] The enclosed nature of Manasses's utterly prosaic death – at home, in bed – somehow emphasizes the domestic, feminized space which is going to prove so important as the narrative progresses, and the idea of a man sustaining a head injury is, as the reader is to discover, later replayed in an altogether more dramatic way. Judith's widowed status has been commented on by author Margarita Stocker as enabling her 'self-election to political action [which] marks her out as a much more challenging figure for traditional views of the public sphere as a masculine arena'.[41]

Again in an emphasis on the subtle primacy of the enclosed, feminized space, it is to her tent that Judith summons Ozias and the Bethulian Elders, berating them for challenging God: 'God is not as a man', she argues, 'that he may be threatened'.[42] Despite Ozias's request that Judith pray to God for rain to break the drought she instead utters a statement remarkable in its imperative assertiveness and in its ambiguity: this is a very literary narrative, suspenseful for the reader. 'Hear me', she says, 'and I will do a thing, which shall go throughout all generations to the children of our nation'.[43] The men are in thrall to her speaking lips; her silent lips are homologically invoked through the ambiguity of 'I will do a thing' that might ensure the very existence of future 'generations'; invoking 'the children' reinforces the homology still more. Secrecy – in a by-now familiar pattern – is again the key component of a woman's actions: 'enquire not ye of mine act: for I will not declare it unto you, till the things be finished that I do'.[44] Her lips are sealed, for the reader and for the Bethulians, in a tantalizingly suggestive way which the narrator does nothing to dispel in detailing the minutiae of her preparations to go to the Assyrian camp, as she 'decked herself bravely, to allure the eyes of all men that should see her'.[45]

Judith recapitulates the theme of Bethulia as virgin territory under threat from male aggressors. She prays: 'they have purposed to defile thy sanctuary, and to pollute the tabernacle [. . .] and to cast down with sword the horn of thy altar', and she identifies very clearly the focus of her revenge: 'Smite by the deceit of my *lips* the servant with the prince, and the prince with the servant: break down their stateliness by the hand of a woman'.[46] She entreats God to 'make [. . . her] speech and deceit to be [. . . the Assyrians'] wound and stripe'.[47] The 'deceit of her lips' carries, I believe, a quite deliberate ambiguity here (in the King James version, at least); Holofernes's downfall will come about because he does not believe that it is her *speaking* lips which have power, and he eradicates those in his focus on her sexual appeal. That intoxicating eroticism is implicit in the markedly decadent setting Holofernes has staged in order to receive Judith: 'Now Holofernes rested upon his bed under a canopy, which was woven with purple, and gold, and emeralds, and precious stones'.[48] It's a setting which renders him passive.

There's a wonderful dramatic irony at play as Judith addresses Holofernes. 'If thou wilt follow the words of thine handmaid', she tells him, 'God will bring perfectly to pass by thee and *my Lord* shall not fail of his purposes'.[49] The phrase is delicious in its *double entendres*.[50] The idea of 'the thing' had first been used in her address to Ozias and the Elders, leaving them – and the reader – in a state of some confusion. Its evocation here, in Holofernes's tent rather than in her own, *appears* to be without ambiguity: surely seduction is on the cards? Holofernes certainly believes so and, in a fatal act of hubris can't see in her deployment of 'my Lord' any being other than himself and, given his irreligiosity, certainly can't see Judith's God. 'God hath sent me to work things with thee', she tells the recumbent General, 'whereat all the earth shall be astonished'.[51] What form will that 'astonishment' take? Indeed, the idea of 'astonishment', with its etymological connections to 'stony' is particularly resonant given the Gorgonian turn of events the reader's about to witness.[52] Will the reader be 'astonished' at the pious widow's sexual incontinence? Will Holofernes be? He is certainly struggling with his own self-control after Judith and her maid have spent four days in his camp living among gentile soldiers but still keeping kosher. 'It will be a shame for our person', thinks Holofernes, 'if we shall let such a woman go, not having had her company'.[53] Again, in a display of magnificent wordplay Judith tells him that 'whatsoever pleaseth [my lord . . .] I will do speedily, and it shall be my joy unto the day of my death', encouraging Holofernes to drink 'much more wine than he had drunk at any time in one day since he was born'.[54]

Like Tarquin, the rapist in Shakespeare's *Rape of Lucrece*, Judith treads stealthily towards the near-unconscious Holofernes's bed and – remember the reader *still* doesn't know what her plans are – 'said in her heart, O Lord God of all power, look at this present upon the works of mine hands for the exaltation of Jerusalem' and, using Holofernes's own 'fauchion' ('falchion', or 'broad sword'), grabs his hair and 'smote twice upon his neck with all her might, and she took away his head from him'.[55] This is the moment of climax for Judith, her maid, Holofernes and the reader. In the erotic canopied space of his luxurious tented bedroom, Holofernes's own phallic sword has symbolically castrated him, or even sexually defiled him: he wanted to take her *maiden*head; she ended up taking his head.[56] Further, it has been argued that 'the original Book's symbolic plot is such that Judith can even be interpreted as raping the would-be rapist [. . .] it is a reminder that God himself once empowered female vengeance'.[57] Judith has become a 'Delilah for the cause of God' or a 'gorgeous gorgon', and such is her beauty that 'were all women to be like Judith, not only Holofernes would lose his head'.[58] Judith and her maid exit the camp unquestioned, Holofernes's head wrapped in his bed canopy and secreted into their kosher bag which, if read symbolically, becomes Judith's kosher bodily space, her chaste vagina; for it to leave the Assyrian camp tightly wrapped around a severed head has, in a manoeuvre reminiscent of 'voracious women' in *vagina dentata* myths, a 'cannibalistic implication' – it starts life as a *food* bag, after all.[59] On returning to Bethulia, the brave and triumphant Judith displays the head.[60] 'The Lord', she announces, 'hath smitten him by the hand of a woman'.[61]

The very *sight* of the head on Bethulia's walls, coupled with the discovery of his decapitated body in his tent, has a Medusan power such that the Assyrians see it and 'fear shall fall upon them, and they shall flee before [. . . the Bethulians'] face'.[62] The Medusa's power has been transferred via Judith's alluring face in the Assyrian camp to Holofernes to the Bethulian soldiers *en masse*, and is reaffirmed in the songs of rejoicing: 'the Almighty Lord hath disappointed [the Assyrians . . .] by the hand of a woman [. . .] Judith weakened him *with the beauty of her countenance*'.[63] More women have been empowered, is the implication, than Judith alone, since in leading the Israelites and brandishing both sword and head Judith has ensured that 'the female population of Israel [. . .] become both graphically and by their actions phallic women'.[64] This gendered inversion, where heroic triumph is, 'because this hero is female, transformed into a feminine event', powerfully vindicates a reading of Holofernes's assassination, especially as we've seen it rendered by Gentileschi, as a birth-in-death.[65] Stocker argues that 'Gentileschi's painting revealed the feminizing of Holofernes's limbs by Judith's murderous vigour'.[66] Bal, too, is in no doubt of the ambiguity of the Gentileschi's depiction. It is 'needless to insist', argues Bal, 'on the resemblance of Holofernes' arms to *thighs* [. . .] The confusion emphasizes the three major jobs in women's lives according to the tradition to which "Judith" belongs: life-giving, life-taking, and, in between, hard work'.[67]

The *Book* elaborates on this idea of the power of Judith's Gorgon, castrating gaze, and the descriptive sweep *up* her body is almost filmic in its direction: 'Her sandals ravished his eyes, her beauty took his mind prisoner, and the fauchion passed through his neck'.[68] The Medusa has captured Holofernes in a visual untruth; similarly, in gazing on Gentileschi's representation of the assassination we, to use Bal's phrase, 'miss-see' arms for thighs; in just such a way the vagina in art is *always* doomed to some kind of 'miss-seeing that is plausible enough to draw attention to the difficulty of seeing'.[69] In Bal's formulation, miss-seeing is tied closely to the vagina's 'lack' which resides not in Medusa's eyes, nor in Gentileschi's paintings, but which 'is an act of interpretation, of constructing meaning out of nothingness'.[70] The vagina, in its flirtation with the semiotic (im)possibilities of covert visibility, is profoundly miss-seen in all attempts at representation; in this specific instance, in terms of the Biblical *Apocrypha* – those Books which both are, but are not, depending on which edition of the Bible is being read.

The *Book* concludes with Judith's withdrawal from Bethulian society, living in solitude until the age of 105 and, through her actions, guaranteeing that 'there was none that made the children of Israel any more afraid'.[71] Judith's entire story has both subverted and shored up cultural expectations of femininity: transgression is embodied in her chastity. For Holofernes, the Medusan Judith was both womb and tomb: 'all men have one entrance into life', says Solomon, 'and the like going out'.[72] She has given birth to Jewish freedom through Holofernes's death.[73] The construction of Judith as all-conquering, murderous, fearless woman is, argues Stocker, 'almost indistinguishable from the misogynist version that demonizes her. Its motivation is different [from a feminist view], but its reception by the masculine spectator might not be'.[74] On the moral justification for the murder, Stocker explores how the poet Vicki Feaver – somewhat misguidedly, I think, given Judith's powerfully *symbolic* function – attempts to get into Judith's – as she views it – grieving mind. In Feaver's poem 'Judith', the speaker pauses momentarily and considers the possibility of sexual intimacy with Holofernes – just to lie 'sheltered and safe in a warrior's/fumy sweat' – before saying, in a deliberately domestic image: 'I bring my blade / down on his neck – and it's easy / like slicing through fish. / And I bring it down again / cleaving the bone'.[75]

Permission to enter

Bethulia's walls, embellished with the head of Holofernes, are transformed in Judith's story into a boundary at once protective and menacing. They signal to

Assyrians a clear message about 'inside' and 'outside'. If the walls there were an analogue for a woman's body, that analogy has been more vividly and literally rendered in the twenty-first century. Who has permission to 'enter' the 'inside' is a key question in the contestation of the field of representation. Brighton sculptor Jamie McCartney's 2011 work, *The Great Wall of Vagina*, was an installation composed of plaster casts of 400 vulvas. These casts 'were arranged tile-like in a 9m long polyptych' and, according to McCartney, 'have nothing to do with eroticism', but the work is 'a celebration of the person as much as their parts [. . .] The geometry of four rows of 10 casts in each panel is repeated in the 10 panels, creating four lines of 100 casts [. . . in] aluminium frames'.[76] The exhibit, as well as having in its title both a pun and an anatomical inaccuracy (McCartney does, to be fair, address this in his book documenting the exhibition, and I'm aware that it's an issue that applies to the title of my own book, too), actually isn't all that original an idea, either. Julie Bamber, for example, was producing work that was very like McCartney's, but from the mid-1990s.[77] How far does McCartney's *Great Wall* move us past the 1970s, and feminist artists' attempts to grant subjectivity to the objectified female body?[78]

The first section of McCartney's book is made up of a series of first-person testimonials from his 'models'. It's in these diverse accounts that the tremendous value of what he's doing is evident. 'I've done the mirror-squat thing', reports one, 'to no avail, but seeing mine next to everyone else's was sort of a breakthrough moment. None of ours looked alike and none (not one!) looked out of place'.[79] 'If presenting my vulva to the world for all to see helps one single lady out there to face her demons', writes another, a woman who had undergone a radical vulvectomy, 'then I'm filled with a sense of pride'.[80] A third writes of being 'a female to male transsexual, so I have a vulva that has been adapted [. . .] seeing the variety in so many vulvas might make other people feel more comfortable about how theirs looks – they're all different and all have their own beauty'.[81] It's in this diversity that McCartney's project, despite the artist's apparent unfamiliarity with the work of his forebears, does succeed. The 'disembodiment' was intended, he writes, to 'deny any references to pornography' – a claim which doesn't entirely ring true given porn's often disaggregating aesthetic.[82] But the pages of close-up photographs are, quite simply, intriguing. And an education. And, quite often, beautiful. There are trim labia and flamboyant, petal-like labia; pierced clitoral hoods; slits; seashells; wounded, healing, healthy labia; labia with eight rings piercing them; hormonally enlarged clitorises; 'reassigned' cunts with no lips, or two lips or a new vulva; and before and after labiaplasty cunts. Page after page, and no two cunts are alike. There's no denying that, reservations over 'disembodiment' and nomenclature aside, McCartney's *Great Wall* is an astonishing feat, and continues the tradition of representing genital diversity exemplified by, for example, Tee Corinne's *Cunt Coloring Book*.

However, the idea of a wall of vaginas has origins almost as old as the *fabliaux*. In the early sixteenth century, Rabelais imagined just such an idea in his *Gargantua and Pantagruel* (1532). In this text, vaginas become (depending on which translation you use, of course), 'whatchamacallits', 'the void of knowledge' being expressed in 'the gaping void of the vagina: a fearsome and abhorrent reminder of the limitations of individual male experience in the quest for knowledge'.[83] Susan Broomhall writes of the particular power of the female body: 'The frustrations of male scholars unable to comprehend gynaecology by personal experience and observation, rather than the authority of the ancients, manifests itself in Rabelais's work in an abhorrence of the vagina.'[84] In one episode the prophetic sibyl is visited by Pantagruel and his men. Like a *Sheela-na-Gig* she 'showed them her tail. Panurge saw it, and said to Epistémon: "Odsbodikins, there's the sibyl's hole"', the 'gaping jaws' of which lead 'into the depths of the body'.[85] In Rabelais's text the vagina, in its resistance to being *known*, here literalized by Panurge as a physical (rather than epistemic) impenetrability, leads him to suggest using them to build a great wall of Paris since the existing walls are so weak that, he tells Pantagruel, 'a Cow with one fart would go near to overthrow above six fathoms of them'.[86] His solution is to use vaginas, since: 'women's whatchamacallits in this part of the country are cheaper than stones [. . .] There is no metal so resistant to blows.'[87] Panurge's schoolboyish, grotesque plan involves the painstaking arrangement of the whatchamacallits in order of size. Somewhat alarmingly, but also bathetically amusingly, he can only foresee one potential problem with his plan: 'the flies would be so lickorish of them, that you would wonder, and would quickly gather there together, and there leave their ordure and excretions, and so all the work would be spoiled'.[88] Consequently, the walls would need to be 'kept from the flies, and wages allowed to some for wiping of them'.[89] Bored with this idea which is becoming less cost-efficient by the minute, the irrepress-ible Panurge, like a toddler immediately weary of a new toy, turns his mind to another vaginal story, this time of the fox and lion who work together to pack an old woman's 'wound' with moss.[90] After 'full five handfuls and a half' they give up, noticing 'another little hole, that stinks like five hundred devils'.[91]

In these episodes from *Gargantua and Pantagruel* we see several motifs which are, by now, familiar. McCartney has autonomized the 'vagina' – split it from the (w)hole body – in order to construct a wall as an installation piece. In doing this, however, he's apparently unaware that he's heir to Rabelais's Panurge. Further, the wonderful, evasive language of 'whatchamacallits' and 'contrapunctums' that the translators use in recounting the episode evokes the unseen-ness of the c/not-seen word. Finally, there's an abjection in the surreal yet immensely practical dimensions of Panurge's stories which McCartney, in his shaven, clinical, white (and, therefore, not racially diverse?) vaginal wall, doesn't transmit. Does this make McCartney any less of a misogynist than Panurge? Each, after all, separates the hole from the whole in building their walls. While Rabelais was after a smutty laugh, however, the same cannot be said of McCartney. His art is not misogynist: it's phenomenally enabling both for cisgendered (broadly speaking 'born') and transgendered women, since each tile 'speaks', through silent lips, volumes more than any of Eve Ensler's monologues ever did.

Another precursor of McCartney was the British artist Cosey Fanni Tutti. Her 1994 'Lip Service' is a montage of four photographs of vulvas juxtaposed in an almost Warhol screen-print style, especially in its overlay of colour (blue on two, and green and sepia-purple on the others), each vulva depicted with a heavy chain draped from anus to clitoris. It ought – not least from this descrip-tion – to be a violent, menacing image but its construction as 'art' and its conse-quent presentation makes it worlds away from BDSM pornographic images.[92] As the artist herself says: '"Lip Service" was created for my and my partner's personal pleasure and love of the aesthetic of female genitalia. I often used chains in my art actions and the idea of these [was] an extension of both those works and my own love of S&M. The chains may seem to represent the notion of bondage, but the primary message is that of female control and exclusion – that permission to enter is required.'[93]

Why do we give birth a wide berth?

The human body as object of scientific study is [...] always already a cultural object invested with meaning [...] perhaps no flesh is more overdetermined with cultural meaning than the female reproductive body [...] *visual* modes of representing obstetrical and embryological information, which have similar consequences in forming both public and professional opinion [have a] long and persistent history [in] the social work of consensus building that these representations achieve.[94]

For Chicago, the 1980s were taken up by the renewed *Dinner Party* tour and work on the *Birth Project*, for which more than 80 'exhibition units' were produced, since 'A birthing woman flies in the face of most representations of women, specifically those that posit a passive female sexuality. The pulsating vulva giving life directly contradicts the idea of the vagina as anything close to passive.'[95] However, it was not a good time for Chicago. *The Dinner Party* had left her ostracized from the art scene for a while: 'In the '70s I was like a leper [...] I had to start all over again [...] I lost everything as a result of *The Dinner Party* [...] I wanted to keep making art [...] I was very isolated.'[96] The *Birth Project* grew out of Chicago's fascination with 'the birth process as a metaphor for creation'.[97] Similarly to *The Dinner Party*, Chicago's narrative is one of not being able to find any pre-existing images which somehow told the 'truth' about women's experiences, and so having to be a pioneer, talking to women and making the unseen truly seen: 'I knew that I wanted to dispel at least some of this secrecy.'[98] Her first image of birth was the Wollstonecraft runner back we've already seen; it's compelling that the image was one which so powerfully united birth and death, showing the complex contradictions of the vagina. Chicago studied creation myths from around the world and through time and across cultures. The *Creation Drawings* which started the sequence are largely abstract: ova-like shapes, curves and jagged edges.[99] *Creation of the World* (1980) shows a woman prostrate, head tipped back so that her breasts point upwards and beyond our sight at the top of the frame; legs apart and a deep central rift from which come a foetal shape and various creatures. The vulva is at the centre of the piece; chasm-like and powerful and hard to look at because of the associated images of pain and splitting. It's like a visual echo of American poet Muriel Rukeyser's question: 'What would happen if one woman told the truth about her life? The world would split open.'[100]

Chicago's vibrant image 'Birth Tear/Tear' is graphic, painful, umbilical, vaginal (the almost separate uterus, joined by umbilical lines, recalls another of Kahlo's paintings, her 'Henry Ford Hospital' (1932)).[101] In the act of giving birth, is the woman separated from her genitals? Does her vagina become an autonomous part of her*self*? Or is she at one with it? We've seen that such onto-logical dilemmas had their genesis in *The Dinner Party*'s Wollstonecraft runner and associated images, which offer a rejoinder to ideas about the passivity of the woman's body objectified by a voyeuristic viewpoint, and this idea of *view-point* was particularly compelling in considering the Kahlo / Wollstonecraft / Gentileschi / Judith genealogy I've already established. In *The Birth Project* book Chicago describes being present as a woman called Karin Hibma gave birth. Here, the autonomized, or at least somehow alien, or separated, vagina is very much in evidence as Chicago quotes from her journal entry of the time, describing the bottom half of Karin's body being bloodied and battered, as opposed to the top half, which, as Karin held her son for the first time, was bathed in motherhood: '"maternity" surrounded the upper part of Karin's body and suffused her, the baby, and Michael in a kind of unearthly glow that was in total contrast to the animality of her bleeding, cut, lower body.'[102] Chicago's 1980 sketches of the scene, *Karin Pushing* and *Afterwards*, illustrate this contrast viv-idly: 'After the baby was born, I was shocked by the way Karin's vagina looked. She had had an episiotomy and there was blood everywhere. I couldn't believe that a woman's body could sustain such trauma.'[103] Like Courbet's *L'Origine Du Monde*, the second of these two sketches show nothing of Karin's face; she has become separated from her vagina, which occupies the centre of the picture, abstracted and yet very clear. The impact of witnessing Karin's labour is clear in 1983's *Birth*, also clearly a development of *Creation of the World*. In *Birth NP* (1984) the mythological, creation-myth, little-creature aspects of *Creation* have disappeared. Instead the centre of the work is dominated by a zigzagged-cunt reflected on the right by a zigzagged foetus in utero – but the uterus is external to the body. *Birth Tear E2* shows this same primal rift once more, a rift whose explosive power is throwing the woman's body backwards; her face can be seen, her mouth is in rictus and her arms are thrown helplessly outwards. One senses that this is a terrible thing the vagina is doing *to* the woman: it is autonomized in the most destructive sense. This radically opposes the idea of birth as an holistic experience which somehow makes a woman 'a woman'. By contrast, there's something less agonizing about *The Crowning* of 1981, where the baby's head is a circular focus for the work, of which many versions, in different media, exist, perhaps the most beautiful being Q 9/9, in its golden filigree embroidery.[104] Here, the threads seem to pulsate in blues, purples and deep oranges, radiating from the centre of the baby's head to the rippling opening of the floral-celestial vulva. This central vulva is also present in *Birth Power* (1984), where flame-like reds and orange colours pour out of a woman's cunt as she bends forward to embrace it (she is *Sheela*-like, almost, in the stretched, exaggerated centrality of the cunt). The abstracted cunt features in another of Chicago's projects, her illustration of selections of erotic writing by Anaïs Nin (1903–77), *Fragments From the Delta of Venus*, where the cunt is depicted variously as sea urchin, mouth, and 'giant hothouse flower'.[105]

Other artists who have experimented with representing the 'active' female body include Renée Cox. Her towering photographic nude (nude, that is, except for a pair of high heels) self-portrait 'The Yo Mama' (1993), shows her holding her smiling infant son across her front. It's an image simultaneously suggestive of vulnerability and power. Cox also caused controversy in 2001 with her own reworking of the Last Supper, 'Yo Mama's Last Supper' (1996). Here, Cox is the central Christ figure, nude and with black disciples apart from one white man – Judas. The picture prompted Rudolph Giuliani, then Mayor of New York, to withdraw funding from any projects which, like Cox's, he argued, did not meet standards of 'decency'. Cox's massive 9' × 9' 'Kiss' formed part of her 'American Family' exhibit in 2001. It's a video installation which makes two sets of lips kissing seem extraordinary, even other-worldly, by the use of extreme close-ups. The effect is one of fleshy confusion: one initially *expects* to be seeing an interaction that is pornographic – lips seem to become labia – but which, in fact, is not. Controversy – and this is a pattern we'll see repeatedly for these artists – had also surrounded Mary Kelly's 1973–79 'Post-Partum Document'. This is the female body as patriarchy does not want to see it (nor some feminists either, it would appear: Judy Chicago has said of a recent exhibition of Kelly's work:

'My god! It was so boring!').[106] Maternity *is* about shit, blood and piss, and the stained nappies Kelly showed as 'Documentation I' merely confirm this. The art of Rona Pondick is, similarly, discomfiting. Her autonomized mouths, spherical organs without a body, were constructed in the 1990s as part of a series of almost 20 'Teeth' sculptures. The separation of these mouths from any human context makes them ugly, decontextualized, autonomous: they represent part of the human body, and yet are transfigured into, for example, grey spheres, out of which teeth seem to emerge. She has other versions in the same series, some massed together into sweetie jars, others in a sickly pink plastic jumble. The same defamiliarizing unease is apparent in her 'Baby Bottles' (1989) series where, in 'Milkman', white clinical feeding bottles with yellowy teats are placed incongruously in a pair of shoes on what looks like an air bag.

Birth images offer a glimpse of female identity that social propriety keeps elusive. We need to maintain a balance between the theoretical and the embodied experiences of women: the ripped perineum during childbirth is not a construct. It's a real, lived experience. In this kind of reading, the cunt becomes powerfully present and productive – not only of the baby but also of meaning. It challenges the phallocentric order in its radical experience and reality. A baby isn't only a 'meaning' or a 'sign', and its body – like that of its mother – must not be theorized out of existence. Even in attempting to configure their own bodies and organize their own experiences through artistic expression, then, are women doomed to fail, to fall into the 'space between'? Because of the prison house or, more favourably, prism, of language, the female artist (Chicago, Cox, Kelly, Pondick, et al.) is doubly othered, denied sanction for their artistic expression. Perhaps *this* is the space between the pathologized and the eroticized? Perhaps this liminal uncertainty is the only truth the cunt can ever know? And it's here that Griselda Pollock appears to relent somewhat. 'In that space between a necessary and an alien *otherness*', she writes, 'we might begin to look for traces of a shift in the circuits of meaning'.[107] It's the violated or parturient vagina which can, I would argue, most effectively articulate that shift. We'll see shortly how male visual artists, and female artists who have not experienced childbirth first-hand, represent the crowning vagina. The images they create are up for grabs and open to the vagaries of interpretation. In these images, 'sclf' and 'other' are in flux, creating anxiety in the artist. The innovative male film-maker Stan Brakhage, for example, whose work we'll look at shortly, has been described as 'nearly paralyzed by his confrontation with raw life', in filming a live birth, seeking 'refuge from the phenomenal world and its attendant, primal anxieties by retreating behind the camera'.[108]

Birth rites and wrongs

Where, then, is the parturient vagina in twenty-first-century art? Is it actually the case that *all* representational art that shows women's bodies autonomizes the vagina, whether it's parturient or not? I'm going to focus, here, on the work of modern artists who represent 'Birth as Confrontational Image'.[109] The London-based sculptor Ron Mueck's 'Mother and Child' is a visually arresting sculpture which plays with the dichotomies of realism/surrealism, life/death, and autonomy/dependence.[110] Prone, on a disproportionately hefty and spotless white plinth, a mother lifts up her head and shoulders a little in order to look at the tiny new-born baby resting on her abdomen. Her vulva, vividly and realistically represented, is the portal which connects the two – like a telephone cord the umbilicus joins her baby to her, disappearing into her vagina and away from view. Her expression is extraordinary: she looks exhausted, yes, as one might expect, but also puzzled, as though she is not quite sure how to relate to this living being which is so much part and yet *not* part of her own body. The umbilicus signifies the inner being outer; and her labia, although slightly engorged, do seem to be somehow holding on to it, not wanting to release it and let the afterbirth emerge. The mother's apparent disengagement makes the cunt even more separate from herself – alien things happen in this known/unknown place; things over which she has little control. Despite being unnervingly lifelike, the sculpture is actually roughly half-life-size, demonstrating the uncanny manipulation of scale for which Mueck is so well known, and of which he argues 'I never make life-size figures because it never seemed to be interesting. We meet life-size people every day.'[111] The 2003 National Gallery exhibition of 'Mother and Child' provoked a variety of responses and, in a pattern which is depressingly familiar when it comes to artists trying to represent the vagina, not all of them were positive. The curator, Colin Wiggins, viewed the viewers' responses: 'You felt that they were confronting a sacred object. You could see that it was communicating something in a visceral and emotional way.'[112]

What's so utterly compelling to me about 'Mother and Child' is that it's not about the *angriness* of the parturient body, but about an umbilical separation and simultaneous conjunction of individuals via the vagina. The mother's expression is one of puzzlement, not, as in crowning images, of agony or ecstasy. The baby is a little astronaut whose lifeline to the mother ship is precarious and temporary and on which she/he is utterly dependent at the moment of Mueck's representation. Indeed, the baby's tiny face seems as wearily puzzled by this first contact as that of the mother. We get the sense that both of them have been through something traumatic, confusing and wonderful. While anatomically the statue is accurate and hyper-real (the word most critics seem to use in discussing Mueck's works), it is simultaneously, in this world of contrasts, dichotomies and contradictions, *un*realistic. Why has she been transported, with her baby, to this cold, white plinth? Why is she alone? How can the plinth be so non-visceral, clinical, cold, when the affective bond of the figures is so vividly depicted? The answer lies, of course, in the multivalent, ambiguous cunt: it's a portal; a mediating space whose autonomy has brought this mother and baby together but which neither of them look at – we, the visitors to the exhibition, are the ones who see it and who marvel at it. And we know that the body still contains the placenta: this frozen moment in time is on the cusp of another delivery which will never happen because this is, after all, art only imitating life. This vagina's work is not yet finished.[113]

In the spring of 2011, the Manchester-based Birth Rites Collection hosted two symposia considering the representation of birth in visual art. At a session on 'Birth as Confrontational image', three practising British artists, Helen Knowles, Jonathan Waller and Hermione Wiltshire spoke about their work. Waller's *Birth* sequence comprises around 80 images from the mid-1990s and was sparked off by the 'intensity' of the 1995 birth of his first child.[114] In trying to articulate that intensity artistically, Waller found very little work depicting the *act* of birth (a problem Chicago had also identified some years previously), especially by men. Many of his paintings are life-sized and have a liquescent quality to them, as gouache and silk dye and car paint, pastels and charcoal, variously combine to produce an almost veiled effect. Waller compares his painting to the birth process – perhaps with a knowing irony – since both involved a 'hard won' activity in terms of 'getting the image out'. His paintings strip away the medical aspects of the process leaving the female figure in control. Critics of Waller's work, he reported at the two symposia, see the 'infant as a phallus', a bizarre observation which, of course, he refutes. It's one which, it strikes me, says far more about the viewer than the artist and which is spoken from a position of being unable to see the vagina as anything other than erotic. Waller's paintings are, he argues, quite literally 'sensuous': in witnessing the moment of crowning we are witnessing all of the woman's senses on high alert and the emergence, too, of a new human being who has yet to use or discover all *their* senses.[115] What Waller encountered when he attempted to display these paintings in the gallery with which he'd been working for eight years, however, was a version of the seen/unseen paradox of the vagina: we know that vaginal births are natural and common and that they'll have happened numerous times in the time it's taken to read this paragraph. But the issue of representation has to do with the audacity of removing the crowning vagina from the safely controlled, restricted-access, clinical space and into a more public context. Waller's then gallery owner angrily asked him: 'Why are you making these pictures?' The vagina as sensuous, powerful, productive entity has, it would appear, no quarter in the art world. On the first day of the exhibition Waller discovered that one of his *Birth* paintings had been moved off the Flowers East Gallery wall and put into a store room; it was hung again only because of the intervention of Waller's friends and – presumably – regular buyers from the Gallery. Reinforcing the idea of the crowning image as controversial, Waller recounts how he moved his work to the New End Gallery in Hampstead whose owners were, to use his words 'interested in contentious work'. The vagina, it seems, is *always* 'contentious' when it is explicitly shown. An article published in *The Independent on Sunday* about Waller's *Birth* sequence ran the headline 'Birth paintings get a queasy reception' and asked 'Is Birth the last taboo subject in art?'[116] In another review, the columnist asked, with stunning essentialist naivety: 'should a man be portraying this area of women's experience?'[117] As Waller puts it with remarkable understatement, 'In England people find anything to do with the genitalia difficult.'[118]

One of the most striking of Waller's images is *Mother No. 58* (1998) where a baby's torso has emerged, its arms seemingly pulling its body away from its mother whose scrunched-up face shares the baby's own look of bewilderment and determination (see Figure 5.6).[119] The palette is one of dusky reds and browns and the line of the mother's pubic hair is midpoint in the frame. Here is the vulva as active, distended, central and remarkable in its openness and elasticity. It takes on an almost spiritual significance in performing this parturitive function. Photographer Claire Harbottle has argued that the perspective we're so used to seeing in birthing images is deeply engrained into artistic representation where, more often than not, we have 'the foot of the bed perspective, the supine position of the body with the legs (where there are any) spread wide, the foregrounding of the genital area and the cropping out of the woman's non-reproductive body parts [which] continue to be pervasive conventions right up to today, both in medical illustration and in art'.[120] Waller's works are more generous to their subjects than those Harbottle describes. The women often have birthing partners with them, and, in the case of *Mother No. 58*, although she is alone with her baby, we can see her face and share in her energy. The same is true of *Mother No. 59*, which is very similar in appearance to *58*, except for the fact that the mother's pelvis is drawn in cross-section: we can see the unseen – the pelvic bones parting, the baby's feet braced on the top of the uterine wall as if to propel herself into the world, like a swimmer performing a turn at the end of a lane in a swimming pool.[121] It's an astounding image – anatomical but not grotesque; explicit but showing the contained maternal body; static, yet with an overarching sense of momentum to it. The vagina and vulva are active, powerful and remarkable in their elasticity and accomplishment.

This is not, of course, to everyone's taste: many people (men *and* women), I suspect, still yearn for the 1950s clichéd model of the midwifery suite, complete with corridor for pacing up and down in, smoking in and looking relieved in, when a nimble female nurse emerges through swing doors and announces: 'Congratulations, Mr Dull: you've got a beautiful baby girl!' Such people believe the parturient vagina should remain covert, hermetic and distant. So quite why those same people went to the Axiom Arts Centre in the summer of 1998 to see Waller's exhibition called *Birth* is a little mysterious, and their 'Exhibition Comments' display just how far we still need to go to reveal the covert realities of so many women's lives. Male visitors to the exhibition wrote of how 'P'raps a wom[a]n should've done it?'; 'Larger than life. Excellentish'; 'samey'; 'Diagrams a bit cheesy'.[122] Female visitors wrote of how 'This *must* be a male artist. The last thing women need is to have the "idealised" nature of birth claimed by a man and offered up as erotica'; 'This exhibition makes me feel physically sick. I can't bear to look at it and the thought of my daughter (seven years) seeing it makes me sad'; 'I am a trained midwife [. . .] I find these images of childbirth very distressing [. . .] These images should not be [o]n public display without a midwife to give positive counselling'; 'These pictures are not suitable for children walking by. If we must have them, put them in the other room.' There were positive comments from men, too: 'superb draughtsmanship'; 'magnificent portrayals of the emotion and grandeur of normal childbirth'; 'F***ing amazing! Brilliant'; and 'Bollocks to the critics'. Women were also forthcoming in their praise for the 'beautifully sensitive' compositions; and for the 'quite incredible – *very* powerful' images; two female respondents mentioned goddess imagery: 'In all ancient civilisations you can find artefacts of big bellied, open legged women (Sheela na Gig). At least once upon a time women were revered for the Goddesses they are!'; and: 'Absolutely amazing, terrifying but so utterly powerful, that immense power of woman, to be referred to as the *weaker sex* what a *joke*. A celebration of the Goddess in us all.' What saddens me so much about the negative comments is how the cunt – no matter how it's portrayed – is somehow 'indecent' *per se*. The concerns expressed by female visitors to the exhibition about their children being 'exposed' to Waller's images as if they were no different from pornographic representations, startled me, even though it's a sentiment I've, of course, encountered many times in the writing of this book. The woman who wanted to 'protect' her seven-year-old daughter from the images is doing far more harm than the images could do in and of themselves: she's encouraging her daughter to see part of her body as shameful, as something to be moved to 'the other room', as if it were, indeed, quite separate and autonomous.

Claire Harbottle also focuses on the idea of the remarkable cultural and social precariousness of images of the parturitive vagina. In the photograph

'Self Portrait with Dead Mother' (2010), for example, she is seated, naked, holding one of William Hunter's eighteenth-century anatomical drawings between her legs. The positioning means that we know that Harbottle's own genitals are behind Hunter's image of brutally dissected yet beautifully rendered female genitals; similarly, the depicted uterus covers her own. The very way she's positioned Hunter's engraving is roughly anatomically correct and the shock comes from the accurate yet misleading specificity of the work's title. Hunter's 'models' were corpses who died in childbirth. Like Sarah Lucas's 'Chicken Knickers', Harbottle's 'Self Portrait' makes for an uncomfortable and incongruous conjunction of the living and the dead; of that which 'should' be seen, and of that which should not. This is the cunt in its visceral, butchered state, rendered radically non-erotic; dissected by the anatomist's scalpel, the illustrator's pen and the viewer's gaze. In her work, Harbottle shows how much non-western parturitive art, in moving away from the supine form of representation, necessarily adopts a different viewing position and empowers the depicted women more. The mother is rendered primary in such representations where her 'subjectivity is paramount and her process more important than the event of the birth'.[123] Artist Hermione Wiltshire, speaking on the same Birth Rites panel as Waller, in 2011, also stated that the 'actual image of crowning [and of the taut perineum is] really problematic' and can 'frighten people'.[124] Unlike Waller, she articulates the vagina in paradoxically phallic terms – the pregnant body, she argues, pushes into space and indicates sexual activity 'like an erect penis'. Wiltshire is bold about the somatic impact of her work, images which offer the privileged position of the moment of crowning 'before the baby has features [. . .] but has appeared'. Such images could, she states, 'remind people of shitting [. . . or of] an emerging penis'. It is 'quite alien'. Her 'Introduce' piece, a flat photographic surface under a domed glass sculpture, gives the impression of reaching out to the viewer in the gallery. In describing that work, Wiltshire's language is again suffused with the key ideas of the seen/unseen and, strikingly, with phallocentrism: the piece is like 'an eye' and is 'erect and excited'.

We've already seen how Chicago struggled to house her monumental *Dinner Party*. Similarly, these artists sometimes struggle to display their work in public: Knowles recounts how Hermione Wiltshire's reproduction of pioneering midwife Ina May Gaskin's *Therese in Ecstatic Childbirth* (2008), a midwifery image which shows the moment of crowning, and the mother's euphoric face, when initially displayed at the Birth Rites Collection in Salford, was repeatedly covered up by people who, presumably, found its detailed depiction of the moment of crowning offensive; Wiltshire had previously been asked to hide it in a locked office.[125] This act of censorship, a variation of which involved *Therese* being covered by another poster in 2009, is odd because we can infer what's behind. Given only the image of open legs and rapturous face – for that is what the poster covering the image leaves open to view – the viewer might well extrapolate that a pornographic, not a birthing image is what lies behind. To return to the ideological position of the viewer as established by Parker and Pollock, such images can be 'easily retrieved and co-opted by a male culture because they do not rupture radically meanings and connotations of woman in art as body, as sexual, as nature, as object for male possession'.[126] In an important sense the ambiguity created by the placement of the censoring, obscuring poster actually made the image – paradoxically through covering it up – more pornographic. Censorship of the vagina creates its own 'realities' which, as it transpires, are utterly illusory; covert visibilities and possibilities are conjured up, tremulous, disturbing, spectral and on the margins.

Wiltshire herself has much to say about the role of the viewer in observing confrontational images. 'Who is looking' determines the interpretation, and 'the way that we identify with images' constitutes our identities. When we look on the parturient vagina we see realism or threat, depending on our perspective and on the experiences we bring to that moment of artistic encounter. *Therese* differs from images like Courbet's *L'Origine* because those 'pornographic images tend to delink the vagina from the face. [. . . *Therese*] changes that by showing the woman's face as well as her genitals'.[127] Wiltshire's recent photographic works, 'Yoga Positions for Birth' (2008), show heavily pregnant women in seemingly floating Yoga poses emphasizing the power of Yogic breathing, Pranayama, forging a powerful connection between 'the mouth and the perineum'.[128] Again, in pregnancy and birth, the reproductive body is analogous to the mouth – each creates and gives forth, and it's on the mouth that artist Helen Knowles's work focuses, too. Curator of the Birth Rites Collection, Knowles collaborated in 2007 with the graphic designer Francesca Granato to make wallpaper, the pink figures on which brought together images of birthing and lap dancing. In this mixture of the domestic and the erotic the pregnant form is ambiguous and powerful and the figures are sufficiently small that what initially appears to be a geometric design 'entices the audience in' until the 'meaning becomes more evident'.[129] In Knowles's *Ecstatic Birth* pictures this 'detective' work continues – the heavily pixelated close-ups of women's faces, sometimes so close-up that their eyes are not included in the frame, borrow from the work of Gaskin, the midwife on whose work Wiltshire also draws. Knowles's artworks, made up of reassembled stills from YouTube birth videos, show how the facial lips can mirror in their intensity and shape the opening of the labia which are not seen but which remain inferred – there are echoes here of Wiltshire's floating yogis. Is this woman throwing back her head and parting her lips in the ecstasy or pain of childbirth? Or in the ecstasy or pain of a pornographic image? The ambiguity reminds us of the vagina's uniquely paradoxical cultural positioning where its ubiquity hangs in the balance with its simultaneous furtiveness. The depiction of the nudity of natural childbirth is still a taboo where pornography is, increasingly, less so.

That taboo was powerfully challenged in 1959 by Stan Brakhage, who made a 13-minute film called *Window Water Baby Moving*, which documented the birth of his first child. It's a hard film to watch because one feels intrusive as Brakhage zooms in on the blood-red vagina, hands, mouths, the crowning, the delivery, the placenta . . . there's something overwhelmingly visceral and intense about it. It's fleshly and so graphic that Kodak requested a release form from the Brakhages' doctor before handing the film back to them and not to the police.[130] Watching Jane Brakhage's vulva stretch during crowning is quite miraculous; seemingly impossible. One watches, willing the baby to emerge and shares the delight on the faces of Stan and Jane Brakhage at the end of the film as the baby lies contentedly on Jane's chest. Does looking at such close-ups of the woman's genitals make us into voyeurs, little better than pornographers? I'd take issue both with Harbottle's claim that Brakhage's technique is that of a 'possessive objectifying spectatorial voyeurism of an overly intrusive lens', and also with the thoughts of the artist and sometime Warhol Factory member Carolee Schneemann (b. 1939, Pennsylvania), on how 'the male eye replicated or possessed the vagina's primacy of giving birth'.[131] In Brakhage's

film (more properly, I suppose, the Brakhages' film), editing techniques create metaphors for birth.[132] Helen Knowles has described how dynamic and
intense being present at a birth is. There was a 'vacillation', she says, 'between
being the watcher and the watched and being inside and outside of the experience', reporting that this feeling is also 'true of childbirth [. . .] at the time
you're in it but then afterwards there's a hell of a lot of [. . .] contemplation of
what's happened to you'.[133] As Chicago talks about the 'softening' effect of using
needlework in depicting the brutal scene on *The Dinner Party*'s Wollstonecraft
runner back, so Knowles articulates a key aesthetic, and even emotional difference, between the photographic and the drawn: 'something graphic is potentially toned down by a drawing'. Brakhage's refusal to 'tone down' is precisely
what makes his film so extraordinary.

Jessica Clements's paintings are remarkable in their omission of certain factors which make the visceral so real. Her 2009 work 'Eileen and Liam' has a
woman on her own in the by now familiar supine position, her face and neck
taut with the effort of pushing, blood viscously dripping onto the white sheet
beneath her (much like Chicago's Wollstonecraft). Her 'Charity and Isaiah' of
2007 is astonishing, however, in its utter defamiliarization. In a Courbet-style
framing of the image, the woman's neck, face, hands and feet are not shown.
The eye is drawn to the sight of the dilated vulva between the mother's spread
legs, with two little legs dangling down from it. There is no sense of urgency
or alarm because we cannot see the mother's expression, nor any sign of any
assistance for her, but we almost instinctively know that this reimagined crowning, the footling breech birth, is unusual and threatening to both mother and
child. Not enough of the story is revealed to us in the painting and so we can
only view it in a state of anxiety. The vagina, portal to life, is here a dangerous,
defamiliarized place. Clements writes that her 'work and [her] goals in painting have changed during the course of [her] research'. She continues:

> As I started my series of birth paintings, my primary concern was to
> understand and depict the physiological process of childbirth: how a woman's
> body changes to accommodate the birth of a child. Accordingly, my earliest
> paintings in this series were cropped tightly around the genitalia to show
> the birth of the baby [. . .] But I have also become more concerned about

the implication of focusing on so narrow a part of a woman's body, even as she births. While the information from these images is valuable, especially since it is largely unavailable, the image itself becomes depersonalized and removed from the experience of a particular woman giving birth. Over time, I began to shift my visual research away from the pure physiology of birth to the physiology of birth in a broader context: a woman's personal experience of birth in relation to her birthing body, and her support network.[134]

A familiar pattern is present here. Like Chicago, Waller and Wiltshire before her, Clements also experienced aggressive objections when she came to show 'Charity and Isaiah'. 'The Office of the President [of the College] had asked our gallery director to remove the painting', writes Clements, 'When we met with the Chief of Staff, he said that several employees were complaining that the painting made them uncomfortable. They argued that birth is a private affair, and here it was displayed in the atrium on their way to the bathroom [. . .] The Chief of Staff [. . .] thought about it, and [. . .] decided that the painting could stay up.'[135] This idea of not *seeing* what we all know is there to be seen – indeed, many of the College staff members would have touched their own vaginas in 'the bathroom' – is precisely the covert visibility enacted because of anxiety around the vagina.[136] Harbottle herself sums it up: 'The Nativity, acted out annually in thousands of school halls, conventionally entirely ignores the actuality of birth in a play almost entirely devoted to the subject.'[137] Monica Sjöö also had a birth image, her 1973 'God Giving Birth', a work celebrating the home birth of her second son in 1961, made into something of a cause célèbre when it was hung as part of the *5 Women Artists – Images of Womanpower* exhibition at Swiss Cottage Library in London. As Sjöö herself wrote, 'I nearly ended up in Court on the charge of "obscenity and blasphemy".'[138] For women to give birth, then, is fine; for them to do so *and* to read into the experience something so profound that they need to convey it artistically, and without recourse to artistic metaphor, is not.

Ghislaine Howard's 1993 'Birth Painting' reproduces the prostrate birthing pose, but her 'Birth Painting No. 2' completely reverses the point of view so that the viewer is placed behind the mother's head, looking down on her but also *with* her as she too observes the painterly confusion between her legs. Clements has argued that Howard's paintings 'though beautiful, feel like disembodied experiences to me'.[139] I don't agree. Clements's own work is photographic in its clarity and realism (almost *surrealism* in the case of 'Charity and Isaiah'), but she still, in her earlier works at least, to some extent defamiliarizes Charity by removing her head from the frame, focusing instead on the gravid abdomen. By contrast, Howard's more muted, blurry and impressionistic technique conveys something of the fervid atmosphere of the delivery room and the radical shift in perspective in 'Birth Painting No. 2' is remarkably effective and enabling.

Renaissance?

Judy Chicago's work may be read as a figurative intervention, an attempt to *represent* the female body beyond the bounds of phallocentric discourse. Depicting the parturient body is not an essentialist enterprise, then, but becomes one which, in scholar Elizabeth Grosz's words, is 'a contestation of patriarchal representations *at the level of cultural representation itself*.[140] This 'contestation' takes many forms. In a sense, Artemisia Gentileschi embraced it, and depicted Judith doing likewise. The confrontational positioning of the birthing body in Frida Kahlo's 'My Birth' was echoed – unwittingly – by Chicago in her Wollstonecraft place-setting, and other artists, male and female, parents and child-free, have developed the theme, in order to depict the vulva as a place of vital potential, not of agonizing jeopardy. In fact, every one of McCartney's 400 'models' could be said to have made small but significant interventions into the field of 'contestation'. Foundations are in place, and walls are being built.

Notes

1   Julia Kristeva, *Powers of Horror: An Essay on Abjection*, trans. Leon S. Roudiez (New York, NY: Columbia University Press, 1982), p. 101.

2   Judy Chicago, *The Dinner Party: From Creation to Preservation* (London, NY: Merrell, 2007), p. 257.

3   Griselda Pollock, *Differencing the Canon: Feminist Desire and the Writing of Art's Histories* (London: Routledge, 1999), p. 98.

4   On the relationship of truth, meaning and desire, and how 'desire is gendered, hence it is always political', see Pollock, *Differencing*, p. 112.

5   Thus my memories of myself as a child seeing for the first time a copy of Édouard Manet's last major painting, his 'Bar at the Folies-Bergère' (1882). I loved what appeared to be the initial simplicity of the picture: a pretty woman in a pretty dress. But I also loved the impossibilities of the painting, and these would cause me to tilt my head to my left shoulder in a pose of puzzled concentration, creasing up my forehead in an attempt to understand, to 'get' it. But, of course, Manet's painting does not satisfy that childish desire to understand. It's a painting which does not 'work' on us in terms of the physics and mechanics of reflection, bodies, objects, but which utterly *does* work on us from an imaginative position of wonderment. Even as an adult the painting gives me an almost childlike frisson; it is a work to be somehow not only *seen* but also *felt* – the zenith of Impressionism, perhaps.

6   Chicago writes of Kahlo that 'I didn't know her work at that time as it was almost unknown in the States', Judy Chicago, personal email correspondence with the author, 22 May 2012.

7   Of his dead wife, William Godwin writes that 'She considered herself as standing forth in defence of one half of the Human species [. . .] She saw, indeed, that they were often attempted to be held in silken fetters, and bribed into the love of slavery'. See William Godwin, *Memoirs of the Author of 'A Vindication of the Rights of Woman'. By William Godwin. The Second Edition, Corrected* (London: J. Johnson, 1798), p. 79.

8   Judy Chicago, *The Birth Project* (New York, NY: Doubleday & Co, 1985), p. 6.

9   Chicago, *From Creation to Preservation*, p. 273.

10 Amelia Jones, 'Sexual Politics: Feminist Strategies, Feminist Conflicts, Feminist Histories', in Amelia Jones (ed.), *Sexual Politics: Judy Chicago's 'Dinner Party' in Feminist Art History* (Berkeley, CA: University of California Press, 1996), pp. 20–38 (p. 27).

11 On the 'known narrative' see Pollock, *Differencing*, p. 115.

12 On 'seeking a gap' for interpretation, see Pollock, *Differencing*, p. 115.

13 For Meyer on Gentileschi's 'vulvar drapery folds', see Laura Meyer, 'From Finish Fetish to Feminism', in Jones, *Sexual Politics*, p. 69. See also Chicago, *From Creation to Preservation*, p. 154.

14 Chicago, *From Creation to Preservation*, p. 154.

15 Salomon, quoted in Pollock, *Differencing*, p. 108.

16 Pollock, *Differencing*, p. 97.

17 Ibid., p. 95.

18 Mieke Bal, 'Head Hunting "Judith" on the Cutting Edge of Knowledge', in Athalya Brenner (ed.), *A Feminist Companion to Esther, Judith and Susanna* (The Feminist Companion to the Bible, 7. Sheffield: Sheffield Academic Press, 1995), pp. 253–85 (p. 277).

19 Bal, 'Head Hunting "Judith"', p. 282; my emphasis.

20 Margarita Stocker, *Judith: Sexual Warrior, Women and Power in Western Culture* (New Haven, CT: Yale University Press, 1998), p. 17.

21 Marcia Pointon, 'Artemisia Gentileschi's *The Murder of Holofernes*', *American Imago*, 38.4 (Winter 1981), pp. 343–67 (p. 345).

22 Pointon, 'Artemisia Gentileschi's *The Murder of Holofernes*', p. 351.

23 Ibid., p. 352.

24   Pollock, *Differencing*, p. 116.

25   Pointon, 'Artemisia Gentileschi's *The Murder of Holofernes*', p. 351.

26   Bal, 'Head Hunting "Judith"', p. 269.

27   Pollock, *Differencing*, p. 124.

28   Ibid.

29   Agnès Merlet, *Artemisia* (1998), subtitles to the French voiceover and dialogue.

30   Pollock, *Differencing*, p. 126, n. 44.

31   David A. de Silva, *Introducing the Apocrypha: Message, Context, and Significance* (Ada, MI: Baker Academic, 2002), p. 17. See also the *OED* for more on the definition and etymology of the term 'Apocrypha'.

32   de Silva, *Introducing the Apocrypha*, p. 26; on the possibility of a female author (which would, of course, provide a powerful female lineage through to Gentileschi's own 'authorship' of the story in her paintings), see Jan Willem van Henten, 'Judith as Alternative Leader: A Rereading of *Judith 7–23*', in Athalya Brenner (ed.), *A Feminist Companion to Esther, Judith and Susanna* (The Feminist Companion to the Bible, 7. Sheffield: Sheffield Academic Press, 1995), pp. 224–52 (p. 225, n. 3).

33   On the etymology of the name 'Judith' see O. Odelain and R. Séguineau, *Dictionary of Proper Names and Places in the Bible,* trans. Matthew J. O' Connell (London: Robert Hale, 1982), p. 229; on Judith as emblem, see Amy-Jill Levine, 'Sacrifice and Salvation: Otherness and Domestication in the *Book of Judith*', in Athalya Brenner (ed.), *A Feminist Companion to Esther, Judith and Susanna* (The Feminist Companion to the Bible, 7. Sheffield: Sheffield Academic Press, 1995), pp. 209–23 (p. 208).

34   de Silva, *Introducing the Apocrypha*, p. 85.

35   On the tent as *sukkâ*, see van Henten, 'Judith as Alternative Leader', p. 250.

36   *The Book of Judith*, 7:12–13, the Bible, *Authorized King James Version with Apocrypha*, intro. and notes by Robert Carroll and Stephen Prickett (Oxford World's Classics. Oxford: Oxford University Press, 1998); hereafter simply 'Jdt.'.

37   Jdt., 7:14.

38   On the etymological debates around the name of the fictional city of Bethulia, see John Barton and John Muddiman (eds), *The Oxford Bible Commentary* (Oxford: Oxford University Press, 2001), p. 638.

39   Jdt., 7:27.

40   Ibid., 8:2–3.

41   Margarita Stocker, *Judith: Sexual Warrior, Women and Power in Western Culture* (New Haven, CT: Yale University Press, 1998), p. 11.

42   Jdt., 8:16.

43   Ibid., 8:32.

44   Ibid., 8:34.

45   Ibid., 10:4.

46   Ibid., 9:8; 9:10 (my emphasis).

47   Ibid., 9:13.

48   Ibid., 10:21.

49 Ibid., 11:6 (my emphasis).

50 On the role of the *double entendre* in the story see, for example, van Henten, 'Judith as Alternative Leader', p. 227.

51 Jdt., 11:16.

52 On Judith's Medusan qualities see Mieke Bal, 'Head Hunting "Judith"', pp. 253–85.

53 Jdt., 12:12.

54 Ibid., 12:14 (note the ambiguous usage of 'my lord' here); 12:20.

55 Ibid., 13:4; 13: 6; 13:8; on Judith as mirror image of the 'coded erotic norm' of Lucretia's tale whereby 'Lucretia is Judith's analogue in chastity and resolution, but her opposite in terms of sexual narrative', see Stocker, *Judith: Sexual Warrior*, p. 20.

56 Of course, as a widow, Judith is not a virgin but is renowned in Bethulia for her piety and chastity. The *Book* makes a point of the fact that she did not ever remarry. Levine goes even further, suggesting that 'Judith *had* to be a widow – that is, sexually experienced but unattached – in order for her to carry out her plan.' See Levine, 'Sacrifice and Salvation', p. 213; my emphasis.

57 Stocker, *Judith: Sexual Warrior*, p. 17. Stocker reads another artist's representation of the assassination scene, that of Jan de Bray (1627–97), as playing with sexualized imagery in the positioning of the phallic sword raised above Judith's head, and the feminized basin and casually snuffed-out candle sitting in the picture's foreground. The painting 'is a representation of sex as a mediating term between life and death, as an expiration into orgasmic oblivion' (Stocker, p. 16).

58 The 'Delilah' quotation is from de Silva, *Introducing the Apocrypha*, p. 85; the 'gorgeous gorgon' description is from Stocker, *Judith: Sexual Warrior*, p. 2; Levine writes about losing one's head in 'Sacrifice and Salvation', p. 212.

59 Stocker, *Judith: Sexual Warrior*, p. 9.

60 On this triumph, see Stocker, *Judith: Sexual Warrior*, p. 46. Stocker's book is a quite brilliant examination of the endurance and multiple reinventions of the Judith mytheme. She discusses the erotic representations of Judith which Gustav Klimt depicted in the early twentieth century and considers Judith as avatar for the late-nineteenth-century's 'Punch and Judy' shows, persuasively arguing that by the *fin de siècle*, 'New Women are born of Victorian Judiths'. See Stocker, 'Judy and Punch: *Marriage and 'Fallen Women'* in her *Judith: Sexual Warrior*, pp. 135–49 (p. 148).

61 Jdt., 13:15.

62 Ibid., 14:3.

63 Ibid., 16:6–7; my italics for emphasis.

64 Levine, 'Sacrifice and Salvation', p. 218.

65 Stocker, *Judith: Sexual Warrior*, p. 7.

66 Ibid., p. 106.

67 Bal, 'Head Hunting "Judith"', pp. 267, 269.

68 Jdt., 16:9.

69 Bal, 'Head Hunting "Judith"', p. 272.

70 Ibid.

71 Jdt., 16:25. De Silva contends that, after her heroic action 'there simply is no place for her in society, no institution that can accept her continued presence as a leading figure (not priest, not king, not senator)'. See de Silva, *Introducing the Apocrypha*, p. 105.

72 *Wisdom of Solomon*, 7:6, the Bible, *Authorized King James Version with Apocrypha*, intro. and notes by Robert Carroll and Stephen Prickett (Oxford World's Classics. Oxford: Oxford University Press, 1998).

73 On how Judith her 'delivering her people is an analogue to the delivery of birth', see Stocker, *Judith: Sexual Warrior*, p. 244.

74 Stocker, *Judith: Sexual Warrior*, p. 18; Stocker examines how so many artists have been inspired by Judith's story, since she is a character who is 'iconized as an integration of rationality, physicality and emotion'. Stocker, *Judith: Sexual Warrior*, p. 245.

75 On Feaver's treatment of Judith see Stocker, *Judith: Sexual Warrior*, p. 241.

76 Jamie McCartney, *The Great Wall of Vagina* (Brighton: Jamie McCartney, 2011), pp. 8–9.

77 See the review of Bamber's work in David Greene's 'Nether Nether Land' in the *Los Angeles Reader*, 17 June 1994, 18. According to Susan Kandel, Greene fails to situate Bamber's work in terms of women artists – instead tracing a male artistic lineage from Gustave Courbet and Frederic Church. See Susan Kandel, 'Beneath the Green Veil: The Body in/of New Feminist Art', in Jones (ed.), *Sexual Politics*, pp. 186–200 (p. 199, n. 6).

78 On how difficult it is to 'identify a positive mode of representing the female body in order to *reclaim* it from its patriarchal construction as passive object, fetishized through structures of male desire', see Jones, *Sexual Politics*, p. 97.

79 McCartney, *The Great Wall*, p. 65.

80 Ibid.

81 Ibid., p. 40.

82 Ibid., p. 74.

83 Susan Broomhall, 'Rabelais, the Pursuit of Knowledge, and Early Modern Gynaecology', *Limina*, 4, 1998, pp. 24–34 (p. 32).

84 Broomhall, 'Rabelais', p. 30.

85 Ibid., pp. 31–2.

86 *Selections from the Works of Francis Rabelais, 'Gargantua and Pantagruel'*, trans. Sir Thomas Urquhart and Peter Anthony Motteux (London: John Westhouse, 1945), p. 173.

87 Quoted in Broomhall, 'Rabelais', p. 32. In Urquhart and Motteux's translation, the 'whatchamacallits' become 'sine quo [*sic*.] nons, kallibistris, or contrapunctums of the women', p. 173.

88 *Selections from the Works of Francis Rabelais*, p. 174.

89 Ibid., p. 176.

90 Ibid., p. 175.

91 Ibid., pp. 175, 176.

92 Cosey Fanni Tutti's 'Lip Service' was first shown at the First International Female Artists' Art Biennial, Stockholm, 1994.

93   Cosey Fanni Tutti, personal email correspondence with the author, 31 May 2012.

94   Karen Newman, *Fetal Positions: Individualism, Science, Visuality* (Stanford, CA: Stanford University Press, 1996), pp. 4–5.

95   Chicago, *From Creation to Preservation*, p. 274; in Chicago, *The Birth Project*, p. 7, an 'exhibition unit' is defined as 'a work or works of art plus accompanying documentation'.

96   Judy Chicago, interview with Helen Knowles and Francesca De Biasco, in Chicago's studio in Belen, New Mexico (February 2012): http://birthritescollection.org.uk/#/judy-chicago-podcast/4565041214.

97   Chicago, *The Birth Project*, p. 6.

98   Ibid.

99   Ibid., p. 12.

100 Muriel Rukeyser, 'Käthe Kollwitz', quoted in Chicago, *The Birth Project*, p. 25.

101 Chicago, 'Birth Tear/Tear' (30" × 40"; 1982). See Chicago, *From Creation to Preservation*, p. 273.

102 Chicago, *The Birth Project*, p. 28.

103 Ibid., p. 29.

104 On how gold thread 'accentuated the spiderweb quality of the uterus shape', see Chicago, *The Birth Project*, p. 36.

105 Judy Chicago, *Fragments From the Delta of Venus* (New York, NY: PowerHouse Books, 2004), n.p.

106 Chicago, interview with Knowles and De Biasco.

107 Pollock, *Differencing*, p. 110.

108 William R. Barr, 'Brakhage: Artistic Development in Two Childbirth Films', in Brian Henderson and Ann Martin with Lee Amazonas (eds), *Film Quarterly: Forty Years, A Selection* (Berkeley, CA: University of California Press), pp. 536–41 (p. 538).

109 This title is taken from a presentation at the Birth Rites Collection symposia in Manchester and London in 2011.

110 Ron Mueck, 'Mother and Child', 2001, mixed media (pigmented polyester resin on fibreglass); 24 × 89 × 38 cm.

111 Ron Mueck, quoted by Sarah Tanguy, in 'The Progress of *Big Man*: A Conversation with Ron Mueck' in *Sculpture: A Publication of the International Sculpture Center*, 22:6 (July/August 2003), at: www.sculpture.org/documents/scmag03/jul_aug03/mueck/mueck.shtml.

112 Colin Wiggins, quoted by Sean O'Hagan in 'Ron Mueck: From Muppets to Motherhood', *The Observer*, 6 August 2006, www.guardian.co.uk/artanddesign/2006/aug/06/art2. In the same article, Marina Warner is quoted as saying 'I think Ron is a sacred artist working in a secular way'.

113 The clinical presentation of Mueck's sculpture is somewhat reminiscent of Rineke Dijkstra's 1994 photographs of three mothers holding their new-born babies (one born one hour before the photograph; one a day; and one a week) close to them, standing naked against white, hard-surfaced backgrounds that contrast with and thereby offset the warm humanity of the images. Dijkstra's photographs may be

viewed at the Tate: www.tate.org.uk/servlet/ArtistWorks?cgroupid=999999961&
artistid=2666&page=1.

114 Jonathan Waller, audio recording from the 'Birth as Confrontational Image' panel
at the Whitworth Gallery in Manchester (9 May 2011) and at the Whitechapel
Gallery in London two days later. See: http://birthritescollection.org.uk/#/
birth-in-contemporary-art/4552208619. All quotations from Waller in this section
are from this same source. *Birth* showed at the Axiom Centre for the Arts in
Cheltenham, United Kingdom, from 27 June–26 July 1998. In the exhibition guide,
Waller reveals that Ruth, his wife, was in labour for 37 hours with their daughter,
Eva. The sequence was originally shown in London, at the New End Gallery in
Hampstead, from 22 June–20 July 1997.

115 On how the pictures' mixture of 'pain and sensuality' is 'an inherent part of the
psyche of Western culture. The tortured crucified Christ has been portrayed
throughout ecclesiastical art, and Waller sought inspiration [. . .] in Renaissance
artist Mathias Grunewald's series of religious paintings for the Isenheim Altarpiece',
see Suzanne Bisset, 'Growing Pains: Is Birth Art's Last Taboo?', *Venue* (26 June–10
July 1998), p. 74.

116 Keren David and Mark Rowe, 'Birth Paintings Get a Queasy Reception', *The
Independent on Sunday*, 6 July 1997, www.independent.co.uk/news/birth-paintings-
get-a-queasy-reception-1249258.html.

117 Jo Stanley, 'Male View of a Woman's Labour Pains', *Morning Star* (11 July 1997), p. 8.

118 Jonathan Waller, quoted in David and Rowe, 'Birth Paintings Get a Queasy
Reception'.

119 Jonathan Waller, *Mother No. 58*, mixed media on paper, 144 × 84 cm (1998).

120 Claire Harbottle, 'Lilla's Birthing: Re-appropriating the Subjective Experience of
Birthing in Visual Art', http://claireharbottlebirthwork.blogspot.com/p/lillas-birthin
g-re-appropriating.html.

121 Jonathan Waller, *Mother No. 59*, mixed media on paper, 125 × 69 cm (1998).

122 Axiom Centre for the Arts in Cheltenham, 'Exhibition Comments' document for
Birth, by Jonathan Waller, 27 June–26 July 1998. My grateful thanks to Jonathan for
sharing this document with me.

123 Claire Harbottle, 'Lilla's Birthing'.

124 Hermione Wiltshire, audio recording from the 'Birth as Confrontational Image'
panel at the Whitworth Gallery in Manchester (9 May 2011) and at the Whitechapel
Gallery in London two days later. See: http://birthritescollection.org.uk/#/
birth-in-contemporary-art/4552208619. All quotations from Wiltshire in this
section are from this same source.

125 See journalist Joanna Moorhead's interview with Hermione Wiltshire, 'The
Art of Creation', in the *Guardian*, 28 May 2008. Also see: www.guardian.co.uk/
lifeandstyle/2008/may/28/women.art. For an image of *Therese* covered by a
scientific-looking diagrammatic poster see Claire Harbottle, 'Visual Representation
of Birth: A Paper', Figure 22, http://claireharbottlebirthwork.blogspot.com/p/
visual-representation-of-birth-paper.html.

126 Parker and Pollock, *Old Mistresses*, p. 130.

127 Wiltshire, quoted in Moorhead, 'The Art of Creation'.

128 Wiltshire, quoted on the Birth Rites Collection website, http://birthritescollection. org.uk/#/yoga-positions-for-birth/4542010765.

129 Helen Knowles, audio recording from the 'Birth as Confrontational Image' panel at the Whitworth Gallery in Manchester (9 May 2011) and at the Whitechapel Gallery in London two days later. See: http://birthritescollection.org.uk/#/ birth-in-contemporary-art/4552208619. All quotations from Knowles in this section are from this same source.

130 On this incident when 'the Kodak lab threatened to destroy the film', see Peter Michelson, *Speaking the Unspeakable: A Poetics of Obscenity* (Albany, NY: State University of New York Press, 1993), p. 247.

131 Claire Harbottle, 'Lilla's Birthing'; Carolee Schneemann, 'Interview with Kate Haug', in Schneemann (ed.), *Imaging Her Erotics*, pp. 21–44 (p. 23).

132 On how 'openings and passageways metonymically suggest transitions' and 'become metaphors for the very process of birth itself', see James Peterson, *Dreams of Chaos, Visions of Order: Understanding the American Avant-Garde Cinema* (Detroit, MI: Wayne State University Press, 1994), p. 55.

133 Helen Knowles, audio recording.

134 Jessica Clements, 'The Origin of the World: Women's Bodies and Agency in Childbirth', unpublished Master of Fine Arts thesis, George Mason University, pp. 78–9.

135 Clements, 'The Origin of the World', p. 11.

136 Helen Knowles, in a recent interview with Judy Chicago, expressed her surprise that the docents (gallery guides) at the gallery in Albuquerque which houses a large number of *Birth Project* works, were embarrassed to have them on display. Chicago responded: 'What does that tell you about women's shame about their own experiences? And part of it is that they're so unfamiliar with images about their own experience. They think [. . .] they're shameful'. Chicago, interview with Knowles and De Biasco.

137 Claire Harbottle, 'Visual Representation of Birth: A Paper'.

138 See Sjöö's own account at: www.monicasjoo.com/exhibition/1_god_giving_birth. html. Sjöö's obituary in *The Guardian* describes her as not only a painter but also a 'writer, feminist, formidable networker and activist, eco-witch, anarchist, founder member, in 1969, of Bristol Women's Liberation and inspiration behind Amu Mawu, a Bristol women's spirituality group'. See Pat West, 'Monica Sjöö: a feminist artist working to glorify the goddess and the earth', *The Guardian*, 23 November 2005, www.guardian.co.uk/news/2005/sep/23/guardianobituaries.artsobituaries1.

139 Clements, 'The Origin of the World', p. 63.

140 Grosz, quoted in Pollock's *Differencing*, p. 102; italics in the original.

6

Revealing the Vagina on Film and TV

Anatomies of hell

I've already mentioned Caryl Churchill's play *Top Girls*, and want briefly to return to it here. One of the guests at Marlene's meal was Dull Gret, a figure taken from Brueghel's painting *Dulle Griet*. In the play, the fairly inarticulate Gret recounts the moment Brueghel so vividly rendered:

> We come into hell through a big mouth. Hell's black and red. It's like the village where I come from. There's a river and [. . .] a bridge and houses. There's places on fire like when the soldiers come. There's a big devil sat on a roof with a big hole in his arse and he's scooping stuff out of it with a big ladle, and it's falling down on us, and it's money [. . .] I'd had enough, I was mad, I hate the bastards. I come out my front door that morning and shout till my neighbours come out and I said, "Come on, we're going where the evil come from and pay the bastards out." And they all come out just as they was [. . .] we go through a big mouth into a street just like ours, but in hell.[1]

The 'mouth' Gret describes is at the left-hand side of Brueghel's painting (see Figure 6.1).[2] It looks somewhat fish-like, but it's topped by a humanoid nose and eyes, has a thin lip and a row of serrated teeth. This folkloric hell's mouth motif is widespread in medieval and early-modern European paintings, sermons, sculptures and plays. Its similarities to the gaping orifice of the *vagina dentata* are clear. As the Jungian psychologist Erich Neumann wrote,

'The *positivity* of the womb appears as a mouth; that is why "lips" are attrib-uted to female genitals, and so the basis for the positive symbolic equation [of] the mouth as the "upper womb", [as] the birthplace of the breath and the word, the Logos. Similarly, the *destructive* side of the Feminine, the destruc-tive and deadly womb, appears most frequently in the archetypal form of a mouth bristling with teeth.'[3] In other words, the imagined lips/lips likeness is deeply rooted psychoanalytically, operating, 'in the wonderful algebra of the unconscious', at least, as 'a reversible equation'.[4] Many film-makers have exper-imented in one way or another with ideas of disjointed female identity, and, more importantly, with how the fissure relates to, or originates in, women's sexual organs. This fracture is manifested on film and TV in female characters' strange – hellish – relationships not only with other *characters*, but with their own *anatomies*, too.

Abandon every hope, all you who enter[5]

The title of Catherine Breillat's 2004 *Anatomie de l'enfer* (*Anatomy of Hell*) is ambiguous.[6] If the film 'anatomizes' hell, then what is that 'hell'? It's both the Woman's (she remains unnamed, and is played by Amira Casar) relationship with the Man (Rocco Siffredi takes this unnamed role), but the 'hell' is also, in Neumann's terms, 'the destructive and deadly womb'. This French-language film's opening subtitles suggest that: 'A film is an illusion, not reality-fiction or a happening, it is a true work of fiction', and immediately emphasize the fluidity and precariousness of identity: 'For the actress's most intimate scenes, a body double was used. It's not her body, it's an extension of a fictional character.' The film is in explicitly sexualized territory almost from the outset, as the camera focuses on one man performing fellatio on another in a crowded nightclub. A woman looks on, anomalous in this almost exclusively male setting, moving ethereally between men who scarcely seem to notice her. Her face remains impassive even as she steadily drags a razor blade across her wrist in the club's bathroom. When a man asks her 'Why did you do that?' she replies: 'Because I'm a woman'. And it's this idea of what makes a woman a 'woman' that so preoccupies Breillat, just as it preoccupies the Woman who wears her blood like a badge on her pale pink satin skirt. The graphic nature of the film's beginning is utterly in keeping with its core philosophical tenets. Can we 'watch the unwatchable'? If we can, then do we become initiates? Breillat cuts a deal with her viewers as the Woman does with the Man, when she offers to pay him to 'watch me where I'm unwatchable. No need to touch me. Just say what you see'. The movie operates primarily in the visual, not aural realm – there's no soundtrack to speak of, for example, to guide the viewer's emotional responses, and so the claustrophobic nature of the two protagonists' intimacy is amplified visually. In an interview, Breillat emphasized the idea that it's scrutiny which makes phenomena 'known', and several times compared herself to an entomologist, anatomizing tiny insects, trying to understand and 'own' the physical minutiae of their existences.[7] Following the deal between the Man and the Woman, the action takes place over the course of four nights in the Woman's bedroom, which is unadorned, save for a large eighteenth-century crucifix on one of the walls.

On night one, the Woman looks ashamed as she undresses awkwardly in front of the Man. She's the embodiment of 'abjection', as conveyed by the French philosopher Julia Kristeva: 'A massive and sudden emergence of uncanniness [. . .] now harries me as radically separate, loathsome. Not me. Not that. But not nothing, either.'[8] Her hesitancy is reasonable, given how the Man talks to her, communicating his own Kristevan horror: 'The fragility of female flesh', he says, 'inspires disgust or brutality'. He continues:

It's not what we see, though when you spread your legs we're revolted by the overly bright colour, the sloppy, shapeless aspect of your hidden lips [. . .] a skin that sweats, that oozes, a pestilential skin, like the skin of frogs. Frogs, at least, have the decency of being green, but their thighs, symbolically, can be spread as wide as yours. It's not what we see. Your denial of the obscenity is what frightens us most.

The first-person plural usage here introduces another ambiguity into an already abstract narrative: does the Man mean to speak for all men? Are they the 'we'? Or, because he's a man who identifies as homosexual, does the horror arise from the fact that he finds female anatomy disgusting because it's somehow unknown to him? Are 'we' gay men? Or are 'we' anyone who isn't 'she';

anyone who is watching the Man watch her? In saying that 'it's not what we see', the Man is suggesting a powerfully connotative quality for the female genitals: he cannot imagine any scenario in which their 'obscenity' could possibly be negated. The close-up of the Woman's crotch is accompanied by a female voice-over which compares it to 'a just-hatched bird, still wet from the egg'. The scene abruptly shifts to a presumably analeptic (flashback) moment of a little boy finding, and accidentally killing, a newly hatched chick. Breillat confirms that the boy's terrified because he's 'looking down into a chasm horrifies us'. She argues, though, that the 'chasm' is 'also alluring' and 'frightening' because it's 'something that shouldn't exist'. This is why covert visibility is so potent a cultural presence/absence: 'It exists, and we all know it' but 'There's this whole conspiracy of the human race' making obscenity 'a social concept'. As with the 'we', so here, the 'it' is ambiguous. 'It' could be the cunt, of course, but it could equally be human materiality, the offensive certainty that flesh decays. Either way, the 'conspiracy of the human race' depends in part on the phenomenon of covert visibility.

Back in the bedroom, the Woman masturbates, and the film's leitmotifs fuse together in one moment: life, death, *la petite mort*, vulnerability, desire and disgust. The Man finally walks over to the bed and parts the Woman's legs. This time it's *her* moment of analepsis: the same voice-over (it's actually Breillat voicing the parts of both Man and Woman) accompanies a scene of a young girl being tormented by little boys. A game of 'Doctors and Nurses' ensues; what's so shocking here is not the sight of the female child's genitals, but how the boys treat them. One of the boys removes the glasses from his companion's face and, off-camera (*ob-scena*), inserts one of the arms into the child's vagina, before laughingly investigating the discharge on it. The boy has found a surrogate penis with which to penetrate the girl. The child's body is emblematic of covert visibility: in its purity, in a Kristevan formulation, 'the sexual component being everywhere is actually nowhere'.[9] That the surrogate takes the form of *looking*-glasses is symbolic in a film so preoccupied with scopophilia (voyeurism) – but also with scopo*phobia*, the rubbernecking desire to look at that which is a source of repugnance. Back in the film's present, the Man inserts his finger – in extreme close-up – into the woman's vagina while talking to her about the relative 'honesty' of an anus, versus the vagina's mystery. The

Woman again implores him: 'Watch me where I'm unwatchable', and, 'Look at me when I can't see myself!' As Breillat has said: 'By looking at it, I'd like the sin to disappear' so that 'we'll love ourselves more'. The synonymy of lips/labia is emphasized as, with a combination of childish inquisitiveness, and very adult malice, on his face, the Man takes a red lipstick and uses it to draw around the sleeping Woman's labia and anus. Then he paints her facial lips, but in a distorted, careless way. Finally, he fucks her insensate body. The facial lips are seen; the labia are hidden. The man's purposeful collapsing of the distinction between them accords with Breillat's belief that 'This film is a theorem [. . .] of what is unspeakable [. . .] Our society is based on this consensual hypocrisy which forms a social bond and it's considered completely necessary [. . .] It's a film about transcendence.' I'm really persuaded by Breillat's personal/political argument here: we are taught not to look on the taboo, and governments are quite happy for this to be the case, for the populace that has revealed 'transcendent truths' is ungovernable. And the route to transcendence, according to Breillat's philosophy? *La jouissance* (sexual transcendence): 'the Word, as in "the Word of Jesus Christ"'. In Kristeva's words: 'The mystic's familiarity with abjection is a fount of infinite jouissance.'[10]

On night two, the camera lingers on the crucifix on the bedroom wall, that oversees – like the director herself, and like her audience – all that passes between the Man and the Woman. The Man sucks the Woman's menstrual blood off his fingers before leaving the house to find a trident-like rake in the garden, the handle of which he inserts into the still-sleeping Woman's body. The associations – with Neptune and with the devil – are powerful. 'It's really beautiful', argues Breillat: 'even if it does [. . . risk] being ridiculous'. The Woman's white skin is exceptionally pale, especially in relation to the Man's. In the foetal position she looks, as Breillat wanted, like a Brancusi sculpture: smooth, ovoid, abstracted. It's a scene that anticipates the end of the film, when the Woman falls into the ocean. 'She returns to the sea, not fire', says Breillat, 'so in a way Neptune becomes a kind of feminine deity'. The rake scene is a tough one to watch because, as Breillat knew, it does verge on the absurd. The bizarre incongruity of soft body, determined Man and garden implement, is distracting, especially as the Man moves away from the bed and the rusty brown rake stays erect, poking out of the woman's body. The veils of propriety have been torn away in this scene, both for the protagonists and for the viewer. The next morning, the Woman says: 'the veils they adorn us with ritually, anticipate our shrouds'.

The taboo of the menstruating body is the focus of night three, too. With her encouragement, the Man removes the Woman's tampon. 'See?' she says: 'That's all there is to it'. She drops the tampon into the bedside glass of water and gently stirs it to make the water incarnadine. 'Tiens! Bois!', she commands ('Take! Drink!'), and, in this ritualistic, Eucharistic moment of communion, he does as she asks, and she drinks, too. It is a revolting act – in the literal meaning of that word, where 'revolting' comes from the French *révolter*, to turn or to rebel. It's a moment when the learned behaviour of bodily disgust overwhelms natural, intellectual curiosity and, in Kristeva's words, imbues an object with a 'loathsome' quality.[11] We rebel against the image – and this is exactly what Breillat wants: there's a solemnity and dignity in drinking Christ's blood in the Christian tradition, or an enemy's blood in a martial one, but *female* blood is (much of what the Woman says in this scene is taken from the Torah) tainted, impure. 'Tampons should never be seen [. . .] I didn't want to make them hidden', says Breillat, exposing once again the covert visibility of the female genitals: 'After all, men know such things exist!' This paradox underpins culture and tradition, and it's one which is powerfully conveyed here. 'I feel nothing' says the Woman, as she inserts a fresh tampon. It's both a literal, and a powerfully metaphorical, statement.

Another startling close-up occurs on the fourth and final night. We see a glistening, smooth black shape being pushed out of the woman's distended vulva onto the bed. It's a moment of shocking defamiliarization. We both know, and yet do not know, what's going on, what we're seeing. It's a moment of a perverse, inanimate birth; it's also the man's symbolic birth – the culmination of his initiation into the powers and wonders of the cunt, and it matters to the woman that he should truly see her body's physical capabilities, so that she might become a subject, or metaphorically give birth to an 'I'.[12] The woman continues to question why he finds her blood so revolting (as he withdraws after intercourse, his penis is stained red with it). Her talk is about goddesses, myth, fertility and curses, but he can take no more: he leaves, saying that because she has finally paid him (as agreed in the original contract), 'I exited from the myth'. In the film's final scenes, the house is deserted and the

Man lifts the bloodied sheet from the dismantled bedstead in a reverential way, as though it were, indeed, the Turin-like shroud of which the woman spoke earlier. The ocean, earlier portrayed as a powerful feminine force, reclaims the body of the Woman as we see her fall (or is she pushed? We never find out.) away from the Man on the cliff top into the foaming waters beneath. 'For me', says Breillat, 'he doesn't kill her [. . .] It's a tale of initiation, it's a legend [. . .] That's the kind of death it is'.

Anatomy of Hell is a film which has authenticity and seeing as its core governing principles. But the whole situation is abstract – in a bar at the end of the film, the Man realizes that he never knew the Woman's name. And neither did we. The mythical, transcendent qualities of the film jar with its visceral 'realism'. 'There's no need', said Breillat, 'for fear, or obscenity, or guilt'. Yet those strong emotions were what the film's critics focused on most, and were what cost the director her health. 'This film destroyed me', she says prophetically (she had a stroke shortly after filming the interview for the film's DVD release):

> What really destroyed me were things I read. I don't understand it [. . .] I felt that, if words had been acid, I'd be disfigured. Suddenly, I felt surrounded by barbarity [. . .] But we mustn't let ourselves be murdered by mediocrity [. . .] When confronted with images which, in spite of everything, are considered 'unwatchable', a way of protecting yourself is to watch them with derision. Then you don't actually see them; you refuse to see them. It's a protection [. . .] To me, the point of this film is not to faint, not to be horrified, but to understand it. After all, it's beautiful. It's human and it's beautiful.

If the abstract, infernal aesthetic of *Anatomy* is informed by Brueghel, then that of *Antichrist* (2009) owes much to Hieronymus Bosch. *Antichrist* is an intense, grotesque film directed by Lars Von Trier, pioneer of the Danish 'Dogme 95' film collective. It has a stage-play quality, despite being shot on location: it's divided into a 'Prologue', 4 'Chapters' ('Grief', 'Pain (Chaos Reigns)', 'Gynocide' and 'The Three Beggars') and an Epilogue. It shows, in astonishingly intimate detail, the breakdown of a relationship between a man (acted by Willem Dafoe but known only as 'He') and a woman (Charlotte Gainsbourg, 'She'), whose toddler son, Nic, has died after falling from a window. The fall (or, perhaps, more properly, 'Fall', given the biblical motifs that permeate the film) is the main subject matter of both Prologue and Epilogue. Handel's achingly beautiful aria 'Lascia ch'io pianga' ('Leave me to weep'), from his early eighteenth-century opera *Rinaldo*, is the dominant soundtrack for these visual set pieces. 'Leave me to weep' pleads Almirena, the soprano who is rebutting the advances of the unkind King Argante.[13] And it's being 'left' to weep that She wants in Von Trier's film, as she experiences 'atypical' (as her doctor puts it) grief at the loss of her son. To recuperate, husband and wife go to 'Eden', the cabin in the woods where She spent what turned out to be her last summer with Nic, writing her thesis on the sixteenth-century European witch craze.

The natural world around 'Eden' is potent and menacing. 'Nature is Satan's church' says Gainsbourg's character gnomically at one point, as the woods slowly encroach on the cabin and on the couple. As though to mirror the bereaved mother's pain, many young die in the woods: a deer miscarries her fawn; a fox tears at her own flesh; a chick falls from a nest and is swooped on by a bird of prey; even the oak tree showers the cabin in acorns that bounce noisily and uncannily off the roof. In an Irigarayan sense, the females of various species are enacting their roles as 'guardians of "nature"'.[14] The self-hatred of Gainsbourg's character stems, Von Trier leads us to believe, from guilt. The couple were having sex when Nic climbed out of his cot and fell to his death. Gainsbourg's genitals are the focus for her hatred: her vagina is the site which brought her little boy into the world, but, as a sexualized entity, it is, in her imagination at least, the reason for his departure from it. And so it is that the couple's sexuality becomes the focus of her psychosis. She slams a large block of wood into Dafoe's erect penis; masturbates his unconscious body until he ejaculates blood; and then penetrates his shin with an old-fashioned manual drill. 'Freud is dead, isn't he?' she said earlier to Dafoe, her therapist husband, but in this scene the powerful manifestation of transference is all too clear. She inserts her finger into the hole she's drilled almost out of curiosity, as though she wants to feel what it's like to be the penetrator and not the penetrated. She pushes a metal pole through his wound, and fastens it using a whetstone and bolts. A fox-hole which Von Trier has clearly shown to be a source of terror for the female character comes into prominence at this point as Dafoe's character agonizingly slides into it to hide from his wife. When she finds him, she tries to drag him out feet first, as though carrying out a breech delivery, but he cannot be 'delivered' to her in that way. Fetching a shovel she digs, rigorously jabbing at the dry earth, forcing a penetration into the burrow beneath. She pulls him up through it, head-first this time, birthing him from the natural world with and against which she seems simultaneously to work.

On returning to the house with her husband, Gainsbourg's character takes a pair of large, old-fashioned scissors and, hand shaking, slices downwards between her open legs. Clitoris and labia are framed in an extremely uncomfortable close-up; blood spurts as she snips them off, excising her sexual identity and, with it, all of the guilt which Von Trier has had her carry. For the act of excision is intercut (if that's not too inappropriate a word) with a recapping of the 'Prologue' scenes, and this time, as she and her husband have sex, she is shown passively watching the boy climb up to the window through which he falls. In this, her last terrifying vision, she equates sex with death; Eros and Thanatos are united; *la petite mort* is pitilessly literalized. As the French writer Georges Bataille wrote in 1939, 'human beings are only united with each other through rents or wounds [. . .] Circumcisions and orgies show adequately that there is more than one link between sexual laceration and ritual laceration; the erotic world itself has been careful to designate the act in which it is fulfilled as a "little death" [*petite mort*]'.[15] Gainsbourg has made her genitals her literal wound, metonymically referencing the site of her psychical wound. When Dafoe's character ultimately strangles his wife, and burns her body, a Boschian procession of white-limbed women marches through the woods, seemingly unaware of him, heading instead for 'Eden', the hellish earthly garden which is a place not of delights, but of mutilation, atrocious cruelty and death.

Chatterbox: Speaking up for one self

What might the great 1970s feminists Gloria Steinem and Betty Friedan have in common with a little-known cult movie in which a woman's vagina suddenly develops a voice and embarks on a singing career? *Chatterbox*, a 1970s Sexploitation movie, plays with ideas of nonunitary selfhood, and examines issues of silence, sexual identity and social participation, while charting the protagonist's desperate attempts to assimilate her 'body-self'.[16] The film's director, Tom DeSimone, spent much of the 1970s working in the Exploitation/ porn margins of the American film industry. He made several gay porn movies under the pseudonym of Lancer Brooks (*How to Make a Homo Movie* (1970)), and has had artistic forays into the camp horror genre, such as 1973's *Sons of Satan* which features a gang of satanic homosexual vampires. In the 1990s, DeSimone moved into television work, directing the soap opera *Acapulco Bay*. While Breillat and Von Trier depicted menacing facets of a radical crisis of selfhood, with women's genitals at its core, DeSimone's 1977 film *Chatterbox* is, in its low-budget, kitsch approach, less intense and is not as much of an explicit take on themes which had been explored in Claude Mulot's earlier porn movie *Le Sexe qui Parle* (*Pussy Talk*, 1975). The issues to which *Chatterbox* gives rise are important, focusing as they do on a particular 'crisis' of female identity which was articulated by second-wave feminists, and which motivated so many of the writers and artists I'm considering in this book.

The movie's aesthetic is less Breughel or Bosch, then, than Benny Hill, and the US poster makes quite clear the 'Exploitation' genre to which the film belongs: a woman (we later find out that she's the film's protagonist, Penelope) is dressed in a bikini and heels, her right leg drawn up in a pose which could be read as provocative or self-defensive. From her crotch comes a speech bubble which tells us that this is going to be 'the story of a woman who has a hilarious way of expressing herself', and that audiences will 'roar when she sits down to talk!' Above her is the movie's title, the 'o' of *Chatterbox* being made up of a woman's heavily lipsticked open mouth. 'It speaks for itself!' the poster exclaims, asking: 'she talks with her *what?*' The Belgian version of the film poster is even more explicit in that it dispenses with Penelope's head and torso altogether, leaving instead a pair of stockinged legs balancing that lipsticked open mouth, the ages-old equivalence of lips and labia being quite clear. 'Madam', the poster asks, 'how would you react if your "you-know-what" suddenly began to talk and sing?' Penelope, star – or, crucially, as we shall see, *co*-star – of *Chatterbox*, is a self-effacing, socially naïve hairdresser whose vagina – later named 'Virginia' – does suddenly begin to talk and sing. Penelope seeks psychiatric help from a Dr Pearl who later becomes Virginia's manager and the film, in a structure reminiscent of the porn features DeSimone also directed, unfolds as a series of vignettes. These tableaux are linked only by the central premise, and are occasionally punctuated by musical routines featuring songs such as 'Wang Dang Doodle' and 'Cock a Doodle Do'. Viewers follow Penelope as she searches for romance, at the same time that *Virginia* is searching for sex and fame.

At the height of her celebrity, Penelope goes to a restaurant with her mother (who has with alarming alacrity set aside her concerns for her daughter once she realizes how profitable Virginia's fame can be) and Dr Pearl and is quickly surrounded by fans. One says: 'I can't tell you how much I admire you, Virginia; you put Gloria Steinem to shame!' 'Thanks', replies Virginia, 'I put them all to shame!' 'Them all' is an interesting concept in this context since a moment later a live TV crew bursts in on the restaurant, the host demanding of Virginia 'Is there any truth to the rumour that Betty Friedan has challenged you to a debate?' Any answer that there might have been is obscured as a priest is next to rush in, attempting, in a pastiche of the concerns we saw Robert Coover rather more darkly address, to exorcize Penelope. DeSimone's conjuring up of Friedan and Steinem here casts light on the role of the film in terms of second-wave feminism. *Virginia* reverses Friedan's credo that biology is not destiny so that *Penelope*'s destiny is fame or notoriety on tour throughout the United States as Virginia.

In her initial visit to Dr Pearl, the psychiatrist, Penelope tells him about 'That foul-mouthed little beast [. . .] All she wants to do is have sex [. . .] But what about me? Am I supposed just to let her take over my life?' This question taps directly into the cultural concerns informing the context of the film and of 1970s feminism. In finding an answer to Friedan's slogan of isolation and despair – 'Is this all?' – that relies on an awakened and voiced libido, Penelope is radically disaggregated: her mind and body are at war. Her abjection is inescapable: to be human is at once to loathe the abject body and at the same time to need it, in all its gross physicality.[17] Penelope epitomizes reticent domestic femininity; Virginia revels in sexual liberation. This liberatory impulse, however, in DeSimone's rendition, is experienced by Penelope as a paralysing constraint. Paraded before the American Medical Association, 'The 8th wonder of the world: Virginia the talking vagina!' is in her element. The same cannot be said of Penelope, however, as she turns her head from the audience in horror and shame. Penelope is imprisoned after Virginia has sexually propositioned a traffic cop. Female sexuality is both spectacle and predicament: it runs counter to notions of liberation because Penelope is not in control. A female prisoner in the adjacent cell says to her, without realizing the irony of the statement: 'You can button your lip!' Bailed out of jail by a former boyfriend, Penelope is taken under Dr Pearl's wing. Clearly an entrepreneurial Freudian, he has recognized the freak-show potential of Penelope's unruly id and must persuade her to perform so that he can profit from her celebrity:

> Up to now you've had a different notion about sex and about your sexual organs. You have been conditioned to feel guilty. Look. Virginia is simply that part of you that is speaking up to be heard. She doesn't want to be just another anonymous organ, something that you never think about, like a pancreas. Nobody thinks about their pancreas. She is pure libido. All Virginia wants you to do is to enjoy yourself totally.

One of the many ironies of what Dr Pearl says here lies in his insinuation that Penelope's conditioned guilt came from the suppression of her sexual identity, when every indication in the film is that once that sexual identity *is* expressed, Penelope experiences a very public guilt or humiliation on the showbiz circuit (see Figure 6.2). After this point in the film, with Dr Pearl bent almost double in talking directly to Virginia, the camera replicates the sense that Penelope's identity is becoming increasingly fragmented, by framing her body from the neck down as she melancholically walks the city streets at night. Later, Dr Pearl is very keen to continue to urge Penelope towards acceptance of Virginia as a mode of coming into being and maturity. 'You may have come in here feeling like a frightened little girl' he tells her, 'But when you leave here everyone in America's gonna know you're a total woman!' As Virginia excels by singing on television and then at venues throughout the States, the camera does take time to show the audience Penelope's very evident discomfort: the more Virginia speaks, the more Penelope is railroaded into silence.

A lot has been written about the diversity and richness of women's voiced identities; less on how silences can be powerful too. We need not read Penelope's silence as emblematic of disempowerment, but as strength: a choice or resistance in the dilemma of coming into being. Feminist psychologist Carol

Gilligan has argued that a woman's silence signals a subordination which is most keenly felt at the onset of adolescence, that is, when sexual identity begins to be most strongly expressed, and when selfhood starts to be stifled. The problem with Gilligan's concept is that silence can actually add to the anxieties felt by the subject whose *choice* it is to be silent, or who feels unable to speak. Gilligan's reification of the individual's 'authentic voice' is only of value or meaning when it is heard, but 'authenticity' of identity may reside in silence, too.[18] Penelope inhabits the mode of being Virginia with varying degrees of defiance and unease. Indeed, the viewer cannot read the instability of identity – 'You're not *our* mother! You're *my* mother!' – as positive or playful. In this partitioning of self into public and private roles, the character experiences a profound conflict. As Mangogul's female courtiers quickly came to realize, according to Diderot scholar Thomas Kavanagh, 'the voice of the sex, speaking its mistress's truth only on the condition she be reduced to pure object, is finally no different from those other voices of gossip and rumor making up the world of the Sultan's court. It is the question of how we might respond to these voices that constitutes the real center of this text.'[19] So, how might we respond to quiet, resistant Penelope, who is at the mercy not only of her own body, but of exploitative hangers-on, too, as vociferous Virginia's celebrity grows and grows?[20]

In the incident with the TV crew in the restaurant, the evocation of Betty Friedan is informative in terms of that by-now familiar conflation of facial lips and labia. In her *Feminine Mystique*, Friedan had asked the '*silent* question', bringing into language issues that she felt had for too long remained unspoken. Friedan wrote that:

> The problem lay buried, unspoken for many years in the minds of American women. It was a strange stirring, a sense of dissatisfaction, a yearning that women suffered in the middle of the twentieth century in the United States. Each suburban housewife struggled with it alone. As she made the beds, shopped for groceries, matched slipcover material, ate peanut butter sandwiches with her children, chauffeured Cub Scouts and Brownies, lay beside her husband at night, she was afraid to ask even of herself the silent question, "Is this all?"[21]

This is fundamentally the question which Penelope is asking in her pre-Virginia manifestation: 'Is this all?' In a sense, it's the question which precipitated so many of this book's concerns. Chicago's 'Womanhouse' project, for example, as we have seen, in building tableaux such as the *Menstruation Bathroom*, exposed the 'secret', suburban, hellish life of so many women in the 1960s to 1970s. In *Chatterbox*, the TV host's question about a Friedan/Virginia debate may not have been as confrontational as he hoped. Both Friedan and Virginia are struggling to allow women to experience a 'real' selfhood where sexual, social, professional and familial identities could be lived fully and with integrity. Penelope signals rebellion in her silence and refusal to participate in what her mother disparagingly terms 'this moral revolution' of mid-1970s America. The film, in its playfulness with voice, silence and selfhood, constructs a dilemma for the feminist critic as issues of agency and power surface. Speech is not wholly liberating for Penelope, but is a source of shame which lays her open to the greed and exploitation of those around her, even her mother. The relationship of Penelope to Dr Pearl and her mother is not unlike that of sex worker and pimp but, oddly (or, maybe, predictably given her lack of a voice), Penelope does not resist. In the final sequence, however, a transference has taken place, as it did in Coover's play, when the 'pricks' of the Man and the Priest began to speak: Penelope's vagina finds a soul mate as her boyfriend's genitals beseech her not to commit suicide. On a cliff top, Virginia has pleaded of Penelope: 'When you jump, keep your legs crossed'. Oddly, DeSimone's Exploitation movie suggests a viable voice for women. It is a voice that's concurrently silent and private, and voluble, sexual and public. As the director himself put it, 'it was our intention to imply that Penelope and Virginia accepted each other'.[22]

An eye for an eye: Lichtenstein's *Teeth*

Diderot's *Bijoux*, as we've seen, is a crucial model in understanding the development of the idea of the 'autonomized cunt'.[23] Film texts are like Diderot's novel because of the desires they arouse of wanting to *know*.[24] The idea Diderot projected, of the involuntary aspect of the revelation of sexual knowledge, is key: in the 2007 film *Teeth*, written and directed by Mitchell Lichtenstein, the protagonist has no more control over her 'jewel' than Mirzoza had over hers, or Penelope over hers. Her vagina is autonomized, as Mirzoza's ultimately comes to be, but, in this film, that autonomization is enacted in an altogether bloodier and more spectacular manner. Lichtenstein plays with cultural fears by literalizing the phenomenon of the *vagina dentata*. It is not – initially, at least – a weapon of choice for Dawn O'Keefe, the film's protagonist, but is, in a model for which Diderot's novel has prepared us, autonomized. It's the dramatization of Luce Irigaray's question in *Speculum of the Other Woman*: 'But what if the "object" started to speak? Which also means beginning to "see", etc. What disaggregation of the subject would that entail?'[25] Irigaray's notion of a 'disaggregation' of identity, of a ruptured self, is fundamental to the films I've looked at, and to Lichtenstein's in particular. What's more, the horror Dawn experiences on realizing how different or unnatural her body is, recalls Irigaray's thoughts on shame (remember – *pudendum* is the Latin word for 'that of which one ought to be ashamed'):

> the reminder, in reverse, of the compromise and the disavowal at work in the fetish. Though her body is beautiful [. . .] woman will still be reserved, modest, shameful, as far as her sex organs are concerned. She will discreetly assist in hiding them. Ensuring this *double game* of flaunting her body, her jewels, in order to hide her sex organs all the better. For woman's 'body' has some 'usefulness', represents some 'value' only on condition that her sex organs are hidden. Since they are something and nothing in consumer terms. Are pictured in fantasy, what is more, as a greedy mouth. How can one trade on something so empty?[26]

The insistent orality of the female form is invoked again, later in Irigaray's text, as the woman's 'two lips, parted to receive other embraces, soon become dry and retracted over their mourning, if the wait is too long. No voice is hers to call, no hands can fill the open hungry mouth with the food that both nourishes and devours'.[27]

The mouth's 'alimentary logic', its perceived libidinal equivalence to the vagina, is shifted to the woman's genitals which, in turn, become overwhelmingly threatening.[28] For, as we've seen, mouths have teeth and can sever, ingest and eradicate. It's the myth of the *vagina dentata*, of course, which collapses and fuses the constituent elements of this precarious, imaginary relationship. Lichtenstein's film teasingly but viciously focuses on what's presented as a liberation or reclamation of the vagina into realms of articulation and autonomization. In a scene early in *Teeth*, Dawn is in a biology lesson. The male teacher struggles to *say* the word 'vagina', eventually saying 'female privates'. The relevant pictures in the textbook have been blanked out by a large circular sticker. Significantly, the pictures showing diagrams of male genitalia have not. The attempts of nearly every student in the class to remove the stickers lead to the picture underneath – of the female reproductive system – being torn and defaced beyond recognition.[29] Dawn leaves the sticker in her biology textbook in place. It's an emblematic act, for the censorship is, for Dawn, directly related to her lack of knowledge about her own sexuality. Her first appearance in the movie as a young adult establishes her as a leading force in her school's sexual abstinence movement, advocating the wearing of a 'promise ring', sporting an 'I'm waiting' T-shirt, and sharing her thoughts on celibacy with younger children. However, the audience has already met Dawn, as a very young child, in the opening sequence, even before the titles, as one of two small children playing in a paddling pool. The boy in the pool suddenly screams: his finger has somehow – mysteriously – been bitten. Dawn appears frightened and puzzled.

It's in the abstinence meeting that Dawn first meets Tobey. Lichtenstein exploits conventional love-story film formulae in visual and auditory ways: at first their eyes meet as Dawn delivers her talk; she hesitates momentarily; he looks down, embarrassed, and then back up, smiling. As the assembled children display their ringed fingers Tobey joins in – but hesitantly. When the two get the chance to talk to each other Lichtenstein once more puts classic romance-genre signs in place – a close-up of Dawn's wide-eyed expression is mirrored by one of Tobey. This careful establishment of innocence and love at first sight is radically undermined by the film's later introduction of the darker elements which accompany the deployment of another film genre laden with expectations and specific auditory and visual cues – the horror genre. If Brad, Dawn's step-brother, was the first 'victim' (a term I'll return to later) of Dawn's vengeful vagina, years ago in the paddling pool, then Tobey is going to be the second. At a tranquil lake, the teenagers swim into the mouth of a mossy cave (Lichtenstein's visual imagery is not subtle, here – earlier, in the same setting, the camera lingered for a moment on a tree characterized by a vulva-shaped hole in its trunk). Initially it is Dawn who swims deeper into the cave: Tobey treads water at its opening, delaying this act of symbolic penetration. When both teenagers are sitting on a ledge inside, the camera cuts away momentarily to take in the folded, complex structure of the cave's roof. Tobey takes little time in turning on Dawn, raping her and stifling her cries by placing his hand over her mouth. With her actual mouth violated by Tobey's hand, Dawn's *symbolic* mouth, her *vagina dentata*, clamps down on him and severs his penis. The initial shots are of the horrified expressions of the youngsters. To eradicate any possibility of ambiguity, Lichtenstein's camera pulls away to show the rest of Tobey's body, with blood pouring from his crotch. Both teenagers then recoil at the sight of his severed penis lying on the ledge between them. We next see Dawn in contemplative, shocked mode, her T-shirt bearing the ironic slogan: 'Warning. Sex changes everything.'

Confronted with the spectacle of the amputated penis, the healthy sexual organ which has been rendered abject, has fallen away from the body, like waste, we have to wonder how far it's legitimate for the viewer to consider Tobey, the rapist, as a 'victim'. *Teeth* is a rape-revenge thriller that differs in several key aspects from others often discussed by feminist film critics, such as *Thelma and Louise*. It differs, too, from a more recent graphic depiction of rape-revenge in the film *The Girl With the Dragon Tattoo*. In Niels Oplev's original, Swedish film (2009), the revenge is effected by means of Lisbeth Salander's promise of pleasure to her rapist who actually believes she has returned to his apartment in order – this time – to have *consensual* sex with him. The revenge is also carefully planned – Lisbeth has brought with her a Taser, ropes or cords, the secret recording of her rape and a tattooist's kit. Lisbeth's revenge is not a spontaneous act, then, but a highly planned, strategic one. The ethics of that are, in a civilized society, problematic, but something that Stieg Larsson did so well in the novel on which the film was based, was to demonstrate how 'civilization' is a façade anyway; a mask for systematic social and individual corruption, exploitation and abuse. If society has been seen so clearly by Salander, then her response-in-kind becomes somehow justifiable – at the very least it is entirely logical, even necessary. The revenge in *Teeth*, by contrast, comes about independently of Dawn's volition. In a significant sense, then, she is *doubly* abused in the scene, because two entirely non-consensual acts are played out (the rape and her body's response to it). Unlike Lisbeth, Dawn has had no opportunity to plan or to prepare. Her response has been beyond her control, so through her revenge she is liberated and threatened in equal measure.

Dawn's *vagina dentata* is initially an autonomic mechanism. As the film's narrative gains momentum, however, the radical disaggregation of that first episode diminishes in response to encounters with different, predatory men. After the incident with Tobey, Dawn throws her purity ring away and goes back to her biology textbook. Peeling off the sticker she reveals a diagram which is a mystery to her, so a search engine enlightens her: she types 'adaptation', then 'mutations' and then 'female genital mutations' into a search engine instead. Lichtenstein situates Dawn's discovery of the phenomenon of the *vagina dentata* firmly – virtually parodically – within the horror film tradition: she claps her hand to her mouth and menacing music plays. Next, we see Dawn setting out to visit a gynaecologist. She cycles past billboards which parody the overt commercial display of women's bodies ('Perfect' says one, over an image of a woman's crotch; 'tasty new [...] banana split' advertises another), accompanied by a stereotypically portentous male voice-over which warns of the womb, that 'dark crucible'. Arriving at the gynaecologist's office, Dawn is immediately pathologized: we see her perched on the end of an examination table wearing a hospital gown. As the gynaecologist proceeds with his rather unorthodox examination (he puts the cover on the workbench instead of over Dawn's body, and purports to be undertaking a spurious test for 'flexibility'), he tells her chirpily, and deliciously ironically for the viewer: 'Don't worry. I'm not gonna bite you!'

During the examination, the motif of physical and psychical fragmentation is visually replayed. We see Dawn only in close-up – her face, in assorted expressions of anxiety, fills the frame. This is intercut with close-ups of the doctor peering at Dawn's genitals – they are in *his* frame of reference, under *his* control. Or so he thinks. He removes his gloves and sexually assaults Dawn. Her body is still split – we are given shots of her face which suggest that she is beginning to understand the motives behind the doctor's unconventional approach. As in the scene with Tobey, the action is conveyed by the characters' expressions of wide-mouthed disbelief. 'It's true!' shrieks the doctor, 'Vagina Dentata! Vagina Dentata! Vagina Dentata!' He struggles to release his hand from Dawn's vagina, and stares, horrified, as four of his fingers plop onto the floor of the examination room.[30]

Dawn's first consensual sexual experience is with a schoolmate, Ryan. 'I'm the hero!' he says, capitalizing on the romantic fantasy Dawn has created for herself. 'I can't believe you're still alive!' she tells him after sex. This moment of relief and release is crucial in Dawn's psychosexual development. She looks at herself in a mirror, seeing herself as whole, a moment of virtually reverential incorporation shared by the viewer – who has previously seen her mainly in parts. However, the tenderness of the post-coital scene is soon shattered as Ryan reveals he slept with Dawn as a bet. Talking of her vows of abstinence he says to her: 'Your mouth was saying one thing, babe [. . .] Your sweet pussy's saying something very different'. The viewer is by now, of course, expecting what comes next. The autonomic *vagina dentata* is slowly, evolutionarily, being understood by Dawn *and* by the audience, and is coming under her control. This illicit shared knowledge heightens our pleasure and anticipation, and when Dawn severs Ryan's penis we believe that it *is* Dawn and not some part of her. She is whole. 'Some hero!' she exclaims. Dawn evolves into a revenger more in the Lisbeth Salander mode. She sets out to seduce her abusive step-brother Brad: 'This is too fuckin' weird' he exclaims. 'Just wait!' she calmly replies. Brad experiences the return of the repressed as he recalls the paddling-pool incident with which the film opened, but his desire for dominance cancels this out. His aggressive libido has seemingly deafened him to all the warning signs: in his recall of the paddling pool scene, Baby Dawn is smiling, not frowning; the music from the horror film he's watching seems purposeful; and Dawn, previously a paragon of abstinence is now – as he constructs her, at least – his seducer. The last we see of Brad is his amputated penis being eaten by his pet dog, who has the presence of mind, at least, to regurgitate the pierced glans.

As Dawn cycles away, Lichtenstein's playful generic self-consciousness comes to the fore. Dawn is alone on a country road. Dawn is virginal in a simple white dress. Dawn fails to fix a puncture. And Dawn hitches a lift with a lone male driver. It's an archetypal teen 'slasher' movie set-up. At the dimly lit 'Super Quick' petrol station, the driver propositions Dawn. Her reaction is one of disbelief tempered by ennui – she has had to come to learn the way of the world. She turns slowly back to the man, and the last frame focuses on her expression of triumph and control. She is whole and unassailable. She is Medusa, in French philosopher Hélène Cixous's terms, at least: 'You only have to look at the Medusa straight on to see her. And she's not deadly. She's beautiful and she's laughing.'[31]

Covert visibility on TV

In 2000, Brit Mark Mylod directed the 3-part *Last Fast Show Ever* for the BBC. *The Fast Show* had been a highly successful sketch show which ran for three series in the mid-1990s. Episode 1 of *The Last Fast Show Ever* featured Johnny Depp in an encounter with the sycophantic, sexually obsessed 'Suit You Tailors', Ken and Kenneth, played by Paul Whitehouse and Mark Williams respectively. Depp begins the scene looking somewhat discomfited by the tailors' explicit innuendo but, by the end of the scene, he has joined in, uttering the tailors' catchphrase 'Ooh! Suit *you*, sir!' with real gusto. Initially the tailors fantasize about the American's insatiable sexual appetite and:

Kenneth: A gushing torrent of young ladies.

Ken: An avalanche of quim.

Kenneth: A mountain of minge. A cornucopia of

Ken: ___ Suit you, sir![32]

Whitehouse's interruption at once neutralizes and emphasizes the spectral word. The humour lies in knowing, of course, what Williams was about to say, and in following what philologist Matthew Hunt describes as their recitation of a 'list of alliterative vaginal synonyms'.[33] 'Cunt' is both unheard but also *heard* in this example of covert visibility. The shared experience of hearing what is *not* said enhances the humour and makes the audience bask in collective self-congratulation for being 'in' on the joke.

'You'd be surprised at things that can talk'

South Park, the animated TV series which has been broadcast on the American cable channel Comedy Central since August 1997, is an enormously successful cultural phenomenon.[34] It's a show which focuses on the lives of a group of four ten-year-old boys: Stan Marsh, Kyle Broflovski, Eric Cartman and Kenny McCormick, who live in the eponymous town in Colorado. The success of the series is almost entirely attributable to the surreal and irreverent imaginations of its creators, Trey Parker and Matt Stone. Unapologetically, and with tremendous panache, they lampoon society – any and all societies: Parker and Stone are equal opportunities satirists for whom no human foible, disease, creed, political stance, sexual identity or race, is out of bounds. They've killed off the Queen, satirized the Prophet Muhammad, ridiculed children with Asperger's, murdered the Kardashians, and had Japanese whalers kill the Miami Dolphins American football team. Each of *South Park*'s more than 200 episodes also has a title which is inventive, puerile and offensive in fairly equal measure. For example, in season 3 'The Red Badge of Gayness' aired; 'Do the Handicapped go to Hell?' was a season 4 episode; and 'Krazy Kripples' was in season 7. In season 8 there was 'The Passion of the Jew'; the 'Breast Cancer Show Ever' features in season 12; and 'The Tale of Scrotie McBoogerballs' was told in season 14. More recently, season 16 has had episodes called 'Reverse Cowgirl' and 'Jewpacabra'.

In April 2006, in season 10, the team took on the idea of the autonomized cunt in an episode called 'A Million Little Fibers'. The title and the basic premise of the episode come from a real-life controversy which centred on a 2003 book called *A Million Little Pieces*, written by James Frey. The book was marketed by Random House as a memoir of addiction and recovery, and, after Oprah Winfrey selected it for her Book Club in September 2005, it was all but guaranteed global commercial success. In January 2006, however, the book was exposed as a fabricated account and not a memoir at all. Frey and his publisher appeared on *The Oprah Winfrey Show,* along with his publisher, to apologize for having misled 'the Empress of Empathy' and her millions of viewers.[35] Fewer than three months after Frey's contrite confession on Winfrey's show, Parker and Stone devised and broadcast 'A Million Little

Fibers'. It was an unusual episode – weird subject-matter aside – because of the absence of the show's four key protagonists. Instead, the focus was firmly on a minor character, Towelie, whose first appearance on the show was in the fifth season. Towelie is a genetically engineered and often-stoned speaking towel, created by Parker and Stone to satirize the phenomenally successful, but often irrelevant, global merchandize market that accompanies TV shows, including *South Park* itself.[36]

In 'A Million Little Fibers', Towelie's memoirs are rejected by a publisher, Porcupine Press, on the grounds that they simply are not sufficiently exciting. They are, after all, written by a towel. Towelie rethinks his strategy, goes through his manuscript replacing the word 'towel' with 'person'; adopts a disguise of a jaunty hat and a fake moustache; and takes the pseudonym 'Steven McTowelie'. He is immediately picked up by the publishers 'Arbitrary House'. As had been the case with James Frey's *Million Little Pieces*, Towelie's book is a massive commercial success chiefly on account of Oprah Winfrey's seal of approval. What happens next is utterly bizarre (not that what's happened before it *hasn't* been bizarre). The peculiar nature of the episode, and its departure from a more familiar format involving the four boys, was a source of consternation to the show's fans. Eric Goldman, for example, wrote that 'it's rare to see an episode of a hit series focus almost entirely on a pot-smoking towel and the talking orifices of a popular talk show host. Yet that's what *South Park* did'.[37] Yes. That is what this episode does. Oprah, it is quickly revealed to the viewer, is not a united entity, but has autonomous organs. During an interview on *The Oprah Winfrey Show*, Towelie is suspected of subterfuge not by Oprah herself, but by her talking vagina, 'Minge'. 'A minge needs attention', complains this disaffected organ, 'at least a scratch once in a while!' Minge is not the only autonomized organ, however. Gary is Oprah's talking anus, whose greatest desire is one day to go to France to visit Paris.

So far, so surreal. The sense of weirdness is intensified by Minge's deep male voice (with an appalling English accent), and Gary's querulous, more high-pitched, but again male tones which are delivered in a very strange and very camp hybrid of Scottish and American. Winfrey's success is the target of the satire. She has achieved what she has, the narrative goes, because she is a workaholic. The cost of this has been the neglect of her body and her sexual identity. The only way Minge and Gary can think of to get her to spend more time with them, and maybe even take them to Paris, is to try to get her fired by revealing that she's been duped by Towelie. They phone the talk show host Geraldo Rivera one night as Oprah sleeps, blissfully unaware of the blue telephone balanced in her crotch. 'A talking towel?' he exclaims, 'That doesn't make any sense'. 'You'd be surprised', replies Gary, 'at things that can talk'. Consequently, Towelie's duplicity is uncovered, thanks to the efforts of the talking organs, who expose 'Steven McTowelie' for the mere towel he is. Even though this is a playful, albeit fairly tasteless representation of the autonomized cunt, it's still predicated on that ancient idea, stemming from the *fabliaux* tradition, that the genitals speak the truth in a way that betrays or undermines their 'owner'. In confronting Towelie with the terrible truth during his second appearance on her show, Oprah grows increasingly angry – 'You're a lying sack of shit!' She turns the studio audience against him, calling out for a 'good old-fashioned lynching'. The audience members look under their chairs (a motif often employed on the *Oprah Winfrey Show*, where anything from a pot of Vaseline to keys for a brand new car would await every audience member) and find primitive torches which they set alight. Minge takes fright, draws a revolver which points out through Oprah's pink trousers and takes hostages, having first shot a police officer. Lieutenant Nelson, the hostage negotiator, steps in and says to his colleagues with some alarm: 'We don't have any time. This is the most unstable vagina I've ever talked to.' Gary wants to surrender; Minge is more vocal than that. He's a wanted man (or, rather, a wanted vagina): 'Don't be stupid, Gary! I've killed a policeman! They'll fry me, and lock you up for life.' It's down to Towelie to hatch a plan to free the hostages by surreptitiously leading them into a nearby bank. In the resulting scuffle, a police officer shoots at Oprah's crotch and kills Gary. Minge commits suicide, having first berated Oprah, calling her 'you stupid cow', but Oprah – mercifully, since to kill off the primetime maven might have been too much for some viewers to bear – survives. 'Oprah's going to be OK', says Nelson, gravely, 'Wish I could say the same for her vagina and asshole'.

In their DVD extras commentary, even Parker and Stone describe the episode as flawed, and talk about its weirdness as being like putting a hat on top of a hat (wearing one hat looks fine; putting another hat on top of the first looks eccentric): 'If [we . . .] had to George Lucas one episode it would probably be this one' say the creators.[38] So, what's the episode for? What cultural function does it fulfil? On the one hand, the brutal equation of guns and genitals, the focus on Winfrey's crotch, the violence of having a police officer shoot directly at a woman's genitals, are arguably unnecessarily vicious and crude, even misogynist. On the other hand – and I'm far from offering an apologia for the puerile nonsense (interspersed, admittedly, with moments of brilliantly wry humour) Parker and Stone largely peddle – the episode does caricature modern media and the hype it creates around itself and around 'celebrities'. It's also an episode which – albeit unwittingly – plays into a long and well-established representational tradition of the autonomous cunt. To mock and objectify any woman is, of course, unacceptable, but to reduce Oprah to the essentials of her physicality is surely also to make a powerful statement about her almost regal identity and power in the eyes of the millions of viewers of her OWN (Oprah Winfrey Network); and the millions of readers of her (fittingly titled, given the subject-matter of *The Vagina*) *O* magazine (which has, over more than 12 years, only a handful of times had Winfrey share its glossy cover with anyone else). Winfrey's stock in trade is the confessional: her particular gift is to make people open up to her, putting themselves at the mercy of her thankfully fairly sound sagacity and advice. To have Oprah's vagina and anus speak, then, is, when viewed in the *fabliaux* tradition, or from a Diderotian perspective, an entirely logical consequence of her overriding passion for 'living the best life' and, essentially, for getting to the 'truth'.[39]

Powerful women are regularly denigrated on *South Park*. Hillary Clinton features in a spoof of the TV series *24* where a 'snuke' (a suitcase containing a nuclear bomb) has been hidden in her 'sniz'. 'We have reason to believe', says Alan Thompson, head of the CIA, 'That Mrs Clinton may have a nuclear device up her snatch [. . .] it's the technical term for a vagina'. The episode plays with the myth of the *vagina dentata*, too: Clinton's aide, Brian, volunteers to clamber into the 'sniz' to defuse the 'snuke', a dangerous task, since 'that snatch has not seen action in over 30 years. It could be toxic!' 'I'm nearing her sniz now', Brian reports: 'Wait! There's something else here. There's something [. . .] Oh God! It's looking at me! [. . .] Aargh! It's eating my head! It's eating my head!', and then Brian explodes in a mess of vivid red blood. Mostly unperturbed, her feet still in the gynaecologist's stirrups, Clinton softly exclaims 'Oh my!' Like Oprah, she is separated from an unruly, uncanny vagina and survives without it. What's the message here? Is it even worth finding one? Yes. Given how many millions of people have watched both 'The Snuke' and 'A Million Little Fibers', there's no doubt that *South Park* both reflects and creates public opinions. This opinion seems to be very firmly – as in the episode 'Stupid Spoiled Whore Video Playset', which shows Paris Hilton inserting a large pineapple into her vagina, only to be subsumed, in turn, by Mr Slave's anus – that women's vaginas are unruly and dangerous if the women themselves have public profiles. The parodies beg the question: do powerful women like Oprah and Clinton sacrifice their sexual identities in order to be successful? How better to diminish a woman's power and to ridicule her than to show her vagina as a place unknown, alien, autonomous and dangerous, even to her? Indeed, isn't the show contributing to a cultural tradition which has long portrayed powerful women as being somehow 'like men', without acknowledging their 'possession' of a vagina?

When *South Park*'s female characters *do* have a degree of control over their genitals, they are treated with fear and suspicion. In 2009's 'Eat, Pray, Queef', Martha Stewart stuffs star and moon shaped confetti into her (pixelated) vulva so as to demonstrate how to make 'queeves [. . .] more dynamic for the holidays [. . .] See how pretty that was? It's a good thing'. And a woman senator can 'queef', or audibly expel air out of her vagina, in three different ways: 'The Sneezing Unicorn', 'The Resuscitator' and 'The Road Warrior'. As a result, queefing is banned. (Imagine that: men saying what women are and are not allowed to do with their own bodies. Preposterous.) The episode ends by critiquing the double standard that 'allows' men to fart but forbids women to 'queef', and showing South Park's men recording a charity record called 'Queef Free' ('You're a woman now, and you're free to queef'). The double standard idea also pervades 'Stupid Spoiled Whore Video Playset' as Wendy Testaburger refuses to be seduced by the over-sexualized items for sale in a Paris-Hilton-themed store in the mall, where products include the eponymous 'Playset' so that girls can make their own sex tapes and 'Let everyone see your cooch'.

A 'cooch' was also significant in 'Mr Garrison's Fancy New Vagina', an episode first shown in 2005, as the opener to the ninth season of *South Park*. The boys' teacher, Mr Garrison, undergoes MTF (male to female) gender reassignment surgery or, as his doctor says, a 'Vaginaplasty' in the course of which he proceeds to 'slice' Mr Garrison's 'balls', and turn his 'penis inside out'. 'Do I look like a woman?' the patient asks after the speedy operation. 'Pretty much', declares the surgeon. The show maintains its humour for ten-year olds in the episode. Mr Garrison's anatomical knowledge is sketchy: 'I can't wait to get my first period!' he tells horrified onlookers in a supermarket, and 'I'm about to pee out my vagina for the first time'. Complications arise when Mr Slave, Garrison's S&M partner, responds to Garrison's 'I got some tampons. I should be getting my period really soon. Hope I don't get too emotional and drive you crazy with my PMS [. . .] I wanna try out my new snooch', with the simple: 'I'm gay. I don't like vaginas'. The misogyny is very much at home with the transphobia and racial stereotyping in this episode. The short, white Jewish boy, Kyle Broflovski, undergoes a 'Negroplasty' in order to play basketball; his father Gerald, undergoes a 'Dolphinplasty', in order to . . . well . . . to be a dolphin.

The ugly surrealism of the Broflovskis' surgery emphasizes that 'you must match on the outside what you feel you are on the inside', and takes it to darkly satirical lengths. The absurdity effectively spills over into Mr Garrison's flippant and speedy surgery so that the show equates the desire to undertake gender reassignment with ridiculous, unrealistic desires. The ugliness pervades the episode: when he thinks he's pregnant, because of the no-show of his period, Mr (now 'Mrs') Garrison wants an abortion: 'if you want, you can just scramble it and I'll queef it out myself'. Because of his lack of a female reproductive system, Garrison doesn't believe the gender reassignment can have worked. 'I'm just a guy with a mutilated penis', he says. The vagina is, in this episode, the poor relation of the penis; a mutilated version of it. In itself it *lacks* significance – it cannot bleed or conceive without the reproductive organs too. Parker and Stone are conveying a message that no amount of hormone treatment or surgery can make a 'man' a 'woman'; the vagina is not only autonomized but also commodified – bought on a whim by Garrison. 'What kind of woman can't have abortions and bleed out through her snatch once a month?' he furiously demands of his surgeon: 'You made me into a freak; that's what you did!' So, MTF transsexuals are 'freaks' in the *South Park* universe. Is it transphobia? Or a more sophisticated riff on the view that MTF transsexuals are not 'women'? Does the signified 'vagina' accord with the signifier 'woman'? Resemblance theory is flawed: Garrison's body has been made to *resemble* a woman's body. But how does one determine which criteria of resemblance to employ? Part of the joke is, of course, that Garrison is utterly unconvincing as Mrs Garrison: he is portrayed as still having facial features and male-pattern baldness which patently point to a resemblance to 'man', not 'woman'. Garrison finally embraces his identity (at least until the episode in season 12, called 'Eek, a penis!'), and, for good measure, homophobia is thrown into the general misogynist/transphobic maelstrom: 'Even though I'm not truly a woman, I think I still like the new me. I'd rather be a woman who can't have periods than a fag. Hey, guys! This girl is staying a woman! Who wants to pound my vagina? Girl power!' As I've already said, the creators of *South Park* are equal opportunities misanthropes who, in the style of over-tired and petulant children, poke fun at so many of western culture's taboos, among them – of course – the paradoxical, troubling, insistent, seen/unseen *c*-word. However much they think they're pushing boundaries, the show's motifs, characterized in the French *fabliaux* by the *vagina loquens*, have been around for centuries: Matt Parker and Trey Stone are the *chevaliers* of twenty-first-century Colorado.

Between women

Sex and the City is a hugely popular American TV show which ran for six seasons until its finale in 2004. There are 94 episodes and the series was loosely based on author Candace Bushnell's semi-autobiographical columns for *The New York Observer*, which were collected together into book form – called *Sex and the City* – in 1997. The TV episodes focus on the lives of four white, affluent, female Manhattan residents: Carrie Bradshaw (a journalist); Samantha Jones (a PR impresario); Charlotte York (who works in an art gallery); and Miranda Hobbes (a lawyer). Two film spin-offs were produced, in 2008 and 2010, presumably because the show had proved itself to be immensely bankable during its TV run: *Sex and the City* (henceforth '*SATC*') had won 7 Emmys (it got 12 nominations in 2003 alone); 8 Golden Globes (5 nominations in 2004); and 3 SAG (Screen Actors Guild) Awards.[40] In 2007, *Time* Magazine's TV critic

James Poniewozik named it one of the top TV shows of all time.[41] Carrie, played by Sarah Jessica Parker, frames and narrates each episode, the events of which she is ostensibly writing up for her weekly newspaper sex column. As the series developed, however, it became apparent that Carrie was more feted for her 'kooky' style of dressing, than for her writing. When Carrie's life isn't revolving around her friends or her wardrobe, it's men – or, rather, the tedious pursuit of men – who take up most of her emotional energy.[42] Samantha Jones (played by Kim Cattrall), like Carrie, is carnally exuberant (*un*like Carrie, who is never filmed without a bra, Samantha's breasts are shown on screen); Charlotte York (Kristin Davis) has a more romantic worldview, firmly directed towards mar-riage; and Miranda Hobbes (Cynthia Nixon) is depicted as the archetype of the exhausted 'wants it all' career woman and, later, mother. So far, so clichéd. But the show's strengths, for all its triviality, lay in some groundbreaking moments where, because of the four women's stories, primetime, 'respectable' TV began to redefine the boundaries of how female sexuality might be represented.[43] The glamorous aspects of the women's lives (and salaries) were not something with which many of the series' viewers could readily identify; but their emotional and sexual antics and predicaments *were* familiar – even while being, at times, preposterously exaggerated for the sake of plot momentum. The women in the show redefine libidinal drives, modifying them to accommodate female friendship and expending as much energy (emotional and temporal), on each other as on men. Without female friendship, Carrie, as scholar Jane Gerhard splendidly expresses it, 'would be adrift in a sea of orgasms, shoes, and inad-equate boyfriends'.[44]

British journalist Tanya Gold excoriated the *SATC* phenomenon in 2010 when the second (almost unanimously critically slated) film was released. In an article called 'Sorry sisters, but I hate *Sex and the City*', Gold's argu-ment started with the frankly contentious assertion that '*Sex and the City* is embraced as a feminist Bible on screen'.[45] There's – at least on the surface of things – so little that's 'feminist' about the *SATC* franchise that Gold's opening 'Biblical' hypothesis mightn't hold water. To be fair to Gold, though, she does mitigate this statement by declaring: 'be warned, sister – *Sex and the City* is to feminism what sugar is to dental care'. Gold rightly attacks the series' infanti-lization (Carrie's wearisome on/off relationship with her paternalistic lover,

'Mr Big', is a case in point); and objectification of women, as well as its vacuous pseudo-intellectualism: 'the only book [Carrie . . .] ever picks up is *Love Letters of Great Men*'. (That's not actually the case – in one of the two episodes on which I focus, Carrie is seen briefly reading a Martin Amis novel.) Gold also comments on how what is initially premised as liberating sex for the women ends up as conservatively retributive instead: Samantha, the most sexually experimental and voracious of the four, develops cancer, while Charlotte, 'by far the most conventional [. . .] plays by the rules and is rewarded'.[46]

But is it really the case that there's no feminist axis to the show? Isn't the chimera of '*post*feminism', postmodernism's odd bedfellow, shot through with contradictions and inconsistencies? *SATC*'s story arcs, it must be said, focused on the taboo topic of the sexually autonomous and fulfilled woman, and on primetime TV, too. Not only did the choice of many and varied sexual partners become the province of women, not the exclusive domain of men, but 'tougher' subjects also got coverage. In the first season, group sex featured in a storyline focused on Charlotte; in season 2 the same character discovers 'Mr Pussy', a man whose particular gift is for performing cunnilingus.[47] Here, at least, if 'cunnilingus signifies active female sexuality, with the clitoris symbolising female potency', then *SATC* does engage, albeit it in an idiosyncratic way, with third wave feminism.[48] Charlotte's life is anything but mundane: she contracts an STI from another sexual encounter and, in season 4, she has infertility issues, falling, in season 5, for a Jewish man and eventually converting so as to be able to marry him. Samantha is the oldest of the four women and even though she was only in her early forties when the series started, she does represent the idea of women continuing to be sexually attractive – and, crucially, sexually *active* – beyond the age of, say, 21. 'In its insistence on female orgasm as fundamental right and essential part of sex', feminist researcher Astrid Henry argues, '*Sex and the City* challenges dominant media images of heterosexuality, such as pornographic ones, in which female orgasm is secondary to male pleasure'.[49] But in that very challenge, the show remains resolutely heteronormative, despite the women's occasional forays into alternate sexual set-ups. Samantha 'I'm a trisexual: I'll try anything once' Jones's character allowed the series' producers to address issues – the menopause; HIV – which hadn't previously been given exposure in the same way.[50] Similar storylines to those of *SATC* (STIs, menstruation, unwanted pregnancies) have more recently been exuberantly and fearlessly examined by the wonderfully talented Lena Dunham in HBO's *Girls*. In *SATC*, Samantha's menopause storyline also challenged the menstrual taboo, as she rejoiced at the appearance – in coitus, no less – of her period.[51]

In the show's final season, Samantha undergoes chemotherapy for breast cancer. And, if we were in need of any further evidence for the present, albeit erratic, feminist credentials of *SATC*, the fact that the right-wing British tabloid *The Daily Mail* disapproved of it, ought to suffice. The *Mail*, never a newspaper to advocate moderation where panic is an option, ran a story in 2008 based on a report in *The American Journal of Paediatrics*, and headed 'Sexually charged shows such as *Sex and the City* and *Friends* to blame for rise in teenage pregnancy.'[52] Yes, *Daily Mail*. It's what our daughters watch on TV – and not underfunding of sex education in schools, economic anxiety, low self-esteem, not even owning a vocabulary for talking about their bodies, young men with their own feelings of social inadequacy or being exposed to the *Mail*'s insatiable obsession with 'famous' women's body shapes – which gets them pregnant. The logical conclusion to the *Mail*'s frankly inexplicable reasoning is that if we throw out all the TVs and close down all the cinemas (as well as the libraries; in the United Kingdom, the Tories are on it already), then teenage pregnancies will cease. And unicorns with rainbow manes will frolic merrily down the nation's high streets, pages from *The Daily Mail* billowing from their horns like just so many party streamers.

In *Sex and the City*, how Samantha deals with her cancer diagnosis is a powerful plotline, and illness figures in Miranda's character arc, too. She is diagnosed with chlamydia and later supports her partner (eventually her husband) when he develops testicular cancer. The great American taboo of abortion is also dealt with in a progressive way in *SATC*: two of the four lead characters have had abortions (Samantha more than once), and a third considers having one. Ultimately, however, the show does err on the side of normative walking-off-into-the-sunset fulfillment for its four central protagonists: Bradshaw's last omniscient voice-over rings somewhat hollow, coming as it does from a woman who was once nearly left homeless because, over the course of a few years, she spent around $40,000 on shoes.[53] 'The most exciting, challenging and significant relationship of all is the one you have with yourself', goes the voice-over. It all sounds very 'self-help' manual. But, in this heterosexual Manhattan bubble where women *need* men (but not always marriage) like they *need* oxygen, the mawkish finale is inevitable: 'And if you find someone to love the you *you* love', intones the narrator, 'well, that's just fabulous'.[54] For all the show's emphasis on finding a *man* 'to love the you *you* love', it's *female* friendship which is the mainstay of the series. This is precisely the point of the episode called 'The Power of the Female Sex'.

Having acknowledged the complications of the feminist/postfeminist fault-lines which traverse *SATC*, it's time to consider how they are manifested in terms of female sexual identity. In other words, is 'woman', as promulgated by the *SATC* franchise, a cohesive individual, or is she irremediably fractured in the face of so many incompatible ideological demands? I'm interested in two specific episodes in respect of this question, both of which feature Charlotte and her vagina, because in each episode the genitals are depicted initially as unruly, autonomous and frightening, even to Charlotte herself; but they have the potential – not always realized, as we shall see – ultimately to be shown in an empowering manner. The first episode I'm going to consider is the fifth of the 94-episode run, and is called 'The Power of Female Sex'; the second is episode 50, called 'The Real Me'.

'The Power of Female Sex' (written by Jenji Kohan; broadcast in the United States in July 1998), signalled a groundbreaking moment for US channel HBO, as the first of its programmes to broadcast the word 'cunt'.[55] The episode was shown in the United Kingdom seven months after its screening in the States, and caused something of a stir. Richard Brooks, writing in the *Observer* newspaper in 1999, called *SATC*'s use of the word 'the last television taboo'; its peculiar power meant that the United Kingdom's Channel 4 had a dilemma on their hands, but came to the conclusion that the episode was acceptable because 'cunt' was used in it 'to describe the female genitalia, not as a swear word'.[56] This denotative use, then, made the word acceptable, and – as we shall see – even made it 'decent', in a scene set apart from Manhattan's world of moral vacuum and sleaze masquerading as sophistication.[57] How is the word deployed, then? How might its pioneering usage not only have been self-legitimating, but actually *acceptable*, to the point of increasing the show's popularity, or, at least of lending the show a complexity which one might miss on a first viewing?

Charlotte in Connecticu(n)t

After failing to get a table for lunch at a fashionable new Manhattan restaurant called Balzac, Carrie goes shoe shopping, as she puts it, 'to unleash the creative subconscious'. Yes. A pair of shoes: that's what a woman needs to be able to be creative (I must have missed that moment in Virginia Woolf's *Room of One's Own*). When her credit card is declined and rudely cut in two by the shop assistant (this *is* Dolce & Gabbana, not Walmart) an old friend, Amalita, who's in the same shop with her partner Carlo, steps in to pay. The act of kindness by an acquaintance is undercut almost immediately, however, by Carrie's direct-to-camera admission, over Amalita's shoulder, as they embrace, that she's not a close friend at all. The sense is that Carrie doesn't much like this woman, but that she *does* like the shoes – a lot – and so, in Carrie's consumerist universe, the exchange of fake bonhomie for expensive shoes is acceptable. A different version of female friendship is represented in the next scene as the four stalwarts play poker. Charlotte reveals (in such a clunky way that one only hopes it's deliberately postmodern and ironic) that 'Neville Morgan, the notoriously reclusive painter, paid a visit to the gallery' where she works. Charlotte's dilemma is that she's concerned that Morgan's invited her to his remote Connecticut farm in order, as Carrie puts it, to 'hold his brush'. Miranda says in passing that she'll sue, should any sexual impropriety take place, to which Samantha replies: 'I can't believe what I'm hearing! You're like the Harvard Law Lorena Bobbitt!', referring to the infamous 1993 case of the woman who deliberately amputated the penis of her physically abusive husband. Samantha's remark is spoken in jest, but serious issues underlie it. The implication is that, in Samantha's worldview, were Morgan to assault Charlotte, the involvement of the law would be both unnecessary and extreme. Further, in likening Miranda to Lorena Bobbitt, Samantha's articulating something wholly offensive about how a female lawyer's successes, especially over men, function as a form of emasculation.

After the card game, Carrie settles into bed to read Martin Amis's *Night Train*. It's an interesting choice: an intelligent novel which plays with unconventional versions of American femininity. The death of a beautiful female scientist is being investigated by a tough female cop, Mike Hoolihan, who's had several unsuccessful heterosexual relationships. The choice of Carrie's reading matter can hardly have been an accident on the producers' behalf; it can be seen as a knowing gesture to the complexities of living authentically as a woman in the United States – difficulties which Carrie and her friends also face. Carrie doesn't read for long, however, as she's interrupted by a phone call from Amalita inviting her to Balzac. It's there that she meets the gallant Frenchman, Gilles. When Gilles leaves the morning after having had sex with Carrie, she's horrified to find $1,000 in cash next to the bed. Because the dominant stylistic motif of the programme is strongly confessional, as the insistent voice-over, and to-camera moments suggest, Carrie's next step is to discuss what's happened with Charlotte and Samantha.[58] Samantha is characteristically blasé about the whole thing, to the point that Miranda calls her 'the dime store Camille Paglia'. Meanwhile, Carrie's voice-over shifts the narrative to Charlotte who has, after all, gone to Neville Morgan's 'secluded Connecticut home'.

Morgan is charming, solicitous and flattered by Charlotte's praise of his back catalogue. He ushers her into a dark barn and, in a slow, deliberate, Anglo-American accent, launches into his arty spiel. 'The canvases you're about to see', he begins, 'I consider to be the apotheosis of every great idea I've ever had. It's the closest I've ever come to pure, universal God force!' With this, Morgan switches on the lights and declaims: 'The Cunt!' Charlotte's face registers surprise; the camera shows the viewer close-ups of Morgan's very large, very colourful semi-abstract canvases in the style of Betty Dodson, each of which, indeed, depicts a cunt. Morgan goes up to one and strokes it tenderly, even reverentially, saying: 'The most powerful force in the universe! The source of all life and pleasure! And beauty!' Charlotte looks politely on, stiffly silent (the sight of the labia has sealed her own lips); her facial expression registers extreme discomfiture. Morgan, momentarily Mangogul, continues: 'I used to paint full nudes, but as I got older I realized that the truth was to be found only in the cunt!' This idea of 'truth' proves to be the cornerstone of the plot and is key to understanding the episode's deployment of female sexuality and the cunt. But more of that in a moment. As we focus on Charlotte's tight-lipped(!), surprised, but fastidiously polite, tongue-tied expression, we learn from Carrie's voice-over that: 'Charlotte hated the c-word. But Neville Morgan was not a man to be corrected.'

Neville's wife, Gertrude, is played by Phyllis Somerville, who was only 54 at the time the episode was made, but who was made to look at least ten years older than that. She comes into the barn with a large tray of homemade lemonade and cookies, and immediately anchors the exchange in more socially conventional territory. The ease of interaction between husband and wife utterly defuses any latent threat in the situation. As Charlotte takes a glass of lemonade from Gertrude, Neville continues with his discourse: 'Each of these portraits is of a woman who's touched my life.' Charlotte's quiet response of 'Incredible!' is quickly followed by what the viewer has perhaps expected, as Morgan asks: 'I wonder – would you consider posing for me sometime?' The positioning and reactions of the two women are crucial as Morgan asks his question. Charlotte's body language is completely closed down. Her suit is prim, and sharp; she has one arm across her body, and her other is closed across her chest, even as she grips her lemonade glass. Her expression is fixed in a rictus of decorum. Next to her, in the same shot, Gertrude is altogether more open. Her red shawl has slipped, leaving the softer, rounded flesh of her left shoulder exposed. Her expression is relaxed, unlike Charlotte's, who can only stumble over her words as she forces out the equivocal: 'I'm very flattered.' Morgan puts his arm around her, and the most splendid line of the vignette is delivered by grey-haired Gertrude, in what has by now been established as her comfortable, natural way: 'I bet you have a beautiful cunt, dear.' The use of 'dear' is particularly potent: it's affectionate, as suits Gertrude's gentleness, and it reconfigures the use of the word 'cunt' in the same compliment. In fact the entire scene is about reconfiguration. First, the anxious expectations shared by the friends at the poker game and by the viewers have to be reassessed radically by Gertrude's presence, which neutralizes the archetypal 'vulnerable woman' setting (like that which Lichtenstein subverted at the end of *Teeth*): a deserted location; a darkened barn with a closed door; a reclusive man whose reputation has been built on painting nudes. Second, Charlotte's own belief system has been transformed: Gertrude uses 'the c-word', previously 'hated' by Charlotte, in a positive, denotative way. 'Cunt' has become something unthreatening, comfortable and warm. There is no longer any space for Charlotte's 'hate'.

The episode shifts to the restaurant, Balzac, where Amalita's wealthy Venetian companion invites Carrie to join him at the Venice Film Festival. Carrie's voice-over is spectacularly epiphanic. 'I couldn't say I wasn't tempted', says our narrator, 'I realised that I could leverage myself like the human equivalent of a sexy joint bond. I'd parlay that $1,000 [from Gilles] into a trip to Venice; into a nice piece of jewellery; a rich husband; followed by a richer divorce'. And she walks away, her own world-view having been as profoundly reconfigured as Charlotte's. Commodification isn't what Morgan is doing with his cunt canvases; it isn't in the 'transgressive' art, but it's in the quotidian socio-economic exchanges of the kind into which men and women enter in swanky restaurants, bars, clubs and parties everywhere. Morgan's paintings show as much beauty as Amalita's coterie displays ugliness. It is in the women's lavatories at Balzac, this least likely of settings, Carrie's voice-over tells us, that an exchange of honesty and integrity takes place, and where shallow posturing is utterly deflated: 'And then the most powerful woman in New York asked me for a favour'. The supercilious restaurant hostess who had previously twice turned away Carrie and Samantha, sticks her head out of her cubicle and asks Carrie for a tampon. Carrie finds one in her handbag and willingly hands it over. This handover is a fundamentally important moment of exchange in the episode's dramatic and ethical trajectory. It isn't just a tampon Carrie provides: it's solidarity, it's an acknowledgement of the cunt that bleeds, that is natural, that is powerful – like those portrayed on Morgan's canvases – in a positive, enabling way. It's an act of authenticity which Amalita and her female companions could never truly understand, as they pick up yet another $1,000 dollars from the (one-)nightstand. In order to maintain her lifestyle, Amalita has to compromise her bodily and moral integrity, separating cunt and selfhood in a series of libidinal transactions. The restroom exchange is not one Amalita would recognize as important, because of its profoundly feminocentric formulation. The tampon has more *authentic* worth in the specific economy Carrie and the hostess have privately generated than any Venetian palazzo will have for Amalita and her crowd. The fact that Carrie admits to the viewer that she is keeping from Samantha how come Balzac's doors are now always open to them, endorses the prized intimacy of the restroom exchange.

Intimacy is the subject of the concluding scenes of the episode, too: the four friends are at Charlotte's gallery to see the Neville Morgan exhibition. The women try to guess which of the paintings is of their friend's cunt. Charlotte herself is relaxed and joyful, teasing her friends and initially refusing to reveal which is 'her' canvas. The intimacy of the four women is emphasized because we, the viewers, are excluded from their verbal exchanges: Charlotte whispers to Carrie, who shares with Samantha, who finally tells Miranda. They rush to the specific canvas and, in the voice-over, Carrie tells us: 'They say a picture is worth a thousand words but in this case I was speechless.' Our exclusion continues as we look at the faces of the women who are looking at the painting. The perspective does shift, so that we're behind the four – but we have no more privileged a viewing position than any of the gallery visitors. As the camera zooms out, we see more – but *not* all of the painting, because the women's bodies partially, perhaps protectively, obscure it. We still cannot *see* the c-word; neither canvas nor cunt is revealed to us. And this isn't an act of censorship or overt decorum: we have seen others of Morgan's paintings in full, after all. It is, rather, an act that underscores female friendship.

The episode, then, has delivered a significant commentary about honesty and openness. The cunts on Morgan's canvases are more incorporated – as Charlotte learns – than Amalita is, in her materially rich, but emotionally poor, life. But a slightly nagging feeling persists after the episode's end, that, perhaps, Charlotte *has* somehow sold herself for the cachet of a Neville Morgan exhibition at the gallery. Alternatively, might we interpret her gains as far less material? She is clearly in her element, is joyful – perhaps even *jouissante* – at the gallery. Her inhibitions have apparently dissolved because of her bodily and psychical assimilation of her sexual organs via the medium of Morgan's *authentic* canvases. Carrie's earlier voice-over about Charlotte not liking the 'c-word' was presumably because of the connotative associations it held. Once painted by Neville Morgan, however, the cunt's associations have become *denotative* for Charlotte. For her, at last, there's more power in the thing signified than in the signifier. The title of the episode implies all sorts of versions of the idea of 'The Power of Female Sex'; it's ambiguous: the literal 'sex' organ – the cunt – *has* proven empowering; by contrast, the hackneyed idea of women using their sexual attractiveness for material reward has been exposed as shallow and debased. Women may use their sexuality like Amalita, or, as Carrie, Charlotte, and the hostess have learned, power can reside in the intimate bonds that unite those women who are truly at one with their 'sex'. In these gallery scenes, the women's inability to guess which canvas shows their friend's cunt, and Charlotte's game of whispered revelation, indicate that the canvases and cunts don't have to speak: the truth (in a narrative reversal of the *vagina loquens fabliau* convention), can come from Charlotte – unified, incorporated, whole Charlotte – *herself.*

Coda

The name of the restaurant, in its evocation of Honoré de Balzac, is provocative: as Graham Robb, Balzac's biographer records, the writer added the nobiliary particle 'de' to his name in 1830 not merely as a hollow show or pretence of lineage, but rather to show how his writing success had *earned* him – to his own mind – the right to claim it. 'Like a new set of clothes', writes Robb of this addition, 'it allowed its possessor to circulate more freely in society [. . .] Above all, it could stand for something far more important than an accident of birth'.[59] This is the case for Carrie, too – it no longer matters *who* she knows; during the episode she's learned something important about emotional authenticity. Her indefinite guarantee of a table at the Balzac restaurant has been *earned* through an act of kindness to a stranger; an important, simple and private exchange between women.[60]

'You can't see what I see'

The establishment and development of the four protagonists' sexual identities is a crucial element, then, of 'The Power of Female Sex'. For the viewer, being able see through *SATC*'s tiresome aesthetic of Blahnik blarney is empowering; Charlotte and Carrie, in particular, have begun to reframe their world views and their understanding of their sexual identities. The later episode was called 'The Real Me' (written by Michael Patrick King; broadcast in the United States in June 2001), and it also focuses on Charlotte. It's worthy of brief consideration, here, because it threatens to fragment precisely that bodily integrity which was consummated in Charlotte's encounter with Neville Morgan's cunt canvases. Despite the episode's name, it's a far less 'real' representation of female sexuality than its predecessor, some 45 episodes earlier.

As with 'The Power of Female Sex' this episode has a restaurant as the story's establishing scene, which Carrie's opening voice-over situates firmly in the realm of Manhattan *fabulousness*: 'Brasserie Eight and a Half, located on the corner of Right Now and Everyone Was There; it was the place to see, and be seen'.[61] Immediately, then, the idea is of the visual as more potent than the intellectual, of form as having more value than content. This is undeniably a disappointment, given the claims I've made about Carrie's renegotiation of ideas of exchange and value in 'The Power'. Stanford, Carrie's friend, is experiencing a crisis of confidence – not about his abilities, but about his looks.[62] Carrie boosts his self-esteem by saying that, if he thinks he's unattractive, 'then you can't see what I see!' and by telling him that he needn't go to 'Hookerville' to meet a man. Shortly after this exchange, when a producer friend tells Carrie she really must model in an upcoming fashion show, the tables are turned and Stanford responds to Carrie's protestations that she's 'not a model' with exactly the same phrase: 'then you can't see what I see'. Later, Miranda et al. confirm to Carrie that she 'struts', even on the sidewalk. Despite each character's expressed anxieties around their appearances, they outwardly profess a fundamental belief in the supremacy of the value of what's invisible. But this is by no means a clear position in an episode which, as a whole, never adopts a satisfactory position on the tension between superficiality and depth.

The next sequence shows the four friends at lunch. Samantha announces that she's going to have a nude photo shoot, and Miranda wryly enquires if it's so that she can have postcards made up 'to hand out to prospective dates'. Within just first three-and-a-half minutes of the episode, then, there have been two playful references to prostitution. Carrie outwardly really wants to be *seen* to be a writer; this sentiment is expressed by her several times in the episode. We do see her write in one scene, although the utter triteness of her ideas does undermine her social performance as 'Serious Writer'. In musing on Narcissus, for example, Carrie wonders: 'did he have no best friends to mirror back a healthy review of himself? And why is it that we see our friends perfectly, but when it comes to ourselves, no matter how hard we look, do we see ourselves clearly?' This continuation of the 'see and be seen' theme first established in the Brasserie reiterates the episode's ethical ambiguity: looking *at*, and *self*-examination are incompatible, as interiority and externality battle it out. This incompatibility is most evident in the episode's treatment of Charlotte – the same Charlotte, the viewer recalls, who was empowered after allowing Neville Morgan to commit her cunt to canvas.

Samantha's absolute confidence during her nude photo-shoot is emphasized by her saying 'I'm comfortable', dropping her robe and, without a second's hesitation, putting her right foot up on a box (much to the astonishment of the momentarily poleaxed young man assisting the photographer). So, here's Samantha: powerful and 'comfortable', showing her body to two strangers in a studio. This self-assurance is robustly juxtaposed with, and established as being powerfully antithetical to, what happens in the next scene. Here, Carrie and Charlotte – certainly *not* strangers to one another – have a discussion in which the full frontal power of the female body just established through Samantha's actions is thoroughly negated.[63] The rainy setting of a Manhattan street means Carrie and Charlotte are sharing an umbrella, thus placing them in intimate proximity, while still being in a public place. I've transcribed the exchange so as better to convey the remarkable solipsism Carrie exhibits in her abrupt non sequitur which allows her to monopolize the conversation's direction:

Charlotte: Do you like your gynaecologist?

Carrie: Yeah. She's amazing. Why?

Charlotte: I think I might want to see someone else.

Carrie: What's happening?

Charlotte: Well, Trey [her estranged husband] and I are still just talking; we're not ready to move back in yet . . .

Carrie: . . . [*loudly*] No! What's happening with your *vagina*?

Charlotte: Shhh!

Carrie: Sweetie, I'm not bugged! It's just us listening.

Charlotte: May be a yeast infection, but my gynaecologist says 'No'. But something's definitely off.

Carrie:	Well, what are the symptoms?
Charlotte:	I don't want to talk about this! Can you just call my machine and leave her number?
Carrie:	Hey! Do you know anyone that Stanford could go out with? If we don't find him someone he's going to start dating hookers!
Charlotte:	Hookers? Eeuw!
Carrie:	Hmm. Exactly. Charlotte, would you say that I'm 'strutting' right now?

And here the conversation ends, with Charlotte, oddly, given the complete lack of concern, interest or compassion her best friend has shown, smiling indulgently. This is not the only inconsistency of representation between the two episodes under consideration here, but it is an important one because Charlotte has moved *so* far from the literally incorporated selfhood she revealed as Neville Morgan 'exhibited' her in the gallery. All of the hard work of that episode in normalizing and enhancing the reputation of the 'cunt' – both signifier *and* signified – is rapidly unravelling here. Charlotte's embarrassed 'Shhh!', and irritated 'I don't want to talk about this!' and the apparent lack of concern – or even interest – of her best friend, also undo the solidarity between women which was also crucial in that earlier episode.

The reportage-style photographer who takes pictures of Carrie in her fitting at Dolce and Gabbana makes her feel 'uncomfortable' (along with Samantha's earlier confident statement to *her* photographer, 'comfort' is developing as central to the women's experiences in this episode). But it's when Carrie's voice-over says 'and speaking of uncomfortable' that the real cognitive dissonance between the worlds of exterior show and interior reality comes into focus: the next shot is a close-up of Charlotte's pained face. The *mise en scène* – blue, utilitarian paper gown, examination couch – quickly establishes that this is a clinical setting, a world away from the fashion studio and yet Carrie's narrative has bridged, and has made an unproblematic connection between, the women's very different experiences of 'discomfort'. Charlotte's gynaecologist is brusque. 'OK', she says, 'You can put your legs down now; it is *not* a yeast infection [. . .] I have an entire file of women all with the same symptoms

[. . .] it could be vulvodynia.' Charlotte is prescribed an antidepressant and is clearly confused when the medic explains: 'It's not for you; it's for your vagina.' This statement is important, and I want to pause for a moment to bring in the themes of this book encapsulated within it. The most obvious parallel is with Kaysen's *The Camera My Mother Gave Me*. Kaysen's narrator had chronic vulvodynia, and its effects were presented as utterly debilitating (as the TV series format perhaps demands, Charlotte's own illness is quickly healed). Kaysen's book's title also made sense through the lens (pun intended) of Buñuel, whose influence also resonated in Kamvyselli's own 'photographic' novel, *f/32*. The most important lens missing from this *SATC* episode, and one which was very much in evidence in the infinitely more thoughtful 'Power of Female Sex' episode, is the lens of *self*-reflection. That's particularly ironic, given the title 'The Real Me', and the many cameo roles within it: Heidi Klum plays *herself*; Kevyn Aucoin, Domenico Dolce and Stefano Gabbana and – remarkably – Ed Koch – all play *themselves*, too. Carrie's half-hearted exasperation with her photographer; Samantha's no-holds barred confidence in front of hers; and Charlotte's more literal specular moment, all tap into the narcissistic resonances of the episode. There's also a point to be made here about incorporation in its literal sense. Even the gynaecologist forces the separation between 'cunt' and 'self'. It's a serious psycho-sexual issue, as I've explored elsewhere in *The Vagina*, but I want to draw this section to a close by considering what happens in its humorous treatment in 'The Real Me'.

The women – all bar Samantha – meet in a restaurant and laugh at the concept of Charlotte's 'depressed vagina'. Carrie stumbles, flippantly, over the word: 'Vulvowhatia?,' and Miranda, having teased Charlotte about writing a journal recording her chronic pain, announces: 'I'm fine, but Charlotte, maybe your *hmm-hmm* would like an order of fries?' The viewer needs to bear in mind as the three women giggle that even Charlotte doesn't precisely understand what, or how serious, her condition is, and yet laughter is legitimated only by the separation between 'Charlotte' (immaculately, preppily dressed) and 'Charlotte's cunt' (hidden, unknown, unspeakable). Samantha joins the women at their table and has her nude contact sheets with her. Charlotte almost immediately looks up, shocked, maybe even disgusted, from scrutinizing the pictures: 'That's not very arty', she exclaims, 'I can see your [and here there's a significant pause] *everything.* Samantha's response is characteristically down-to-earth: 'What's the big deal? It's just a vagina!' And Charlotte's reply is conspiratorial in tone: 'It's *magnified*! I've never even seen *mine* that close!' The three other women are astonished. 'I don't wanna look; I think it's ugly!' says Charlotte, to which Miranda immediately retorts: 'Well, maybe that's why it's depressed.'

The episode concludes with another absurd comparison drawn by Carrie. She claims that walking down the catwalk; then falling (she was elegantly stepped over by Heidi Klum, prompting Stanford to exclaim: 'Oh my God! She's fashion road kill!'); and then getting up and carrying on, is on a par with Charlotte facing up to her own 'fear' of 'seeing *herself*.' The viewers see Charlotte's head and torso as she contorts with a hand mirror. As she lowers the mirror, the camera remains on her face, which registers consternation initially, and then fascination. This, for the woman diagnosed with vulvodynia, is of a different magnitude of 'bravery' from that Carrie has just claimed for herself. Carrie's rhetoric becomes more and more preposterous, as she tells the viewers that 'just like Narcissus before her, Charlotte became so mesmerized by what she saw that . . .' – and the voice-over trails off as we see Charlotte fall, and hear a thud closely followed by an 'Ow!' Samantha's encouragement of Charlotte to look at her own genitals (she had even, during the lunchtime conversation, offered her powder compact as a mirror), momentarily promises a healthy attitude to women's bodies. But it is only a transitory attitude – both for Charlotte as she falls down, and for the viewer who still hasn't 'seen' the female body in this episode. And it's in comparison with the powerfully liberatory message of the earlier 'Power of the Female Sex', that this episode *so* agonizingly fails. The inconsistency is exasperating: Charlotte, we know, has incorporated her cunt and has happily – even proudly – publicized it (or, rather, an explicit depiction of it) to her friends at Morgan's exhibition. The later episode, however, in its reversal of everything the earlier one established, is 'safer'; more 'sanitized'. And the price of that 'sanitation' is a sense that the characters really understand neither their own bodies (the 'cunt' is, once more, un*seen*), nor their relationships with one another. Charlotte is *not*, to use Carrie's simile, 'like Narcissus' in 'The Power of Female Sex', because she should be a more fulfilled, complete woman as a result of her interactions with Neville and Gertrude Morgan. The 'narcissism' portrayed in 'The Real Me' signifies a far more superficial, damaging and divisive (in terms of 'Charlotte' and 'Charlotte's vagina') dramatic arc than was ever the case in the earlier episode.

The Vagina isn't – couldn't be – a book about *all* representations of women's sexual organs. The focus is, rather, on episodes such as these, centring on Charlotte, where the female 'self' and the female 'body' experience, on the one hand, a union, and, on the other, a split of such magnitude that the 'cunt' is represented as autonomized, unincorporated, alien. And the idea of the whole woman, so elegantly dealt with in 'The Power', but apparently abandoned by the time of 'The Real Me', pervades *SATC* in pernicious ways. Even though the narrator, Carrie, can *see* the lack of authenticity which her lifestyle promulgates, she recurrently refuses to risk any enduring transgression of heteronormative ideals. In the fairly early days of her relationship with Mr Big, Carrie protested that she found herself abjuring a unified sense of self, performing various roles in his company, to please him. 'You should see me around him!' she complained: 'I wear little outfits: "Sexual Carrie", "Casual Carrie". Sometimes I catch myself actually *posing*. It's just – it's just exhausting!'[64] She could – *should* – have learned much from Charlotte's 'posing' for Neville Morgan in the more sophisticated days of *SATC*'s first season, that brought with it a completion, not a division, of self.

Notes

1　Caryl Churchill, *Top Girls* (London: Methuen, 2005), pp. 27–8.

2　Pieter Brueghel de Oude, *Dulle Griet*, Museum Mayer van den Bergh, Antwerp.

3　Erich Neumann, *The Great Mother*, as quoted in Grisel Gómez-Cano, *The Return to Coatlicue: Goddesses and Warladies in Mexican Folklore* (Bloomington, IN: Xlibris, 2010), p. 89, my italics for emphasis.

4　Pat Carr and Willard Gingerich, 'The Vagina Dentata Motif in Nahuatl and Pueblo Mythic Narratives: A Comparative Study', in Brian Swann (ed.), *Smoothing the Ground: Essays on Native American Oral Literature* (Berkeley, CA: University of California Press, 1983), pp. 187–203 (p. 192).

5　Dante Alighieri, *The Divine Comedy. Volume 1: Inferno*, trans. Mark Musa (London: Penguin, 2003), Canto III, line 9, p. 89.

6　Catherine Breillat's *Anatomie d'enfer* (2004), is based on her 2001 novel, *Pornocratie*.

7　Breillat's *Anatomie d'enfer* (2004), Tartan DVD extras.

8 Julia Kristeva, *Powers of Horror: An Essay on Abjection*, trans. Leon S. Roudiez (New York, NY: Columbia University Press, 1982), p. 2.

9 Kristeva, *Powers of Horror*, p. 164.

10 Ibid., p. 127.

11 On how 'the loathsome is that which disobeys classification rules peculiar to the given symbolic system', see Kristeva, *Powers of Horror*, p. 92.

12 'During that course in which "I" become' writes Kristeva, 'I give birth to myself amid the violence of sobs [. . .] If it be true that the abject simultaneously beseeches and pulverizes the subject, one can understand that it is experienced at the peak of its strength when that subject [. . .] finds the impossible within'. Kristeva, *Powers of Horror*, pp. 3, 5.

13 I am indebted here to Derek Alsop of the University of Chester, whose knowledge of Handel is second to none.

14 Luce Irigaray, *This Sex Which is Not One*, trans. Catherine Porter (New York, NY: Cornell University Press, 1985), p. 77.

15 Georges Bataille, 'The College of Sociology', in *Visions of Excess: Selected Writings, 1927–1939*, ed. and trans. by Allan Stoekl, *Theory and History of Literature, Volume 14* (Minneapolis, MN: University of Minnesota, 1985), pp. 246–56 (p. 251).

16 Kym Martindale uses the term 'body-self' in discussing Monica Wittig's *Lesbian Body*, which 'endeavours to resite [. . .] authority by proposing the lesbian as the "author" of her own anatomy, as the subject who anatomizes, maps and names her body-self'. See Martindale, 'Author(iz)ing the Body: Monique Wittig, *The Lesbian Body* and the Anatomy Texts of Andreas Vesalius', *The European Journal of Women's Studies* 8.3 (2001), pp. 343–56 (p. 347).

17 As Barbara Creed expresses it: 'Although the subject must exclude the abject, the abject must, nevertheless, be tolerated for that which threatens to destroy life also helps to define life'. See Barbara Creed, *The Monstrous Feminine: Film, Feminism, Psychoanalysis* (London: Routledge, 1993), p. 9.

18 On silence as empowerment, see Maureen A. Mahoney, 'The Problem of Silence in Feminist Psychology', *Feminist Studies* 22.3 (1996), pp. 603–25.

19 Thomas M. Kavanagh, 'Language as Deception: Diderot's *Les Bijoux Indiscrets*', *Diderot Studies XXIII*, ed. Otis Fellow and Diana Guiragossian Carr (Geneva: Librairie Droz, 1988), pp. 101–14 (p. 110).

20 To suggest the passage of time and Virginia's ascendant celebrity, DeSimone uses Hollywood old-school *Citizen Kane* spinning newspapers with their headlines charting Virginia's fame. 'CIA bugs Virginia' declaims the Washington Post; 'Police Close Up Virginia's Opening' is the headline on the Boston Globe.

21 Betty Friedan, *The Feminine Mystique* (Harmondsworth: Penguin, 1965), p. 13.

22 Tom DeSimone, personal email correspondence with the author, June 2007.

23 On how, through the 'conventions of Enlightenment literary erotics, a philosopher imagines a female bodily discourse fantasized, elicited and recorded for posterity', see Nancy K. Miller, *French Dressing: Women, Men, and Ancien Régime Fiction* (London: Routledge, 1995), p. 4.

24 On how both Diderot's novel and modern films 'exhibit misogynistic regimes of sexual relationships', and 'are narrative vehicles for the spectacular, involuntary presentation of the knowledge of pleasure as confessions of socially disruptive "sexual truths"', see Linda Williams, *Hard Core: Power, Pleasure and the 'Frenzy of the Visible'* (Berkeley, CA: University of California Press, 1999), p. 30. In Diderot's tale, of course, the revelation is less literally 'spectacular' than auditory.

25 Luce Irigaray, *Speculum of the Other Woman*, trans. Gillian C. Gill (New York, NY: Cornell University Press, 1985), p. 135.

26 Irigaray, *Speculum*, p. 115.

27 Ibid., p. 195.

28 On this 'Alimentary Logic', see Kaja Silverman, *The Acoustic Mirror: The Female Voice in Psychoanalysis and Cinema* (Bloomington, IN: Indiana University Press, 1988), p. 67.

29 Far-fetched though this episode may seem, the director has suggested that he was intentionally making reference to the infamous Kanawha County textbook controversy (Lichtenstein, director's commentary, DVD). In this small West Virginian community, for several months in 1974, fundamentalist Christians successfully called for a boycott of local schools after the School Board listed new books for use in schools, hundreds of which, the protesters argued, were indecent. Books such as *Paradise Lost*, *Lord of the Flies*, *The Crucible* and *Animal Farm* were deemed to be anti-family or anti-God or communist. The Kanawha controversy is the most prolonged violent episode in the history of West Virginia: during it, schools were dynamited, homes were stoned and school buses were shot at. A prominent church leader announced that he was praying for God to kill several School Board members. Happily, that leader's God didn't oblige, the Board backed down, and the most 'controversial' books were withdrawn. For more on the Kanawha County Textbook Controversy, see Jonathan Zimmerman, 'Where the Customer Is King: The Textbook in American Culture', in David Paul Nord, Joan Shelley Rubin and Michael Schudson (eds), *The Enduring Book: Print Culture in Postwar America*, Vol. 5 of *A History of the Book in America* (Chapel Hill, NC: University of North Carolina Press, 2009), pp. 304–24 (pp. 318–24).

30 As Smith and Ferstman argue in *The Castration of Oedipus*, 'The castration sacrifice of the penis [or, in this case, the gynaecologist's fingers] to the (M)other transforms the male into the consort. We therefore have a chain of signification whereby the phallus is the privileged signifier but is possessed, owned, and controlled by the womb and the breasts', which are the material components of female sexual difference. J. C. Smith and Carla J. Ferstman, *The Castration of Oedipus: Feminism, Psychoanalysis, and the Will to Power* (New York, NY: New York University, 1996), p. 149.

31 Hélène Cixous, 'The Laugh of the Medusa', trans. K. and P. Cohen, *Signs: A Journal of Women in Culture and Society* 1.4, pp. 875–93 (p. 893).

32 Mark Mylod (dir.), *Last Fast Show Ever* (BBC, 2000).

33 Matthew Hunt, www.matthewhunt.com/cunt/etymology.html.

34 *South Park* was one of James Poniewozik's, 'All-TIME 100 TV Shows', *Time Magazine*, 6 November 2007; *Entertainment Weekly* ranked *South Park* the twelfth-greatest TV Show of last 25 years, 18 June 2007; in 2004 Channel 4 ranked the '100 Greatest Cartoons' and *South Park* came in 3rd place (behind *Tom & Jerry*, and, at the top of

the list, *The Simpsons*). The show has been Emmy-nominated 11 times, winning 4 times (see: www.imdb.com/title/tt0121955/awards).

35   See Maureen Dowd on Winfrey as the 'Empress of Empathy', in 'Oprah's Bunk Club', *New York Times*, 28 January 2006.

36   One has to wonder how much the invention of Towelie was a satirical move, and how much it was actually a shrewd, if cynical, marketing decision. A quick glance at eBay shows many (probably unauthorized) Towelie-related items for sale, ranging from wristbands to stickers to T-shirts. The parody of spin-offs has spin-offs.

37   Eric Goldman, '*South Park*: "A Million Little Fibers" Review', http://uk.tv.ign.com/ articles/702/702516p1.html, 20 April 2006.

38   'To George Lucas' probably refers to that director's inability to leave well alone, but almost compulsively revisit, for example the *Star Wars* franchise, in an attempt to 'improve' the movies. Parker and Stone are suggesting that they'd like to revisit and rejig their 'Million Little Fibers' episode.

39   On Winfrey's 'Live Your Best Life' slogan as 'the perfect nondenominational and popular motto for a serious spiritual message: that finding [. . .] eternal truth within is the purpose of our lives', see Marianne Williamson, 'Living Her Best Life', in *The Oprah Winfrey Show: Reflections on an American Legacy*, ed. Deborah Davis (New York, NY: Harry N. Abrams, 2011), pp. 128–9 (p. 128).

40   For the list of *Sex and the City*'s Emmy successes, see: www.emmys.com/shows/ sex-and-city; for its Golden Globes, see: www.goldenglobes.org/browse/film/24922; a search of SAG Awards press releases gives information on the show's wins there: www.sagawards.org/awards/search. In 2001 the show 'won the Emmy for Outstanding Comedy series, the first time a cable television show has ever taken top honours for best series in any category'. See Jane Arthurs, '*Sex and the City* and Consumer Culture: Remediating Postfeminist Drama', *Feminist Media Studies*, 3.1 (2003), pp. 83–98 (p. 89).

41   See James Poniewozik, 'All-TIME 100 TV Shows', *Time*, 6 September 2007: http://entertainment.time.com/2007/09/06/the-100-best-tv-shows-of- all-time/#sex-and-the-city.

42   On how *SATC* 'publicly repudiates the shame of being single and sexually active in defiance of the bourgeois codes that used to be demanded of respectable women' see Arthurs, '*Sex and the City* and Consumer Culture', p. 85.

43   On this issue of 'primetime' TV and the influential role HBO had to play in content development, see Arthurs: 'the forces shaping programmes in the digital, multichannel era of television [. . .] allow for innovation in its sexualised mode of address'. Arthurs, '*Sex and the City* and Consumer Culture', p. 83.

44   Jane Gerhard, '*Sex and the City*: Carrie Bradshaw's Queer Postfeminism', *Feminist Media Studies*, 5.1 (2005), pp. 37–49 (p. 43).

45   Tanya Gold, 'Sorry Sisters, But I Hate *Sex and the City*', *The Telegraph*, 21 May 2010: www.telegraph.co.uk/culture/film/7746119/Sorry-sisters-but-I-hate-Sex-and-the-City. html.

46   All quotations in this paragraph are from Gold, 'Sorry Sisters'.

47   In episode 18, 'The Cheating Curve', Charlotte keeps company with the 'Power Lesbians', 'Manhattan's Choicest New Social Hive', unofficially overseen by the

extremely wealthy Patty Aston. Patty asks Charlotte if she's gay, and Charlotte talks fairly unconvincingly about the 'company of all these women'; the 'safe, warm, environment'; and how 'there's a very powerful part of me that connects to the female spirit'. Patty's wonderfully unambiguous response is: 'Sweetheart, that's all very nice, but if you're not going to eat pussy, you're not a dyke'. Many thanks to Louisa Yates of the University of Chester for bringing this particular episode to my attention.

48   Astrid Henry, 'Orgasms and Empowerment: *Sex and the City* and the Third Wave Feminism', in Kim Akass and Janet McCabe (eds), *Reading Sex and the City* (London: I.B. Tauris, 2006), pp. 65–82 (p. 77). Henry's reading of *SATC* through the lens of third wave feminism is both ingenious and plausible.

49   Henry, 'Orgasms and Empowerment', p. 76. In episode 56, 'My Motherboard, My Self', Samantha's 'loss' of her orgasm is presented as a dilemma of almost existential importance, remedied only by her release of grief at the funeral of Miranda's mother.

50   Samantha declares this in episode 34, 'Boy, Girl, Boy, Girl . . .'.

51   'Far from suffering shame over bleeding on a man she has just met, her obvious relief reveals a far greater taboo, that surrounding the menopause': see Kim Akass and Janet McCabe, 'Ms Parker and the Vicious Circle: Female Narrative and Humour in *Sex and the City*', in Akass and McCabe (eds), *Reading Sex and the City*, pp. 177–200 (p. 192).

52   Barry Wigmore, 'Sexually charged shows such as *Sex and the City* and *Friends* to blame for rise in teenage pregnancy', *The Daily Mail*, 4 November 2008: www. dailymail.co.uk/news/article-1082571/Sexually-charged-shows-Sex-And-The-City-Friends-blame-rise-teenage-pregnancy.html.

53   Shoes perform a crucial, almost fetishistic, role in *SATC* which, alas, lies beyond the subject-matter of this current book. However, to see more on how 'the autoeroticism legitimated by the narcissistic structure of the look in consumer culture offers the possibility of doing without men at all', see Arthurs, '*Sex and the City* and Consumer Culture', p. 93. On the maths behind shoe-buying, see episode 64, 'Ring a Ding Ding'.

54   *SATC*, episode 94, 'An American Girl in Paris (Part Deux)'.

55   On how the word had first been broadcast on US TV some four years earlier as Phil Donahue 'uttered [. . .] *cunt* on his talk show (in relating and condemning an employer's insult to a female employee) without any sort of bleep, and without any noticeable reaction from the audience', see Jesse Sheidlower (ed.), *The F-Word: The Complete History of the Word in all its Robust and Various Uses* (London: Faber and Faber, 1999), p. xii. My thanks to Matthew Hunt for bringing this reference to my attention.

56   Richard Brooks, 'Last Taboo Broken by Sex and the C***', *The Observer*, 14 February 1999: www.guardian.co.uk/uk/1999/feb/14/richardbrooks.theobserver.

57   On how the specifics of the episode's usage arguably brought 'respectable connotations [. . .]. Uttering it in this context lifts prohibitions, rescues it from taboo and inspires laughter', see Akass and McCabe, 'Ms Parker', p. 192.

58   This technique of breaking the fourth wall was dropped in subsequent series.

59   Graham Robb, *Balzac: A Biography* (London: W. W. Norton, 1994), pp. 168–9.

60   Alternatively – and this is a far less elegant, but equally fun, interpretation – it might simply be that 'Balzac' is roughly homophonous with 'Ball sack', and that Jenji

Kohan – in this episode so focused on *female* anatomy – was having a little laugh with the viewers.

61 *8½* is the name of a semi-autobiographical 1963 film by Federico Fellini; it's also the name of a restaurant in Vancouver.

62 Stanford Blatch, played by Willie Garson, is an intriguing character since he is almost – but not entirely – part of the female friendship group established by the four leads. His homosexuality is portrayed as enhancing his affinity with the four women (he has been referred to as Carrie's 'gay gal pal') and gently complicates the show's dominant paradigm of heteronormativity. See *Out*, January 2006, p. 24. Elsewhere, Ron Simon refers to how *SATC*'s 'creative dialogue between the gay sensibilities of the male executive producers and the multitudinous real-life experiences of the female writing team gave the series its unique voice'. See Ron Simon, '*Sex and the City*', in Gary R. Edgerton and Jeffrey P. Jones (eds), *The Essential HBO Reader* (Lexington, KY: The University Press of Kentucky, 2008), pp. 193–203 (p. 199). Thanks to Anna Mackenzie and Louisa Yates, both of the University of Chester, for drawing Stanford's importance to my attention.

63 The women's intimacy was emphasized in episode 18, 'The Cheating Curve', as Samantha helps Carrie release a stuck diaphragm. In a sense, Carrie's cunt here 'speaks' to her friend: it reveals to her (and, by extension, to Charlotte and Miranda, too), that Carrie's back in a sexual relationship with Mr Big. (Again, many thanks to Louisa Yates for her invaluable input here.)

64 *SATC*, episode 11, 'The Drought'.

7

Revealing the Vagina in Performance Art

My body, my art

As 'the words "explicit" and "explicate" stem from the Latin *explicare*, which means "to unfold"', we might expect performance art literally to 'unfold' the customarily concealed cunt.[1] Depending on how we interpret it, the innermost folds and secrets of the vagina are a cause for celebration – liberation, even – as details are revealed; or, in their mystery, they are a source of anxiety and doubt. 'The male fear', write Lawyer J. C. Smith and UN Human Rights Monitor Carla Ferstman, 'is of the marshland of female fecundity; the terrible stench of a wet, dank interior; the humid horror of the female body'.[2] It's a statement which truly resonates with the Man's attitude and language in Breillat's *Anatomy*, where 'hidden lips' had 'a skin that sweats, that oozes, a pestilential skin, like the skin of frogs'. To 'unfold' the female body *should* mean a renunciation of such fears, but women continue to be punished for the mysteriousness of their bodies – hence the routinely mechanical and soulless pornographic character of the global sex trade. Explicit performances can be seen as one part of the lucrative exploitation of women. Sheila Jeffreys reminds us (should we ever need reminding) in *The Industrial Vagina*, her riposte to apologists for the sex industry, that: 'live girls and women do have their orifices penetrated to produce pornography. They take drugs to service the pain and humiliation, and they bleed. Pornography has the harmful physical effects on women's health of other forms of prostitution, which include abraded vaginas and anuses, and considerable pain'.[3] However, and this is the point of this chapter, explicit performances *by* women – that is, under the control, direction and fiscal ownership of women – can be poles (or pole *dancers*?) apart from the degradation Jeffreys brings to mind. Rebecca Schneider argues the case for perspectivalism: what really matters when we watch the explicit body-as-entertainment is 'who determines the *explication* of that body, what and how it *means*'.[4] Performance art, as opposed to, say, painting or sculpture, operates outside of the orthodox frame and so demands of the viewer different ways of looking at the female body. Further, the writer, in *describing* performance art that has already taken place, weaves 'shrouds of words for bodies long gone'.[5] Performance breaks down distinctions between the chaotic raw material of 'life', and the organized realm of 'art', and the body is the nexus of this breakdown. As Jeffreys asks, is it the case that pornography may be read through the lens of *art*'s discourses if it takes place 'under the validating authorship of the art-established' individual?[6] In order to look at the body in *new* ways, however, one must first be aware of the *old* ways. For the *female* performer there is an immediate double bind: 'as "woman" she is [. . .] preceded by her own markings, standing in relation to her body in history as if beside herself'.[7] The female performance artist must grapple with 'the ghosts' of 'explication'.[8] Schneider imagines a world where Manet's Olympia 'steps out of his frame to authorize her own framing [. . .] claiming space as art *and* artist', and casts Carolee Schneemann in the role.[9]

Schneemann's detractors, one might reasonably assume, did not regard her nudity per se as an issue: 'Sexual display was not the problem. *The agency of the body displayed, the author-ity of the agent* – that was the problem with women's work'.[10] Thus Yves 'Le Monochrome' Klein's *Anthropometrie* Series of the late 1950s and early 1960s, where he dragged, rolled and pressed blue-painted women's bodies onto paper or canvas to create his work, is 'art', even *Gesamtkunstwerk* ('total' art). By contrast, a woman using *her own body* in performance is 'transgressive'. A 'woman *with* [paintbrush] was in some way [a] woman *with* phallus and thus unnatural, monstrous, threatening'.[11] Annie Sprinkle sold 'tit prints' (an appropriation, perhaps, of the *Anthropometries*) from her website for many years, since the printing 'works great when you want to send out a bunch of postcards and don't have time to write them'.[12] Works like Schneemann's *Interior Scroll*, and Shigeko Kubota's 'Vagina Painting'

(New York, 1965), are at once processes *and* ends in themselves, performances *and* constructions: the woman is both artist *and* object. She has entered into a closed, autonomous and necessarily self-referential signifying relationship, liberated from the controlling, dictatorial concerns of patriarchy. But being the 'viewing subject' *as well as* the 'viewed object' brings with it difficulties, too, if a woman artist is occupying a position where, as Lynda Nead wrote in *The Female Nude*, she is 'forming and judging her image against cultural ideals and exercising a fearsome self-regulation.'[13] That 'self-regulation' anticipates a range of self-harming activities for women, from anorexia to cutting. Performance art enables women, by unfolding identity – specifically, *sexual* identity – to delimit their own sets of 'regulations' and to reset boundaries. In describing her early artistic/sexual experiences Schneemann describes painting a nude self-portrait which was criticized for being too explicit, for 'unfolding' *too much*: 'The female was the constant preoccupation of the male imagination, but when I wanted to examine it fully myself and have actual parts depicted, I was accused of breaking essential aesthetic boundaries.'[14] The unfolding is a rejection of the polarized discourses which most commonly frame the female body in culture: the pathologized and the 'erotic'. Feminist performance art, or kinetic theatre (Schneemann's favoured term), confronts this binary, opening up – often literally – new views and horizons.[15] As it innovates, it rejects traditional modes of (patriarchal) representation in order to reimagine and *re*present female identity. A woman can be a muse, a nude, an Olympia, a 'fetishised object', but 'the vulva itself, which the fetish seeks to displace, is "obscene"', observes art historian Lisa Tickner.[16] The wonderfully confrontational performance artist Karen Finley sees her work as fundamentally democratic: 'I didn't want to channel my "art" into a painting that some rich person would buy and hang in his study and then close the door. So I made a conscious decision to do something that couldn't be bought or sold.'[17] For while the body *can* in some senses be both bought and sold – is, to use Jeffreys's term, 'industrial' – the 'live' moment of a physical performance is evanescent. It possesses a unique transience that operates quite beyond commonplace commercial exchanges, and, in terms of sexually explicit performance pieces, acknowledges that 'sexual pleasure is far too important a commodity for women not to seek their own desire and agency in it.'[18]

Since the 1960s, Schneemann has continued to produce provocatively explicit works, but not solely to shock. Rather, in her relationships with her body, with her cats and with her life-size models of dead swans (more of those shortly), she does not 'claim transgression, rather she claims quotidian norma-tivity – and that claim of quotidian becomes, ironically, her transgression'.[19] And that's one of the challenging factors of her performances: she's evidently a woman who *needs* an audience to see film or photographs of her in inti-mate moments, or for whom she can perform live, recreating such intimate moments verbally and visually. And that is not 'quotidian behaviour': to hide 'transgression' would be, for Schneemann, to hide her artist persona. From her early short film, *Fuses* (1964–67), Schneemann felt a particular kind of vulner-ability in using her body as her art, not on account of her nudity, but 'because the culture was going to trash this'.[20] The heterosexual sex acts of Schneemann and her then partner James Tenney, which were filmed for *Fuses*, were received in a variety of ways by Schneemann's audience. Importantly, the film's refusal to conform to pornographic convention led to some women using it as the starting-point for a more integrated understanding of their sexuality: 'Women would come up to me after a showing', recalls Schneemann, 'and say, "Thank you for restoring me to my whole body; I have always been in some alienation from my own genital self – thank you!"'.[21]

Schneemann somewhat self-importantly describes herself as having 'trans-formed the definition of art, especially discourse on the body, sexuality, and gender'.[22] From 1993 to 1997 she performed a show called *Ask the Goddess*, during which 'Vulva's direct interaction with the viewer creates a visual, ver-bal and experiential dialogue with the audience' and 'the Vulva speaks: If the traditions of patriarchy split the feminine into debased/glamorized, sanitized/bloody, madonna/whore . . . fractured body, how could Vulva enter the male realm except as "neutered" or neutral . . . "castrated"?'[23] Many times in her art she depicts herself as belonging 'to the realm of "cunts" – about to enter my culture in motion and speaking'.[24] In the performance of *Ask the Goddess* at the Owen Sound Festival in Ontario in 1991, Schneemann 'personifie[d] the vulvic realm'.[25] Goddess images – and images from Vietnam, maternal images, images of crucifixion and images of Schneemann's own vulva – were projected onto a screen behind her. She wore a horned headdress, sometimes howled like a wolf or wore a cat mask and made cat noises, all the while interacting with the audience. To be fair, Schneemann does describe *Ask the Goddess* as 'a very funny piece', continuing: 'I am not the Goddess; the Goddess is actually a set of double slides that are continuously projected behind me.'[26] She's a vulvar magic-8 ball; a labial Dear Abby or Marjorie Proops; she is directed by the audience and has to pose in whatever way a randomly selected card dictates, and answer audience questions. She might, for example, take a double-headed axe and hack at a piñata-like pillow hanging from a washing line until feathers cascade over the stage. Later, she covers a life-sized model of a swan with red paint, upending it so that the bird 'bleeds' all over her, paint pouring from under its tail.

As I watched the Ontario performance of *Ask the Goddess* on YouTube (it's about a 7-minute long extract edited by Schneemann herself from a 20-minute film), I know that I *should* have been engaging with grandiose thoughts about the permeability of bodies; about how audience and performer become one; about the provocative reappropriation of the Leda myth. I *should* have been in thrall to Schneemann's 'frame'-breaking and audacious transgression. So was I? Was I really contemplating how the cunt speaks – *and is heard* – in feminist performance art? Was I full of admiration for Schneemann's Lacanian enactment of the tension between *connaissance* and *savoir* (there's a big mirror on stage, too, reflecting many of Schneemann's actions)? No. No. Not at all. The performance looks like a parody of itself (and of the important work Schneemann was doing far earlier, in the 1960s); it has the air about it of an overenthusiastic but under-prepared first-year drama student's attempts at 'performing feminism', and my overriding preoccupations as I watched, were: 'Someone's going to have to clean up those tickertape feathers and that red paint that spewed out of that fake swan's arse' (as I rarely worry about cleaning *anything* up, this all came as quite a shock). Schneemann wanted a provocative show, and she got one: I'd have been provoked into asking for my money back. How does this performance advance our understanding of the female body? *How* does it suggest that, to quote Schneemann again, the personified 'vulvic realm' really has *anything* of import to say? Schneemann's scroll – as we'll see – is by, and of, her, but it emphasizes that, although the homology of lips and labia remains playful, her body is not one whole: her cunt is autonomized.

Some ten years prior to *Ask the Goddess* came *Fresh Blood – A Dream Morphology*. Again audience participation is key (might my prim Britishness be at the root of my deep disquiet with Schneemann's style?): this is a 'co-generative piece'.[27] The audience who are to 'co-generate' meaning, may wish to reflect on her own claim on her website, that she is 'regarded as one of the few who consistently create a heterosexual eroticism truly based in the feminine'.[28] As was the case with *Ask the Goddess*, so *Fresh Blood* is a multimedia performance: projected sounds and images merge with the spoken word. There are live video feeds, and 'a red umbrella, red pajamas, watering can, door, [and a] raised table'.[29] The title of the piece somewhat gives the game away: the artist had a vivid dream about menstruation and compulsively revisits and enacts the manifest content in a quest for its latent meaning. Must, for the woman performer, meaning always be as elusive and surreal as the world of dreams? '*What*', asks Schneemann, '*do a red umbrella and a bouquet of dried flowers stuffed with little dolls have in common?*'[30] Quite. A primal 'V' shape, representing 'Venus Vectors', is repeatedly reproduced in the piece in a variety of ways: scratched into a wall; made by the artist opening her legs in the air while lying on her back; and, as Schneemann is 'joined by her double – a black woman as nurse, judge, western union – they present unconscious and active links in a shared history which is personal, racial, political and sexual'.[31] What does it all *mean*? I quote Schneemann verbatim from her website:

> 'Fresh Blood – A Dream Morphology' posited female physicals [...exposing] the feminine as normative. In examining our most taboo [... viscera] I was built an ethos in which male phobias were eliding. I would invert the projects of the unsanitary leakage, abject, I could posit all the wet bloody cyclic not only in [its] physicality, but in a conceptual frame of positive range so that the phobic [... masculine] would have to shrivel and cower ... the functions of my body would not be symptomatic or all that is not male.[32]

So that's clear, then. I know that I'm coming across as snippy and sarcastic – Schneemann is, after all, a performance artist and not a writer – but if your performance needs an explicatory rationale in the first place, or even a description subsequently, such a statement needs to be clear and to the point. But these performances of the 1980s and 1990s are a disappointment because

Interior Scroll was *so* ground-breaking and important that it feels as though the artist's been attempting to recreate its potency ever since. Similarly, 1995's *Vulva's Morphia* shared with *Ask the Goddess* 'Vulvic personification', but this time presented 'a visceral sequence of photographs and text [. . .] an ironic analysis [. . .] to undermine Lacanian semiotics, gender issues, Marxism, the male art establishment, religious and cultural taboos'.[33] That's a lot of work for a lone 'vulvic personificiation'.

And so to the substance: to the brave and innovative *Interior Scroll* performance Schneemann gave just twice: in August 1975 in East Hampton, New York, and in September 1977 in Colorado at the Telluride Film Festival.[34] Here the labia are the lips, the cunt speaks, the secrets of the female genitals are – literally – unfolded before the audience's eyes. In New York, Schneemann stood naked on a table in a dimly lit corner of an exhibition hall; painted her face and body and read from her self-published book, *Cézanne: She Was a Great Painter*. She then dropped the book and, as if extracting a tampon, gently parted her labia and began to remove a long (36 × 2.25") concertinaed paper scroll from her vagina, reading from it, inch by inch. In Telluride, the paint was replaced by mud from a local mining stream, and the performance functioned in part as a protest about the session's title ('The Erotic Woman'), and as an introduction to a screening of her *Fuses* and *Plumb Line*, along with short films by other artists including Severson. 'Perhaps this "erotic woman"', said Schneemann, 'will be seen as primitive, devouring, insatiable, clinical, obscene, or forthright, courageous, integral'.[35] This is woman producing art from within; making her body voluntarily penetrable and bringing truth from deep inside herself: 'Schneemann centers the body in the truth of the spaces that are negotiated between made and imagined worlds'.[36] 'In this performance', writes Jane Blocker, an art historian, 'Schneemann unites bleeding, speaking, and writing. Her script [. . .] is birthed as the umbilicus, is uttered from silent lips'.[37]

The event was portrayed by Schneemann as powerfully mystical, constructing the vagina, as she saw it 'physically, conceptually, as a sculptural form, an architectural referent, the source of sacred knowledge, ecstasy, birth passage, transformation'.[38] In a thought-provoking nod to the *vagina dentata* motif, Schneemann characterized 'the vagina as a translucent chamber of which the serpent was an outward model: enlivened by its passage from the visible to the invisible'.[39] The potency of describing the scroll as a serpent (and, indeed, the scroll which was exhibited hanging down in a Plexiglas box, 39 × 8 × 7" after the performance, does have something of an exuvial (shed snakeskin) appearance) is evident here, and I'm very taken by the idea that the movement was from the 'visible to the invisible', as though female sexuality enters the realm of the ineffable and unseen once it is made public: real female 'visibility', as in 'connotation', lies in the *indiscernibility* of the vagina, cervix and uterus. Schneemann describes the serpentine qualities of the 'spiraled coil', the scroll, and denotes the birth canal as having 'the shape of desire and generative mysteries, attributes of both female and male sexual power. This source of interior knowledge would be symbolized as the primary index unifying spirit and flesh in Goddess worship'.[40] The 'uncoiling serpent' of scroll bore Schneemann's feminist texts and drawings, that is, 'actual information (like ticker tape, rainbow, Torah in the Ark, chalice, choir loft, plumb line, bell tower, the umbilicus, and tongue)'.[41] Scroll 1 warns the audience to 'BE PREPARED: to have your brain picked/to have the pickings misunderstood', and warns women 'NEVER [to] justify yourself just do what/you feel carry it strongly yourself'.[42] Scroll 2 again has a cautionary tone: 'PAY ATTENTION TO CRITICAL / AND PRACTICAL FILM LANGUAGE / IT EXISTS FOR AND IN ONLY / ONE GENDER', and, 'he ['a happy man / a structuralist filmmaker'] told me he had lived with / a "sculptress" I asked does / that make me a "film-makeress"? / "Oh no," he said. "We think of you / as a dancer."'[43]

We're not really so far, here, from Mangogul's magic ring; the woman's body speaks the truth, opens the closed, unfolds the hidden, speaks the unspeakable, initiates powerful visual and auditory allusions. Repeatedly, Schneemann characterizes herself as a conduit for bigger ideas about selfhood and female sexuality: 'I'm a conscious form available for use [. . .] I'm using myself in a culture that surrounds me with artifice, lies, obfuscations, grandiosity'.[44] This sense of the utility of the female body as a *self*-objectifying entity in the face of misogynist or pornographic objectification is an important one. Schneemann is driven by a compulsion to control the means of explication of the female body. 'I didn't *want* to pull a scroll out of my vagina and read it in public', she has said, 'it was because the abstraction of eroticism was pressuring me that this image occurred'.[45] For Schneemann, 'the world is a great vulva that mirrors and imprints the phallic shape, not the reverse! [. . .] This is the work, and I'm an element in it, the best available material for investigation.[46]

Around 20 years after *Interior Scroll*, Schneemann produced *Vulva's Morphia* (1992–97), after a dream (much of Schneemann's work is triggered by her vivid dreams) in which a voice told the artist to let the vulva do the talking. The work is the personified Vulva's pictorial biography: 36 hand-coloured prints set in a grid formation interspersed with lines of text protesting at the cultural denial of the cunt.[47] At school, hegemonic forces conspire to deny the validity of Vulva's own experiences: the Church, psychoanalysis, Masters and Johnson and even branches of feminist theory erode Vulva's being in the world. Her very name is changed by the vulgar discourses of slang, and she 'strips naked, fills her mouth and cunt with paint brushes, and runs into the Cedar Bar at midnight to frighten the ghosts of de Kooning, Pollock, Kline.'[48] This is the rebellious, creative autonomous cunt; the speaker of truth and authenticity; a voice struggling to be heard above the raucous clamour of male depictions of female sexual identity. In her written account of *Vulva's Morphia*, Schneemann shares the content of the lectures she gave to accompany – or, rather, to be integral to – the piece. Gendered binaries are discussed, and goddess culture is invoked. FGM is explored, and 'Vulva ruminates on "negative space": if cock is a thing and cunt is a place.'[49] Text and image and, on occasion, perform-ance, coalesce and images of toothed jaws, primitive sensual shapes and ana-tomical diagrams confront the viewer and make the usually invisible visible. In Schneemann's display, Vulva is a presence, not a lack, has agency, not merely passivity, and is autonomous, not dependent. But that autonomy is not to deny the holistic being of Schneemann: Vulva both is *and is not* the artist. As Jane Blocker writes of pain and how it can evoke something like authenticity, 'we do not merely *have* bodies; we *are* bodies.'[50]

The vulva monologues

Annie Sprinkle (the name gestures at her predilection for 'waterfalls, piss, vagi-nal fluid, sweat, cum – anything wet') was born Ellen Steinberg in Philadelphia in 1954.[51] She's a porn-actor-turned-performance artist, sexologist and activist and in many ways is the original 'cunty' voice. Her first encounter with porn was when, at 18, she sold popcorn at the Empress cinema in Tucson; the film which was showing – fittingly – was *Deep Throat*, the story of a woman with a clitoris in her throat who can, therefore, only be sexually satiated by means of fellatio. 'I had absolutely no idea that people filmed sex in graphic, juicy detail', recalls Sprinkle, in her characteristically playful way, 'I was so shocked I watched the whole movie twice. I felt like I had discovered some very valuable, yet forbidden, treasure.'[52] Her 'first performance in front of an audience' came in court, when she was subpoenaed to give evidence in the trial of the cinema where *Deep Throat* had been screened, and it was here that she met Linda Lovelace, the film's star, and the director Gerard Damiano, who became Sprinkle's lover and porn mentor.[53] Sprinkle went on to make 150 porn films and 20 videos.

Sprinkle's performance art – much analysed by critics including Terri Kapsalis and Chris Straayer – makes heard a voice which embraces a non-unified multiplicity of identities.[54] Despite pushing the boundaries of propriety perhaps more than any other performance artist (in 1989 she read verses from the Book of Genesis in an erotic voice, in front of a 'vulva-on-a-crucifix sculpture'), Sprinkle remains an approachable, amiable and pro-woman woman.[55] Further, she depicts herself less as a taboo-breaker than a taboo-revisionist: 'I felt I was fixing taboos that were not in our best interest, like using a speculum without a medical degree and looking at our beautiful genitals in bright light and in public.'[56] Perhaps her most celebrated and controversial performance art sequence – which did, indeed, take place 'in bright light and in public' – was her *Public Cervix Announcement* of the late 1980s/early 1990s. Part-evangelical and part-educational, part empowerment and part celebrating the power to shock, this exhibitionism made public the private and spoke volumes in its open contestation of the idea of the 'shameful' pudendum. Rebecca Schneider lucidly discusses Sprinkle's performance project. 'At the site of the cervix', she writes, 'the name of art would slap against the name of porn across the stage within the stage, the proscenium' of the body.[57] Sprinkle's key theoretical concern is with the woman's body as an unstable site, a Platonic cave onto the walls of which all manner of thoughts and desires are projected. She makes instability an opportunity, not a threat: she plays with personae, even in terms of effecting her transformation from Ellen Steinberg to Annie Sprinkle (and even later to the goddess 'Anya'), to the point that she refused 'to be cast by anti-porn feminists in the *unitary* role of victim'.[58] Similarly, in her 1990 series of photographs 'The 16 Sluts and Goddesses Within Linda Montano', Sprinkle urged her subject to experiment with different identities, ranging from 'Linda *Hell* – Professional Dominatrix' to '*Prissy* – Prom Queen'.[59] In 1982, Sprinkle's *Deep Inside Annie Sprinkle*, the film she scripted, acted in and produced, became a best-selling adult video.[60] It was a conceptually self-conscious film which showed how, during screenings of her earlier films, Sprinkle would break the fourth wall by going 'into a movie theater where one of my porn movies is playing and have sex with several of the porn fans who are watching me on screen'.[61] In her art through the late 1980s and into the 1990s Sprinkle was her own subject, and object; her own observer, and observed. This trend was established in 1976 when Sprinkle had her first centrespread: 'I was really shocked at how graphic it was. Hundreds of thousands of copies hit the stands – my pink, open pussy was there to see on every city street corner [. . .] I remember thinking that it was the first time *I* could really take a long look at my pussy and anus'.[62]

Ideas about the 'truth', and its attendant problems, are articulated by Sprinkle in *Herstory of Porn: Reel to Real*, a seven-part 1999 performance in which her persona is reproduced multiple times in the images of her, taken from 25 years' worth of her hardcore films, playing on a screen; and again in her live presence on stage, interacting with the films.[63] She is the woman in the film, but she also is not; she is both commentator and actor; subject and object. As Gabrielle Cody, a drama professor at Vassar College, astutely expresses it: 'the most radical element of this event is not the pornographic content of the clips Annie shows us, but rather, the boldness and vulnerability of the *speech acts* she performs alongside' those film clips.[64] *Herstory* enacts complex narrative manoeuvres which promise 'truth' and cohesion, but which instead emphasize a breach in the series of binaries around which Sprinkle's identity is predicated: lips/labia, speech/silence, the visual/the aural, the porn actor/the educator, young Ellen/mature Annie. The script for *Herstory* enacts the interplay between lips and labia: the film shows Annie inserting a toothbrush into her vagina while the live Annie on stage explains: 'That was my idea, to use the toothbrush. I brush after every meal. Look ma, a big cavity!'[65]

In the same sequence, or 'loop', Annie is shown with another female actor, Vanessa Del Rio, who is putting 'Cocksucker Cranberry' lipstick onto Annie's labia.[66] The different identities Annie plays in the film clips are echoed by those she takes on as she addresses the audience: dominatrix, Hollywood starlet, New Age goddess. In the *Deep Inside* section of *Herstory*, Annie on stage masturbates her screen self with the same vibrator, a tiny figure against the graphic backdrop of the film. 'One of her most sexually marked body parts becomes pure imago', writes Cody, 'an infinitely readable surface of continually available information and pleasure.'[67] Even when Sprinkle is onstage '*as her present self*', it is a performance, that little word '*as*' suggesting that the performativity never stops.[68] Sprinkle's art blurs the boundaries of fantasy and reality, and acknowledges the futility or, at best, the inauthenticity, of representational art. This is emphasized in the third loop of *Herstory* where, in a palimpsest of shifting subject/speaking positions, '*ANNIE slowly and sexily walks (mimicking her walk in the video) across stage to where a cardboard standee of ANNIE in a corset is set up with a black feather boa around its shoulders. ANNIE is wearing the same dress that she is seen wearing in the film. ANNIE mimics the on-screen dialog.*'[69] So, here we have Annie on screen, on stage and onstage but in cardboard cut-out. She mimics herself – but at what point does self-mimicry actually become the self? Sprinkle's work has been described by Schneider as being 'problematically emblematic of the tense stand-off between the literal, material body and her complex ghosting, the symbolic body of "woman"'.[70] Unable to settle on a coherent identity Sprinkle instead adopts the more contentious position of permitting the co-existence of apparent opposites in her work:

> It's very strange looking back at those old movies from twenty-five years ago. I had never watched them before and when I saw them I had very mixed feelings. On the one hand, they seem so silly, immature, very unerotic, and some are outright violent, and in retrospect, very misogynist. And on the other hand, some were very creative, and funny, they were baby steps and there's a wonderfully uninhibited quality about them.[71]

Like Schneemann's performances, Sprinkle's also owe a debt to goddess worship and the power of the female body. In her one-woman *Post-Porn Modernist* (later *Post-Post-Porn Modernist*), a show she performed for four years from 1990, Sprinkle summons the persona of 'the ancient sacred prostitute, a healer and teacher', in the 'Pornstistics' section of the show.[72] 'Bare-breasted, and vibrator in hand', writes Cody, 'Annie invokes the myth of the ancient temple and re-creates a masturbation ritual' which, in its authenticity and openness moves past – *post* – pornography and artificiality.[73] Indeed, Sprinkle has written of the masturbation ritual section of *Post-Porn Modernist* (the part of the show which she regards as the most important) that her goal 'was to be authentic and be in the moment, whatever it was. I could see absolutely no point in faking an orgasm, and I never did'.[74] Masturbation is central to the work of performance artist and musician Lydia Lunch, too. In a conversation with Andrea Juno, Lunch (not unlike *SATC*'s Samantha) light-heartedly urged women to get familiar with their genitals 'it's not like they don't have mirrors in the house, honey. They're all *over* the place. Get down there and start doing a little investigative research – unlock those mysteries'.[75] Linda Williams emphasizes how, in Sprinkle's work, specifically in *Post-Post Porn Modernist*, the orgasm is empowering because it is 'a solo and the point is the self-sufficiency of the female body'.[76] Sprinkle's cunt works *for* her and – even more importantly in this field of incorporation and corporeal integrity – *as* her.

The political tenor of *Post-Porn Modernist* was explicitly stated in the 'Post Porn Modernist Manifesto' by Veronica Vera. Here, the 18 or so signatories advocated 'sex-positivism', and declared that they embraced their 'genitals as part, not separate, from [their] spirits'.[77] The *Public Cervix Announcement* segment of *Post-Porn Modernist* is firmly situated in a tradition of cunt performance art which had as its harbingers both Yoko Ono's 1964 'Cut Piece' and Kubota's 'Vagina Painting'. Sprinkle began her *Public Cervix Announcement* by giving herself an onstage douche while making small talk with the audience. 'So what should I see in [this town]?' she would ask, 'I hear there's a nice botanical garden.'[78] She would then present an anatomical chart before parting her labia, and opening her vulva with a metal speculum.

Audience members were invited to take turns to shine a torch to see Sprinkle's cervix (about 40 can do so during a performance), being invited to comment into a microphone at the same time. Sprinkle estimates that around 25,000 people participated in the years she performed the *Public Cervix*

Figure 7.1 *Annie Sprinkle,* Public Cervix Announcement. By kind permission of Annie Sprinkle

Announcement (Figure 7.1).[79] 'A line quickly forms', writes Sprinkle, 'like worshippers at communion or kids waiting to see Santa.'[80] She continues:

> There are those who say my purpose is to 'demystify the female body', but that is an impossibility. The female body will always be a very great mystery, no matter how many you see or how much knowledge you achieve. You can never demystify a cervix. It's a magnificent miracle – the doorway to life itself. One reason why I show my cervix is to assure the misinformed, who seem to be primarily of the male population, that neither the vagina nor the cervix contains any teeth. Maybe you'll calm down and get a grip. Lots of folks, both women and men, know very little about female anatomy and so are ashamed and/or afraid of the cervix. That's sad, so I do my best to lift that veil of ignorance.[81]

Sprinkle's teasing here around the idea of the *vagina dentata* belies a more serious agenda: in allowing her *silent* cervix to do the talking for her she is articulating an identity for herself which is at once consistent *and* non-unitary. She is, additionally, playing with the idea of autonomization: the cervix may not have teeth, but it does seem to return the viewer's gaze, unblinkingly, like a 'theoretical third eye' of the sort Bataille imagined: 'in *Simone's* hairy vagina, I saw the wan blue eye of *Marcelle*', writes the narrator of *Story of the Eye*.[82] The honesty and integrity – both bodily and spiritual – of Sprinkle's performances were, perhaps predictably, reviled by some reviewers: 'Watching a fat, Jewish, middle-aged New Yorker masturbate on stage is not art' said one particularly contemptible critic, 'Hitler, where are you now that we need you?'[83] Such abhorrent critiques, which so utterly and wilfully miss the point of Sprinkle's work, scarcely warrant further comment.

The premiere of *MetamorphoSex* in 1995 (the year *before* Ensler's first draft of *The Vagina Monologues*) saw Sprinkle, Linda Montano, Barbara Carrellas and more than 20 volunteer women perform 8 ritualistic acts.[84] Montano had, in the early 1980s, immersed herself in an exploration of such 'Living Art' by spending an entire year tied by an 8' rope to, but never touching, the male artist, Tehching Hsieh.[85] Act 2 of *MetamorphoSex* was called 'Voices from the Vulva', where 'Cast members get into a V-shaped line and chant' while 'each woman individually takes the "talking pussy puppet", steps up to a microphone, and says something from her vulva – as if her vulva is speaking'.[86] It was performed as a series of stream-of-consciousness narratives spoken by each woman's 'vulva' and the aim was – as is the case with so much of Sprinkle's work – authenticity: 'whatever comes to mind, we speak it. This way the audience gets to know us all a bit as individuals'.[87] The climax of the performance was an enabling space for the volunteer performers who, through the last 6 'Acts', were directed and encouraged to 'build erotic energy [. . . to] an energetic climax [. . . and to surrender] to whatever feelings are there, or not there. There is no talking'.[88] The embodied spiritual aspects of the collaborative, amateur performance mean that language is renounced; the body-as-signified exists free of it.[89] In the penultimate 'Act', the Quaker-like (Sprinkle's own simile) invitation to participants who wish to speak to do so, emphasizes the spiritual qualities of the show and, again, it is the vulva which speaks.

Schneider draws an explicit parallel between Courbet's *L'Origine* and Sprinkle's *Public Cervix Announcement*. I remain unconvinced by this, for it is clear to me that Sprinkle, as a woman opening her own vulva and putting her own cervix on view is radically reconfiguring centuries' worth of preconceptions about the objectifying gaze of heterosexual men (men like Courbet).

Sprinkle is securing an authoritative position for herself.[90] Her cunt vociferously – *autonomously?* – offers a retort to Gilligan's formulation (which I established in discussing *Chatterbox*) of silence as subjugation. *Public Cervix* subverts the pornographic gaze by forcing the compliance of the relationship onto the observer, and away from Annie, who takes control, and directs the gaze: she establishes an *anti*-pornographic rapport with the viewer.[91] Sprinkle, despite some theorists' claims that she is complicit in misogyny 'if she doesn't act *against* the system that constructs women as whores and objects of pornography', *knowingly* allows her cunt silently to dictate a strident agenda of female sexual identity and empowerment.[92] In this way, Sprinkle successfully unites *Chatterbox*'s Penelope and Virginia in a literally spectacular rejoinder to Friedan's question of 'Is this all?' The vulva, vagina and cervix shout that 'no: there is so much more', the labia speak a language – of possibility, performativity, identity and desire – it is a language which other lips do not speak. As Sprinkle's friend and porn colleague Veronica Vera has said, capturing precisely the ideas of authenticity, and its complicated cousin, intention, which structure much of the analysis in this book: 'The world is always ready to make its own interpretations and simplifications, we need to stay vigilant that what we mean is clear, especially to ourselves.'[93]

Talkin' 'bout my (organs of) generation

When Eve Ensler first published *The Vagina Monologues* in 1998, she asked the maven of second-wave feminism, Gloria Steinem, to write the Foreword. Steinem does a good job of exploring the idea of the vagina as a sacred space, featuring in global religions. She alludes to the Hindu Yoni and its male equivalent, the Lingam; she discusses the crucial ritual role of the vulva in Tantric Buddhism; and mentions Kali, too. She argues that the traditional heart shape is a 'residual female genital symbol', and sees classical church architecture as representative of the female genitalia, where there is 'a central vaginal aisle toward the altar [. . .] in the sacred center, the altar or womb, where the miracle takes place – where males give birth'.[94] Ensler's primary aim was, like Schneemann's, to produce a performance which makes the unseen-c-word *seen*. *The Vagina Monologues*, an edited collection of first-person narratives and testimonials, is interspersed with 'Vagina Facts', one of which persuasively points to this idea of the speaking body and how it is demonized. In the late sixteenth-century, the readers are told, a witch trial called the clitoris the third teat – the one which was believed to be (or, rather, was *constructed* as being) the devil's teat, since it was found 'adjoining to so secret a place which was not decent to be seen'.[95] In a later work, her *Vagina Warriors*, Ensler claims that her eponymous Warriors 'work to make the invisible seen'.[96] This ocular motif is a theme which runs throughout *The Vagina*, from Buñuel's grotesque envisioning of the eye to Bataille's surreal invaginating of it; to Schneemann's, and Sprinkle's opening of the vagina to the gaze, and to the little-recorded and, therefore, *confrontational* images of crowning which so many birth artists reproduce. Reading *Vagina Warriors* does leave one with the feeling that there's darkness to be conquered, not light to be shone (literally, if Betty Dodson or Annie Sprinkle are our guides) – but more of that shortly. In *The Monologues*, too, stories of abjection and fear are associated with the 'vagina' (and there's much more to be said in a moment about Ensler's terminology). While menstruation, orgasm and birth are featured as what the 'vagina' does, narratives of rape and genital mutilation are also presented. 'Connecting with the vagina is fundamental', Ensler has said, 'I think that by focusing on a piece that has been cut off we can end the fragmentation, we reabsorb it [. . .] into the entire body.'[97] Women's experiences in the *Monologues* are articulated by their vaginas, not in the sense of ventriloquism, or of Schneemann's unfolding scroll, but in the form of a series of secular confessionals. Indeed, it is through the vagina – '*My vagina, my vagina, me*' – that Ensler sees a quasi-religious transformation being effected for and by women, with Ensler herself as their evangelist leader.[98] *Is* 'my vagina me'? Is this a statement of intent to unite Penelope and Virginia (in *Chatterbox*)? To bring together the voice of the Cunt and the silent Woman of Coover's *Theological Position*? Is Ensler going to yoke Courbet's *L'Origine* to his *Clairvoyante*? Can we *all* speak with our lips if we speak about our *lips*? Can we offer praise to the Goddess? Hallelujah!

No.

Not really.

For all her attempts to construct a unitary selfhood for women, Ensler recounts stories of women for whom there is little experience of a peaceful intimacy of lips and labia. Even in her work, the vagina is a dark, unknown place, a focus for misogynist fears, violence and rage. Ensler's vaginas are far from happy. Although we're told that we're going to learn 'how I came to love my vagina', a Bosnian woman constructs her body topologically in her rape account: 'my vagina was my village'.[99] FGM is another aspect of the vagina recounted by Ensler but – and here's the sticking point – it's *not* usually the *vagina* that is directly mutilated as labia are excised and clitoridectomies are performed. The very name of Ensler's performance is a misnomer. This is not just to split hairs. It's an important point. If we're aiming at a union, truthfulness, openness of expression and of selfhood, then *The Vagina Monologues* as a title will not work. In short, if Ensler's performance is aimed at a joyous moment of collective female genital restitution, then these stories should called *The Cunt Monologues*. But that would not sell; theatre producers and advertisers would be scared off; and Ensler would not have gained the colossal mainstream respect and acclaim she has today (I'm not suggesting pure self-interest here: the success of *The Vagina Monologues* has enabled Ensler to raise a lot of money for caring for victims of FGM in the developing world).

In an HBO documentary filmed at New York's Theatre Workshop, which first aired on Valentine's Day 2002, Ensler performed the show solo. This was a mistake. She came across as smug and was a weak performer. If the *Monologues* are to embrace a diversity of women's experiences, then each must be performed by a different voice. The recording makes for uncomfortable viewing – for the studio audience too, it appears. They're unsure whether to laugh, and the result is that 'serious' accounts, such as those about rape, are not strongly enough differentiated from more flippant ones. This is the autonomized cunt which does *not* get to speak. At times in the performance it's unclear whether it's Ensler's subjectivity we're witnessing, or that of one of the hundreds of women she interviewed in compiling the show ('You cannot love a vagina unless you love hair', she intones at one point. Really? Says who? I mean, literally – whose voice *is* this we're hearing?).[100] 'I was really sucked down this vagina trail', says Ensler, apparently oblivious to how very odd an image that is (it precedes Nicholson Baker's novel *House of Holes* by a decade, of course, but it still suggests to me the kind of fanciful vaginal theme park he created there). Ensler spends quite a lot of her stage time demeaning and patronizing her (male) stage-hands, and the entire venture is something of an embarrassment. She grimaces and gurns her way through the 'Reclaiming Cunt' section and, despite her claim that the performance is unedited, in the 'Coochie Snorcher' story about the seduction of a 13-year-old girl by a far older woman, the child's age has been changed to 16, presumably at HBO's instigation. While the consciousness-raising she's doing (e.g. sharing horrific US rape stats) is commendable, the performance is not. It's a ragbag of uncomfortable (and not in the 'positive' sense of 'we need to talk about "uncomfortable" issues') juxtapositions and uneasy concessions to essentialism: *why* is the 'my vagina's pissed off' woman not an '*I'm* pissed off' woman? As Christine M. Cooper states, Ensler's women 'are replaced by, or subsumed within, their fully emotive body parts [. . .] vaginas serve as the crux of women's lives, their purpose or motivation [. . .], their now as well as their future [. . .] I cannot see a celebratory liberation of vaginas – the word or the women for whom they stand – without reservations'.[101] The birth segment of Ensler's performance is very moving and beautiful but watching her fake orgasms for the 'moaning' segment is unbearably embarrassing (not a patch on Meg Ryan), and it made me appreciate where – if you'll forgive the unintended pun – Ensler's vociferous detractors such as Betty Dodson are coming from.

Annie Sprinkle has spoken of how she 'was a bit irritated by the anatomically incorrect' name of *The Vagina Monologues*. But she admits to admiring what Ensler accomplished.[102] Further:

I know how Betty [Dodson] felt about the show. I think many of us were a bit jealous of Eve's success, and many of us felt we had done a lot of work before her on the same topics. But Eve managed to make it mainstream and make a ton of money doing it. I was impressed by the money she made and the money she raised for women's causes. That was a very good thing. And [I] think it was great that she gave it all away free to colleges to perform. That was smart and generous. Betty didn't like it that Eve talked about pleasure and also about rape in the same show. That never bothered me. But of course, I had done my show *Post Porn Modernist*, where I did my *Public Cervix Announcement* and sex magic masturbation ritual years before Eve. So I felt like the pioneer, as Betty did too, and Eve was in some ways the settler. But in some ways she was also the pioneer – getting into more mainstream and big time theaters.[103]

This notion of the *mainstream* cunt is an interesting one. The *Monologues* provided a space where 'respectable' women could yell 'cunt!' in theatres in what Schneemann would call a 'co-generative' moment; and a call did go out in February 2012 for 'Vaginas [to] occupy Wall Street' (replete with a picture of two red hands with thumbs and index fingers pressed together and splayed into a kite shape – the American Sign Language sign for 'vagina'); and Oprah, Jane Fonda, Glenn Close, Erica Jong and many other high-profile women did perform the work in 2001 in Madison Square Garden, but there are *still* 3 million girls having their genitals butchered in Africa every year.[104] Ensler isn't reclaiming 'cunt'; she's participating in keeping it compliant, not in keeping it real, and while thousands of educated theatregoers flock to see Z-list soap stars performing the *Monologues* in theatres all over the western world and feel themselves emancipated by shouting 'Cunt!' in unison, how much do they actually then change? How many of them even whisper the word once they've left the theatre? Žižek maintains that *The Vagina Monologues* is flawed because 'it is *the* Woman who speaks through her vagina, not *vagina-truth itself that speaks*'.[105]

Dodson, certainly an advocate of Žižek's search for '*truth*', and Sprinkle's 'number-one role model in life', led the initial counterblast to Ensler's project.[106] She, too, felt that not only was the terminology wrong but went further, arguing that it was potentially dangerously misleading. She wanted, she wrote, for Ensler's performance piece to be called *The Clit Conversations*, and for women to embrace their own sexuality in a positive way rather than to focus on its negative aspects.[107] Women, according to Dodson, should worry about their own sexual gratification and the increasingly right-wing political climate in the United States and the United Kingdom, and not overlook this by *only* looking to, for example, Bosnia. 'Standing on stage and screaming CUNT', Dodson writes, 'offers no practical healing', and it's such practical healing that she worked for nearly 40 years to offer women, as the 'mother of masturbation'.[108] Ensler's insistence on the word 'vagina' in her title, argues Dodson, vindicates Freud's ideas about 'mature' and 'immature' orgasm in its exclusion of the clitoris which, as Natalie Angier reminds us, is 'a bundle of nerves: 8,000 nerve fibers, to be precise. That's a higher concentration [. . .] than is found anywhere else on the body [. . .] and it is twice the number in the penis'.[109] I'm aware, of course, that I'm critiquing the title of Ensler's work in a book called *The Vagina*. The irony is by no means lost on me. My book was, for a long time, going to be called *Can't*, suggesting in that word the insufficiencies, the 'cannot', of language and making the *Cunt* covertly visible. The pronunciation of *Can't* in most British English accents comes very close to *Cunt*. In many *American* English accents, however, as an American friend pointed out to me, there is little similarity in the sound of 'can't' and 'cunt'. And so that title was ruled out (the wonderful Inga Muscio had already published a book called *Cunt*, so even *had* any publishers been willing to take on my book with that title, it would not have been original). I toyed briefly with *Vulvanomics* (the *Freakonomics* authors sold 4 million copies!); had an email exchange with Betty Dodson about using her art in a book called *The Vagina* (I allayed some of her anxieties by explaining that my Introduction actually deconstructs the whole idea of genital language); and realized, finally, the power of the straightforward title in an age of search engines. So, *The Vagina* it is. But I digress. Camille Paglia's anxieties in 2001 about 'the garish visibility of Eve Ensler' in her piece for Salon.com is also, like Dodson's, a thoughtful – albeit harsher – repudiation of Ensler's venture.[110] Paglia argued that *The Vagina Monologues* and V-Day in particular ('a grisly memento mori of violence against women'), were bad news for feminism, and she worried about the 'positively criminal' spreading of 'the psychological poison of Ensler's archaic creed of victimization [. . .] to impressionable women students'.[111]

In a talk she gave in the summer of 2004, the conservative philosopher Christina Hoff Sommers really tore into *The Vagina Monologues* (but was sufficiently generous to give credit to Ensler's global humanitarian work in passing). 'The woman who "discovers" that her clitoris is her "essence" and says, "My vagina, me," is insulting herself and all women', argued Sommers, continuing:

> One of the many laudable goals of the original women's movement was its *rejection* of the idea that women are reducible to their anatomy. Our bodies are not our selves. Feminist pioneers like Susan B. Anthony and Sojourner

Truth fought long and hard so women would be respected – not for their sexual anatomy – but for their minds. The struggle for women's rights was a battle for political and educational equality. Feminist foremothers like Mary Wollstonecraft or Elizabeth Cady Stanton demanded that women have the opportunities to develop their intellects and to make full use of their cognitive powers.[112]

Of course, on one level Sommers is right (although it pains me to agree with her), but on another level she's very, very wrong. Ensler never claimed to be doing *everything* to end the abuse of women and girls everywhere. But she probably did make some women more comfortable with the 'v-word' and maybe with the 'c-word', too. Dodson's objections are far more compelling. Women can be political but anorgasmic. In Dodson's ideology, *nosce te ipsum* ('know thyself') precedes – and does anything *but* annul – the 'political and educational equality' of which Sommers writes. If our labia are unknown to us then how can our lips speak out about political issues? Performances such as those by Schneemann, Sprinkle and even Ensler require us to reassess our understanding of how explicit representation functions when it's for, and by, women.

The power of pussy

The performance artist Kembra Pfhaler (b. 1961), who, in the early 1990s, had her labia (temporarily) surgically sewn together in Richard Kern's short film *Sewing Circle*, also choreographed and performed a piece in 2011 which she called *The Great Wall of Vagina* (there's no evidence that she was aware of British artist Jamie McCartney's work of the same name). In this, five naked 'Girls of Karen Black', covered in bright body-paint, lay one on top of the other, legs spread and stacked vulvas directed at the audience. A sixth member of the group then squirted a turkey-baster full of white cream from the top vulva so that it trickled downwards, eventually dripping off all five. In an interview, Pfhaler claimed that her group is 'making fun of female sexuality', compelling the reporter to declare that Pfhaler's 'well-orchestrated rejections [of] standards of feminine beauty and seductiveness resonate even during quiet moments of the act as the women stood still, horrifying, wide-eyed and robotic, conjuring semblance to an army of demonic inflatable sex dolls'.[113] Pfhaler was co-curator with Julie Atlas Muz of the 2007 *Womanizer* exhibition at the unconventional Deitch Projects Gallery in New York City. As Andrew C. Robinson wrote in *Gay City* News, 'the outsider, the queer, the goth rock priestess, the pandrogyne, the side show freak, the trannie, and the power of pussy are on parade in the current exhibition'.[114]

One of the exponents of 'pussy power' was Muz, who was best known at the time for her alter ego, Mr Pussy. In the fine tradition of the all-male Australian group 'Puppetry of the Penis' who had had worldwide success in the late 1990s and early 2000s with their 'genital origami', Muz dressed up her labia and vulva in various costumes to create the various guises of Mr Pussy in a series of photographs.[115] In doing so, she styled her pubic hair into moustaches and beards; would insert items such as cigars into her vulva, and balance jolly hats or spectacles on her pubic bone and lower abdomen. Mr Pussy, a complex, radical version of the ventriloquist's dummy, would 'speak' as Muz manipulated her own labia and vulva to mimic a mouth moving. What's really interesting here – bizarre images aside – is that Muz purposefully enacts a separation of herself from her cunt when the performance is underway: 'I don't know that much about him', she has said of Mr Pussy, 'I don't understand him – he's come out of me. As an exhibitionist, I don't have any shame. That's a positive thing'.[116] Despite the odd decision to personify her genitals as male, Muz is making important visual statements about female sexuality and identity. The performance relies on Muz having pubic hair. And not just the 'airstrip' pubic hair, or even utterly absent hair, of pornography, but full, natural hair sufficient in quantity to be Freud's moustache and beard (his 'mouth' in between the two, of course); dreadlocks are a tall order, and so when Mr Pussy is in Rastafarian mood, he dons a wig, complete with woollen tam (hat); he wears a turban in another guise (and carries a tiny bottle of tequila when he's a cowboy). In an alternate identity, the 'anatomically perverse "Mr. Pussy," [. . .] eschewed *vagina dentata* in favor of the relatively ineffectual *vagina mustachio* (Muz styles her "down there" as a crooning mariachi)'.[117] It puts a whole new spin on the mariachi classic, 'Soy un hombre muy honrado'.[118]

Although Mr Pussy 'comes out' of the artist, he is ultimately – essentially – under her control. He's only partially autonomized or – if we refuse to suspend our disbelief – is utterly without autonomy; he's an extension of Muz. In May 2005 Muz had written – as Mr Pussy – to *Village Voice*. 'I don't like that bitch Julie Atlas Muz', wrote Mr Pussy: 'She is a whore, and I do not want to be associated with her in any way. I am my own person, a simple Cuban-Chinese-immigrant faggot who just wants to have my own children's network television show. I love children; they are our future.'[119] This is an unconventional but ultimately affirmative performance because the cunt is not covert: the vulva is open and touched and healthy and glistening (Muz has said that she uses *lip*-gloss to achieve this last effect). It's a witty, clever act: the cunt is being made explicit but *erotic* associations are secondary to the primary performance (if, indeed, they're there at all). Complex issues of gender performativity come into play when one sees this as a drag act. Are we watching Muz's genitals in drag, pretending to be a ('faggot') male character? Is the cunt – that most identifiably 'female' marker of identity – here having a crisis of identity? Judith Butler usefully problematizes the complexities of drag: 'There is no original or primary gender that drag imitates, but *gender is a kind of imitation for which there is no original*; in fact, it is a kind of imitation that produces the very notion of the original as an *effect* and consequence of the imitation itself.'[120] Muz's performance is delectably complicated by this idea of the body's 'essence': Mr Pussy is *and is not* Muz's genitals. In an interview, Muz has said of Mr Pussy: 'He does not approve of me running around naked. So I support him, but he's a little more touch and go with me.'[121] In Butler's formulation, it is not a case of a 'she' performing a 'he', but of a 'she' performing a 'she', performing a 'he'. The talking cunt both is *and is not* autonomous.

Changing the subject

'Does a transsexual *change subjects*? Or just bodies – or body parts?'[122] This provocative question was posed by Marjorie Garber in her essay, 'Spare Parts: The Surgical Construction of Gender'. Garber tries to trace what happens to the 'I' after someone who has undergone MTF (male to female, although some dispute the binary which is implicit in this terminology) SRS (sex reassignment surgery) sees her new vagina for the first time: 'I saw [. . .] a normal looking introitus [vulva] but incredibly distinctive because it was mine.'[123] 'The "I" of this statement' argues Garber, 'is, at least in part, [the man], however much the "mine" belongs to [the woman]'.[124] Medical discourses themselves, in their construction of the gendered 'insignia' of FTM and MTF SRS (the non-penetrable vagina, the non-menstruating body, a high or low voice, an absence of penis and so on), blur 'categories and boundaries', since so many of these insignia – length of hair, for example – are *social* constructs.[125] How do MTF and FTM transsexuals enter this space of (vulvar) performance art? Do their lips 'speak' the same language as those of 'cisgendered' women (i.e. those women who are comfortable with their natally assigned gender identities)?[126] Something I've shown in the course of *The Vagina* is that ciswomen experience a disaggregation of self. Is that experience even more distinct in the lives of transpeople? Along with Betty Dodson and others, I find *The Vagina Monologues* problematic for a number of reasons, among them the absence of the trans voice. Ensler worked to remedy this with a group of transsexual women who performed *The Vagina Monologues* in February 2004. A film, *Beautiful Daughters*, directed and produced by Josh Aronson and Ariel Orr Jordan, recorded the event and had its premiere early in 2006, including Ensler's new monologue. In subsequent productions, however, this monologue is presented as something of an 'optional extra' for the actors wishing to perform the show, and, in 2003, men were encouraged to compose ensemble pieces to participate in V-Day activism and activities. As Christine M. Cooper expresses it, Ensler's '"community of vaginas" has its limits, and it encompasses heterosexual male experience more easily than the experience of menopausal or transgendered women or the intersexed'.[127] This marginalization is ironic in a play that – ostensibly – aims to dismantle ostracism and otherness. In this aim it falls short, and so other, non-Ensler-authored versions of the confessional dramatic model have started to emerge.

The visual artist Simon Croft's poster for the show of the British *(Trans)Mangina Monologues, a Celebration of Trans Male Sexuality* is startling because of the immediate connotative interpretations that spring to mind (see Figure 7.2). For what we appear to be looking at is a perfectly symmetrical vulva, with labia on each side; trimmed pubic hair; and a pronounced clitoral hood at the top. Turn the picture through 90 degrees, however, and what you see is a picture of a man's top lip, surrounded by a moustache and beard, with his tongue peeping cheekily out to one side, and reflected in mirror-image to create the (w)hole. The visual pieces fall into place: here's his nose, for example, previously unnoticed in the shock of the optical illusion in the vertical plane. It's a wonderfully effective, provocative image. It challenges what we see, what we *think* we see, and what we think it's appropriate, or 'decent', for us to see. 'Facial hair is a really important male signifier for many transmen', writes Croft, 'so I felt that aspect was key; plus body hair generally is a very gendered thing and the pressures on what is expected regarding pubic hair in particular have become quite intense, so those twin aspects played on the visible/invisible. The mouth is about speech, and the closed mouth is about the idea that there isn't a word for it (yet)'.[128] Dramatist Laura Bridgeman recalls that 'the image was in a vertical position because of the position of the text and people would recoil; we had complaints. It's a really powerful image and we just countered any complaints with the answer it's just two mustachioed lips. It's tongue in cheek and it's really clever. Maybe too clever for some people'.[129] The (*Trans)Mangina Monologues*, trans-masculine stories and memoirs, were compiled, edited and written by Bridgeman and Serge Nicholson, and directed by Lois Weaver. Two performances took place in the summer of 2009, and were the result of a collaboration between *Transfabulous* (a London-based transgender arts festival which took place annually from 2005–08), and *Girlboy* (Bridgeman's project), presenting 'a cast of trans guys' in order to showcase 'a contemporary slice of the trans male experience [. . . which] actively challenges prejudice and discrimination'.[130] Bridgeman says that she and Nicholson 'always had this idea that we would go around the country and collect new stories all the time and invite guys from those regions to join us on stage, if they wanted to contribute. [. . .] We had the idea to do a sort of roadshow'.[131]

In 2011, Bridgeman and Nicholson published their book, *There Is No Word For It*, based on their *Monologues*.[132] One speaker recalls mixing with 'artistic trans men' and feeling 'jealous. Left behind. To be defined trans was to be respected. They seemed to occupy a radical space far away from my own experience'.[133] Another has a more detached tone: 'I wasn't in crisis. I wasn't depressed [. . .] I'm objective; I can observe myself'.[134] The authors' aim was not only to explore 'love, sexuality, daily life and finding a new language. The desire was to *discover words for the unmentionable* and unlock stories that had never been told'.[135] The notion of the inadequacy of language has been so dominant in my own work that this struck a chord with me. Ciswomen experience misogyny because they are 'women'. If a trans-person rejects gendered binaries, or inscribes alternatives in his or her flesh, how much *more* elusive must 'the word for it' be? If to have a vagina is to have (in Freudian terms) a 'lack', then does having a penis constructed in the place of the vagina double that 'lack'? Can I 'lose' my 'lack'? Is the 'lack' eradicated through the substitution of a surgically constructed penis? Or what if surgery is not the route chosen by the individual, but hormone therapy is used on its own? Does *he* still have *her* vagina? 'There is no word for it [. . .] It's just anatomy', says another *(Trans)Mangina* speaker, with dry wit and understatement: 'Mangina is a nice one. No word for it. I haven't found the word'.[136] Another also struggles with language, and then rejoices in it: 'The male nurse calls the inside of me, my vault. I like the idea of a vault because it reminds me of a treasure chest. Like I have treasure to find'.[137] To return to Garber: *has* the individual 'changed subjects'? Is the cunt even more alien to her than it has been to the numerous disaggregated ciswomen we've met in this book, because its presence no longer accords with the trans-body? It's an astonishingly troubled and troubling linguistic, cultural and socio-political problem, and, in a sense, warrants a book all of its own.

Another of the many writers and thinkers who engage with the complexities of the transgendered experience is the American-born activist Riki Wilchins.[138] In the spring of 2010, Wilchins performed in her *MANgina Monologues*, a stand-up show which is, in Wilchins's own words, 'Transgender 101. It tracks the arc of a transition'. In an interview Wilchins said that: 'I realize I can't do regular stand-up: *bump-bump-joke, bump-bump-joke*, about my mother-in-law and how women shop. I'm up there because I am passionate about transgender politics and transgender experience and transgender oppression. That's why I want to be up there. It's a way to educate people about how gender-queer folks get hurt'.[139] In her routine, Wilchins argues that: 'Transgender is supposed to be "in" now.

We're supposed to be the new "gay" [. . .] I gotta tell you: it's really tough changing sexes [. . .] I'm not trapped in anyone's body.'[140] She argues that gender reassignment surgery should be treated in the same way as other procedures: 'consider America's favourite surgery: the ever-popular rhinoplasty, or nose job. I think that little dialogue with your surgeon would go something like this: [. . .] "You should live as a small-nosed woman for two years. Just to make sure". She talks, too, about how difficult the transition period is in everyday terms (queuing for the bathroom, travelling and airport security, etc.), that is, how best to perform the 'insignia' of which I wrote earlier. And film representations of the transgendered body are also the object of her critique: 'For years now they've been building up trannies as killer evil villains.' Wilchins playfully investigates other, essentialist insignia, too, saying sardonically at one point during her routine: 'Now that I'm growing older, I'm actually having the pleasures of going through menopause.'

Owning up

Artists who display their own bodies in explicit ways are endeavouring to make their lips heard above the raucous din of misogyny or transphobia. Those who make the unseen seen, and who, in doing so, defy the prevalent cultural dread of the covert, threaten to extinguish conventional definitions of decorum. They own, and own up to, their identities, in this perilous world where guilt and shame and fear would have them suppressed. The anthropologist David Valentine, writing with Riki Wilchins, 'noted that although the genital area accounts for only 1 per cent of the body's surface area, genitals "carry an enormous amount of cultural weight in the meanings that are attached to them"'.[141] In his work, Croft engages with the significance of speaking and unspoken 'lips'. 'Everyone makes assumptions and quite often they aren't correct', he writes: 'Most people simply don't know what transmen might or might not have physically, or what we might or might not want to do with it. There's a whole range of transmale physicalities, sexualities, etc. and you can't assume anything about any particular individual. If you're going to get intimate with a transman, you have to talk about it (politely) – and that closes the loop back to speech.'[142] So we need to resist silence. We need to talk, and listen, and engage with artists like Schneeman, Sprinkle, Pfhaler and Muz. It's why they do what they do; and it's also what Ensler, perhaps despite herself, has inspired.

Notes

1   Rebecca Schneider, *The Explicit Body in Performance* (London: Routledge, 1997), p. 2.

2   J. C. Smith, and Carla J. Ferstman, *The Castration of Oedipus: Feminism, Psychoanalysis, and the Will to Power* (New York, NY: New York University, 1996), p. 235.

3   Sheila Jeffreys, *The Industrial Vagina: The Political Economy of the Global Sex Trade* (Abingdon: Routledge, 2009), p. 76.

4   Schneider, *The Explicit Body*, p. 3.

5   Jane Blocker, *What the Body Cost: Desire, History, and Performance* (Minneapolis, MN: University of Minnesota Press, 2004), p. xi.

6   Schneider, *The Explicit Body*, p. 16.

7   Ibid., p. 23.

8   Ibid., p. 52.

9   Ibid., p. 29; Schneemann defines herself thus on her official website. See www.caroleeschneemann.com/bio.html. For Schneemann posed as Olympia, see Robert Morris's installation piece, *Site* (1963), as reproduced in Carolee Schneemann (ed.), *Imaging Her Erotics: Essays, Interviews, Projects* (Cambridge, MA: The MIT Press, 2002), p. 122.

10 Ibid., p. 35.

11 Ibid., p. 38.

12 Annie Sprinkle, *Post-Porn Modernist: My 25 Years as a Multimedia Whore* (San Francisco, CA: Cleis Press, 1998), p. 100.

13 Lynda Nead, *The Female Nude: Art, Obscenity and Sexuality* (London: Routledge, 1994), p. 10.

14 Carolee Schneemann, 'Interview with Linda Montano', in Schneemann (ed.), *Imaging Her Erotics*, pp. 131–4 (p. 133).

15 On the coinage of the expression 'kinetic theatre', see Carolee Schneemann, 'Interview with ND', in Schneemann (ed.), *Imaging Her Erotics*, pp. 113–26 (p. 125).

16 Lisa Tickner, 'The Body Politic: Female Sexuality and Women Artists Since 1970', *Art History* 1.2 (June 1978), pp. 236–49 (p. 242).

17 Karen Finley, interview with Andrea Juno, in Andrea Juno and V. Vale (eds), *Angry Women* (San Francisco, CA: Re/search Publications, 1991), pp. 41–9 (p. 42).

18 Linda Williams, 'A Provoking Agent: The Pornography and Performance Art of Annie Sprinkle', *Social Text*, 37 (Winter 1993), pp. 117–33 (p. 130). Amelia Jones has argued that there's no such thing as an unmediated viewing of a performance, since 'we only apprehend live bodies through our own perceptual apparatuses, already filtering experience through memory'. See Amelia Jones, 'Lost Bodies: Early 1970s Los Angeles Performance Art in Art History', in Peggy Phelan (ed.), *Live Art in LA: Performance in Southern California, 1970–1983* (Abingdon: Routledge, 2012), pp. 115–84 (p. 117).

19	Schneider, *The Explicit Body*, p. 49.

20	Carolee Schneemann, 'Interview with Kate Haug', in Schneemann (ed.), *Imaging Her Erotics*, pp. 21–44 (p. 29). *Fuses* was banned in Russia once censors saw its content, having first invited Schneemann to the 1989 Moscow Film Festival. On Schneemann as a 'pornographer and dangerous woman', see Schneemann, 'Notes from the Underground: a Feminist Pornographer in Moscow', in Schneemann (ed.), *Imaging Her Erotics*, pp. 217–23 (p. 223).

21	Carolee Schneemann, interview with Andrea Juno, in Juno and Vale (eds), *Angry Women*, pp. 66–77 (p. 71).

22	www.caroleeschneemann.com/bio.html.

23	www.caroleeschneemann.com/works.html.

24	Carolee Schneemann, '"Maximus at Gloucester": A Visit to Charles Olson', in Schneemann (ed.), *Imaging Her Erotics*, pp. 52–3 (p. 53).

25	www.caroleeschneemann.com/works.html.

26	Carolee Schneemann, 'Interview with Carl Heyward', in Schneemann (ed.), *Imaging Her Erotics*, pp. 196–207 (p. 205).

27	Carolee Schneemann, *Fresh Blood – A Dream Morphology*, 1981–87. Performance: two slide carousels/zoom lens, dissolve unit (projection area 8 × 12 feet), ceiling side-lights, raise platform, microphone, speakers, metal watering can, transparent umbrella, door, etc., two monitors, video camera, live video relay.

28	www.caroleeschneemann.com/works.html.

29	Ibid.

30	Carolee Schneemann, 'Fresh Blood – A Dream Morphology', in Schneemann (ed.), *Imaging Her Erotics*, pp. 234–49 (p. 234).

31	www.caroleeschneemann.com/works.html. 'Venus Vectors' became a standalone installation piece in 1987: Carolee Schneemann, *Venus Vectors*, 1987. Sculpture/video installation: acrylic, aluminium, video monitors, 2-channel video, photographs on mylar between 10 radiating Plexiglas panels, each 42 × 50 in. Overall radius 72 in.

32	www.caroleeschneemann.com/works.html.

33	Ibid.

34	Schneemann faced the double bind of the artist: the idea that work, designed, after all, for public display, is, once it's actually *on* display, as much the property of the observer as of the originator, whose 'body can be reappropriated for meanings quite other than those originally intended'. Nead, *The Female Nude*, p. 68.

35	Schneemann, 'Interior Scroll', in Schneemann (ed.), *Imaging Her Erotics*, pp. 150–61 (p. 155).

36	Kristine Stiles, 'The Painter as an Instrument of Real Time', in Schneemann (ed.), *Imaging Her Erotics*, pp. 3–16 (p. 16).

37	Blocker, *What the Body Cost*, p. 125.

38	Schneemann, 'Interior Scroll', p. 153.

39	Ibid.

40	www.caroleeschneemann.com/works.html.

41 Schneemann, 'Interior Scroll', p. 154. On the same page Schneemann acknowledges her indebtedness to two other filmmakers of the period, Sharon Hennessey (*What I Want*) and Anne Severson (*Near the Big Chakra*), encountered by Schneemann at Buffalo University early in 1974.

42 Ibid., p. 156.

43 Ibid., pp. 159, 160.

44 Carolee Schneemann, 'On Censorship: Interview with Aviva Rahmani', in Schneemann (ed.), *Imaging Her Erotics*, pp. 211–16 (p. 215).

45 Schneemann, 'On Censorship: Interview with Aviva Rahmani', p. 215; my italics for emphasis.

46 Ibid.

47 Carolee Schneemann, *Vulva's Morphia*, 1992–97. Suspended photogrid: 36 hand-painted color laser prints on paper, mounted on board, each 11 × 8.5 in.; text strips, 58 × 2 in. Four small electric fans, side-mounted. Total wall installation 60 × 96 in.

48 Carolee Schneemann, 'Vulva's Morphia', in Schneemann (ed.), *Imaging Her Erotics*, pp. 298–307 (p. 300).

49 Schneemann, 'Vulva's Morphia', p. 305.

50 Blocker, *What the Body Cost*, p. 34.

51 Annie Sprinkle, interview with Andrea Juno, in Juno and Vale (eds), *Angry Women*, pp. 23–40 (p. 27).

52 Sprinkle, *Post-Porn Modernist*, p. 24.

53 Ibid., p. 25.

54 See Terri Kapsalis, *Public Privates: Performing Gynecology from both ends of the Speculum* (Durham, NC: Duke University Press, 1997); Chris Straayer, 'The Seduction of Boundaries: Feminist Fluidity in Annie Sprinkle's Art/Education/Sex', in Pamela Church Gibson (ed.), *More Dirty Looks: Gender, Pornography, Power* (London: BFI, 2004), pp. 224–36.

55 For a picture of this approximately 8' tall crucifix sculpture, see Sprinkle, *Post-Porn Modernist*, p. 98.

56 Sprinkle, *Post-Porn Modernist*, p. 166.

57 Schneider, *The Explicit Body*, p. 55.

58 Gabrielle Cody, 'Introduction: Sacred Bazoombas', in Gabrielle Cody (ed.), and Annie Sprinkle, *Hardcore From the Heart: The Pleasures, Profits and Politics of Sex in Performance* (London: Continuum, 2001), pp. 1–19 (p. 3; my italics for emphasis).

59 For more on 'The Many Faces of Linda Montano', see Linda Montano, interview with Andrea Juno, in Juno and Vale (eds), *Angry Women*, pp. 50–65 (pp. 51, 58–9). However, in a personal email conversation (23 April 2012) with the author, Annie Sprinkle wrote that 'The series is called "The 16 Sluts and Goddesses Within Linda Montano". I never called it "Many Faces".

60 Cody, 'Introduction', p. 8; *Deep Inside Annie Sprinkle*, a full-length 35mm feature film, written and directed by Annie Sprinkle, 1982.

61 Sprinkle, *Post-Porn Modernist*, p. 27, quoted in Cody, 'Introduction', p. 7.

62	Ibid., p. 37; my italics for emphasis.

63	Annie Sprinkle, *Annie Sprinkle's Herstory of Porn – Reel to Real*; multimedia one-woman show directed by Emilio Cubeiro; 1997 to present.

64	Cody, 'Introduction', p. 17; my italics for emphasis.

65	Annie Sprinkle, 'Annie Sprinkle's Herstory of Porn', in Gabrielle Cody (ed.), and Annie Sprinkle, *Hardcore From the Heart: The Pleasures, Profits and Politics of Sex in Performance* (London: Continuum, 2001), pp. 44–64 (p. 47).

66	Sprinkle identifies this film as being *Bizarre Styles* (1981). See Sprinkle, *Post-Porn Modernist*, p. 203.

67	Gabrielle Cody, 'Commentary: *Annie Sprinkle from Reel to Real*', in Cody (ed.), and Sprinkle, *Hardcore From the Heart*, pp. 65–9 (p. 67).

68	Annie Sprinkle, 'Annie Sprinkle's Herstory of Porn', p. 60.

69	Ibid., p. 51.

70	Rebecca Schneider, 'Foreword: Ooouuuhhh, Professor, I Love It When You Talk Academic', in Cody (ed.), and Sprinkle, *Hardcore From the Heart*, pp. vii–x (p. viii).

71	Annie Sprinkle, 'Annie Sprinkle's Herstory of Porn', p. 61.

72	Cody, 'Introduction', p. 13; *Annie Sprinkle Post-Porn Modernist* (1990–95), written and performed by Annie Sprinkle; Directed by Emilio Cubeiro, and later by Willem de Ridder as *Post-Post-Porn Modernist*. For some of the 'Pornstistics' illustrated slides, see Sprinkle, *Post-Porn Modernist*, pp. 96–7.

73	Cody, 'Introduction', p. 13.

74	Sprinkle, *Post-Porn Modernist*, p. 171.

75	Lydia Lunch, interview with Andrea Juno and V. Vale, in Juno and Vale (eds), *Angry Women*, pp. 105–17 (p. 113–14).

76	Williams, 'A Provoking Agent', p. 129.

77	Sprinkle, *Post-Porn Modernist*, p. 196. This sense of bodily integration shows how far Sprinkle had moved since her early days in porn magazines such as *Annie Sprinkle's Bazoombas* which emphasizes a real sense of fragmentation in its frankly surreal tag line: 'If you love big, bulbous breasts . . . and the women they live on'. See Sprinkle, *Post-Porn Modernist*, p. 39.

78	Ibid., p. 165.

79	Ibid., p. 166.

80	Ibid., p. 165.

81	www.anniesprinkle.org/html/writings/pca.html. This position differs from Sprinkle's 1991 claim that she performs her *Public Cervix Announcement* in order 'to demystify women's bodies'. See Sprinkle, interview with Andrea Juno, p. 34.

82	Georges Bataille, quoted in Schneider, *The Explicit Body*, p. 83. Schneider argues that Bataille 'suggests that this vision will result in his own beheading, or castration, as he likens his experience to the guillotine'. See Schneider, *The Explicit Body*, p. 84. On the 'theoretical third eye of the cervix', see Schneider, *The Explicit Body*, p. 55.

83	Quoted in Sprinkle, *Post-Porn Modernist*, p. 174.

84 Annie Sprinkle, *MetamorphoSex*: a week-long sexuality workshop with more than 20 local women, culminating in three sex-magic performance/rituals which the public was invited to attend (premiered December 1995).

85 For more on 'Living Art', see Montano, interview with Andrea Juno, pp. 56, 62, 65.

86 Annie Sprinkle, 'MetamorphoSex', in Cody (ed.), and Sprinkle, *Hardcore From the Heart*, pp. 31–5 (34). The author asked Sprinkle about the puppet in a private email conversation (23 April 2012): 'It was called the "Vulva puppet" and was made by Dor[rie] Lane of the House O'Chicks. She gave it to me. Various sex educators were using them. WE all loved them.' I discuss Lane's puppets in my Introduction.

87 Sprinkle, 'MetamorphoSex', p. 34.

88 Ibid., p. 35.

89 In Lacanian terms, it is no longer the case that 'the *symbol* manifests itself first of all as the murder of the *thing*'. Jacques Lacan, *Écrits: A Selection*, trans. Alan Sheridan (New York, NY: W. W. Norton, 1977), p. 104; my italics for emphasis.

90 On Bataille and the gaze, see Schneider, *The Explicit Body*, p. 84. Women may experience or deploy the female gaze, then, but only in a surrealist scenario where one woman 'looks' through another's vagina.

91 On how Sprinkle maintains 'an identity and a relationship with the viewer', and how 'the whole point of [. . .] pornography is that you're not having that kind of confrontation', see Richard Schechner, in conversation, 'Dinner with Richard Schechner and Gabrielle Cody: She Wanted a Better Life', in Cody (ed.), and Sprinkle, *Hardcore From the Heart*, pp. 105–110 (p. 106).

92 Williams, 'A Provoking Agent', p. 121. Williams does later acknowledge, via Judith Butler's writing, that Sprinkle plays with 'the very constructedness of the woman's identity' in *Deep Inside Annie Sprinkle*. See Williams, 'A Provoking Agent', p. 124.

93 Annie Sprinkle, 'Annie's Breakfast with Veronica Vera: The Art of Sex Work', in Cody (ed.), and Sprinkle, *Hardcore From the Heart*, pp. 86–92 (p. 91).

94 Gloria Steinem, 'Foreword' in Eve Ensler, *The Vagina Monologues* (London: Virago, 2001), pp. ix–xix (xiv, vii). This architectural analogy is oddly Christian in its bias, although Steinem does say she's describing 'most *patriarchal* buildings of worship', p. xvii; my italics. It's also a visual used by Faith Wilding in *De/Reconstructa* (see my Conclusion).

95 Ensler, *The Vagina Monologues*, pp. 31–2.

96 Eve Ensler, *Vagina Warriors* (New York, NY: Bulfinch Press, 2005), p. 6.

97 Virginia Braun in conversation with Eve Ensler, 'Public Talk about "Private Parts"', *Feminism and Psychology* 9.4 (1999), pp. 515–22 (p. 519).

98 Ensler, *The Vagina Monologues*, p. 50.

99 Ibid., pp. 53, 61.

100 Eve Ensler, *The Vagina Monologues*, an HBO performance and documentary first aired on 14 February 2002. Ensler just does not seem to know when to stop, and who would not cringe at the mention in *Vagina Warriors* of the actor Tonya Pinkins describing Ensler as her 'shero'? See Ensler, *Vagina Warriors*, p. 88.

101 Christine M. Cooper, 'Worrying about Vaginas: Feminism and Eve Ensler's *The Vagina Monologues*', *Signs*, 32.3 (Spring 2007), pp. 727–58 (p. 733).

102   Sprinkle, private email correspondence with the author (24 April 2012).

103   Ibid.

104   On the American Sign Language sign for 'vagina' see Ensler, *Vagina Warriors*, p. 104. The Occupy Movement's version appears to be upside down, with the index fingers pointing up, and the thumbs down. The sign caused consternation in November 2011 for American footballers and cheerleaders at the University of Oregan who thought they were signing an 'O' for 'Oregon'. See www.sportsgrid.com/ncaa-football/oregon-o-sign-vagina/. And on the front cover of the December 2011–January 2012 *Reader's Digest* magazine, Michelle Obama is shown making what appears to be the same sign, much to the delight of internet conspiracists and those with a puerile sense of humour everywhere. See, for example, www.popsessive.com/2011/12/04/first-lady-michelle-obama-covers-readers-digest/. On the numbers of girls annually being subjected to FGM in Africa, see WHO's (the World Health Organization's) Fact Sheet No. 241, February 2012: www.who.int/mediacentre/factsheets/fs241/en/.

105   Slavoj Žižek, *Organs Without Bodies: On Deleuze and Consequences* (London: Routledge, 2004), p. 173; emphases in original.

106   Sprinkle, *Post-Porn Modernist*, p. 178.

107   http://dodsonandross.com/sexfeature/bettys-response-vagina-monologues.

108   Ibid.; on Dodson as the 'mother of masturbation', see Sprinkle, *Post-Porn Modernist*, p. 178.

109   Natalie Angier, *Woman: An Intimate Geography* (New York, NY: Anchor Books, 1999), p. 63.

110   www.salon.com/writer/camille_paglia/page/8/.

111   Ibid.

112   Christina Hoff Sommers, 'Sex, Lies and the *Vagina Monologues*', a paper delivered on 03.08.04 at the *Young America's Foundation 26th Annual National Conservative Student Conference* in Washington, DC, and later reprinted at FrontPageMagazine. com on 25 August 2004, http://archive.frontpagemag.com/readArticle. aspx?ARTID=11662.

113   Jacquelyn Gallo, 'Kembra Pfahler and The Girls of Karen Black: *The Wall of Vagina*', *Artcritical: The Online magazine of Art and Ideas*, 27.06.11. www.artcritical. com/2011/07/09/wall-of-vagina/.

114   Andrew C. Robinson, 'Post-Gender Pandrogyny', *Gay City News*, 18 January 2007, www.deitch.com/files/projects/womanizer_gaycitynews.pdf.

115   'Genital Origami' is the group's own description of their art. See: www. puppetryofthepenis.com/.

116   Robinson, 'Post-Gender Pandrogyny'.

117   Michael Wang, 'Mother's Courage', *Artforum*, 5 July 2005, www.artforum.com/diary/id=9212.

118   'Soy un hombre muy honrado' ('I am a very honest man') has been recorded by a variety of artists including the actor Antonio Banderas, and by The Gipsy Kings.

119   Julie Atlas Muz, Mr Pussy, 'Hola señor editor de *La Voz de la Villa*', Letters, *Village Voice*, 3rd May 2005. www.villagevoice.com/content/printVersion/191883/.

120	Judith Butler, 'Imitation and Gender Subordination', in Henry Abelove, Michèle Aina Barale and David M. Halperin, *The Lesbian and Gay Studies Reader* (London: Routledge, 1993), pp. 307–20 (p. 313; italics in original).

121	Tony Phillips, 'Inside Downtown "It Girl" Julie Atlas Muz', *Edge*: www. edgepalmsprings.com/entertainment/theatre/features//40398/inside_downtown_%E2%80%99it_girl%E2%80%99_julie_atlas_muz.

122	Marjorie Garber, 'Spare Parts: The Surgical Construction of Gender', in Henry Abelove, Michèle Aina Barale and David M. Halperin, *The Lesbian and Gay Studies Reader* (London: Routledge, 1993), pp. 321–36 (p. 331).

123	Garber, 'Spare Parts', p. 331.

124	Ibid.

125	Ibid., p. 332.

126	*Cisgendered*: 'cis' as the antonym of 'trans', means that the subject identifies with the gender ascribed to her at birth. 'The term cis challenges the taken-for-granted normalcy of consistency among sex, gender, and gender identity': see Julia T. Wood, *Gendered Lives: Communication, Gender, & Culture* (Boston, MA: Wadsworth, 2009), p. 26.

127	Cooper, 'Worrying about Vaginas', p. 740, n. 27.

128	Simon Croft, private email conversation with the author, 6 June 2012.

129	Caroline Simpson, 'Genderful: An Interview with Laura Bridgeman and Serge Nicholson' (December 2011): http://foggysapphires. wordpress.com/2011/12/14/genderful-an-interview-with-laura-bridgeman-and-serge-nicholson/.

130	See the website: www.transmanginamonologues.com/.

131	Simpson, 'Genderful'.

132	Laura Bridgeman and Serge Nicholson, *There Is No Word for It* (London: Hot Pencil Press, 2011).

133	Anon, 'Drag Kings', in Bridgeman and Nicholson, *There Is No Word*, pp. 19–20 (p. 20).

134	Anon, 'Crisis What Crisis?', in Bridgeman and Nicholson, *There Is No Word*, p. 39.

135	Bridgeman and Nicholson's 'Hot Pencil Press' blog: www.hotpencilpress.com/word. html; my italics for emphasis.

136	Anon, 'Naming it', in Bridgeman and Nicholson, *There Is No Word*, pp. 102–3 (pp. 102, 103).

137	Anon, 'Treasure', in Bridgeman and Nicholson, *There Is No Word*, p. 72.

138	Riki Wilchins is also a theorist, author of *Read My Lips: Sexual Subversion and the End of Gender* (1997); *Queer Theory/Gender Theory: An Instant Primer* (2004); and co-editor of *GenderQueer: Voices from Beyond the Sexual Binary* (2002).

139	Will O'Bryan, 'Punch-Line Politics: Riki Wichins's "one trans show" takes her from serious to stand-up, but her mission stays the same', *Metro Weekly* (December 2009): www.metroweekly.com/feature/?ak=4716.

140	Riki Wilchins, 'The MANgina Monologues (A One Trans Show)': www.youtube. com/watch?v=82UU5JE12ZM.

141 David Valentine and Riki Wilchins, quoted in Katrina Karkazis, *Fixing Sex: Intersex, Medical Authority, and Lived Experience* (Durham, NC: Duke University Press, 2008), p. 147.

142 Croft, private email conversation with the author, 6 June 2012.

8

Revealing the Vagina: Conclusion

Seeing the obscene

In the early 1930s, the American etymologist Allen Walker Read defined 'obscenity' in a way that's still utterly pertinent and fresh nearly 80 years later. 'The determinant of obscenity lies not in words or things', he wrote, 'but in attitudes that people have about words and things'.[1] His a posteriori suggestion that 'it is the existence of a ban or taboo that *creates* the obscenity where none existed before', is intriguing, because it offers a radical approach to the 'problem' of obscenity.[2] Writing in the 1930s, Walker Read can scarcely have been expected to have anticipated that Europe would so shortly see in the death camps at Auschwitz, Buchenwald, Treblinka and more, the true extent of humanity's capacity for obscene acts. Our little word features pitifully insignificantly on any obscenity scale that can measure such events. Walker Read saw in 'obscene' words an anthropological purpose, as 'scapegoats' which 'canalize a certain emotion and thus leave the remainder of the language free from it'.[3] To Walker Read, then, taboo *precedes* obscenity. Further, to use an obscene word does not neutralize the taboo, but, rather, *emphasizes* its power, because of the strong reactions and sensations to which it may give rise. Here is Walker Read arguing for the denotative neutralization which I started *The Vagina* by considering for *cunt*: 'the only way that a taboo can be actually broken is to use the word unemotionally in its simple literal sense'.[4] Walker Read died in 2002, at the age of 96. That's some 68 years after the publication of his remarkable article 'An Obscenity Symbol'. And while some words have changed in that time, western culture's warped sensibilities, remarkably, have not, especially when one considers the chaotic socio-cultural and political nature of those same 68 years. As Walker Read put it, reflecting on the First World War, 'The supporters of a civilization that can send forth its young men to kill each other ought not to be squeamish about the misuse of a few words'.[5] Quite.

This dilemma is remarkably similar to the one articulated in The Greatest Film Ever Made (and this, as I tell my students, is an Objective Truth): Francis Ford Coppola's *Apocalypse Now* (1979). The elusive Colonel Walter E. Kurtz, played magnificently by the monumental (in both stature and role) Marlon Brando, reflects on the fatal illogicality of the conflict in Vietnam and Cambodia. 'We train young men to drop fire on people', he muses, 'but their commanders won't allow them to write "fuck" on their airplanes because it's obscene!'[6] What, precisely, then, is obscene about *cunt*? Whatever *is* seen as obscene about it appears to legitimate and perpetuate the fractured identities, literally or meta-phorically, of so many women. The un-*seen*-word is, by the smoke and mirrors of patriarchal culture, seen but hidden, and heard although silenced. It is vis-ible and covert. The logical destinations of this radical dissociation are sexual abuse, female genital mutilation or the complex self-harming rituals enacted in labiaplasty procedures.

Surprisingly, similar ideas about obscenity and the female body arise in an altogether different film: *South Park: Bigger, Longer & Uncut* (1999).[7] Love-struck ten-year-old Stan asks Chef: 'How do you make a girl like you more than any other guy?' 'Oh, that's easy!' comes the reply: 'You just gotta find the clitoris'. Stan, of course, has no idea what this means and the adult chef quickly realizes his mistake. 'Is that like finding Jesus, or something?', asks Eric, when Stan asks him. In this film, we have the only example I've discov-ered – thus far – of the talking clitoris. It features at the end of this charac-teristically chaotic movie in which the United States and Canada go to war because of the 'obscene' language in the Canadian film spin-off of the chil-dren's TV show starring serial farters, Terrance and Phillip. The film is show-ing at South Park's cinema, and all the children want to go and watch. There's a delightful, self-referential mischievousness at play, of course, in Trey Parker and Matt Stone using 'bad' language in a film spin-off from a popular TV series in order to show the South Park parents' uproar about a film which uses 'bad' language. The satire is unsubtle but effective: if we get caught up in 'obscene' language, we risk missing the real obscenities. The bloody cartoon battle scenes between Canada and the United States at the end of the film emphasize this. And there's a warning to the Right in showing the absurd consequences of trying to 'protect' children by killing people. Stumbling away from the fighting, Stan encounters a large, pink, benign blob with soothing tones, a luminous aura and a soundtrack of heavenly choirs. In a pastiche of the heroic quest narrative, Stan lies prostrate before the almighty Clitoris which speaks with the mystic omniscience of the Delphic Oracle. 'Be not afraid!' she says, in a magnificently inappropriate echo of Jesus addressing his disciples in Matthew 14:27, 'Behold my glory! [. . .] I am the Clitoris!' Stan is disappointed, however, when this heavenly vision won't tell him how to make his classmate Wendy Testeberger like him, but instead asks him to protect Terrance and Phillip. The organ's last words to Stan before it disappears are: 'Now go! Hurry! The Clitoris has spoken!' And it's the only one I know of that has.

The disaggregation of the female body occurs because of the paradoxical covert visibility of her sexual organs. They become liminal, 'othered', are everywhere and nowhere. The often-nightmarish visions of the autonomized vagina which I've considered in this book may seem far-fetched. But the truth is that *literal* disaggregation is being forced on real women's bodies globally. Political engagement will come about, I'd hope, as one compelling consequence of this book. Writing in the mid-1990s (but, sadly, with an applicability to today), the art historian Amelia Jones vividly articulated the interrelationship of 'theory' and 'activism':

> I would have hoped by now – especially with world politics in such alarming disarray and under right-wing sway – that the theorization of oppression, via philosophers [. . .] would not be opposed to the physical act of protest: feminists must continue to attack racism, homophobia, classism, imperialism and sexism on every possible front. Theory is an activist intervention in the *real* of discrimination which, as many cultural theorists have pointed out, takes place textually, institutionally, psychologically and otherwise. All these intersecting aspects of oppression (which are never discrete) support and inform one another.[8]

There are clearly far more pressing issues facing humanity – global poverty, war, famine, disease, sexual violence – than *cunt*. The arguments around obscenity are useful distractions from the everyday issues, problems and fights in women's lives, where, for example, they're victims of violence, walk miles to get clean water for their families or miss out on an education because of a lack of sanitary protection. The impulse for activism is neutralized in the quotidian wrangling about a little word, and philosophical debate is depicted as something of an extravagance. Except, of course, the *fragmentations* identified in that exact debate are real and urgent and impact on the lives of women. To conclude *The Vagina*, I want to touch on where it might lead, and how its two central governing principles – the covert cunt, and the fragmentation of self – can actually underpin the fundamental activist responses which are needed right now in the international community.

The covert visibility of female genital mutilation

On the 22nd April 2012, the Sunday Times newspaper devoted its Leader to the issue of FGM. 'Britain Must end this Horrific Mutilation', ran the title.[9] The article reported on how 'the barbaric practice' is endemic in Africa and in parts of the Middle East, where '90% or more women in Sudan and Somalia have been mutilated this way'. Additionally, the abuse has been 'inflicted on perhaps 120m women alive today and on 3m girls a year in Africa alone'. The practice is illegal in the United Kingdom but various factors, including what the paper calls 'a warped sense of respect for different cultural traditions', mean that very few prosecutions have been brought. The rhetoric of the Leader's last paragraph did make me feel uncomfortable, however, since it is so close in tenor to far-right sentiments. I had to struggle to see the equanimity in it:

> When people from these mainly African countries come to Britain they should leave behind these practices which, like witchcraft, forced marriages and honour killings, have no place here. They must integrate and abide by British laws. Cultural diversity has its limits as Trevor Phillips, chairman

of the Equality and Human Rights Commission, has pointed out. Female genital mutilation goes well beyond these limits. It is unacceptable and must be stopped.

The sentiment of the last couple of sentences is beyond doubt; the facts are inarguable. What troubles me is that rhetoric of the 'when *they* come over *here*' school of thought. FGM is not a problem *only* because it is still – illegally – being carried out on British soil. Nor is it a problem *only* because very young British girls are being taken out of 'our' country to undergo FGM, eventually being brought back to 'our' country, irrevocably changed. No. It's a problem in and of itself. It's a *global* debate; not an opportunity for buttressing national identity politics. Anne Phillips complicates the debate still more. 'Western feminists', she writes, 'express anger and revulsion at the practice of burning, cutting or removing female genitalia, but they might usefully consider how a practice like implanting polyurethane-covered silicone into one's breasts must appear to those not used to this practice'.[10]

On the reverse side of the same page of the newspaper was a captioned, topical photograph intended to illustrate the geo-political complexities of the F1 Grand Prix being hosted in Bahrain. In the photograph, three young women in makeshift niqabs and long, black gowns are running, clearly in a state of some agitation, towards the photographer. The oldest of the three has a speech bubble coming from her (veiled) mouth: 'It's the last time I agree to be an F1 pit babe!' It is the case that, sometimes, having a modicum of respect for 'different cultural traditions' is not a bad thing, especially if its absence makes a newspaper appear appallingly culturally insensitive. And, in the same newspaper's *Style* magazine, dated 4th September 2011, the weekly 'cultural barometer' ridiculed the 'gross' efforts of the Shoreditch Sisterhood who had made a quilt out of numerous vulvar and labial images as a protest about FGM; this visibility was one step too far. But, credit where it's due: the same newspaper, the *Sunday Times*, was, as long ago as 1992, responsible for breaking the story of the occurrence in the United Kingdom of what was then called 'female circumcision'. It continues to make details of this sinister covert procedure visible, right next to Middle England's toast and marmalade on a Sunday morning, when many readers might otherwise (prefer to?) remain ignorant of it. In the exposé of April 2012, the paper revealed that there are still doctors in the United Kingdom willing to carry out the procedure for around £750. For this, you can have your daughter's clitoris cut off, and her vulva sewn-up (both offences under the FGM Act of 2003), without her having to go any further than London.[11]

Four types of FGM are widely practised on girls as young as three years old: Types 1 and 2 'account for about 80% of all FGM' procedures.[12] In Type 1, the clitoris is sliced off; Type 2 has the additional removal of the labia. Type 3, 'infibulation', includes the excision of the labia and clitoris, but the vulva – or any raw edges – are also stitched shut (a small twig or matchstick may be inserted in order to create a small passageway through which menstrual blood may pass; if the urethra is also blocked by this stitching, it can take up to 20 minutes to urinate, since that same tiny opening is the only outlet). Type 4 is an amalgam of the previous 3 Types, with the inclusion of 'corrosive substances [. . .] The victims endure excruciating pain, the risk of bleeding or infection and often carry the physical and emotional scars for years'.[13] Further, the vaginal walls might be lacerated with 'a fragment of glass, a razor blade, or a potato knife', followed by the girl's legs being bound together, 'so that the walls of the vagina can grow together', thereby 'preserving virginity'.[14] 'Somali girls', writes Somali–Dutch activist Ayaan Hirsi Ali, 'are brought up with the motto, "Just keep your stitches intact". The moment of truth comes on the wedding night. If it turns out that your vaginal walls are no longer stitched together, you are a whore'.[15] The historian Margot Badran attributes Egyptian FGM practices to Islamic texts which credit women with 'enormous sexual appetites (far greater than those of men)', so that their 'whole being, body and voice constitutes [*sic.*] a sexualised entity' and women 'must be contained, therefore, to preserve social order'.[16] However, FGM 'is not prescribed by Islam, according to classic Islamic jurisprudence and standard Islamic interpretive methodologies', and the Qur'an makes no direct mention of it; FGM, 'except in Southeast Asia, has less to do with the Islamic law schools than with socio-cultural customs in the various countries'.[17] Hirsi Ali encapsulates the problems of this particularly insidious type of covert visibility. 'Because of the hidden effects of the ritual – genitals are by definition covered parts of the body – society can disapprove of the ritual while at the same time denying that it is the problem,' she writes: 'If children had their noses, or parts of their ears cut off, the [in this instance, Dutch] government would not be able to get away with its policy of passive tolerance.'[18]

If you've read this far in *The Vagina*, then, hopefully, you'll be able to work out what I think about these systematic acts of callous, misogynist abuse. I'll end this section, then, with a quick anecdote. One of the delights of writing at Gladstone's residential library in North Wales is the diversity of people one meets. A young man and woman from a large city in the west of the United Kingdom were staying there as I was writing a draft of this conclusion. They asked what I was working on (actually, when I first said 'I'm finishing a book', one asked: 'Is that *reading* one, or . . .?'), and the woman, a teacher, told me of how, in her class, a young girl of Somali ethnicity had inexplicably stopped attending school for a couple of months. The girl had been a fairly lively, happy ten-year-old. But on her return, she stopped speaking. Just stopped. The covert, repugnant trauma that had been enacted on her labia was made visible in her lips. Mutilation had rendered her mute, as the theoretical synonymy was violently, literally, confirmed.

The covert visibility of labiaplasty procedures

In 'Revealing the Vagina in Visual Art (1)', I looked at subRosa, the 'cyber-feminist cell'. The same group made a short but effective film called *Vulva De/Re Constructa*, which was produced by Faith Wilding and Cristina Nguyen Hung.[19] It begins with collage of medical and drawn sections of an anatomically laid out vulva. A woman's clear voice speaks: 'Question: when is the image of a cunt not pornographic? Answer: when it is medicalised'. A male voice next talks about 'aesthetic surgery of the female external genitalia', the awareness of which has increased 'due to media attention, both from magazines and video'. This voice claims that many women 'feel self-conscious about the appearance of their *labia majora*, the outer lips, or more commonly, *labia minora*, the inner lips'. Then: 'what does woman want?' asks a man's disembodied, bearded lips, 'My god! What does she want?' In silhouette, 'Ms Lack' and a male doctor sit across a table from one another and talk. She reads back to him an article he's written about 'women who, for whatever reason, lack an overall optimum architectural integrity of the vagina'. She says that she really, really desires 'overall optimum architectural integrity of the vagina', and a floor plan of a cathedral, in the early German Gothic style, is superimposed on a picture of a vulva.

Drawings by Faith Wilding emphasize the absurdity of such purely aesthetic procedures. 'Augmented "rococo" labia', for example, bloom in one shot, in Rorschach-symmetrical pinks and pale browns; this idea of 'augmentation', for which the silhouetted woman is asking, perplexes the doctor. He clearly sees the dollar signs before his eyes, however, and hypothesizes with her, with the aid of diagrams, about how he might perform such a procedure, using collagen, skin grafting and silicone. 'Isn't that dangerous?', asks the client at one point. 'Y'know', replies the doctor, 'I don't believe so. I don't believe the hype.' It's an effective, full-frontal piece of satire. The complexities and clear dangers which accompany the procedure are downplayed. The viewer is left wondering why anyone would want such an operation – and the fact that the question is being asked demonstrates the contingency of aesthetic surgery: who's to say an 'augmentation' is any more or less absurd than a reduction, a cutting away, a mutilation? The clinicalized setting of the one forces the viewer to question the barbarity and ludicrousness of the other. subRosa's fictional surgeon has real-life counterparts. Dr David Matlock, owner of the 'Laser Vaginal Rejuvenation Institute' in LA, offers 'a "boutique cosmetic gynaecological laser surgery programme" [and] Laser vaginal rejuvenation, for the enhancement of sexual gratification. Designer laser vaginoplasty, for the aesthetic enhancement of the vulva structures. I also do liposculpting'.[20] The procedures can cost more than £40,000. For the bargain price of £1,000, though, one may purchase the 'G-Shot. This is when a quantity of collagen – the same stuff that goes into lips – is injected into the rough area inside the vagina that is *supposed* to constitute the G-spot'.[21] Depressingly, one journalist recently argued that, with the NHS performing over 2,000 surgical labial procedures annually in the United Kingdom, and many thousands more being done privately, 'Media images of labial perfection are more likely to dictate trends than feminist blandishments. Labial sculpting, then, along with Botox, boob jobs and highlights, looks as if it's here to stay' – and this is the same newspaper that argues so vociferously against FGM.[22]

In the summer of 2012, the UK-based filmmaker Ellie Land launched her *Centrefold*, a documentary about the huge increase in the numbers of women requesting cosmetic labiaplasty procedures.[23] The animated film used the real voices of three women recounting how they felt about their genitals prior to surgery. One reports that their labia 'looked disgusting. Shrivelled up'; another talks about the 'embarrassment. A day didn't go past when I didn't think about them – in a bad way'. And the third reveals a deep-seated insecurity which had had an impact on her sexual relations with her partner: 'I thought I didn't look the way that women's bits were meant to look.' It's a beautiful, sensitive film which asks crucial questions about why women feel that there is a 'way that women's bits' should look. Where does this message come from and, more importantly, how can we change it? Lih-Mei Liao, one of the consultants working on *Centrefold*, is a clinical psychologist who is 'vehemently opposed to such surgery. "It has become a social phenomenon," she says. "It is nothing to do with a recognisable disease or condition".[24] The columnist Camilla Long does not regard this problem quite so seriously. 'One morning', she writes, 'I joined 50 feminists on a march [. . .] in protest against labiaplasty [. . . which is] the process of surgically nipping and tucking your Violet Elizabeth.'[25] Long sees such protests as the territory of the privileged few, an opportunity between Pilates classes and salon blow-dries to wear sparkly merkins and carry witty placards: 'I felt a sense of discomfort. I began to wonder if we weren't missing the point. If feminism was drowning in a sea of dubious publicity and stick-on fannies. If the real issues had been obscured by a bizarre new hobby. If women's rights were now just a lifestyle choice.'[26] This is contentious writing from Long, culminating in a glib witticism which entirely omits the possibility of a *continuum* of 'real issues' regarding women's psychological and physiological health. My concerns about labiaplasty do not mean that FGM is not also a practice which profoundly troubles me: activism about one issue does not prohibit activism about another.

As Wilding expresses it: 'women from quite different economic, social/cultural backgrounds and geographical origins are undergoing vulvar surgery and alterations for completely different reasons – and with differing results – all of which however have their roots in patriarchal gender practices'.[27] I do not demean the concerns of women who have body dysmorphia, who see images of symmetrical, hairless, almost lipless cunts and feel that they come up short. And, as Alyssa Dweck and Robin Westen put it in *V is for Vagina*, 'It's not wholly about L-looks. Sisters can suffer from chronic irritation, infection, poor hygiene and pain during sex or sports because of their flabby labia'.[28] After all, to whom are these women, in a culture that doesn't fairly represent and reveal the cunt, able to *talk* about their distress? Wilding argues that 'the new vulvar and vaginal surgical technologies would be put to much better use in helping women seeking reconstruction and healing of sexual organs mutilated and damaged by FGM practices, than in making unnecessary "aesthetic" interventions on perfectly healthy women'.[29] Absolutely; and the money spent on those technologies would also be put to better use in educating our daughters about their own bodies, ridding them of the self-hatred and low self-esteem which make their genital *appearance* (not 'health', nor psychological 'appropriacy') their be all and end all. Where there's discomfort or damage then, yes, of course surgery is appropriate, if that's what the woman desires, or if that's what the trans person needs. But this pathologizing of healthy female bodies is lining the pockets of the 'aesthetic' industries, and it has to stop.

The covert visibility of the menstruating woman

As the director Catherine Breillat says of the tampon scene in her film *Anatomy of Hell*, 'the more obscenity and disgust that's attributed to women's bodies, the fewer rights they'll have. It's statistical. It's a tool used to dominate and subjugate women. [. . .] The deliberate attribution of disgust and obscenity to women's bodies makes it necessary to "save them from themselves" [. . .] reducing them to the state of an animal'. In my analysis of that scene, I argued that the taboo around menstruation has a long way to go before it's altered. Studies already exist, including Karen Houppert's *Curse*, which examine the psychical separation that can occur when women see menstruation as something happening *to* them, as a period during which their bodies betray them. They feel fragmented and, often, in pain. Toppling age-old cultural taboos is a superhuman task, but works like Houppert's do a great job of exposing previously covert practices and rituals around menstruation, and of bringing them to light. 'What does it mean for a girl, or woman, to say simply, "This happens to me"', asks Houppert, 'and for society to say, "No it doesn't"? Not in movies. Not in books. Not in conversations'.[30] Chris Bobel's *New Blood* also explodes the myths and silences around socio-cultural discourses of menstruation, which have 'been used to prove women's inferiority and unsuitability for everything from pursuing a college education [. . .] to being elected president of the United States or nominated to the Supreme Court (Oh, the dangers of PMS!)'.[31] Bobel also exposes how symptoms of premenstrual syndrome are hijacked and exaggerated to the point where 'sorting out the real problems from those conjured up in the service of sexism is difficult work'.[32] Lunapads, in a riposte to the evasive language and images employed by Always and Femfresh, sell soft toy uteri (in pink, with blue ovaries) and 7.75" × 6.25" ovaries, 'the brainchild of an anatomically obsessed illustrator who loves internal organs and all they do'.[33] Either option is also available as a lapel pin: both personify – autonomize – the organs they represent by giving them eyes and mouths. In terms of menstruation, once again, we need to think globally, and consider the excellent work of organizations like ACTSA (Action for South Africa), whose 'Dignity! Period' campaign, since 2005, 'has delivered over 7 million sanitary products' to Zimbabwe's women, meaning that they no longer have to resort to using 'newspapers, rags, leaves and bark as a substitute [for] sanitary pads [which] leads to infections [or, sometimes] infertility and causes social embarrassment [to the point where] many women cannot go to work and girls cannot go to school' when they're menstruating.[34]

Where *The Vagina* might lead

Finally, two key areas which have been touched on in this book, and in which theory needs to mesh with activism, are, first, the *trans*-experience of covert visibility, and, second, the role of pornography in perpetuating the discourse of autonomous anatomy. What I've written about performance art in this book has taken on board the idea that 'the vagina' is a contested site in gender politics. In our theoretical discussions we need to be mindful of the lived realities of transphobia for many trans-women who may have vaginas, and trans-men who may have, as I put it in that chapter, 'lost the lack'. As Lisa Lees movingly writes: 'I know transphobia exists. I have seen and experienced the change that comes over people when they find out I am transsexual [. . .] Those people who continue to admit that I exist do get over their initial fear and stop treating me like an exhibit in a freak show. Still, there is usually a noticeable permanent shift in behaviour that indicates I have been assigned to a category of "other" and am not to be included in certain kinds of conversations and interactions'.[35] We also need to avoid the pernicious binaries which exclude intersex people, and recognize each individual's selfhood. Simon Croft, the designer of the poster for the *(Trans)Mangina Monologues*, saw the core of that particular project as being about 'speaking the "unspeakable"'.[36] He writes:

> I reflected on how we literally shape words with our flesh; our mouths and tongues. [. . .] I can appreciate that some people found the image difficult, or didn't like it, and I think reasons for that included people who felt that the image didn't represent their physicality (people who have phalloplasties, for example) – felt that people might assume that that's what they had; or people who maybe thought it was reductive. However, for me that misses the core point of the image. The image isn't representing a physicality – it's representing a principle; an idea – that everyone makes assumptions and quite often they aren't correct [. . .] I do like the fact that the image has been a little controversial, that it has generated a reaction, because then people do start talking, start breaking down the taboo, the silence.

If we can 'name the parts', then we can effect a change in cultural perceptions: the c-word can be *seen*.

I have also touched on the issues around pornography and the meaning of the 'explicit' in terms of women's bodies. Heterosexual men are more willing than ever to consume vast quantities of pornography, happily, it seems, fulfilling the 'demand' half of the basic supply and demand marketing equation.[37] As legal scholar Clare McGlynn has written, succinctly summarizing the complexities of the feminism/pornography debate, 'In the area of pornography regulation, radical feminists consider that restricting pornography will help in the fight against domestic violence, while anti-censorship feminists fear that it will further limit women's sexual choices and that it is a distraction from other, generally costly, policy options.'[38] These distractions, as I wrote at the start of this conclusion, are often welcomed by patriarchy, since they conveniently prevent activism in other areas. The 'docile bodies' of which Michel Foucault wrote in the 1970s aren't only those which are explicitly punished or controlled; they are also, in the pornographic realm, subject to more *covert* strategies of surveillance and regulation.[39] And 'docile bodies' may, of course, transmute into resistant, activist bodies. Much more work remains to be done to identify and expose the functioning of 'covert visibility', and of the 'autonomous cunt', in the manifold discourses of pornography in the twenty-first century.

'Good' language

And, please, let's agree on a *name* for it. The *OED* defines 'clitoris' thus: 'a homologue of the male penis, present as a rudimentary organ, in the females of many of the higher vertebrata'. Would the sky *really* fall, were the *OED* to define 'penis' as: 'a homologue of the female clitoris, present as a pretty unsophisticated organ, really, in the males of many of the higher vertebrata'? (It doesn't.) If we salvage language, if we make the c-word *seen*, might we fundamentally reclaim the right to talk about the significant issues it currently eclipses? Alternatively, if 'cunt' *has* gone too far into the dysphemistic realm, then let us find another: a powerful word, an accurate word, one that acknowledges the richness of women's sexual identities and desires, and one that does not infantilize, by sounding 'cute'. We need a *name* that will help us to discuss, and to celebrate, to reveal, and to assimilate, the *named*. This is imperative: it is not a task that we can abandon to the vagaries of serendipity.

Notes

1 Allen Walker Read, 'An Obscenity Symbol', *American Speech*, 9.4 (December 1934), 264–78 (p. 264).
2 Walker Read, 'An Obscenity Symbol', p. 264; my italics for emphasis.
3 Ibid., p. 267.
4 Ibid., p. 274.

5 Ibid., p. 275. Walker Read's own deployment of covert visibility is beautifully – if not contradictorily – executed here. His most important work of the period was about the word 'fuck', and yet the word is not mentioned once in the entirety of 'An Obscenity Symbol'.

6 Francis Ford Coppola, dir., *Apocalypse Now* (1979).

7 Trey Parker, dir., *South Park: Bigger, Longer & Uncut* (1999).

8 Amelia Jones, 'Power and Feminist (Art) History' (Review Article), *Art History*, 18.3 (September 1995), pp. 435–43 (p. 440).

9 'Britain Must End This Horrific Mutilation', Leader in the *Sunday Times*, 22 April 2012, p. 20.

10 Anne Phillips, *Culture and Gender* (Cambridge: Polity, 2010), pp. 63–4. Of course *consent* is present in breast augmentations in a way it's categorically not in genital infibulation.

11 Mazher Mahmood and Eleanor Mills, 'I can circumcise them here: £750 for the first daughter', *Sunday Times*, 22 April 2012, p. 10.

12 Mahmood and Mills, 'I can circumcise them here', p. 11; some Islamic commentators draw a distinction between 'removal of the clitoral prepuce [hood]' and 'clitoridectomy [. . .] similar to amputation of the penis'. See Anne Sofie Roald, *Women in Islam: The Western Experience* (London: Routledge, 2001), p. 240.

13 Mahmood and Mills, 'I can circumcise them here', p. 11.

14 Ayaan Hirsi Ali, *The Caged Virgin: An Emancipation Proclamation for Women and Islam* (New York, NY: Free Press, 2006), p. 15.

15 Hirsi Ali, *The Caged Virgin*, p. 86.

16 Margot Badran, *Feminism in Islam: Secular and Religious Convergences* (Oxford: Oneworld, 2009), pp. 170–1.

17 Badran, *Feminism in Islam*, p. 180; Roald, *Women in Islam*, p. 244.

18 Hirsi Ali, *The Caged Virgin*, p. 107.

19 *Vulva De/Re Constructa*: http://artfem.tv/id;9/action;showpage/page_type;video/ page_id;Vulva_de_reConstructa_by_subRosa_2000_flv/.

20 Jessica Brinton, 'David Matlock, aka Dr Sex, can "fix" you down there', *Sunday Times* 'Style' Magazine, 20 June 2008, pp. 36–7 (p. 36).

21 Brinton, 'David Matlock, aka Dr Sex', p. 37 (italics added for emphasis).

22 Lois Rogers, 'Do Looks Matter?', *Sunday Times* 'Style' Magazine, 9 October 2011, pp. 50–1 (p. 51).

23 To learn more about the *Centrefold* project, see: www.thecentrefoldproject.org/.

24 Rogers, 'Do Looks Matter?', p. 50.

25 Camilla Long, 'Feminism? I Was a "Muff March" Virgin', *Sunday Times Magazine*, 8 January 2012, p. 5.

26 Long, 'Feminism?', p. 5.

27 Wilding, 'Vulvas with a Difference', p. 154.

28 Alyssa Dweck and Robin Westen, *V is for Vagina: Your A-to-Z Guide to Periods, Piercings, Pleasures and so Much More* (Berkeley, CA: Ulysses Press, 2012), p. 103.

29   Wilding, 'Vulvas with a Difference', p. 153. Virginia Braun writes compellingly
      about women's various motivations for undergoing labiaplasty procedures – 'the
      psychological response to genital morphology', for example. See Braun, 'In Search of
      (Better) Sexual Pleasure: Female Genital "Cosmetic" Surgery', *Sexualities* 8.4 (2005),
      pp. 407–24 (p. 411; emphasis in original).

30   Karen Houppert, *The Curse. Confronting the Last Unmentionable Taboo: Menstruation*
      (London: Profile Books, 2000), p. 7. Houppert writes on the same page of how, 'After
      a while, it becomes psychologically disorientating to look out at a world where your
      reality does not exist.'

31   Chris Bobel, *New Blood: Third-Wave Feminism and the Politics of Menstruation* (New
      Brunswick, NJ: Rutgers University Press, 2010), pp. 35–6.

32   Bobel, *New Blood*, p. 36.

33   See: Lunapads.com.

34   www.actsa.org/page-1022-Dignity!%20Period..html.

35   Lisa Lees, *Fragments of Gender* (Lulu.com), p. 98. See also: lisalees.com.

36   Simon Croft, personal email correspondence with the author, 6 June 2012.

37   On how 'the fact remains: the success of the porn industry largely depends on the
      willingness of heterosexual men to buy its products, to enter into a contract which
      provides them with (vicarious) use of a female body for their arousal or amusement',
      see Karen Boyle, 'Introduction: Everyday Pornography', in Karen Boyle (ed.),
      Everyday Pornography (Abingdon: Routledge, 2010), pp. 1–14 (p. 1).

38   Clare McGlynn, 'Marginalizing Feminism? Debating Extreme Pornography Laws
      in Public and Policy Discourse', in Boyle (ed.), *Everyday Pornography,* pp. 190–202
      (p. 201).

39   '[D]iscipline produces subjected and practised bodies, "docile" bodies. Discipline
      increases the forces of the body (in economic terms of utility) and diminishes these
      same forces (in political terms of obedience). In short, it dissociates power from
      the body.' See Michel Foucault, *Discipline and Punish: The Role of the Prison*, trans.
      Michael Sheridan (New York, NY: Random House, 1995), p. 139.

Bibliography

Primary

Acker, Kathy, *Algeria: A Series of Invocations Because Nothing Else Works* (London: Aloes Books, 1984).

Alighieri, Dante, *The Divine Comedy. Volume 1: Inferno*, trans. Mark Musa (London: Penguin, 2003).

Arden, Jane, *Vagina Rex and the Gas Oven*, Playscript 58 (London: Calder and Boyars, 1971).

Aschenbrand, Periel, *The Only Bush I Trust is my Own* (London: Corgi, 2006).

Baker, Nicholson, *House of Holes* (London: Simon and Schuster, 2011).

— *The Fermata* (London: Vintage, 1994).

Bataille, Georges, *Story of the Eye* (London: Penguin, 2001 [1928]).

Bridgeman, Laura and Serge Nicholson, *There Is No Word For It* (London: Hot Pencil Press, 2011). [Contains: Anon, 'Drag Kings', pp. 19–20; Anon, 'Crisis What Crisis?', p. 39; Anon, 'Treasure', p. 72; Anon, 'Naming it', pp. 102–3.]

Burroughs, William, *The Naked Lunch: The Restored Text* (London: Harper Perennial, 2005).

Chaucer, Geoffrey, *The Miller's Tale* in *The Canterbury Tales* in Larry D. Benson (ed), *The Riverside Chaucer* (Oxford: Oxford University Press, 2008), pp. 68–77.

Chicago, Judy, with photography by Donald Woodman, *Holocaust Project: From Darkness Into Light* (New York, NY: Penguin, 1993).

Chicago, Judy, *Fragments From the Delta of Venus* (New York, NY: PowerHouse Books, 2004).

Churchill, Caryl, *Top Girls* (London: Methuen Drama, 2005).

Cody, Gabrielle (ed.), and Annie Sprinkle, *Hardcore From the Heart: The Pleasures, Profits and Politics of Sex in Performance* (London: Continuum, 2001). [Contains: Rebecca Schneider, 'Foreword: Ooouuuhhh, Professor, I Love It When You Talk Academic', pp. vii–x; Cody, 'Introduction: Sacred Bazoombas', pp. 1–19; Sprinkle, 'Annie Sprinkle's Herstory of Porn', pp. 44–64; Cody, 'Commentary: *Annie Sprinkle from Reel to Real*', pp. 65–9; Sprinkle, 'Annie's Breakfast with Veronica Vera: The Art of Sex Work', pp. 86–92; 'Dinner with Richard Schechner and Gabrielle Cody: She wanted a Better Life', pp. 105–10.]

Coover, Robert, *A Theological Position: Plays* (New York, NY: EP Dutton & Co. Inc., 1972).

Corinne, Tee, *Cunt Coloring Book* (San Francisco, CA: Last Gasp, 2005 [1988]).

Diderot, Denis, *Encyclopédie ou Dictionnaire raisonné des sciences, des arts et des metiers* (Paris, 1755), trans. Philip Stewart in *The Encyclopedia of Diderot & d'Alembert: Collaborative Translation Project* (Ann Arbor, MI: Scholarly Publishing Office

of the University of Michigan Library, 2002), http://hdl.handle.net/2027/spo.
did2222.0000.004.

— *The Indiscreet Jewels*, trans. Sophie Hawkes (New York, NY: Marsilio, 1993).

Donne, John, 'A Valediction Forbidding Mourning', in Theodore Redpath (ed.), *The Songs
and Sonnets of John Donne* (London: Methuen, 1983), pp. 260–1.

D'Urfey, Thomas, *Wit and Mirth: Or Pills to Purge Melancholy* (London: Pearson, 1719).

Ellis, George, 'Preface' to M. Pierre Jean Baptiste Le Grand d'Aussy, *Fabliaux or Tales,
Abridged from French Manuscripts of the XIIth and XIIIth Centuries* (London: Bulmer
and Co., 1796).

Ensler, Eve, *The Vagina Monologues* (London: Virago, 2001).

— *Vagina Warriors* (New York, NY: Bulfinch Press, 2005).

'Eurudice' [Eurydice Kamvyselli], *f/32: The Second Coming* (London: Virago, 1993).

Feaver, Vicki, 'Judith', in *The Handless Maiden* (London: Jonathan Cape, 2009).

Freely, Maureen, *Under the Vulcania* (London: Bloomsbury, 1994).

Gaiman, Neil, *American Gods (Author's Preferred Text)* (London: Headline, 2005).

Garin, *Le Chevalier Qui Fist Parler Les Cons*, prose trans. Helen Nicholson, http://
homepage.ntlworld.com/nigel.nicholson/hn/indexKnight.html.

Gómez-Cano, Grisel, *The Return to Coatlicue: Goddesses and Warladies in Mexican
Folklore* (Bloomington, IN: Xlibris, 2010).

Godwin, William, *Memoirs of the Author of 'A Vindication of the Rights of Woman'. By
William Godwin. The Second Edition, Corrected* (London: J. Johnson, 1798).

Grose, Francis, *A Classical Dictionary of the Vulgar Tongue*, 2nd edn (London: S. Hooper,
Facing Bloomsbury Square, 1788).

Home, Stewart, *Cunt* (London: The Do-Not Press, 1999).

Judith, The Book of, *Authorized King James Version with Apocrypha*, intro. and notes
by Robert Carroll and Stephen Prickett (Oxford World's Classics. Oxford: Oxford
University Press, 1998).

Kamvyselli, Eurydice, see 'Eurudice'.

Kaysen, Susanna, *The Camera My Mother Gave Me* (New York, NY: Vintage, 2001).

— *Girl, Interrupted* (New York, NY: Random House, 1993).

Lewis, G. R., *Illustrations of Kilpeck Church, Herefordshire: In a Series of Drawings made
on the Spot. With an Essay on Ecclesiastical Design, and a Descriptive Interpretation*
(London: Pickering, 1842).

John, *King James Version*.

McCartney, Jamie, *The Great Wall of Vagina* (Brighton: Jamie McCartney, 2011).

Mellick III, Carlton, *Razor Wire Pubic Hair* (Fountain Hills, AZ: Eraserhead Press, 2003).

— *The Haunted Vagina* (Portland, OR: Eraserhead Press, 2006).

Néret, Gilles, *Pussycats* (Koln: Taschen, 2003).

Rabelais, Francis, *Selections from the Works of Francis Rabelais, 'Gargantua and Pantagruel'*,
trans. Sir Thomas Urquhart and Peter Anthony Motteux (London: John Westhouse, 1945).

Riccoboni, Marie-Jeanne, *Les Lettres de Mistriss Fanni Butlerd*, 'XXVᵉ Lettre', *Oeuvres
Complètes de M*me *Riccoboni*, Vol. 4 (Paris: Foucault, Libraire, Rue des Noyers, 1818).

Sanger, Margaret, *The Autobiography of Margaret Sanger* (New York, NY: W. W. Norton
[1938], 2004).

— *The Selected Papers of Margaret Sanger: Volume 1: The Woman Rebel, 1900–1928*, ed.
Esther Katz (Champaign, IL: University of Illinois Press, 2003).

Schneemann, Carolee (ed.), *Imaging Her Erotics: Essays, Interviews, Projects*
(Cambridge, MA: The MIT Press, 2002). [Contains: Kristine Stiles, 'The Painter as
an Instrument of Real Time', pp. 3–16; Schneemann, 'Interview with Kate Haug',

pp. 21–44; Schneemann, '"Maximus at Gloucester": a Visit to Charles Olson', pp. 52–3; Schneemann, 'Interview with ND', pp. 113–26; Schneemann, 'Interview with Linda Montano', pp. 131–4; Schneemann, 'Interior Scroll', pp. 150–61; Schneemann, 'Interview with Carl Heyward', pp. 196–207; Schneemann, 'On Censorship: Interview with Aviva Rahmani', pp. 211–16; Schneemann, 'Notes from the Underground: a Feminist Pornographer in Moscow', pp. 217–23; Schneemann, 'Fresh Blood – A Dream Morphology', pp. 234–49; Schneemann, 'Vulva's Morphia', pp. 298–307.]

Scholder, Amy, and Dennis Cooper (eds), *Essential Acker: The Writings of Kathy Acker* (New York, NY: Grove Press, 2002). [Contains: Jeanette Winterson, 'Introduction', pp. vii–x; Scholder, 'Editor's Note', pp. xi–xiv; also contains extracts from: Acker, *Blood and Guts in High School*; *Don Quixote*; *Empire of the Senseless*; *Florida*; 'New York City in 1979'; *Kathy Goes to Haiti*; *Pussy, King of the Pirates*; *The Burning Bombing of America: The Destruction of the U.S.*; *The Childlike Life of the Black Tarantula*.]

Self, Will, *Cock and Bull* (London: Bloomsbury, 2006).

Shakespeare, William, *Hamlet*, ed. Ann Thompson and Neil Taylor (London: Arden Shakespeare, Third Series, 2006).

— *Twelfth Night*, ed. Roger Warren and Stanley Wells (Oxford: The Oxford Shakespeare, 2008).

Solomon, Wisdom of, *Authorized King James Version with Apocrypha*, intro. and notes by Robert Carroll and Stephen Prickett (Oxford World's Classics. Oxford: Oxford University Press, 1998).

Sprinkle, Annie, 'MetamorphoSex', in Gabrielle Cody (ed.), and Annie Sprinkle, *Hardcore From the Heart: The Pleasures, Profits and Politics of Sex in Performance* (London: Continuum, 2001), pp. 31–5.

Steinem, Gloria, 'Foreword' in Eve Ensler, *The Vagina Monologues* (London: Virago, 2001), pp. ix–xix.

Thomas Ellis, Alice, *God has Not Changed* (London: Burns and Oates, Continuum, 2004).

Walker, Barbara G., *The Woman's Encyclopedia of Myths and Secrets* (San Francisco, CA: Harper Collins, 1983).

Updike, John, *Americana: and Other Poems* (New York, NY: Knopf, 2001).

Secondary

Akass, Kim and Janet McCabe, 'Ms Parker and the Vicious Circle: Female Narrative and Humour in *Sex and the City*', in Akass and McCabe (eds), *Reading Sex and the City* (London: I.B. Tauris, 2006), pp. 177–200.

Allan, Keith and Kate Burridge, *Forbidden Words: Taboo and the Censoring of Language* (Cambridge: Cambridge University Press, 2006).

Angier, Natalie, *Woman: An Intimate Geography* (New York, NY: Anchor Books, 1999).

Atwood, Craig D., 'Deep in the Side of Jesus', in *Pious Pursuits: German Moravians in the Atlantic World*, ed. Michelle Gillespie and Robert Beachy (Oxford: Berghahn Books, 2007), pp. 40–64.

Badran, Margot, *Feminism in Islam: Secular and Religious Convergences* (Oxford: Oneworld, 2009).

Bal, Mieke, 'Head Hunting "Judith" on the Cutting Edge of Knowledge', in Athalya Brenner (ed.), *A Feminist Companion to Esther, Judith and Susanna* (The Feminist Companion to the Bible, 7. Sheffield: Sheffield Academic Press, 1995), pp. 253–85.

Barr, William R., 'Brakhage: Artistic Development in Two Childbirth Films', in Brian Henderson and Ann Martin with Lee Amazonas (eds), *Film Quarterly: Forty Years, A Selection* (Berkeley, CA: University of California Press), pp. 536–41.

Barthes, Roland, 'Deux Femmes/Two Women', *Artemisia*, an issue of *Mot Pour Mot/Word For Word*, 2 (Paris: Yvon Lambert Gallery, 1979), pp. 8–13.

Barton, John and John Muddiman (eds), *The Oxford Bible Commentary* (Oxford: Oxford University Press, 2001).

Bataille, Georges, 'The College of Sociology', in *Visions of Excess: Selected Writings, 1927–1939*, ed. and trans. Allan Stoekl, *Theory and History of Literature, Volume 14* (Minneapolis, MN: University of Minnesota, 1985), pp. 246–56.

Benedict, Ruth, *Zuni Mythology* (New York, NY: Columbia University Press, 1935).

Blackledge, Catherine, *The Story of V: Opening Pandora's Box* (London: Weidenfeld & Nicolson, 2003).

Blake, Norman F., 'Nonstandard Language in Early Varieties of English', in Irma Taavitsainen, Gunnel Melchers and Päivi Pahta (eds), *Writing in Nonstandard English* (Philadelphia, PA: John Benjamins, 1999), pp. 123–50.

Bloch, R. Howard, 'Modest Maidens and Modified Nouns: Obscenity in the Fabliaux', in Jan M. Ziolkowski (ed.), *Obscenity: Social Control and Artistic Creation in the European Middle Ages* (Leiden: Koninklijke Brill, 1998), pp. 293–307.

Blocker, Jane, *What the Body Cost: Desire, History and Performance* (Minneapolis, MN: University of Minnesota Press, 2004).

Bobel, Chris, *New Blood: Third-Wave Feminism and the Politics of Menstruation* (New Brunswick, NJ: Rutgers University Press, 2010).

Boyle, Karen (ed.), *Everyday Pornography* (Abingdon: Routledge, 2010).

Broude, Norma and Mary D. Garrard (eds), *The Power of Feminist Art: Emergence, Impact and Triumph of the American Feminist Art Movement* (London: Thames and Hudson, 1994).

Burns, E. Jane, 'This Prick Which is Not One: How Women Talk Back in Old French Fabliaux', in Linda Lomperis and Sarah Stanbury (eds), *Feminist Approaches to the Body in Medieval Literature* (Philadelphia, PA: University of Pennsylvania Press, 1993), pp. 188–212.

— *Bodytalk: When Women Speak in Old French Literature* (Philadelphia, PA: University of Pennsylvania Press, 1993).

Butler, Judith, 'Imitation and Gender Subordination', in Henry Abelove, Michèle Aina Barale and David M. Halperin, *The Lesbian and Gay Studies Reader* (London: Routledge, 1993), pp. 307–20.

Caputi, Jane, *The Age of Sex Crime* (Bowling Green, KY: Popular Press, 1987).

— *Goddesses and Monsters: Women, Myth, Power and Popular Culture* (Bowling Green, KY: Popular Press, 2004).

Carr, Pat and Willard Gingerich, 'The Vagina Dentata Motif in Nahuatl and Pueblo Mythic Narratives: A Comparative Study', in Brian Swann (ed.), *Smoothing the Ground: Essays on Native American Oral Literature* (Berkeley, CA: University of California Press, 1983), pp. 187–203.

Castle, Terry, *The Apparitional Lesbian: Female Homosexuality and Modern Culture* (New York, NY: Columbia University Press, 1995).

Chicago, Judy, *The Dinner Party: from Creation to Preservation* (London: Merrell, 2007).

— *The Birth Project* (New York, NY: Doubleday & Co, 1985).

Clements, Jessica, 'The Origin of the World: Women's Bodies and Agency in Childbirth', unpublished Master of Fine Arts thesis, George Mason University, Fairfax, VA, 2009.

Cook, Elizabeth, *Epistolary Bodies: Gender and Genre in the Eighteenth-Century Republic of Letters* (Stanford, CA: Stanford University Press, 1996).

Cottingham, Laura, 'Eating from the *Dinner Party* Plates and Other Myths, Metaphors and Moments of Lesbian Enunciation in Feminism and Its Art Movement' in Amelia Jones (ed.), *Sexual Politics: Judy Chicago's 'Dinner Party' in Feminist Art History* (Berkeley, CA: University of California Press, 1996), pp. 208–28.

Coxon, Sebastian, *Laughter and Narrative in the Later Middle Ages: German Comic Tales 1350–1525* (London: MHRA Legenda, 2008).

Creed, Barbara, *The Monstrous Feminine: Film, Feminism, Psychoanalysis* (London: Routledge, 1993).

D'Arcy, Chantal Cornut-Gentille, '"The Personal is Political" in Caryl Churchill's *Top Girls*: a Parable for the Feminist Movement in Thatcher's Britain', in Susanna Onega (ed.), *Telling Histories: Narrativizing History, Historicizing Literature*, Costerus New Series 96 (Amsterdam: Rodopi, 1995), pp. 103–15.

de Saussure, Ferdinand, *Course in General Linguistics*, trans. Wade Baskin; ed. Perry Meisel and Haun Saussy (New York, NY: Columbia University Press, 2011).

de Silva, David A., *Introducing the Apocrypha: Message, Context and Significance* (Ada, MI: Baker Academic, 2002).

Dijkstra, Bram, *Idols of Perversity: Fantasies of Feminine Evil in Fin-de-Siècle Culture* (Oxford: Oxford University Press, 1986).

Dittmer, Wilhelm, *Te Tohunga: The Ancient Legends and Traditions of the Maoris* (London: G. Routledge, 1907).

Douglas, Mary, *Natural Symbols: Explorations in Cosmology* (Harmondsworth: Penguin, 1973).

Drenth, Jelto, *The Origin of the World: Science and Fiction of the Vagina* (London: Reaktion Books, 2004).

Dweck, Alyssa and Robin Westen, *V is for Vagina: Your A-to-Z Guide to Periods, Piercings, Pleasures and so Much More* (Berkeley, CA: Ulysses Press, 2012).

Edwards, Gwynne, *A Companion to Luis Buñuel* (Woodbridge: Tamesis, 2005).

Ekwall, Eilert, *Street-Names of the City of London* (Oxford: Clarendon, 1965).

— *The Concise Oxford Dictionary of English Place-Names* (Oxford: Clarendon, 1936).

Evenson, Brian, *Understanding Robert Coover* (Columbia, SC: University of South Carolina Press, 2003).

Federman, Raymond, *Critifiction: Postmodern Essays* (Albany, NY: SUNY Press, 1993).

Finley, Karen, interview with Andrea Juno, in Andrea Juno and V. Vale (eds), *Angry Women* (San Francisco, CA: Re/search Publications, 1991), pp. 41–9.

Foucault, Michel, *Discipline and Punish: The Role of the Prison*, trans. Michael Sheridan (New York, NY: Random House, 1995).

— *The History of Sexuality*, Vol. 1 (Harmondsworth: Penguin, 1990).

Fowler, James, *Voicing Desire: Family and Sexuality in Diderot's Narrative* (Oxford: Voltaire Foundation, 2000).

France, Peter, *Rhetoric and Truth in France: Descartes to Diderot* (Oxford: Clarendon Press, 1972).

Friedan, Betty, *The Feminine Mystique* (Harmondsworth: Penguin, 1965).

Fuentes, Victor, *Buñuel: cine y literatura*, as translated and quoted in Tatjana Pavlović, Inmaculada Alvarez, Rosana Blanco Cano, Anita Grisales, Alejandra Osorio and Alejandra Sánchez, *100 Years of Spanish Cinema* (Oxford: Wiley-Blackwell, 2009).

Furbank, P. N., *Diderot: A Critical Biography* (London: Secker & Warburg, 1992).

Gallop, Jane, *Thinking Through The Body* (New York, NY: Columbia University Press, 1988).

Garber, Marjorie, 'Spare Parts: The Surgical Construction of Gender', in Henry Abelove, Michèle Aina Barale and David M. Halperin, *The Lesbian and Gay Studies Reader* (London: Routledge, 1993), pp. 321–36.

Genette, Gérard, *Narrative Discourse*, trans. Jane E. Lewin (Oxford: Blackwell, 1980).

Green, Jonathon, *The Cassell Dictionary of Slang* (London: Cassell, 1998).

Greene, Sheila, *The Psychological Development of Girls and Women: Rethinking Change in Time* (East Sussex: Routledge, 2003).

Greer, Germaine, *The Whole Woman* (London: Doubleday, 1999).

Gutiérrez-Albilla, Julián Daniel, *Queering Buñuel: Sexual Dissidence and Psychoanalysis in his Mexican and Spanish Cinema* (London: I.B. Tauris, 2008).

Harris, Oliver, *William Burroughs and the Secret of Fascination* (Carbondale, IL: Southern Illinois University Press, 2003).

Henry, Astrid, 'Orgasms and Empowerment: *Sex and the City* and the Third Wave Feminism', in Kim Akass and Janet McCabe (eds), *Reading Sex and the City* (London: I.B. Tauris, 2006), pp. 65–82.

Herbenick, Debby, and Vanessa Schick, *Read My Lips: A Complete Guide to the Vagina and Vulva* (Lanham, MD: Rowman and Littlefield, 2011).

Hirsi Ali, Ayaan, *The Caged Virgin: An Emancipation Proclamation for Women and Islam* (New York, NY: Free Press, 2006).

Holmes, Morgan, *Intersex: A Perilous Difference* (Cranbury, NJ: Associated University Presses, 2008).

Hooijer, Katinka, 'Vulvodynia: On the Medicinal Purposes of Porn', in Merri Lisa Johnson (ed.), *Jane Sexes It Up: True Confessions of Feminist Desire* (New York, NY: Four Walls Eight Windows, 2002), pp. 259–80.

Hopkins, Henry T., 'Foreword' in Amelia Jones (ed.), *Sexual Politics: Judy Chicago's 'Dinner Party' in Feminist Art History* (Berkeley, CA: University of California Press, 1996), p. 10.

Houppert, Karen, *The Curse. Confronting the Last Unmentionable Taboo: Menstruation* (London: Profile Books, 2000).

Hughes, Geoffrey, *Swearing: A Social History of Foul Language, Oaths and Profanity in English* (London: Penguin, 1998).

Hurley, Kelly, 'Reading Like an Alien: Posthuman Identity in Ridley Scott's *Alien* and David Cronenberg's *Rabid*', in Judith Halberstam and Ira Livingston (eds), *Posthuman Bodies* (Bloomington, IN: Indiana University Press, 1996), pp. 203–24.

Irigaray, Luce, *Speculum of the Other Woman*, trans. Gillian C. Gill (New York, NY: Cornell University Press, 1985).

— *This Sex Which is Not One*, trans. Catherine Porter (New York, NY: Cornell University Press, 1985).

— 'When Our Lips Speak Together', reprinted in Janet Price and Margrit Shildrick (eds), *Feminist Theory and the Body: A Reader* (New York, NY: Routledge, 1999), pp. 82–90.

Israel, Jonathan I., *Enlightenment Contested: Philosophy, Modernity and the Emancipation of Man 1670–1752* (Oxford: Oxford University Press, 2006).

Jackson, Kenneth, *Studies in Early Celtic Nature Poetry* (Cambridge: Cambridge University Press, 1935).

Jeffreys, Sheila, *The Industrial Vagina: The Political Economy of the Global Sex Trade* (Abingdon: Routledge, 2009).

Jones, Amelia, 'Interpreting Feminist Bodies: the Unframeability of Desire', in Paul Duro (ed.), *The Rhetoric of the Frame* (Cambridge: Cambridge University Press, 1997), pp. 223–41.

— 'Sexual Politics: Feminist Strategies, Feminist Conflicts, Feminist Histories', in Amelia Jones (ed.), *Sexual Politics: Judy Chicago's 'Dinner Party' in Feminist Art History* (Berkeley, CA: University of California Press, 1996), pp. 20–38.

— 'The "Sexual Politics" of *The Dinner Party*: A Critical Context', in Amelia Jones (ed.), *Sexual Politics: Judy Chicago's 'Dinner Party' in Feminist Art History* (Berkeley, CA: University of California Press, 1996), pp. 82–118.

— 'Lost Bodies: Early 1970s Los Angeles Performance Art in Art History', in Peggy Phelan (ed.), *Live Art in LA: Performance in Southern California, 1970–1983* (Abingdon: Routledge, 2012), pp. 115–84.

Jones, Ruth Felker, *Marks of His Wounds: Gender Politics and Bodily Resurrection* (Oxford: Oxford University Press, 2007).

Kadden, Barbara Binder, and Bruce Kadden, *Teaching Mitzvot: Concepts, Values and Activities* (Denver, CO: A.R.E. Publishing, 2003).

Kandel, Susan, 'Beneath the Green Veil: The Body in/of New Feminist Art', in Amelia Jones (ed.), *Sexual Politics: Judy Chicago's 'Dinner Party' in Feminist Art History* (Berkeley, CA: University of California Press, 1996), pp. 186–200.

Kapsalis, Terri, *Public Privates: Performing Gynecology from Both Ends of the Speculum* (Durham, NC: Duke University Press, 1997).

Karetnikova, Inga, *How Scripts Are Made* (Carbondale, IL: Southern Illinois University, 1990).

Karkazis, Katrina, *Fixing Sex: Intersex, Medical Authority and Lived Experience* (Durham, NC: Duke University Press, 2008).

Kavanagh, Thomas M., 'Language as Deception: Diderot's *Les Bijoux Indiscrets*', in Otis Fellow and Diana Guiragossian Carr (eds), *Diderot Studies XXIII* (Geneva: Librairie Droz, 1988), pp. 101–14.

Kennedy, Randall, *Nigger: The Strange Career of a Troublesome Word* (New York, NY: Random House, 2003).

Kristeva, Julia, *Powers of Horror: An Essay on Abjection*, trans. Leon S. Roudiez (New York, NY: Columbia University Press, 1982).

— *Strangers to Ourselves*, trans. Leon S. Roudiez (New York, NY: Columbia University Press, 1991).

Kubitza, Anette, 'Rereading the Readings of *The Dinner Party* in Europe', in Amelia Jones (ed.), *Sexual Politics: Judy Chicago's 'Dinner Party' in Feminist Art History* (Berkeley, CA: University of California Press, 1996), pp. 148–76.

Lacan, Jacques, 'The mirror stage as formative of the function of the I as revealed in psychoanalytic experience', delivered at the 16th International Congress of Psychoanalysis, Zurich, 17 July 1949, from Jacques Lacan, *Écrits: A Selection*, trans. Alan Sheridan (New York, NY: W.W. Norton, 1977).

— *Écrits: A Selection*, trans. Alan Sheridan (London: Routledge, 2001).

— *The Four Fundamental Concepts of Psycho-Analysis* (The Seminar of Jacques Lacan, Book XI), ed. Jacques-Alain Miller, trans. Alan Sheridan (New York, NY: Norton, 1998).

Lapidge, Michael, *Anglo-Latin Literature, 600–899* (London: Hambledon, 1996).

Levine, Amy-Jill, 'Sacrifice and Salvation: Otherness and Domestication in the *Book of Judith*', in Athalya Brenner (ed.), *A Feminist Companion to Esther, Judith and Susanna*

(The Feminist Companion to the Bible, 7. Sheffield: Sheffield Academic Press, 1995), pp. 209–23.

Levy, Brian J., *The Comic Text: Patterns and Images in the Old French Fabliaux* (Amsterdam: Rodopi, 2000).

Livoti, Carol and Elizabeth Topp, *Vaginas: An Owner's Manual* (London: Fusion Press, 2005).

Lunch, Lydia, interview with Andrea Juno and V. Vale, in Andrea Juno and V. Vale (eds), *Angry Women* (San Francisco, CA: Re/search Publications, 1991), pp. 105–17.

Malotki, Ekkehart, 'The Story of the "Tsimonmamant" or Jimson Weed Girls: A Hopi Narrative Featuring the Motif of the Vagina Dentata', in Brian Swann (ed.), *Smoothing the Ground: Essays on Native American Oral Literature* (Berkeley, CA: University of California Press, 1983), pp. 204–20.

May, Kerstin, *Art and Obscenity* (London: I.B. Tauris, 2007).

McEnery, Tony, *Swearing in English: Bad Language, Purity and Power from 1586 to the Present* (London: Routledge, 2006).

McGlynn, Clare, 'Marginalizing Feminism? Debating Extreme Pornography Laws in Public and Policy Discourse', in Karen Boyle (ed.), *Everyday Pornography* (Abingdon: Routledge, 2010), pp. 190–202.

Meyer, Laura, 'From Finish Fetish to Feminism: Judy Chicago's *Dinner Party* in California Art History', in Amelia Jones (ed.), *Sexual Politics: Judy Chicago's 'Dinner Party' in Feminist Art History* (Berkeley, CA: University of California Press, 1996), pp. 48–74.

Michelson, Peter, *Speaking the Unspeakable: A Poetics of Obscenity* (Albany, NY: State University of New York Press, 1993).

Miles, Margaret, 'Carnal Abominations: The Female Body as Grotesque', in James Luther Adams and Wilson Yates (eds), *The Grotesque in Art and Literature: Theological Reflections* (Grand Rapids, MI: Eerdmans, 1997), pp. 83–112.

Miles, Rosalind, *Who Cooked the Last Supper?* (New York, NY: Three Rivers Press, 2001).

Miller, Nancy K., *French Dressing: Women, Men and Ancien Régime Fiction* (London: Routledge, 1995).

Miller Graham, Mark, 'Creation Imagery in the Goldwork of Costa Rica, Panama and Colombia', in Jeffrey Quilter and John W. Hoopes (eds), *Gold and Power in Ancient Costa Rica, Panama and Colombia* (Washington, DC: Dumbarton Oaks Research Library and Collection, 2003), pp. 279–300.

Montagu, Ashley, *The Anatomy of Swearing* (London: Rapp and Whiting, 1967).

Montano, Linda, interview with Andrea Juno, in Andrea Juno and V. Vale (eds), *Angry Women* (San Francisco, CA: Re/search Publications, 1991), pp. 50–65.

Moran, Joe, *Star Authors: Literary Celebrity in America* (London: Pluto Press, 2000).

Morel, Jacinthe, 'De la Curiosité dans *Les Bijoux Indiscrets*: Propositions de lecture', in Otis Fellow and Diana Guiragossian Carr (eds), *Diderot Studies XXV* (Geneva: Lirairie Droz, 1993), pp. 75–88.

Morton, Mark, *The Lover's Tongue: A Merry Romp through the Language of Love and Sex* (Ontario: Insomniac Press, 2003).

Murphy, Timothy S., *Wising up the Marks: The Amodern William Burroughs* (Berkeley, CA: University of California Press, 1997).

Muscatine, Charles, 'The Fabliaux, Courtly Culture and the (Re)Invention of Vulgarity', in Jan M. Ziolkowski (ed.), *Obscenity: Social Control and Artistic Creation in the European Middle Ages* (Leiden: Koninklijke Brill, 1998), pp. 281–92.

Muscio, Inga, *Cunt: A Declaration of Independence* (New York, NY: Seal Press, 2002).

Nead, Lynda, *The Female Nude: Art, Obscenity and Sexuality* (London: Routledge, 1994).

Newman, Karen, *Fetal Positions: Individualism, Science, Visuality* (Stanford, CA: Stanford University Press, 1996).

Odelain, O., and R. Séguineau, *Dictionary of Proper Names and Places in the Bible,* trans. Matthew J. O'Connell (London: Robert Hale, 1982).

Oliphant, Thomas, *The Old and Middle English* (London: Macmillan, 1878).

O'Reilly, Sally, *The Body in Contemporary Art* (London: Thames and Hudson, 2009).

Parker, Rozsika and Griselda Pollock, *Old Mistresses: Women, Art and Ideology* (New York, NY: Pantheon, 1981).

Pearcy, Roy J., *Logic and Humour in the Fabliaux: an Essay in Applied Narratology* (Cambridge: D. S. Brewer, 2007).

Peterson, James, *Dreams of Chaos, Visions of Order: Understanding the American Avant-Garde Cinema* (Detroit, MI: Wayne State University Press, 1994).

Phillips, Anne, *Culture and Gender* (Cambridge: Polity, 2010).

Pointon, Marcia, *Brilliant Effects: A Cultural History of Gem Stones and Jewellery* (New Haven, CT: Yale University Press, 2009).

Pollock, Griselda, *Differencing the Canon: Feminist Desire and the Writing of Art's Histories* (Abingdon: Routledge, 1999).

— *Vision and Difference: Femininity, Feminism and the Histories of Art* (New York, NY: Routledge, 1988).

Pollock, Sheldon, 'Cosmopolitan and Vernacular in History', in Carol A. Breckenridge, Sheldon Pollock, Homi K. Bhabha and Dipesh Chakrabarty (eds), *Cosmopolitanism* (Durham, NC: Duke University Press, 2002), pp. 15–53.

Prescott, Peter S., *Encounters with American Culture, Volume 2 (1973–1985)* (New Brunswick, NJ: Transaction Publishers, 2006).

Prioreschi, Plinio, *Medieval Medicine* (A History of Medicine, Vol. v – Medieval Medicine. Omaha, NE: Horatius, 2003).

Pucci, Suzanne Rodin, 'The Discrete Charms of the Exotic: Fictions of the Harem in Eighteenth-Century France', in G. S. Rousseau and Roy Porter (eds), *Exoticism in the Enlightenment* (Manchester: Manchester University Press, 1990), pp. 145–75.

Rees, Emma L. E., 'Sheela's Voracity and Victorian Veracity', in Liz Herbert McAvoy and Teresa Walters (eds), *Consuming Narratives: Gender and Monstrous Appetite in the Middle Ages and the Renaissance* (Cardiff: University of Wales Press, 2002), pp. 116–27.

— 'Cordelia's Can't: Rhetorics of Reticence and (Dis)ease in *King Lear*', in Jennifer C. Vaught (ed.), *Rhetorics of Bodily Disease and Health in Medieval and Early Modern England* (Surrey: Ashgate, 2010), pp. 105–16.

Ring, Nancy, 'Identifying with Judy Chicago', in Amelia Jones (ed.), *Sexual Politics: Judy Chicago's 'Dinner Party' in Feminist Art History* (Berkeley, CA: University of California Press, 1996), pp. 126–40.

Roald, Anne Sofie, *Women in Islam: The Western Experience* (London: Routledge, 2001).

Robinson, Hilary, *Reading Art, Reading Irigaray: The Politics of Art by Women* (London: I.B. Tauris, 2006).

Robb, Graham, *Balzac: A Biography* (London: W. W. Norton, 1994).

Róheim, Géza, *Fire in the Dragon and Other Psychoanalytic Essays on Folklore*, ed. Alan Dundes (Princeton, NJ: Princeton University Press, 1992).

Schneemann, Carolee, interview with Andrea Juno, in Andrea Juno and V. Vale (eds), *Angry Women* (San Francisco, CA: Re/search Publications, 1991), pp. 66–77.

Schneider, Rebecca, *The Explicit Body in Performance* (London: Routledge, 1997).

Sheidlower, Jesse (ed.), *The F-Word: The Complete History of the Word in all its Robust and Various Uses* (London: Faber and Faber, 1999).

Showalter, Elaine, *The Female Malady: Women, Madness and English Culture, 1830–1980* (London: Virago, 1987).

Sigel, Lisa Z., *Governing Pleasures: Pornography and Social Change in England, 1815–1914* (New Brunswick, NJ: Rutgers University Press, 2002).

Silverman, Kaja, *The Acoustic Mirror: The Female Voice in Psychoanalysis and Cinema* (Bloomington, IN: Indiana University Press, 1988).

Silverton, Peter, *Filthy English: The How, Why, When and What of Everyday Swearing* (London: Portobello Books, 2009).

Simon, Ron, 'Sex and the City', in Gary R. Edgerton and Jeffrey P. Jones (eds), *The Essential HBO Reader* (Lexington, KY: The University Press of Kentucky, 2008), pp. 193–203.

Smith, J. C., and Carla J. Ferstman, *The Castration of Oedipus: Feminism, Psychoanalysis and the Will to Power* (New York, NY: New York University, 1996).

Sonnendecker, E. W. W., 'Menopause', in T. F. Kruger and M. H. Botha (eds), *Clinical Gynaecology* (Cape Town: Juta and Co., 2007), pp. 332–52.

Spiro, Melford E., 'The Internalisation of Gender Identity', in L. Bryce Boyer and Simon A. Grolnick (eds), *The Psychoanalytic Study of Society*, Vol. 15, *Essays in Honour of Melford E. Spiro* (London: Routledge, 1990), pp. 45–68.

Sprinkle, Annie, *Post-Porn Modernist: My 25 Years as a Multimedia Whore* (San Francisco, CA: Cleis Press, 1998).

— interview with Andrea Juno, in Andrea Juno and V. Vale (eds), *Angry Women* (San Francisco, CA: Re/search Publications, 1991), pp. 23–40.

Steinem, Gloria, 'Foreword', in Eve Ensler, *The Vagina Monologues* (London: Virago, 2001), pp. ix–xix.

Stocker, Margarita, *Judith: Sexual Warrior, Women and Power in Western Culture* (New Haven, CT: Yale University Press, 1998).

Stamelman, Richard Howard, *Lost Beyond Telling: Representations of Death and Absence in Modern French Poetry* (Ithaca, NY: Cornell University Press, 1990).

Straayer, Chris, 'The Seduction of Boundaries: Feminist Fluidity in Annie Sprinkle's Art/Education/Sex', in Pamela Church Gibson (ed.), *More Dirty Looks: Gender, Pornography, Power* (London: BFI, 2004), pp. 224–36.

Swinnerton, Jo, *The London Companion* (London: Think, 2004).

Tone, Andrea, 'Contraceptive Consumers', in Elizabeth Reis (ed.), *American Sexual Histories* (Oxford: Wiley-Blackwell, 2012), pp. 247–69.

Ussher, Jane M., *Managing the Monstrous Feminine: Regulating the Reproductive Body* (London: Routledge, 2006).

Vanderheyden, Jennifer, *The Function of the Dream and the Body in Diderot's Works* (*The Age of Revolution and Romanticism: Interdisciplinary Studies*) (New York, NY: Peter Lang, 2004).

van Henten, Jan Willem, 'Judith as Alternative Leader: A Rereading of *Judith* 7–23', in Athalya Brenner (ed.), *A Feminist Companion to Esther, Judith and Susanna* (The Feminist Companion to the Bible, 7. Sheffield: Sheffield Academic Press, 1995), pp. 224–52.

Wajnryb, Ruth, *Language Most Foul: A Good Look at Bad Language* (Sydney: Allen and Unwin, 2005; republished in the United States as *Expletive Deleted: A Good Look at Bad Language* (New York, NY: Free Press, 2005); appeared in the United Kingdom as *C U Next Tuesday. A Good Look at Bad Language* (London: Aurum, 2004)).

Werner, Stephen, *The Comic Diderot: A Reading of the Fictions* (Birmingham, AL: Summa, 2000).

Wilding, Faith, 'Vulvas with a Difference', in Maria Fernandez, Faith Wilding and Michelle M. Wright, *Domain Errors! Cyberfeminist Practices* (New York, NY: Autonomedia, 2002. A subRosa project), pp. 149–60.

Williams, Gordon, *A Dictionary of Sexual Language and Imagery in Shakespearean and Stuart Literature* (London: The Athlone Press, 1994).

Williams, Linda, *Hard Core: Power, Pleasure and the 'Frenzy of the Visible'* (Berkeley, CA: University of California Press, 1999).

Williamson, Marianne, 'Living Her Best Life', in Deborah Davis (ed.), *The Oprah Winfrey Show: Reflections on an American Legacy*, (New York, NY: Harry N. Abrams, 2011), pp. 128–9.

Wolf, Naomi, *Vagina: A New Biography* (London: Virago, 2012).

Wood, Julia T., *Gendered Lives: Communication, Gender & Culture* (Boston, MA: Wadsworth, 2009).

Zimmerman, Jonathan, 'Where the Customer is King: The Textbook in American Culture', in David Paul Nord, Joan Shelley Rubin and Michael Schudson (eds), *The Enduring Book: Print Culture in Postwar America*, Vol. 5 of *A History of the Book in America* (Chapel Hill, NC: University of North Carolina Press, 2009), pp. 304–24.

Žižek, Slavoj, *Organs Without Bodies: On Deleuze and Consequences* (London: Routledge, 2004).

— *How to Read Lacan* (London: Granta, 2006).

Journal articles

Acker, Kathy, 'A Few Notes on Two of my Books', in Ellen G. Friedman and Miriam Fuchs (eds), *The Review of Contemporary Fiction: Kathy Acker, Christine Brooke-Rose and Marguerite Young*, 9.3 (1989), pp. 31–6.

Anon, 'Dr Johnson at Oxford, and Lichfield', in 'Sylvanus Urban' (ed.), *The Gentleman's Magazine and Historical Chronicle*, Vol. 55 (London, January 1785), p. 288.

Arthurs, Jane, '*Sex and the City* and Consumer Culture: Remediating Postfeminist Drama', *Feminist Media Studies*, 3.1 (2003), pp. 83–98.

Braun, Virginia, 'Breaking a Taboo? Talking (and Laughing) about the Vagina', *Feminism and Psychology*, 9.3 (1999), pp. 367–72.

— 'In Search of (Better) Sexual Pleasure: Female Genital "Cosmetic" Surgery', *Sexualities* 8.4 (2005), pp. 407–24.

— in conversation with Eve Ensler, 'Public Talk about "Private Parts"', *Feminism and Psychology* 9.4 (1999), pp. 515–22.

Braun, V. and S. Wilkinson, 'Socio-Cultural Representations of the Vagina', *Journal of Reproductive and Infant Psychology*, 19.1 (2001), pp. 17–32.

Briggs, Keith, 'OE and ME *cunte* in Place-Names', *Journal of the English Place-Name Society*, 41 (2009), 26–39.

Broomhall, Susan, 'Rabelais, the Pursuit of Knowledge, and Early Modern Gynaecology', *Limina*, 4, (1998), pp. 24–34.

Cixous, Hélène, 'The Laugh of the Medusa', trans. K. and P. Cohen, *Signs: A Journal of Women in Culture and Society* 1.4 (1976), pp. 875–93.

Clune, Michael, 'Blood Money: Sovereignty and Exchange in Kathy Acker', *Contemporary Literature* XLV, 3 (2004), pp. 486–515.

Cooper, Christine M., 'Worrying about Vaginas: Feminism and Eve Ensler's *The Vagina Monologues*', *Signs*, 32.3 (Spring 2007), pp. 727–58.

Cottingham, Laura, 'Interview with Zoe Leonard', *Journal of Contemporary Art*, 6.1 (Summer 1993), pp. 64–77, www.jca-online.com/leonard.html.

Dunham, Judith L., '"Dinner Party" Aftertaste', *Artweek*, 10 (25 August 1979).

Fairman, Christopher M., 'Fuck' (March 2006), pp. 1–74. Ohio State Public Law Working Paper No. 59; Center for Interdisciplinary Law and Policy Studies Working Paper Series No. 39. Available at SSRN: http://ssrn.com/abstract=896790 or http://dx.doi.org/10.2139/ssrn.896790.

Firth, J. R., 'A Synopsis of Linguistic Theory, 1930–1955', *Studies in Linguistic Analysis* (1957), pp. 1–32.

Gallo, Jacquelyn, 'Kembra Pfahler and the Girls of Karen Black: *The Wall of Vagina*', *Artcritical: The Online Magazine of Art and Ideas*, 27 June 2011. www.artcritical.com/2011/07/09/wall-of-vagina/.

Gerhard, Jane, '*Sex and the City*: Carrie Bradshaw's Queer Postfeminism', *Feminist Media Studies*, 5.1 (2005), pp. 37–49.

Hawkins, Susan E., 'All in the Family: Kathy Acker's *Blood and Guts in High School*', *Contemporary Literature* XLV, 4 (2004), pp. 637–58.

Hume, Kathryn, 'Voice in Kathy Acker's Fiction', *Contemporary Literature*, 42.3 (Autumn 2001), pp. 485–513.

Jones, Amelia, 'Power and Feminist (Art) History' (Review Article), *Art History* 18.3 (September 1995), pp. 435–43.

Juhasz, Alexandra, 'It's about Autonomy, Stupid: Sexuality in Feminist Video', *Sexualities* 2.3 (1999), pp. 333–41.

Lee, Janet, 'Menarche and the (Hetero)Sexualisation of the Female Body', *Gender and Society* 8.3 (September 1994), pp. 343–62.

Mahoney, Maureen A., 'The Problem of Silence in Feminist Psychology', *Feminist Studies* 22.3 (1996), pp. 603–25.

Martindale, Kym, 'Author(iz)ing the Body: Monique Wittig, *The Lesbian Body* and the Anatomy Texts of Andreas Vesalius', *The European Journal of Women's Studies* 8.3 (2001), pp. 343–56.

McMinn, Dr Samuel N., 'Insanity Cured by the Excision of the External Organs of Generation', *The Boston Medical and Surgical Journal*, Vol. Xxxii No. 7, Wednesday (19 March 1845), pp. 131–2.

Meyer, Laura, with Faith Wilding, 'Collaboration and Conflict in the Fresno Feminist Art Program: An Experiment in Feminist Pedagogy', *n.paradoxa: International Feminist Art Journal*, 26 (July 2010), pp. 40–51.

Nochlin, Linda, 'Courbet's "L'origine du monde": The Origin Without an Original', *October*, 37 (Summer 1986), pp. 76–86.

O'Connell, Helen, K. V. Sanjeevan and J. M. Hutson, 'Anatomy of the Clitoris', *Journal of Urology*, 174 (October 2005), pp. 1189–95.

Pointon, Marcia, 'Artemisia Gentileschi's *The Murder of Holofernes*', *American Imago*, 38.4 (Winter 1981), pp. 343–67.

Raitt, Jill, 'The *Vagina Dentata* and the *Immaculatus Uterus Divini Fontis*', *Journal of the American Academy of Religion* 48.3 (September 1980), pp. 415–31.

Rian, Jeff, 'What's all this Body Art?' *Flash Art* 26 (January–February 1993), pp. 50–3.

Sciolino, Martina, 'Kathy Acker and the Postmodern Subject of Feminism', *College English*, 52.4 (April 1990), pp. 437–45.

Tanguy, Sarah, 'The Progress of *Big Man*: A Conversation with Ron Mueck' in *Sculpture: A Publication of the International Sculpture Center*, 22.6 (July/August 2003), n.p., www.sculpture.org/documents/scmag03/jul_aug03/mueck/mueck.shtml.

Thorogood, Nicki, 'Mouthrules and the Construction of Sexual Identities', *Sexualities* 3.2 (2000), pp. 165–82.

Tickner, Lisa, 'The Body Politic: Female Sexuality and Women Artists since 1970', *Art History* 1.2 (June 1978), pp. 236–49.

Elwin, Verrier, 'The Vagina Dentata Legend', *The British Journal of Medical Psychology*, 19.3–4 (June 1943), pp. 439–53.

Walker Read, Allen, 'An Obscenity Symbol', *American Speech*, 9.4 (December 1934), pp. 264–78.

Wang, Michael, 'Mother's Courage', *Artforum*, 5 July 2005, www.artforum.com/diary/id=9212.

Wilding, Faith, 'How the West was Won: Feminist Art in California', *Women Artists News*, 6.2&3 (Summer 1980), pp. 15–16.

Williams, Linda, 'A Provoking Agent: The Pornography and Performance Art of Annie Sprinkle', *Social Text*, 37 (Winter 1993), pp. 117–33.

Newspaper articles

Bisset, Suzanne, 'Growing Pains: Is Birth Art's Last Taboo?' *Venue* (26 June–10 July 1998).

'Britain Must End This Horrific Mutilation', Leader, *The Sunday Times* (22 April 2012).

Brinton, Jessica, 'David Matlock, aka Dr Sex, Can "Fix" You Down There', *Sunday Times* 'Style' Magazine (20 June 2008).

Brooks, Richard, 'Last Taboo Broken by Sex and the C***', *The Observer* (14 February, 1999): www.guardian.co.uk/uk/1999/feb/14/richardbrooks.theobserver.

Coren, Victoria, 'Keep our curses in rude health', *The Observer* (27 May 2012).

David, Keren, and Mark Rowe, 'Birth Paintings Get a Queasy Reception', *The Independent on Sunday* (6 July 1997): www.independent.co.uk/news/birth-paintings-get-a-queasy-reception-1249258.html.

Deveny, Kathleen, 'Why the C Word Is Losing Its Bite: Rethinking the Most Taboo Term in English', *Daily Beast* (as an archived *Newsweek* article), 29 August 2009, www.thedailybeast.com/newsweek/2009/08/28/why-the-c-word-is-losing-its-bite.html.

Dowd, Maureen, 'Oprah's Bunk Club', *New York Times* (28 January 2006).

Gold, Tanya, 'Sorry sisters, but I Hate *Sex and the City*', *The Telegraph* (21 May 2010): www.telegraph.co.uk/culture/film/7746119/Sorry-sisters-but-I-hate-Sex-and-the-City.html.

Greene, David, 'Nether Nether Land', *Los Angeles Reader* (17 June 1994).

Harris, Gareth, 'Chris Ofili's The Holy Virgin Mary Returns to London', *The Telegraph* (28 January 2010): www.telegraph.co.uk/culture/art/art-news/7093216/Chris-Ofilis-The-Holy-Virgin-Mary-returns-to-London.html.

Haslam, Nicky, 'Getting a Kick', review of Geoffrey Mark, *Ethel Merman*, in *The Spectator* (9 February 2008).

Kennedy, Maev, 'Library Show for Word Rhyming with Hunt', *The Guardian* (23 October 2004): www.guardian.co.uk/uk/2004/oct/23/education.arts?INTCMP=ILCNETTXT3487.

Kramer, Hilton, 'Judy Chicago's "Dinner Party" Comes to Brooklyn Museum', *New York Times* (17 October 1980), Late City Final Edition. Available at: http://grammarpolice. net.archives/001194.php.

Leitch, Luke, 'Workers 'C' Red over Word-Play at Library', *The Evening Standard* (22 October 2004): www.thisislondon.co.uk/news/workers-c-red-over-wordplay-at-library-6943080.html.

Long, Camilla, 'Feminism? I was a "Muff March" Virgin', *Sunday Times Magazine* (8 January 2012).

Mahler, Richard, 'The Battle of Chicago: [. . .] Feminist Artist Judy Chicago fires back at critics who call her *Dinner Party* obscene and withdraws her gift of it to a university', *The Los Angeles Times* (12 October 1990): http://articles.latimes.com/1990–10–12/ entertainment/ca-2100_1_dinner-party.

Mahmood, Mazher and Eleanor Mills, 'I can circumcise them here: £750 for the first daughter', *Sunday Times* (22 April 2012).

Moorhead, Joanna, 'The Art of Creation', interview with Hermione Wiltshire, *The Guardian* (28 May 2008): www.guardian.co.uk/lifeandstyle/2008/may/28/women.art.

Muz, Julie Atlas and Mr Pussy, 'Hola señor editor de *La Voz de la Villa*', Letters, *Village Voice* (3 May 2005): www.villagevoice.com/content/printVersion/191883/.

O'Bryan, Will, 'Punch-Line Politics: Riki Wichins's "one trans show" takes her from serious to stand-up, but her mission stays the same', *Metro Weekly* (December 2009): www. metroweekly.com/feature/?ak=4716.

O'Hagan, Sean, 'Ron Mueck: From Muppets to Motherhood', *The Observer* (6 August 2006): www.guardian.co.uk/artanddesign/2006/aug/06/art2.

Petridis, Alexis, Review of Jamie Foxx, *Unpredictable*, in *The Guardian* (21 April 2006).

Poniewozik, James, 'All-TIME 100 TV Shows', *Time Magazine* (6 November 2007).

Robinson, Andrew C., 'Post-Gender Pandrogyny', *Gay City News* (18 January 2007), www. deitch.com/files/projects/womanizer_gaycitynews.pdf.

Rogers, Lois, 'Do Looks Matter?', *Sunday Times* 'Style' Magazine (9 October 2011).

Rose, Barbara, 'Vaginal Iconology', *New York Magazine* (11 February 1974).

Spencer, Mimi, 'The Vagina Dialogues. It's time to stop hiding behind euphemisms, for our children's sake', *The Guardian* (18 March 2005).

Stanley, Jo, 'Male View of a Woman's Labour Pains', *Morning Star* (11 July 1997).

Sullivan, Caroline, Review of Jamie Foxx, live at the Café de Paris, London, in *The Guardian* (25 April 2006).

Wardrop, Murray, 'Anti-Semitic abuse "rife among football fans"', *The Telegraph* (14 April 2011).

West, Pat, 'Monica Sjöö: a feminist artist working to glorify the goddess and the earth', *The Guardian* (23 November 2005): www.guardian.co.uk/news/2005/sep/23/ guardianobituaries.artsobituaries1.

Wigmore, Barry, 'Sexually charged shows such as *Sex and the City* and *Friends* to blame for rise in teenage pregnancy', *The Daily Mail* (4 November 2008): www.dailymail. co.uk/news/article-1082571/Sexually-charged-shows-Sex-And-The-City-Friends-blam e-rise-teenage-pregnancy.html.

Films

Breillat, Catherine (dir.), *Anatomie d'enfer* (*Anatomy of Hell*), 2004.

Buñuel, Luis (dir.), *Viridiana*, 1961.

Coppola, Francis Ford (dir.), *Apocalypse Now*, 1979.

DeSimone, Tom (dir.), *Chatterbox*, 1977.
Lichtenstein, Mitchell (dir.), *Teeth*, 2007.
Llosa, Claudia (dir.), *La Teta Asustada* (*The Milk of Sorrow*), 2009.
Mangold, James (dir.), *Girl, Interrupted*, 2000.
Merlet, Agnès (dir.), *Artemisia*, 1998.
Mulot, Claude (dir.), *Le Sexe qui Parle* (*Pussy Talk*), 1975.
Oplev, Niels (dir.), *Män Som Hatar Kvinnor* (*The Girl with the Dragon Tattoo*), 2009.
Parker, Trey (dir.), *South Park: Bigger, Longer & Uncut*, 1999.
Sprinkle, Annie (dir.), *Deep Inside Annie Sprinkle*, 1982.
Von Trier, Lars (dir.), *Antichrist*, 2009.

TV programmes

Avanzino, Peter, Dwayne Carey-Hill, Frank Marino, Rich Moore, Stephen Sandoval and James Purdum (dir.), *Drawn Together* (Comedy Central, 2004–2007).
Burrows, James (dir.), *Will and Grace* (NBC, 1998–2006).
Greer, Germaine (presenter), *Balderdash and Piffle* (BBC2, 30 January 2006).
King, Michael Patrick, et al. (dir.), *Sex and the City* (HBO, 1998–2004).
Mylod, Mark (dir.), *Last Fast Show Ever* (BBC, 2000).
Parker, Trey (dir.) and Matt Stone, *South Park* (Comedy Central, 1997–present).
Schaffer, Jeff (dir.), *The League* (FX, 2009).

Music

Falling in Reverse, 'Good Girls, Bad Guys', *The Drug in Me is You* (Epitaph, 2011).
Foxx, Jamie, 'Storm (Forecass)', *Unpredictable* (J, 2006).
Lady Gaga, 'Born This Way', *Born This Way* (Streamline, 2011).
Lennon, John, and Yoko Ono, 'Woman is the Nigger of the World', *Some Time in New York City* (Apple/EMI, 1972).
Metallica, 'Don't Tread on Me', *The Black Album* (Elektra, 1991).
The Rolling Stones, 'Angie', *Goats Head Soup* (Rolling Stones, 1973).

Personal correspondence

Briggs, Keith, personal email correspondence with the author, 16 February 2012.
Chicago, Judy, personal email correspondence with the author, 22 May 2012.
Coover, Robert, personal email correspondence with the author, October 2011.
Croft, Simon, personal email correspondence with the author, 6 June 2012.
DeSimone, Tom, personal email correspondence with the author, June 2007.
Fanni Tutti, Cosey, personal email correspondence with the author, 31 May 2012.
Hunt, Matthew, personal email correspondence with the author, 2006–present.
Kamvyselli, Eurydice, personal email correspondence with the author, 27 April 2009.

Kunin, Julia, private email correspondence with the author, 30 October 2012.
Sprinkle, Annie, personal email conversation with the author, 23 April 2012.
Wilding, Faith, personal email correspondence with the author, 22 July 2011.

Websites

Bridgeman, Laura and Serge Nicholson, 'Hot Pencil Press' blog: www.hotpencilpress.com/word.html.

British National Corpus: http://corpus.byu.edu/bnc/.

Chicago, Judy, interview with Helen Knowles and Francesca De Biasco, in Chicago's studio in Belen, New Mexico (February 2012): http://birthritescollection.org.uk/#/judy-chicago-podcast/4565041214.

Emmys: www.emmys.com/shows/sex-and-city.

Golden Globes: www.goldenglobes.org/browse/film/24922.

Goldman, Eric, 'South Park: "A Million Little Fibers" Review' (20 April 2006): http://uk.tv.ign.com/articles/702/702516p1.html.

Harbottle, Claire, 'Visual Representation of Birth: a Paper', Figure 22: http://claireharbottlebirthwork.blogspot.com/p/visual-representation-of-birth-paper.html.

— 'Lilla's Birthing: Re-appropriating the Subjective Experience of Birthing in Visual Art', http://claireharbottlebirthwork.blogspot.com/p/lillas-birthing-re-appropriating.html.

Hoff Sommers, Christina, 'Sex, Lies and the *Vagina Monologues*', a paper delivered on 3 August 2004 at the Young America's Foundation 26th Annual National Conservative Student Conference in Washington, DC, and later reprinted at FrontPageMagazine.com on 25 August 2004: http://archive.frontpagemag.com/readArticle.aspx?ARTID=11662

Knowles, Helen, audio recording from the 'Birth as Confrontational Image' panel at the Whitworth Gallery in Manchester (9 May 2011) and at the Whitechapel Gallery in London (11 May 2011): http://birthritescollection.org.uk/#/birth-in-contemporary-art/4552208619.

Lees, Lisa, *Fragments of Gender* (Lulu.com).

Museum of Menstruation and Women's Health, www.mum.org.

'O' for 'Oregon' (November 2011): www.sportsgrid.com/ncaa-football/oregon-o-sign-vagina/.

Phillips, Tony, 'Inside Downtown "It Girl" Julie Atlas Muz', *Edge*: www.edgepalmsprings.com/entertainment/theatre/features//40398/inside_downtown_%E2%80%99it_girl%E2%80%99_julie_atlas_muz.

Portas, Mary, 'Kinky Knickers': www.liberty.co.uk/fcp/content/kinky-knickers-mary-portas/content.

SAG (Screen Actors Guild) Awards: www.sagawards.org/awards/search.

Simpson, Caroline, 'Genderful: an interview with Laura Bridgeman and Serge Nicholson' (December 2011): http://foggysapphires.wordpress.com/2011/12/14/genderful-an-interview-with-laura-bridgeman-and-serge-nicholson/.

Sjöö, Monica: www.monicasjoo.com/exhibition/1_god_giving_birth.html.

Urban Dictionary: www.urbandictionary.com/define.php?term=vagina&defid=2278413.

Waller, Jonathan, audio recording from the 'Birth as Confrontational Image' panel at the Whitworth Gallery in Manchester (9 May 2011) and at the Whitechapel Gallery in London (11 May 2011): http://birthritescollection.org.uk/#/birth-in-contemporary-art/4552208619.

Wiltshire, Hermione, audio recording from the 'Birth as Confrontational Image' panel at the Whitworth Gallery in Manchester (9 May 2011) and at the Whitechapel Gallery in London (11 May 2011): http://birthritescollection.org.uk/#/birth-in-contemporary-art/4552208619.

Wiltshire, Hermione, quoted on the Birth Rites Collection website: http://birthritescollection.org.uk/#/yoga-positions-for-birth/4542010765.

Hunt, Matthew, www.matthewhunt.com.

www.caroleeschneemann.com.

www.cyberfeminism.net/.

http://dodsonandross.com/sexfeature/bettys-response-vagina-monologues.

Internet Movie Database (IMDb): http://imdb.com/.

www.popsessive.com/2011/12/04/first-lady-michelle-obama-covers-readers-digest/.

www.puppetryofthepenis.com/.

www.salon.com/writer/camille_paglia/page/8/.

www.anniesprinkle.org/html/writings/pca.html.

www.transmanginamonologues.com/.

Sh! Women's Erotic Emporium: www.sh-womenstore.com/Sensual+Pleasures/Touch/Vulva_Puppet.html.

Court case

Le Vine v DPP, Royal Courts of Justice, London, 06.05.10. Neutral citation number: [2010] EWHC 1128 (Admin). Co/4271/2010.

Select artworks/performances

Brueghel de Oude, Pieter, *Dulle Griet*, Museum Mayer van den Bergh, Antwerp (1562).

Chicago, Judy, 'Birth Tear/Tear' (30" × 40"; 1982).

Dijkstra, Rineke, photographs of three mothers at the Tate (1994): www.tate.org.uk/servlet/ArtistWorks?cgroupid=999999961&artistid=2666&page=1.

Harbottle, Claire, 'Lilla's Birthing', photograph on paper (2010).

LeCocq, Karen, *Feather Cunt* (1971, remade 1996), mixed media. Original dimensions 12"w × 10"h × 12"d.

Lucas, Sarah, 'Chicken Knickers' (1997). Photograph on paper, 426 mm × 426 mm, Tate Britain.

Mueck, Ron, 'Mother and Child', 2001, mixed media (pigmented polyester resin on fibreglass); 24 × 89 × 38 cm.

Schneemann, Carolee, *Venus Vectors*, 1987. Sculpture/video installation: acrylic, aluminium, video monitors, 2-channel video, photographs on mylar between 10 radiating Plexiglas panels, each 42 × 50 in. Overall radius 72 in.

— *Vulva's Morphia*, 1992–97. Suspended photogrid: 36 hand-painted colour laser prints on paper, mounted on board, each 11 × 8.5 in.; text strips, 58 × 2 in. Four small electric fans, side-mounted. Total wall installation 60 × 96 in.

— *Fresh Blood – A Dream Morphology*, 1981–87. Performance: 2 slide carousels/zoom lens, dissolve unit (projection area 8 × 12 ft), ceiling side-lights, raise platform, microphone, speakers, metal watering can, transparent umbrella, door, etc. 2 monitors, video camera, live video relay.

— posed as Olympia: Robert Morris, installation piece, *Site* (1963).

Sprinkle, Annie, *MetamorphoSex*; a week-long sexuality workshop with more than 20 local women, culminating in three sex-magic performance/rituals which the public was invited to attend; premiered December 1995.

— *Annie Sprinkle Post-Porn Modernist* (1990–95), written and performed by Annie Sprinkle; directed by Emilio Cubeiro, and later by Willem de Ridder as *Post-Post-Porn Modernist*.

— *Annie Sprinkle's Herstory of Porn – Reel to Real*; multimedia one-woman show directed by Emilio Cubeiro (1999).Tutti, Cosey Fanni, 'Lip Service', First International Female Artists' Art Biennial, Stockholm (1994).

Waller, Jonathan, *Mother No. 59*, Mixed medium on paper, 125 × 69 cm (1998).

— *Mother No. 58*, Mixed medium on paper, 144 × 84 cm (1998).

Wilchins, Riki, 'The MANgina Monologues (A One Trans Show)': www.youtube.com/ watch?v=82UU5JE12ZM.

Wilding, Faith, and Cristina Nguyen Hung, *Vulva De/Re Constructa*: http://artfem.tv/id;9/action;showpage/page_type;video/ page_id;Vulva_de_reConstructa_by_subRosa_2000_flv/.

Wilke, Hannah, *S.O.S. Starification Object Series*, 1974–82; 10 b & w silver gelatin prints and 15 chewing-gum sculptures mounted on board (Collection of the Museum of Modern Art, New York).

Organizations

ACTSA's 'Dignity! Period' campaign: www.actsa.org/page-1022-Dignity!%20Period..html.

'Always': www.always-info.co.uk/whats-new/always-acti-pearls-pads.aspx.

Axiom Centre for the Arts in Cheltenham, 'Exhibition Comments' document for *Birth*, by Jonathan Waller, 27 June – 26 July 1998.

The Birth Rites Collection: http://birthritescollection.org.uk/.

The Centrefold Project: www.thecentrefoldproject.org/.

Church & Dwight Co., Inc., *2010 Sustainability Report*: www.churchdwight.com/pdf/Susta inabilityReports/2010SustainabilityReport.pdf.

The Emmy Awards: www.emmys.com/.

Femfresh: www.femfresh.co.uk/.

FORWARD (The Foundation for Women's Health, Research and Development): www. forwarduk.org.uk/about.

The Annual Golden Globe Awards: www.goldenglobes.org/.

'P&G Corporate Newsroom': http://news.pg.com/about.

RB Press Release, '2011: Full Year Targets Exceeded', 8 February 2012: www. rb.com/2011-Full-Year-Results.

'Hygiene is the foundation of healthy living': www.rb.com/Media-investors/ Category-performance/Hygiene.

For 'eco positive periods': Lunapads.com.

Lysol 'Love-quiz . . . For Married Folks Only', 1948: www.mum.org/Lysol48.htm.

Rees, Emma L. E., 'Cultural Attitudes to Female Genitalia' survey (April 2012): hosted by Survey Monkey, www.surveymonkey.com/s/STBH8T9.

The Screen Actors Guild Awards: www.sagawards.org/.

The (Trans)Mangina Monologues: www.transmanginamonologues.com/.

UK Deed Poll Service official website: www.ukdps.co.uk/ AreThereAnyRestrictionsOnNames.html.

WHO (the World Health Organization), Fact Sheet No. 241, FGM in Africa, February 2012: www.who.int/mediacentre/factsheets/fs241/en/.

Index

Note: Numbers in **bold** indicate an extended discussion of a topic, or the location of a black and white illustration within the text.